GOING FULL CIRCLE
A 1,555-MILE WALK AROUND
THE WORLD'S LARGEST LAKE

by Mike Link & Kate Crowley

Lake Superior
Port Cities Inc.

i

First Edition: June 2012

Lake Superior Port Cities Inc.
P.O. Box 16417
Duluth, Minnesota 55816-0417 USA
888-BIG LAKE (888-244-5253)

5 4 3 2 1

Library of Congress Cataloging-in-Publication Data

Link, Mike.
  Going full circle : a 1,555-mile walk around the world's largest lake / by Mike Link & Kate Crowley. - 1st ed.
    p. cm.
  ISBN 978-0-942235-23-4
  1. Hiking – Superior, Lake, Region – Guidebooks.
  2. Superior, Lake, Region – Guidebooks. I. Crowley, Kate. II. Title.
  GV199.42.S86L56 2012
  796.5109774'9 – dc23

                                                    20122014676

Printed in the United States of America

  Editors: Konnie LeMay, Ann Possis
  Design: Tanya Bäck; Cover photo by Amanda Hakala
  Printer: Sheridan Books Inc., Chelsea, Michigan

To our children and grandchildren
And to all of the other grandchildren of the world

Advance Praise for *Going Full Circle*

Funny and personal, yet I learned about things I love like: plants, water quality, animals, research techniques, aging and health, Lake Superior geography and more!

Kate and Mike know how to convey scientific information, awe, beauty, spiritual and emotional connection, what's inside and outside of themselves – all at the same time. They truly know how to keep things interesting. Their journey has enhanced the Lake Superior community tenfold. Coupled with their videos of folk along the shoreline, community survey, point samples, speaking events, articles, scientific notes, this book proves that – for the love of life – Kate and Mike aren't really going to retire. Thank God.

— Ellen Van Laar, ArtAdventures, Batchawana, Ontario

Who but Mike and Kate would have dreamed up this trip, let alone carried it off? An astounding "retirement." While many of us think of playing with grandchildren and gardening, Mike and Kate embarked on a grueling walk to publicize the issue of fresh water, arguably one of the most pressing issues of the century. Speaking your mind for fresh water is one thing. Putting your feet to the pavement is quite another level of passion and leadership.

A great writing style ... so approachable, yet compelling. I was drawn into Mike and Kate's day-to-day journey and the dreams that sustained them. Both high-level science and personal self-discovery. In purpose and substance ... Superior!

— Jerry Phillips, Rittenhouse Inn, Bayfield, former national director of American Bed and Breakfast Association

Mike and Kate's stories, and their prose, are as full of pleasant surprises as their journey around Lake Superior was. They capture the unique landscape and personalities of Lake Superior poetically. Of course, I am partial to the U.P. chapters where the people and stories of the land come alive.

— F. Michelle Halley, Lake Superior manager, Conservation Programs, Great Lakes Regional Center

No one has experienced Lake Superior as Mike and Kate did – one step at a time for 1,555 miles. In their steps, we come full circle, but through their eyes we end in a different place. This is the story of what one discovers in taking a very close look at one of the planet's greatest lakes, its shores and its people.

— Mark Peterson, executive director, Audubon Minnesota

Like Montaigne centuries before them, Mike and Kate have contemplated how to live. Their prescription begins with caring for the planet, and for family and friends; with dreaming and following those dreams (even through pain); with observing closely; and always, living in the moment.

— Beth Blank, retired owner Solbakken Resort, Minnesota

CONTENTS

ONE

Counterclockwise

I wish I was 20 and in love with life and still full of beans.
Self-Portrait, Mary Oliver

Mike:

Journeys seldom start at the beginning and rarely end after the last mile. This would certainly be the rule for our 4½-month, 1,555-mile hike around Lake Superior.

Why attempt to walk – as closely as possible – along the shore of the largest freshwater lake in the world by surface area? Think of lassoing a dream, of creating the perfect summation for your career and life. We wanted this journey to mark the end of my nearly four decades at the Audubon Center of the North Woods. The journey took a year of planning, of raising of funds toward a budget of $25,000, of traversing grueling miles where limited trails existed ... and ending with a series of operations to put my battered body back together.

It was worth every effort.

But as you can see, this complex, time-consuming process did not start on the day we first marched bravely – and naively – from a wind-blasted Lake Superior beach one April morning. No, our months-long journey started with a much shorter hike on the magnificent Lake Superior Hiking Trail paralleling the lake's Minnesota shore.

As we enjoyed the wonderful summer day, talk drifted to my retirement. That day was still a few years off, but the ending significant; I had been director of the Audubon Center in Sandstone, Minnesota, since its founding in 1971. We were not sure when it would be, but we knew it would be within a few years.

"Just walk away," Kate suggested. "Just walk out the door and keep walking."

Yes, not turning my back, just turning the page – I liked it. But I thought I could go farther, about 70 miles north. "Why don't I just keep walking to Duluth?" I countered.

At that point someone should have put on the brakes, but there was only Kate and me, and we had no brakes. The dream grew bolder, finally encompassing the entire shoreline of Lake Superior. The lake became a destination, a cause and a challenge. Then we faced what all dreamers must face: How to make what is spoken into reality.

That was the inception, but the real birth of the idea had roots in our past, in the history of two people who began in different places on their life journey, then came together on paths that made walking around Lake Superior a logical choice in our 60s.

My journey began from an auspicious start as the largest baby ever born in Rice Lake, Wisconsin (12 pounds – a record only recently broken).

Life was not exactly easy. While serving in New Guinea during World War II, my father suffered an injury or illness (the records are lost and my father never talked of the war) that sent him to a military hospital in Washington state, where he was not expected to live. My mother traveled there to marry him. His unexpected recovery qualified him for release from the hospital, but disqualified him from military disability payments. Thanks to his asthma, developed because of his military service, the trucking industry where he worked as a mechanic before the war would not give him a job.

As a result, for the first five years of my life we moved every few months through small towns in Wisconsin and Minnesota to pick up part-time jobs. The three of us (I was an only child) lived on anything he could earn until he finally got a job at Honeywell, which he kept until he retired. On vacations from school, I lived with my grandparents in the peaceful small town of Rice Lake. They introduced me to blackberry picking and we visited the farms

© Lake Superior Magazine

If you traveled on the roads, this is the estimated mileage between towns. We traveled tightly to the shore, so our mileage was different. From Wawa to Marathon, Ontario, we paddled by canoe.

of relatives in nearby Prairie Farm. To this day, I cannot pass up picking blackberries from a bush or eating a blackberry pie.

Visits during my grade school and middle school years to the farm and to the "reserve," as my family called the Lac Courte Oreilles reservation, helped me get a sense of my family background, my Ojibwe heritage. Ogima Binesi Kwe, my great-great grandmother, made the tinkanagon or dikinaagan (cradle board) which I still own, and on which my great-grandmother and grandmother were carried. She is one of three to whom we dedicated our trip, along with our son, Matt, and Kate's brother, John.

My life has always been a little counterclockwise, a bit out of the ordinary, and my first outdoor adventures (when I was 21) began with one of life's unpredictable moments. I happened to meet Neal Hayford, a plumber, who lived in my apartment building in Champlin. His brother had a canoe we could borrow, and he asked if I'd like to take a ride with him.

"Of course," I said, and soon the Rum River became the baptismal font for my love of the outdoors. For Neal, our first landing on the trip was a true baptism, since he rolled into the river.

Every turn of the river gave me a new perspective, and I discovered quickly how invigorating a journey in nature could be. This canoe trip led to a lifetime of paddling, more than 10,000 miles in canoes and kayaks. Paddling rivers that were nothing more than blue lines on a state map and exploring gravel roads led me to write a column called "Link's Lore" for 14 weekly newspapers – another happy accident of fate. The columns were a wonderful outlet, restricted in size and deadline, but wide open in subject and style, which let me experiment and share my adventures in learning about life as well as place.

I enjoy gathering people together for fun and adventure, occasionally on the wacky side perhaps. One time I called together friends for the funeral of my old Pontiac. I was living in south Minneapolis and had a young family to support. The car, a big clunker, seemed like a good value when I bought it, but it kept breaking down at inconvenient times, sapping all available dollars from our small budget. Too cheap to throw it away but too invested to walk away, I finally got relief when the bulky vehicle kicked its bucket seats. I celebrated with a very public funeral that caught the attention of *Minneapolis Tribune* writer Robert T. Smith, who even played taps at the affair. The car lights were painted black, we had a wake, a military-style six cap-gun salute and a cross-city procession to car heaven (a real place on Washington Avenue where they crushed old cars) – where I sent it to rest with a eulogy of "dashes to dashes and rust to rust."

The funeral also meant I was without transportation just when, as unlikely as it might seem, I got a job as tax accountant at Honeywell, headquartered in south Minneapolis. Walking to work would have been a good lead-in to this story, but I actually rode a three-speed English bicycle. When I took another tax accounting job at National Car Rental, the bike continued to transport me 11 miles each way … though that probably was not the right employee image for a car rental company. Without a car, the bike was my transportation. I pedaled through blizzards and past stuck cars. I managed to get to work with a briefcase across the handlebars and I only occasionally hit patches of ice that sent me into a snowdrift or swerving dangerously across the lanes.

All this gave me another wacky idea: Why not mount a midwinter bicycle race? The First Annual Groundhog Day Invitational – I had no intention of having a second, I just liked the name – drew 5,000 to 10,000 people out for a day of laughs. It wasn't actually a race, but people did pedal around Lake Harriet in Minneapolis. What was crazy was the fact that I had no standing, no credibility, but my letters and phone calls seemed to strike the right note and no one said no. Maybe it was collective cabin fever, but I can't explain why thousands of people came ready for a midwinter party. The costumes, the laughter, the absurd fun with officials from MTA (Minneapolis Transit Authority), the lieutenant governor and even the groundhog from Como Park made it special. Just like our hike around Lake Superior, these events brought people together who wanted to celebrate life and enjoy sharing their time without feeling like they were at a commercial event.

I wish I could explain the psychology of these events, but that is beyond me. I just learned that people respond to honesty and there is worth in living by your own values. My career as a tax accountant was five years old, but it did not satisfy my passion for doing things I could be proud of – it was just about money and that was not enough.

In 1971, I said yes to a job that had as its description: "See what you can do." It only guaranteed three months of work, at $300 a month, far below a tax accountant's salary. I was in the job for six months plus 38 years, seeing what I could do as founding director of the Audubon Center of the North Woods in Sandstone, Minnesota.

Over the next three decades I found satisfaction teaching about the environment and standing up for issues like the protection of the Boundary Waters Canoe Area Wilderness, and I met people who were involved in long-term conflicts like the fight over dumping taconite tailings in Lake Superior at Silver Bay. Their efforts impressed me. They had no personal gains in mind or fortunes to spend, just a strong drive to make the future better. I hosted the meetings for them and the people standing up against mining in the BWCAW and joined them in letter-writing and testifying. It was a course in civic response to problems that were serious for the environment and people.

I began to lead adult groups around Lake Superior to explore its beauty in summer and winter. For Northland College in Ashland, Wisconsin, I developed a course that took students around the lake for four weeks in a 15-passenger van. One goal was to understand the natural areas – so we backpacked the Porcupine Mountains, Pictured Rocks National Lakeshore and Isle Royale in Michigan, in Pukaskwa National Park in Ontario and in the Apostle Islands National Lakeshore in Wisconsin. The second was to meet the people living on the lake. In between hikes, we stopped in communities and interviewed people to try to understand their relationship to the Big Lake, just as Kate and I would do on our hike.

My work at the Audubon Center was still "see what you can do" and that meant see what you can do to raise money to support the education programs as well. As crazy as it might seem, this meant that for five years I captained a sailboat on Lake Superior and took people sailing, camping and exploring the islands, with all the revenue going to the center's operations. It was here that Kate and I joined lives, having our wedding ceremony on the *Izmir* (now the *Doris E*). Together we sailed the Apostles, to Duluth, Isle Royale and the Porcupine Mountains in Michigan's Upper Peninsula. We learned to appreciate the lake from the water, as well as from the land that we would dedicate ourselves to a walk around: to explore, to meet people, to gather environmental information and, ultimately, to call attention to the needs of and the concerns for the lake. It seems natural given our histories. Kate's life journey started far differently than mine. I'll let her tell it.

Kate:

Like two asteroids destined to collide, my life and Mike's actually orbited around one another in the 1950s and '60s in south Minneapolis. Our paths may have even crossed at some point, unbeknownst to us. But though we inhabited the same part of the city, the circumstances of our lives were radically different.

Unlike Mike, I was the oldest of seven children (five boys, two girls), not an unusual number for an Irish Catholic family, post-World War II. My family was also nontraditional in that my mom was the major wage earner, working as a full-time dietician, with a master's degree, at the Nicollet Clinic in Minneapolis. My father was an itinerant salesman, who throughout my childhood sold one crazy item after another, from "Spud Spits" (wire holders used to bake potatoes) to silver cardboard ashtrays. We kids accepted this unusual family structure and only realized it was strange when the question would come up in school, "What does your dad do?" assuming my mom was a housewife. My dad for his part went "off to work" each day, though he didn't have an office. My parents were supportive of one another's career choices and if there was discontent or frustration, I never knew about it.

When I was born, we lived in the same brick apartment building by the University of Minnesota where my paternal grandmother had lived. One of my earliest memories was going for walks along the Mississippi River with an elderly lady who lived in the apartment below us. I would kick through fallen leaves and pick up twigs to build "houses." Even in the city, I was introduced early to the wonders of nature thanks to the parks wisely set aside for the general public.

Soon after my first brother was born, we moved to Clinton Avenue in south Minneapolis, just a block from Minnehaha Creek and my maternal grandmother. Even after my mom became director of dietetics at the old Abbott Hospital, new brothers and sisters arrived. As the oldest girl, I was expected to watch over my younger siblings whenever the woman who took care of us during the day wasn't there. I often had to be the enforcer, a role of which my now-adult siblings remind me whenever there is a reunion. They have far different memories than I do, of course. I couldn't have possibly been that mean.

Mom and Dad both grew up on farms, and it seems to me that convinced them never to have anything to do with the outdoors or nature again. My

We took time to do some posing on the shore for photographer Jennifer Johansen before our trip.

introduction to nature and adventure grew solely from my proximity to Minnehaha Creek and to playmates in my neighborhood.

If "enforcer" described part of what I was, "tomboy" covered the other part and still does today. My competitiveness with my next younger brother and my general curiosity and natural craving for movement were responsible. I thrived on outdoor activities and sports and enjoyed roughhousing as often as possible.

With Mom gone during the day, and the babysitter only too happy to have our ever-growing group of wild ones outside, I was free to wander and explore the meandering creek. In the 1950s, fear of strangers and kids playing out of sight was not an issue. As befit a tomboy, I wore my curly hair short, though that was probably because it was easier for my mom to maintain. I absolutely loved my "duck tail" when it was in style. I did not like dolls. Who needed those when there was a real live baby in the house at any given time? But I loved the dresses Mom sewed for me and my sister every Easter and the new corduroy jumpers I got before school started.

Unlike my parents, my grandmother was a woman of the earth, a farmer taken reluctantly off the farm. She lived just one block away in the city, and we kids would cut through the alley and yards to get to her house. She earned money by ironing clothes and caring for one or two elderly people in her home, but her greatest joy and passion were her gardens, one in her backyard and another – a full city lot, which was planted entirely with vegetables. That's usually where we found her on summer days. If there is a nature-lover gene, I inherited mine from her.

Later I would share my love of nature with my youngest brother John. I was 14 when he was born and, in some ways, he felt more like my child than my brother. When he was just a toddler, I introduced him to the moon in the night sky, when we sat on a swing at a park one summer evening. I was

6

encouraged by his interest in nature as he grew up and delighted when, as an adult, he took a job driving and narrating a tour bus in Alaska's Denali National Park. But in 2003, John was diagnosed with a brain tumor. For the next five years, he endured every form of treatment, both conventional and experimental. In the end, the cancer won. John died in January 2009, leaving a young wife and two little girls. John would have loved our Full Circle Walk, as he loved wandering through the Alaskan tundra. So we brought him along with us in our hearts; he was the second person to whom we dedicated our walk.

But long before this sadness, there were the joys of growing up – all of the siblings together. I attended 12 years of Catholic school. For high school, I'd desperately wanted to go to a public co-ed school, but I'm grateful for my four years at the all-girl Regina High School, which reinforced the fact that women are as capable and talented as men.

I started at the University of Minnesota in 1967, got married in 1970 and had my two children in 1973 and 1974. In my late 20s, I bought a motorcycle and tried hang-gliding, both exciting but risky adventures, followed by more outdoor adventures in my 30s. I got my degree in recreation and park administration in 1976. It was through this degree program that I was introduced to my future career as a naturalist and writer, and ultimately, to Mike.

In 1978, I found my calling as a monorail tour guide at the Minnesota Zoo, eventually becoming supervisor. When I began, half of the Northern Trail that the monorail covered was undeveloped – just forest, fields and ponds. We tour guides had to develop a "spiel" that would cover not only the zoo animals but the wild areas as well. This was the beginning of my naturalist training: going out and observing every day, reading about what we were seeing and getting training with other naturalists whenever possible. It was through this job that I met Mike.

I was a member of the Minnesota River Valley Audubon Chapter and each summer it held a fundraiser for North Woods Audubon Center. I hadn't heard of this environmental center, but I would soon learn much more about it. In June 1981, I attended an ice cream social in south Minneapolis. A striking man wearing jeans, looking like a cross between Marty Stouffer and Grizzly Adams, was the auctioneer for the event. He was the director of the center and during the course of the afternoon I learned that the center offered training for naturalists in a variety of programs. Mike smiled and laughed easily with those he met and exuded a warmth and sincerity that drew people to him.

After the social event ended, I waited to talk to him. I introduced myself and explained what I did. Mike characteristically reached out and put his hand on my shoulder. I can honestly say I felt electricity pulsing through my arm. That did it. I wasn't only interested in having him teach my staff, I was interested in *him*. The real deal, he was my dream man. Five years later, my dream came true. We married on a boat on Lake Superior and began our life of adventure together.

Mike:
Having joined forces on the sailboat and in life, Kate and I spent 24 years sharing a love of nature and family in a nice home next to Willow River State Forest. We hiked, skied, traveled and loved life.

But on December 17, 1989, our world was shaken to the core. A call came from New Zealand where my son Matthew was working as an outdoor educator. An avid kayaker, he had been on a difficult class-five river with other instructors, I was told. At the end of the trip, they were playing in a pool beneath a dam. There was a piece of rebar underwater, put in to stabilize the concrete dam. Matt's kayak caught under the metal rod, and he could not escape. He died, and my heart broke.

I hung up the phone and told Kate. We sat and held hands in silence. It was a gray day like so many December days: thick clouds, short on daylight, the woods buried under six inches of snow. I went for a walk. The unnatural hush from the house followed me. The woods were still until I walked beside a copse of pines. Out burst a flock of crows in all their raucousness, tearing the silence. I watched the scattering black birds – the spirit carriers in so many cultures.

On the way back home, life returned to the forest. I heard birds and the clack of branch upon branch. I spotted an otter track trailing from a creek to the Willow River. I had not seen it earlier, and now I followed it with my old naturalist curiosity. Suddenly I knew I was supposed to do this. The otter celebrates snow and rivers, Matt's two passions.

From that moment, the otter became the symbol I needed to renew my own life. I knew then, too, that the only way to honor my son was to live each day in a way that would make him proud. I had my direction. The next year, on every river I traveled in five states, I saw an otter. That has never happened before or since.

We had memorials in the Twin Cities and in Sandstone, and one more, a pipe ceremony, on Lake Superior. Ojibwe teacher Larry Aitkin gave a blessing with a pipe as we gathered on a windy, cold beach to celebrate Matt's life. Two decades later, near the same spot and with similar blustery conditions, our full circle journey would begin. It was natural that Matt should be the third person in whose memory we would dedicate our Full Circle Superior hike.

Remembering Matt, Kate and I also realized that we were embarking on a journey with risk – the risk of wet rocks and steep cliffs, of cold water and storms, of aging bodies and unknown paths. Like many adventures with risk – like the adventures that Matt embraced – this one would also be worth taking.

The spirits that would accompany us on our journey had chosen us and that completed the dreaming. Our trip concept was complete. But as we moved from dreaming about a 1,555-mile hike to actually planning the five-month, shore-hugging walk around the world's largest lake, we began to realize how far from a casual jaunt this would be.

I had been on many one-month expeditions with college students and friends, but this undertaking meant getting ourselves into better condition, figuring out how and when to communicate with people once on the road, and developing a schedule and calculating the costs. And we needed to keep our own bills paid and house safe for the duration. It was mind boggling, but if I could bury a sedan, organize a bicycle race during a Minnesota winter and marry the woman of my dreams on a sailboat in Lake Superior, surely this would be possible. One thing I did know for certain: We'd picked the right lake.

Why Lake Superior?

The whim of a good idea got us started on this journey, but it would take a much more substantial motivator to keep our 60+-year-old hips, knees and legs moving forward every day. For us, Lake Superior would be that motivator. As residents of a water-rich state and as grandparents, we are aware and concerned about fresh water and the future. Lake Superior holds 10 percent of all the fresh water on the surface of the earth. It is not only the largest of the Great Lakes; it could hold the water from all the other four Great Lakes, plus have room left for three extra Lake Eries!

With a depth of 1,276 feet, Lake Superior is not the deepest lake, nor the one with the most water. In fact, 33 other lakes are deeper. Baikal in Russia is more than four times deeper. Even with 3 quadrillion gallons of water, Lake Superior (12,100 cubic kilometers) does not have the most fresh water, beaten out by Lake Baikal (23,000 cubic kilometers) and by Lake Tanganyika in Africa (19,000 cubic kilometers).

Unless someday the Great Lakes are reclassified and Michigan and Huron are considered one lake, Superior is by far the largest and has the wildest and most pristine shorelines. With an area of 117,702 square kilometers (45,445 square miles) we had the symbol of fresh water and the expedition we wanted.

Superior is shared by three states and one Canadian province – Michigan, Wisconsin, Minnesota, and Ontario. It has a nice spread of cities, but no huge urban areas. Thunder Bay, Ontario, is the largest and going counterclockwise you have Duluth, Superior, Ashland, Houghton, Marquette, and the two Sault Ste. Maries,(Michigan and Ontario) representing most of the population.

There are national lakeshores in two states, national historic parks in two states, a national park on an island on Lake Superior and a national park in Ontario, as well as numerous state and provincial parks, historic areas and a geologic landscape that lays bare the Canadian Shield, the heart of the North American continent.

There are still many indigenous populations, with the Lake Superior Chippewa (Anishinabe) and Cree represented all around the lake, as well as a few representatives of the Sioux nation. It is the lake of Naniboujou and Michipeshu (two important spirits of the Anishinabe). Respect for the lake is obvious in the names associated with it: Superior (which actually means the highest elevation of the great lakes), Gitchi Gummi or Gitchi Kami.

As a symbol of fresh water, Lake Superior is an obvious choice. It is one of the few freshwater bodies that can be seen from outer space. The image of the "big blue ball" in the blackness of space is one I will never forget seeing as a boy. As an adult I realized that most of that blue was salt water that, for all its beauty, does not offer much to drink. Having grown up in the Land of Sky Blue Waters, the land of 10,000(+) lakes, near the headwaters of the great Mississippi River and the Great Lakes, fresh water has been integral to our lives. It seems abundant and endless, but you don't need to go to the moon to see that the truth is quite different.

Of all the valuable assets in the earth's biosphere, it still comes down to two key resources needed for all of us to survive – breathable air and drinkable water.

It really is that simple. So the call of this magnificent place of beauty was based on a need to protect the very basis of life on Earth. This is where we would focus our energy. This would be the cause that gave the adventure meaning.

From canoes to kayaks to sailboats, we had a lifetime of freshwater adventure and this would be a continuation of that love of water, but Kate was quite clear from the beginning – this was not going to be a backpack trip. "We are in our 60s: walking is enough!" With that established, we could begin to frame the trek in different ways.

Our goal was to stay on or as close to the shore as possible, which meant trying to find trails, railroad grades, secondary roads and walkable shores. This commitment led us on many wonderful adventures and encounters that would not have happened if we'd taken the highway route. It also placed us in constant contact with our inspiration. I told people that my goal was to keep my left foot wet. In reality, both feet would often be wet.

We also thought that this would be a grand experiment for an aging population, since we are at the cusp of the baby boomer bulge and health is something we are both concerned about. We wanted to observe and record the changes in our bodies. With a four-year age difference and very different life histories, we knew the trip would affect each of us in different ways.

I've led an adventurous life with a few spills, falls and accidents along the way that left me with a spine that acts up. In the winter of 2008 I led a college class on a snowshoe trek and came back with a foot that was hurting. Diagnosed as plantar fasciitis, it affected how I walked. That in turn aggravated my back. I went for an MRI and learned of 11 problems with seven disks. I ended up getting spinal injections and started to walk with a cane. I was not the epitome of a long-distance hiker and Kate watched this until one day she said, "What would you think about being my support person while I do the walk around the lake?" My response was a defensive, "I am not too excited about that. The hike is still two years away; I think this is a little premature!" And it was laid to rest but lingered in the background.

My back pain gradually came under control and we moved on to the next challenges. We managed to find a group of advisers who believed in our plan; they represented all three states and Ontario. In Minnesota, Beth and Bill Blank provided the contacts and background for the Minnesota shore that comes from three decades as Innkeepers and owners of Solbakken Resort. In addition, they provided their home to use for meetings, planning, relaxation and spiritual renewal as we looked ahead.

Lonnie and Kelly Dupre had experience with long expeditions that Lonnie had taken to the North Pole, the Bering Strait and Greenland. During one meeting Lonnie said we needed to take a break every hour, to give ourselves 10 minutes to rest and relax. Kate's response was, "That's a good idea, but what will we do with those 10 minutes?" The concepts of "rest and relax" seemed to float by her! The result was the first of our research projects: taking point samples every three miles when we were on the shore. As freshwater demand and development continue it will not be enough to simply say that "we remember when."

Kate's inspiration came from the fact that we actually know so little about this big body of water. A dot-to-dot set of GPS points with notes and photos in the four cardinal directions will be a great tool if we can find places to store them for access to future researchers and policy makers.

Next, we went to websites to learn about the distance and came up with figures that ranged from 1,350 to 2,975 miles. The islands are included in shoreline figures, which might explain the big number, but was the smaller number simply the road distance? And what about the other numbers – where did they come from? When we were told there were 7,000 streams entering the lake we were amazed and worried. Then someone said there were 350 streams, so we went to the Natural Resources Research Institute in Duluth and asked how there could be such a discrepancy. We were told there were 5,000 interfluvial flows (something we had never heard about). This term includes little seeps and springs we encountered with great frequency, but that reduced the number of actual streams to 1,754 in the final pre-trip estimate.

Jerry Phillips of the Rittenhouse Inn in Bayfield was our Wisconsin adviser. We have known him and his wife, Mary, since we stayed at the Rittenhouse on our honeymoon 25 years ago. Jerry is involved with the arts, tourism, history and just about everything else that is positive and exciting for the Bayfield Peninsula. He was instrumental in connecting us with the Bad River Reservation.

Finally, I retired from the Audubon Center on March 21, 2009. All dates have to have some significance for me and there is nothing that says "renewal" and "fresh start" like the vernal equinox. It was an easier transition than I might have expected because I had the trek to focus on and, although I did not actually walk away that day, in my mind the walking away began there. Kate got an unofficial retirement as people assumed: if I was gone so was she. She continued to work on projects for the center, but for the most part we were both free to concentrate on Lake Superior.

Our daughter Alyssa met us on Wisconsin Point on a blustery day.

We needed to find sponsors who cared about Lake Superior and believed that two people in their 60s could make the hike. Let's just say they were not lining up to be part of our cause at first. We continued to define our goals and hoped interest and support would follow.

Two great people came in to our expedition world early in the planning. Tobias Tan, a former student in one of my field research college classes, was born in Singapore with a heart for the great wilderness and wild places of the world. As a college student in Edmonton, Alberta, he is a genius of web design and computers and filled one of our most pressing needs. Having fallen in love with Lake Superior when he was with us for a winter class, he volunteered to put together our website, www.fullcirclesuperior.org, which gave us immediate credibility. We continue to use the site to update people on Lake Superior and fresh water issues, but we also know that this was one of the first building blocks for our success. It taught us that in this age of exploration, being connected to social networks and Internet media is essential.

The second important person to be added to the team (yes, you need a team to do an expedition) was Amanda Hakala. Amanda had worked at the Audubon Center, been a student in the graduate program for environmental education at Hamline University where I teach, and a house and pet sitter for us over the years, so she had proven her trustworthiness. If our dogs Leopold and Sigurd accepted you, it was a good bet Kate and I would like you, too. She agreed to be our assistant, and Beth and Bill agreed to be back-up support when Amanda was not available. With six months to go we were making good progress, except we still did not have a vehicle to use for transportation and lodging.

The idea of a SAG (Support and Gear) wagon is important for many reasons. We could hike the shoreline in front of homes because the normal high-water mark is also the boundary between private and public land, but camping in front of people's lake homes was not an option.

Getting picked up and dropped off required some long drives in locations like the Upper Peninsula of Michigan. On the Minnesota shore I used my bicycle to facilitate shuttles, but that would not work anywhere else.

At the end of a tough walk (measured in sand, cobbles, streams, as well as miles), we wanted to shower, eat, upload photos, update the website and blogs and do our research notes. And it really helped to have Amanda prepare our dinners and drive our shuttle.

Doing programs for the public along the way meant it would be advantageous to have a support person who could handle programs for young people and get Kate and me to our public presentations.

Duluth was the logical start and end location since it was the closest point to our home, it's where the St. Louis River enters the lake and it's home to a very important sponsor – *Lake Superior Magazine* (the publisher of this book).

When I suggested that we start by walking east, Kate responded with a shocked, "Counterclockwise?" I explained my reasons and thought that I would only explain this once. Next, I was the one who was shocked to learn there was a general expectation we would go clockwise. One person tried to get us to reconsider because the traditional way of the Anishinabe is clockwise for all spiritual journeys. Perhaps it is the result of having never worn a wristwatch that makes me less inclined to walk the direction of the clock, but I thought I'd better check this out.

I told John Morrin, an elder from the Grand Portage Band, how my idea had been received. I did not want to insult the indigenous peoples. I had settled on this direction, first because of the black fly, which begins to hatch in early spring from the fast moving waters of the streams along the lake. If we started walking north in the spring we would walk from one hatch to the next for weeks. I would be singing, under my mosquito netting, the 1949 "Black Fly Song" written by Canadian Wade Hemsworth. It gives me the shivers just thinking of the chorus.

> *And the black flies, the little black flies*
> *Always the black fly no matter where you go*
> *I'll die with the black fly a-pickin' my bones*
> *In North Ontar-eye-o-eye-o, In North Ontar-eye-o*

Second, summer heat is something both Kate and I dislike (we are northerners after all). Even beaches on Lake Superior can be hot in the summer, especially if breezes blow off the land, so I thought it would be better to be in Canada in July and August.

"So John, what do I do? I do not want to insult anyone." His reply was both thoughtful and understated, "It is your journey; you should follow the path that is right for you." Later, I asked Michael Wiggins, the chairman of the Bad River Band, the same question. He said the Ojibwe do follow a clockwise pattern, but the Oneida go counterclockwise. Then after a pause he laughed and added, "Of course, we say they're wrong."

In the summer of 2009 we drove around the lake to check out the logistics (and we did it counterclockwise). This allowed us to meet with Alex Mayer at Michigan Tech in Houghton (one of three Michigan advisers – Bill Rose and Rolf Peterson were the other two). Alex is with the Center for Water and Society and he indicated a need for information about the knowledge and attitude of people around the lake. Thus was the beginning of one of our most important initiatives, which would involve Dr. Tony Murphy from the University of St. Catherine and the author of Minnesota's Environmental Literacy studies, and Dr. Rich Axler of the University of Minnesota's Natural Resources Research Institute.

During the drive we were able to determine just how long and difficult some of the shuttles would be. This helped us to decide to bring two vehicles, even though we still didn't have an RV lined up. In the meantime, Granite Gear, Midwest Mountaineering, Lake Superior Trading Post, Piragis Northwoods Outfitters and Littlbug stoves had come on board as sponsors and were covering our hiking and camping gear.

In Ontario, we met with Dawn Elmore and she introduced us to Mike and Cheryl Landmark from the Voyageur Trail Association, an all-volunteer group that provided us with vital links for the Canadian portion of our trek. They share our dream for a complete trail around the lake. Dawn also introduced us to Errol Caldwell from the Center for Invasive Species in Algoma, Michigan, and what we thought was the last of our biological research observations.

A later discussion with NRRI in Duluth posed a situation that worried us then and continues to concern us. What if the other great lakes draw down Lake Superior to hold their levels, or if some idiocy allows Lake Superior waters to be shipped elsewhere? On our walk, we could measure and photograph all the streams we crossed. NRRI wanted to see how lowering of the level of the lake would impact game fish trying to spawn and return to the lake. It is a potentially devastating change.

We were now just eight months from the beginning of the trek and feeling good about everything, except for lack of money, lack of an RV and lack of a research partner for personal health.

Good friends, Patty and Gary Mondale, allowed us to use their home in Tucson for October and November so we could continue our training and preparation. We used the warm desert climate to put in lots of miles and get ourselves in shape. On the way home we took the long route and went to visit three of our grandchildren in Ohio. Just north of Cincinnati at rush hour, in the midst of traffic and the confusion of road construction, in the center lane, I had the next physical setback.

Suddenly my right eye developed a cascading cloud of reddish brown that seemed to flow from top to bottom and I was immediately impaired, but unable to do anything in the stop and go of the traffic. It turned out to be a torn retina. I was very happy we were in the Dayton area, where I got excellent attention over the Thanksgiving holiday and didn't lose my sight. After a number of procedures, it was stabilized and we continued on with plans and assumptions. In the end, it did affect my depth perception on some days and my eyesight deteriorated as we walked.

Our grandchildren had opened a window on the future. Our commitment to their future became stronger and both Kate and I knew we wanted to leave them a legacy by our example and our dedication to clean water. Our gift would be that we tried our best to leave the planet in as good a shape as we could. Yet, I wanted something for them to relate to and that is where Paddle Lake Superior joined our crew.

Paddle-To-The-Sea by Holling Clancy Holling was published in 1939 and became a classic in children's literature. It describes the journey of a carved canoe as it travels from Nipigon through the Great Lakes to the ocean. It was a book I read to my children and now we gave it to our grandchildren along with an old 1966 Bill Mason video of "Paddle" made in Canada. Amanda created a child-oriented portion of our website called, "Where is Paddle?" Paddle to the Sea had completed his voyage, so now it was time for Paddle Lake Superior.

Wood-carving friends told me it would take six months, but six weeks from departure I got a block of wood and went to work creating my own Paddle. Our crew was now complete, or so we thought, but serendipity is not limited by planning and we added a videographer. Jim Radford had read about our plans and became intrigued. He called and asked if we would be interested. Sure. But we had no money, no video camera and we were within two months of departure. The result was someone who helped bring the trip to life through visuals. Kate found a calling as she put the video camera in her hand and narrated the trip of our lifetime. In the end, it added to our human survey and captured the human aspect of Full Circle Superior – 2010.

In the two months prior to departure many things happened. The most important was when Amanda's mom found a used RV that she bought and rented to us. Then we got the breakthrough for our health research: Health Span (BeneVia), Anytime Fitness and Medica got interested and wanted to help us tell our story. It was too late to get all the baseline studies done that we would like, but Drs. Paul and Dan Dewey helped us get our first aid kits and our basic measurements established.

Speaking of health, Kate was doing great, but my knees began to hurt by mile 2,000 of training. They burned, they ached, they throbbed, and I was in a quandary. Did I exercise too much or was I just getting old too quick? Dr. Paul Dewey suggested that I switch to a bike for training the last few weeks. This helped, but the question was, "Would they make it?"

April 29, 2010 – Our 24th wedding anniversary (remember, I like significant dates). After two months of unseasonably warm and dry weather, the day arrived. Gathered on Duluth's Canal Park boardwalk behind Canal Park Lodge with friends and loved ones, we were treated to music by Doug and Bryan Wood. Then we gathered at the shore and, in the Native American tradition, gave tobacco to the lake for safe passage and inspiration. It was perfect, except the storms and cold weather that had not come in March and April arrived the night before.

The waves rolled in, and the sky was a petulant grey with angry texture in the clouds. This was Lake Superior, Gitchi Gummi, the largest of the Great Lakes, and it was in charge from the moment we began. When the waves wash over the packed sand, you walk in the loose sand. When the wind blows sand in your face, you accept and keep going.

Our friends and family walked with us down the boardwalk. Our grandchildren frolicked, knowing that something was happening, but not able to grasp the extent of what Grandma and Grandpa were up to. It was a marvelous beginning as we walked toward Wisconsin. It was day one, hour one and mile one – only 144 days and 1,549 miles to go!

> To turn, turn will be our delight,
> Til by turning, turning we come 'round right.
> Simple Gifts, A Shaker Song

TWO

Into the Rhythm

I hear lake water lapping with low sounds by the shore
I hear it in the deep heart's core.
William Butler Yeats

Kate:

The 152 miles in Wisconsin would be the shortest shoreline to cover of the 1,555 miles we would walk in the three states and one province that encircle Lake Superior. Walking counterclockwise, Wisconsin would also be the first shore for us to tackle. This would be our pacesetter, we figured, getting us into a routine of solitary hiking broken by stops to take measurements, observe the landscape and, we hoped, chat with local residents.

But each shore, it turned out, would present unique challenges for us. In Wisconsin, it was red clay, born from the ancient bed of Glacial Lake Duluth, an early version of Lake Superior that existed when the ice was still in the basin and the shoreline was far above its current level.

The red clay made the shoreline extremely narrow because the clay slopes are undercut by waves and constantly slump downwards. Three feet of walking space was the best we could find in places. We also met the fewest residents because, in Wisconsin, most of the cabins are perched high on bluffs (some perilously close to the eroding edge) and residents didn't come down to the shore often, it seemed. And red clay became a nemesis for me – but more on that later.

Four of us bounced in a 22-foot bucking boat just after leaving Minnesota Point on that April 29, Day One of our journey. The wind howled, pushing huge waves – too big, really, for our boat – so we decided to land on the harbor side of Wisconsin Point. Our neighbor, Dick Glattly, made several attempts to get next to the pier, but we couldn't grip the cement wall or throw a rope over one of the stanchions. Even within the protection of the pier, the wind pushed the boat away from landing. Would we have to go back to Minnesota and drive across the bay just as we were getting started?

In the midst of this struggle, an angel in blue, Dan Mettner, came running toward us. He caught our line and bought us a few critical moments to throw our packs onto the cement and clamber up after them. Then Dick headed for home and we headed east.

Dan had driven over from our launch celebration in Canal Park. He'd parked at Dutchman's Creek, the first road access after Wisconsin Point, then walked 4 miles to meet us. A long-distance backpacker, this tall man with a salt-and-pepper goatee easily matched our stride as we moved down to the sandy beach.

Waves rolled in with foaming white tops and the wind blew away our words. I had to yell to be heard. It was invigorating and reminded me of visiting Cape Cod as a teenager. These waves, though, looked more like chocolate milk as the mucky bottom churned to the surface.

We were enveloped in the roar of the lake, the call of gulls and a tempestuous wind. The challenge was slogging down a soft sand beach and avoiding the waves that kept sneaking up on us. Wisconsin Point has lots of driftwood and had more garbage than any Lake Superior shore we would see along the rest of the journey, perhaps because in early spring, the lake tends to kick back anything tossed into it. Surgical gloves, empty tampon applicators, fishing lures and plastic bottles and bags were among the debris we noted.

I spotted something colorful near my feet and bent to pick it up. Dan called it "stick bait" – local terminology for a lure with three barbed hooks, which immediately snagged my thin wool gloves. I needed Dan, wearing his bifocal contacts, to unhook me. The lure was my first souvenir. I tucked it into a Clif Bar wrapper and into my pack.

I tend to watch the ground as I walk and began to see yellow-shafted flicker feathers and wings lying in the sand. Dan had seen more up the beach. "Around here they call it the 'yellow hammer,'" he said of the pigeon-sized bird.

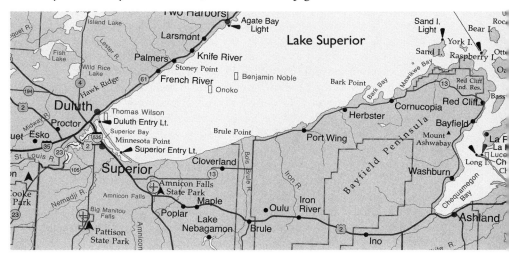

Why were there so many dead flickers on this beach? Later I learned that these ground-feeding woodpeckers might have been casualties of the raptors that also follow the shores on migration, or they may have arrived exhausted when migrating across the lake. Along with the beach garbage, another unfortunate sign of spring.

A psychedelic mix of fluorescent pink, blue and yellow tangled in vegetation caught my attention. Another lure. I began to wonder whether I might be able to open a bait shop after this trip.

We tried to stay on wet sand because it is harder and easier to walk on, but the waves forced us into the softer stuff. Around 10 miles, my right heel began to feel sore. After going up and down a few more sloping ridges, I knew I had sand in my boots. It didn't seem worth stopping, but after a few more minutes, I told Mike and Dan that I needed to check my foot. We climbed a sandy bank and found a long driftwood log to sit on. As soon as I took off my boot and sock, I felt guilty. A large blister had already burst; my heel was red and raw. How could I have been so stupid? Barely into our first day, and I had a handicap that could very well delay our journey.

Mike dug through the first-aid pouch looking for moleskin, and Dan handed me a blister pad. I gingerly tended the wound, then put my sock and shoe back on. That's when we noticed a lone gull down on the sand.

All along Wisconsin Point, we were entertained by flocks of gulls riding the wind, drifting over the water and banking back like gray-and-white kites. Near Dutchman's Creek, the flocks were massive. They were almost all ring-bills, with a few larger herring gulls mixed in. The large concentrations were most likely due to a nearby landfill. Still, it was a beautiful sight, especially when they all lifted up into the wild wind to soar back and forth.

But one gull remained behind. Dan noticed it pulling at something in the sand. We thought it might be a plastic bag, or maybe the gull was caught in fishing line. Dan looked with his binoculars. A sick feeling washed over us when he said, "It has a lure stuck in its foot."

Another wave rolled in knocking the bird down, rolling it tail over head. Mike and Dan went to see what they could do. It tried to run, but was swept up by a retreating wave and rolled farther into the surf. Sure it would drown, I faced away, not wanting to see it die. I heard Mike yell, "Come and help!" I turned to see him carrying the hapless bird on a long piece of driftwood.

The gull dropped off the stick onto the sand and struggled to escape. I tackled it as gently as possible and got my hands around its wings, pulling them in close to its body. My experience handling birds of various sizes at the Audubon Center came in handy. The bird's yellowish green eye stared at us. I talked soothingly, trying to convey our desire to help. The vicious hook was caught in both the webbing of one foot and its beak.

Once I had it pinned down, Dan tried to free its foot, but the hook was in deep. The bird's tongue was bleeding, pierced by the hook. I despaired about the bird's suffering and our inability to help. Then Dan remembered his Leatherman tool and took it out of his pack, first cutting the hook in the bill and then freeing the foot. Other than slight bleeding from its beak, the bird seemed okay.

I held it a little longer, then opened my hands. I held my breath and waited to see what it would do. The gull ran and flapped unsteadily for a few feet, gained air and took off, skimming just above the waves. A gull was not the bird I would have chosen as a totem or symbol of our walk, but we felt a special bond with the species at that moment.

Some people would say it was just a gull. Others call them "flying rats" because of their love of garbage and begging at fast-food restaurant parking lots. I could only think of it as a creature suffering from a human-related cause. The white lure with fluorescent dots of blue, yellow and green went carefully into my growing collection. As I eased it into my pack, I couldn't help but think about another cause of suffering for wildlife and people then much in the news – the oil spill in the Gulf of Mexico spreading onto the beaches and marshes.

The wind continued to blow as we made our way toward Dutchman's Creek. We hugged the slope that came down to the beach – slumping red clay that carried whole trees down to the lake.

We neared the first of what would be many dozens of streams to cross during our next few months. The waves were beginning to creep up farther on the beach, making our approach difficult. When we reached the flow, we looked for ways to cross without getting our feet completely wet.

Dan left us at this point. He was a gift for the first leg of our journey. A nice man, he has backpacked all over the country, walking many thousands of miles. He was an easy hiking companion, not given to non-stop chatter, but knowledgeable about this stretch of shore. Before he left, he snapped photos of us crossing through that first stream.

Soon we got a call from Amanda. Our hosts at Camp Amnicon had suggested that we walk on the road because the current high waves would erase any walkable beach. We climbed a slope and bushwhacked half a mile to Morrison Creek, then found a path to the dirt road that led into the camp.

Mike couldn't tell me exactly how much farther it was to the camp, and this was the first of what would become my late-afternoon low points. For me, the last 2.5 miles of any day were hard ones psychologically. I was ready to be done, and I couldn't see our destination because the road kept curving.

When we finally saw the RV parked ahead, I breathed a sigh of relief. We had walked more than 17 miles – a very long first day and 2 miles farther than we had anticipated. My feet throbbed. My hips creaked almost audibly. I could barely climb into the RV to collapse on the couch. Sheena, Amanda's rat terrier, was not happy about our arrival. She was extremely protective of her mistress and barked aggressively whenever we opened the door. It was an irritation we'd have to learn to swallow to keep peace in our little transient family.

Luckily for me, Camp Amnicon directors Alana Butler and Simon Gretton provided a warmer welcome and a bottle of sparkling white wine. We toasted our inaugural day, and then Alana showed us to the Sunset Hermitage, the cabin where Mike and I would stay that night. Camp Amnicon, connected to the Evangelical Lutheran Church of America, is on 700 acres along the shore of Lake Superior by the Amnicon River and offers retreat and adventure programs for adults and youth. Our hermitage was extra cozy with a gas fireplace, mini-

kitchen and the nicest outhouse we've ever seen. Gratefully, we each took a hot shower. It felt great, but secretly I craved a nice hot soak in a tub. I checked my blistered heel and carefully rebandaged it, wondering how I would protect it in the coming days.

I struggled to stay awake long enough to update the trip journal and record my meals in my food journal in what would become a daily pattern. Only 12 hours into our long-distance hike and I pondered, with some trepidation, the significant events on this first day – stormy weather, a blister and a bird that nearly drowned. Was the giant Naniboujou or maybe Kitchi Gami itself testing us?

With classical music playing on the radio and warm red flames glowing in the little stove, I gave in to sleep. I did hear Mike as he got ready for bed, but soon I was down for the count.

We awoke to cloudy skies and a mix of wind and rain. Our itinerary was already in flux. With the same strong winds as yesterday, we knew there wouldn't be enough beach edge to walk from the Amnicon River down to the Bois Brule River, so we decided to skip ahead to the stretch scheduled for Day 3 on Highway 13 to Herbster. Surprisingly, we both felt good. Mike's knees were not bothering him, maybe because he wore neoprene knee braces the day before. My blister was protected by Band-Aids and moleskin and didn't seem to be a problem.

We drove our car to Brackett's Corner where we parked and started walking down Wisconsin State Highway 13. By the time we started the temperature was in the 40s, with a slight mist falling. We met Amanda for lunch in the RV at Fish Creek, 3 miles up the road where there was a pullout. With the chilly damp weather we were happy to have a hot bowl of minestrone.

As we ate, an older man walked up to and around the RV. He knocked on the door and Sheena went ballistic. When I opened the door, I couldn't hear a word he said, so I stepped outside to speak with him.

"Are you the beach walkers?" he asked. He lived in Port Wing, 6 miles up the road, and wanted to walk with us. Mike explained about the waves, our route change and that we'd be walking the road for the rest of the day. That didn't sound quite so appealing, so he wished us luck and left.

At this point we realized while we had been encouraging people to join us, it would be difficult to pinpoint meeting times and locations. Each day would be a work-in-progress. We often wouldn't know a day's real itinerary until that day.

After lunch, our route took us on a beach, across a stream, bushwhacking through trees, and then back to the road. I felt slow, heavy and too full. When we crossed the bridge over the Iron River 5 miles from our start, we saw mergansers and blue wing teal floating near the mouth. About this time my digestive system declared war. Thank goodness for the thick woods nearby.

The mist changed back into rain, and our rain gear was soon soaked. On the road, cars drove past and most moved over to the middle, reducing the spray shot our way.

The rain finally stopped, and a bit of sun came out as a car slowed down in the other lane and a young woman rolled down her window.

"You the ones walking around the lake?" she asked.

"Yes."

She smiled. "Heard you on the radio last night. That's awesome. Need anything?"

She lived outside of Cornucopia, another small town along Highway 13. We thanked her for her thoughtfulness, but didn't need anything just then.

The plan was to catch up with Amanda at the Port Wing Harbor. Mike said we could walk to the harbor along a sand beach on a designated natural area called the Bibon Marsh. The beach was beautiful – white-capped waves, gulls flying by and lots of hard, flat sand to walk. We watched as an immature bald eagle was harassed by a gull. The eagle soared overhead and hovered for a moment, looking down at us. The gulls just hung in the air, as if suspended by invisible strings. Then two more mature eagles flew up the beach.

I was looking forward to reaching Amanda and was pleased when we finally saw her on other side of the harbor entry, busy talking to a man fishing from the shore. But she didn't see us and was past shouting distance. Then we realized there was no way to reach her; this was where the lake enters the marsh and it was too deep to cross. We had cell phones, but we'd had problems finding service all day and this was no exception. We tried giving hand signals to Amanda, but that wasn't working either.

I was getting my late-day blues at this point. Tired and sore, I was none too happy when we had to walk back up the same beach and return to the road, a

Barely started and I had to stop for a blister break. Ouch.

good mile or more. Mike is always chipper at times like this, which made me even grumpier. I hate going backwards. Mike accepts whatever comes his way.

I slowed down and dropped behind him, in no mood to chat. Another bald eagle flew by, too good not to share. I called to Mike. Then I tried to appreciate the white pines on the beach. Something good would come of the extra mile.

Amanda drove the RV over to our side and found a parking lot where we got in and drove back to Brackett's Corner to get the car. Then Mike went all the way back to Dutchman's Creek to look for a missing first-aid bag, which I later discovered in the bottom of my backpack. Amanda and I drove on to Little Sand Bay, looking for the Wilderness Inquiry cabin we'd use as a base for the next four days.

Once there we plugged the RV into the electrical hookup so we could cook. Showers were built onto the outside of the cabin, with lots of open air above and below the wooden sides. I took a shower, which felt good – nice hot water, even if it was a bit chilly once you turned off the water. I still dreamed of a bathtub, but reminded myself that this was still much better than camping out in a tent.

Mike decided to sleep in the cabin on the couch. I decided on the RV, even though it was sloping slightly to one side and I had to lie diagonally. By 11 p.m. and with journaling done, I passed quickly out … at least for a little while.

I awoke in the wee hours of the morning when the rain from a nighttime thunderstorm pounded the RV roof, making the sound of stones against a tin can. Lightning sparked the sky and wind rocked us. By the time I got out of bed at 6:30 a.m., the skies were absolutely clear with temperatures in the 40s. Mike was still asleep on the couch in the cabin. He didn't even hear the storm.

We thought about tackling the stretch from Amnicon River that we skipped the day before, but the rain may have caused the rivers to swell. I worried about the blister on my heel and didn't relish getting my feet wet. The NOAA weather report predicted strong winds (up to 40 mph) from the southwest. Jim Lynch, the cabin's caretaker, said that sometimes storms funnel up the shore from Duluth, so we decided to check the lake to see if we could walk beside it.

We first went to the Ehler's General Store about 40 miles up the road in Cornucopia to buy tall kitchen garbage bags (to cover my feet on river crossings), then returned to the Port Wing harbor to start walking. Wearing both a fleece jacket and a windbreaker quickly became too much, and I stopped to take one off. Mike walked on, then stopped, turned and stood with his hands on hips. I figured he was upset with my delay, so I imitated his posture in defiance. When I caught up to him, I asked, "What were you upset about?"

"Nothing," he said in surprised and sincere innocence. There are so many ways to miscommunicate.

The sky changed from clear blue to puffy white clouds to thick, dark gray masses. The wind blew hard, but happily at our back, all day. We ran out of beach and were forced back onto the rural highway. I entertained myself looking at houses and gardens. One especially clever design had whimsical garden features – a table with teapot, cups and two wire "ladies" having a "spotta tea."

We ate lunch on the beach, having walked about 7 miles to Herbster. Like Port Wing, Herbster is a small town with businesses along Highway 13 and good access to Lake Superior. I always felt euphoric reaching a beach. The waves, the wind, the sounds, the sights boosted my spirits. This feeling lasted the entire trip. What is it about coming down to the water? Is it an ancient, subconscious genetic memory of our origins? The water surrounding our cells has the same salinity as the ocean. Or is it a latent memory of the nine months we spend floating in another liquid environment? Whatever it is, returning to the shore renews me.

Sticking to the road meant more encounters with people and a realization of how fast news might travel around the Big Lake. On this day, the first encounter was with a middle-aged woman and her mom from Clear Lake, Wisconsin, who own a cabin at Port Wing. They pulled up alongside us and the woman said, "Are you the ones walking around the lake?"

"Yes."

She introduced herself as Renee Edwards. "Bless you. We'll pray for you," she said as they drove off.

A short time later, Renee returned and got out of her car with her camera. She asked if she could take our picture. We posed, she snapped a shot and then handed us a pen from her church and a $20 bill. Her whole church would pray for us, Renee said. She also told us how she and her husband always talked about walking around the lake. We didn't know there were others as crazy as us.

We told Renee how lucky she is to have a place on the lake.

"I feel like we live in God's country up here," she said, smiling. "There's a spiritualness about it."

We agreed completely and Renee went on her way again.

The next car to stop nearly caused an accident as it screeched to a halt with another car coming up fast behind. The man from Dayton, Minnesota, wanted to know where our followers were. Apparently he'd seen us on the news as we'd walked along the beach in Duluth with friends and family on the boardwalk.

"I wasn't sure where to look for you. I thought of going to Highway 2, but remembered you wanted to be close to the lake, so I came over to 13." He wanted to take a photo of us. Then he waved and drove off.

Amanda told us about another guy who had been at the Siskiwit Bay Coffee shop in Cornucopia hoping to meet us, but he gave up and left. It felt strange, this sudden celebrity. But then again, we intended to spread the word about clean fresh water, Lake Superior and healthy lifestyles, and getting our name out there meant a greater opportunity to reach more people. It felt good that people cared. Besides that, the pale green leaves on the aspen were so beautiful, the red maples were in bud and the marsh marigolds, dandelions and wild strawberry were in bloom. What an excellent time of year to walk near the lake.

The third encounter came on the road to Bark Point. We had stopped to do a 3-mile point count, taking photos in the four cardinal directions, recording the flora and fauna in that spot and logging the GPS coordinates, when a pickup truck slowed down. Bill and Dave Mackey recognized us from news articles. Bill has a place on the point with his wife, Karen, an artist.

"My wife and I," Bill said, "keep a scrapbook for things like this."

We talked about the lake and its preciousness. They own land on the Iron and Bois Brule rivers, and Bill said he's trying to arrange for his 900 acres to become public land. He's been worried about sediment runoff into the river and lake. They took our picture and drove on.

The road to Bark Point seemed to never end, and my mood sagged. I kept looking ahead hoping to see some sign of Amanda and the car (and the end of our day), but we didn't find her until we reached a boat launch off the road. By that time, I was moving mechanically. I was learning that whenever we got close to 12 miles for the day, walking hurt my attitude as well as my body.

Sheena was in full territorial mode when we tried to get into our car. We still weren't prepared for her reaction; I jumped every time I opened the door. She always relaxed when we were in the car or RV, but once when Amanda picked us up, the dog lunged and bit my left hand forefinger as I put things into the back seat. Yelling has no effect when Sheena is protecting Amanda (or thinks she is), and while such a guardian was good for Amanda on this trip, it was not so good for the rest of us. Oddly, we had worried about how to handle encounters with aggressive dogs on our hike; we didn't imagine one would be traveling with us.

The day's walk finished short of Cornucopia for a total of 15 miles. Back at the cabin, we showered with the wind blowing over and under the wooden panels. Before dinner we worked on our respective computers, typing up notes and data, while Amanda cooked pork tenderloin, corn and fried potatoes. Mike was ready to sleep by 8 p.m. His feet were burning with nerve pain from his bad back. I made him soak his feet in hot water, then rubbed herbal lotion into them, which seemed to help. I did the same for mine. He was asleep on the couch by 9 p.m., when I went back to the RV. Amanda stayed in the cabin until a mouse ran over her foot in the living room and she scurried back to the RV. You could hear mice racing through the cabin walls, and I'm sure a few ran over Mike during the night, but he didn't begrudge them their space as long as he got a good night's sleep. Little did we know, by the end of this walk, how rare a good night's sleep would be.

Something also happens on taking a walk.
Charles Dickens

Mike:

The purpose of our adventure was to learn, to teach, do research, observe and record. Along the way, we gathered information and talked with people. We came away with a lot of impressions. In between these chapters, I'd like to share some details of our discoveries in our "After Thoughts."

Connecting with people, as well as observing nature, was a goal of our walk. Informally on the road, in restaurants, shops or hotels and at presentations along the way, we wanted to meet people and get their stories of the lake. People actually arrived on the shores of Lake Superior just as a shore was being created by the receding glaciers some 11,000 years ago. People are part of the lake's ecosystem. As you can see in Kate's day-to-day descriptions, we encountered many people. We made new friends and had a great respect for most everyone we met. Their generosity and curiosity bolstered us and gave us a new, positive perspective about how residents understand and intend to care for the lake.

To gather people's attitudes and knowledge about the lake, we used a survey developed with the help Dr. Tony Murphy of St. Catherine University in St. Paul, Alex Mayer at Michigan Technological Center for Water and Society, and Rich Axler at the Natural Resource Research Institute.

We had a video camera to record interviews with people about their feelings and concerns. We captured 70 stories, many on our website, from around the lake, and this serves as a 2010 baseline, just as the survey does. Among the most amazing, happy statistics – we met a grand total of four grumpy people on our 1,555 miles. It helped, of course, that we tried to avoid conflict, walked as a couple (are obviously not homeless), are "seniors" and that we approached people with a smile and a greeting. More importantly, most residents around the lake seem naturally welcoming and friendly.

We also discovered the power of the local media. As our story will show, people frequently greeted us and even waited to meet us, after reading or seeing our story. We needed the media to spread word about our trip and our educational and inspirational goals, and the press did that in print and broadcast, both regionally and farther afield.

Our connection with *Lake Superior Magazine* turned out to be a good endorsement, especially with regional businesses, which respect the publication.

When we met with *L'Anse Sentinel* Editor Barry Drue at a picnic table just north of L'Anse, Michigan, I asked him if he would have given me the time and the column inches if I had just come to the office with concerns about fresh water and Lake Superior. He laughed. We both knew our message was delivered in the context of a story – the story of our walk around the lake – and that was the best way we could tell it.

At times we were overwhelmed with requests to stop and to visit. We tried to accommodate as many as we could, but not everyone got as much time as we or they might have liked. Besides needing to meet a daily mileage goal, we also had Amanda scheduled to meet and pick us up in a designated places at designated times. An offer of something cold to drink on a hot day, though, was always hard to turn down. We even went back a few times to visit with people we'd met during the day.

We surveyed, one way or another, 570 people.

The demographics revealed in the survey give us a cultural picture of Lake Superior people, or at least those who interacted with us. Just more than half identified themselves as politically liberal and 17 percent as conservative. Slightly more than 90 percent were Caucasian; 63 percent were female; and about one-third (35 percent) earned $51,000 to $100,000. Every income bracket, though, was represented. Happily, 61 percent said they spent five to 20 hours outside every week – to live on the lake, after all, usually means to love the outdoors.

We had a pretty fair split on location: 36 percent were Minnesota; 25 percent from Michigan; 15 percent from Canada and 12 percent from Wisconsin. The remainder came from several other states. Of those doing the survey, 85 percent owned a cabin on Lake Superior and 35 percent lived permanently within the watershed.

So how did they answer some of the key questions?

78 percent did not think the laws and regulations on global warming were doing enough to protect the lake.

64 percent saw global climate change as a very serious threat to the lake. We found that the Canadians were more likely to talk about climate change. Our impression was that they did not have the same aversion to the term or concept as some U.S. citizens do and were willing to engage in conversation about it.

63 percent did not think that the laws and regulation were doing enough to control development.

82 percent did not think enough was being done to protect the lake from pollution. However, 65 percent did not expect a decline in the water quality of the watershed over the next 10 years, though 35 percent felt it had declined in the last 10 years.

75 percent felt invasive species were a very serious threat. In our conversations, we heard a strong fear of Asian carp getting into the Great Lakes through Chicago's waterways. It concerned homeowners, fishermen and just about every group we met.

46 percent felt that failing septic tanks posed a somewhat serious threat to water quality and another 44 percent thought it was a very serious threat.

58 percent thought agriculture runoff was a serious threat. Considering the limited areas of agricultural development around the lake, this was an interesting finding.

67 percent thought dumping chemicals down the drain was a serious threat to the lake and 30 percent thought it was somewhat serious.

70 percent saw industrial emissions as a very serious threat to the lake.

53 percent thought run off from driveways was very serious and 41 percent felt it was somewhat serious.

76 percent saw the destruction of wetlands as very serious; 94 percent believe wetlands are a filter for the quality of lake water and 81 percent knew that phosphorus promotes excess plant and algae growth. Studies have shown that the hard and soft stem bulrushes (part of the wetland system) actually remove the most phosphorus from a water system.

56 percent of those surveyed thought that coal-burning power plants were the main source for mercury, but 28 percent did not know how mercury might get into the water.

68 percent believed that the lake temperature is rising.

79 percent recognized that the lake's water level has been decreasing for a decade.

Our broad conclusions from our surveys and interviews were that first and foremost, people truly love Lake Superior. Perhaps because they love it, they know their bay, their home site and their area particularly well. However, they did not seem to know as much about what is happening in other places around the lake.

Imagine Lake Superior as a big bowl of cereal with people all around the sides, dipping their spoons into it. Wouldn't you want to know if one of the others spit in the bowl or had a contagious illness? Lake Superior is a big bowl, and we hope people will become more connected all around the lake. We need to be informed about the lake, what threatens it and its conditions on all shores. People are intelligent and they care, but we have to work together.

THREE

Red Clay & Balloons

To see a world in a grain of sand,
And heaven in a wild flower,
Hold infinity in the palm of your hand
And eternity in an hour
Auguries of the Innocence, William Blake

Kate:

A breathtaking morning to start our Day Four – clear and calm, with a waning moon in the pale blue sky. The morning routine was nearly settled: Up around 6 a.m., write at the computer, do yoga (sometimes), get dressed, eat breakfast, make and pack lunches, load our backpacks, head out.

We drove to the Siskiwit Bay Coffee shop in downtown Cornucopia and met owners Barb and Dennis Edwards. They had been reading newspaper articles about our walk and told other patrons what we were doing. They generously gave us coffee and T-shirts. After checking email, we headed back to the Amnicon River to complete the leg we'd missed earlier.

Cornucopia, a town of about 200, essentially has two "business" districts. Along Highway 13 there is a pull-off area toward the lake that has a marina and, in season, several retail stores. This is the best known part of Cornucopia, being the part most visited. It's also where the retired boats are left to decompose, almost an icon of the town nicknamed "Cornie." Residents and savvy visitors are more familiar with the other retail area, the downtown, found by turning off the highway onto Superior Avenue to find Ehler's Store, the coffee shop and a restaurant.

The wind blew out of the west and started to pick up, but the sun was shining on the beach. I took a deep breath, looked ahead and thought, "This could very well be our best day and our worst day." The best because there was no better place than a remote beach. But it would also turn out to be slow going because the clay banks complicated travel.

We immediately realized we were remote only from people. The beach abounded with tracks – coyote, wolf, bear, raccoon, deer, otter and even eagle. At the first stream, five vultures soared and a couple of eagles perched in the trees. A nearby deer carcass was the attraction.

We saw wolf tracks nearly all day and constantly scanned the shore ahead in hopes of seeing a wolf trotting our way or a bear shuffling out of the woods. Tracks were all we spotted, though the track makers may have been watching us.

Once again I found yellow-shafted flicker feathers on the beach, as well as perfect round balls of clay with pebbles imbedded in them. Then I began to see and collect beach glass. Of all the Lake Superior beaches I would walk, Wisconsin offered the most of these bits of wave-tossed opaque glass. I spent a lot of time bending down to pick up the green, white and blue pieces until my pockets bulged. During the whole trip, I continued to stuff my pockets with treasures.

At one point, I saw a pair of teeth in the sand. We believe they belonged to a deer. So fascinating was the beach combing that I had to remind myself to look up and appreciate the broader beauty along the shore and among the trees. No matter the direction – forward, backward, across the lake, across the beach, to the sky or to the land – there was so much to see.

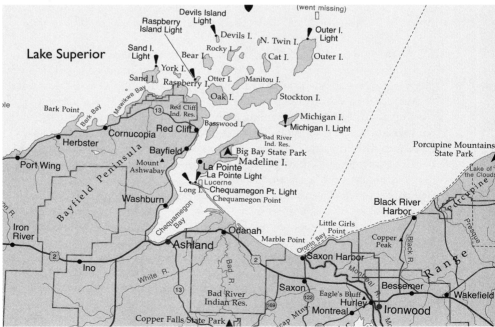

My blister was healing nicely, but I didn't want to get my foot wet. That proved impossible. We crossed many streams, most tiny and easy to jump, but some were bigger. When possible, I tried to cross on logs. Mike, blisterless, just slogged through. He took off his socks and shoes. I covered mine in green plastic bags, holding them up around my knees. The makeshift waders worked well for crossing streams, but when I used them to get around a bulge of clay bank, the waves washed over the tops and my boots got soaked. Frustrated, I gave up the pretense of staying dry and, like Mike, just slogged along and hoped for the best. At least, Mike would say later, I'd gotten biodegradable bags.

There were no logs to use at the Poplar River, so Mike walked across at the river mouth in water to his knees. Then he came back to lead me. On the other side, we sat on a log, wrung out our socks and I changed my blister covering. We decided it was a good time and spot to eat our sandwiches. But as the clouds thickened and the wind picked up, we got both chilled and sandblasted.

When the clay banks forced a choice, we tried to go up and over them rather than walk in the lake. Mike went first; I followed. Usually this worked well, but one time I found myself standing on a slow-moving escalator going the wrong way – down. My right foot and trekking pole sunk in the clay. In slow motion and with no way to stop, I lost my balance, spun and rolled backwards down the bank. I saw Mike's distraught face as I slid away. Two thoughts flashed in my mind: "This doesn't feel too bad," followed quickly by "Crap. I'm going to have mud all over me." When I finally slid to the bottom of the slope – only about 5 feet – Mike called down, "Are you OK?" Nursing a severely bruised ego, I nevertheless tried to answer civilly. To Mike's credit, he never burst out laughing at the ludicrousness of it all. Had our roles been reversed, I probably would have.

I stood up and reached behind me. Thick clay caked my butt, my back, my sleeves, my boots, pants and poles. It could've been worse; I could have gone down face first.

I tried to wash off in the lake, but that just made the clay, already thick enough for pottery, turn slicker. I nearly cried about my brand-new pack and my pretty purple rain jacket now coated with this ocher dye. We were in the middle of nowhere – no shower, no gas station, no hotel. This actually was a lesson – accept it because there isn't anything to do about it until we returned to the cabin many hours hence. Even though the sun still shone, I felt a dark cloud roll over my head and a deep sigh in my heart. And I still had to get up the slope. Mike bent a sapling down for me to grab, and I scrambled beside him, ready to go on.

Getting my bearings again, I took a good look at the shore. Because of the clay banks, much of the land appeared to be gradually slipping into the lake. In places it looked as if an earthquake had split the land and created crevasses. In other places, the clay oozed out like lava. All of it eventually washes into the lake, tinting the water brick-red for a long way out.

We bushwhacked through thick speckled alder, and I sweated with the exertion. Mike often went around the base of the clay banks, but since I didn't want to walk in water, I went up along them. After I struggled through one section, muttering and grumbling, a branch hit me in the eye. That was just about enough for the day. About to launch into a complaint against the universe and in Mike's general direction, I rubbed my eye and stopped as I spotted an otter swimming parallel to the beach. Mike saw it, too, and began taking photographs. We both held our breath as it swam calmly past. Perfect timing on the otter's part. One of our totemic animals, it brought back to us the spirit of Mike's late son, Matt, who loved to play in the water and snow. We felt Matt with us in spirit on this walk. And while I don't think he gave me the poke in the eye, he – as an otter – definitely boosted my mood at just the right time.

At another small stream we came upon a young porcupine munching new green leaves in a tree. Nearby, someone had placed a deer skull on a tall branch poking out of the sand. It was a strange, almost mystical combination – the quick and the dead.

I found myself envying the gulls and eagles (12 counted this day) and their ability simply to set their wings and glide on the wind – above the clay. Lots of sharp-shinned hawks soared along the shore toward Wisconsin Point on their northerly spring migration. We noted even more wolf tracks on the beaches, but still no living example.

We also made another major discovery on this shore – balloons, all colors, in all kinds of places from the middle of the beach to beneath downed trees. I crawled under one birch next to the water and came eye to eye with an orange balloon. Most still had some air in them. Some were still attached to strings. They were buried in sand, under tree roots, in tree branches. Some were latex; others were Mylar. I should have started keeping count but didn't realize at the time how common they would be during the whole trip. These were not left behind by local party-goers. What this phenomenon demonstrated for us was how far airborne pollution might carry. Many of the pollutants into Lake Superior, such as PCBs, are airborne and may blow here even from countries across the ocean.

Our day ended at the Bois Brule River, which we couldn't cross; it was too deep, filled with waves and running fast. Amanda had come down the Clevedon Road to pick us up, but joined us as we completed our walk to the mouth of the river, where we turned around and walked back to the car.

Amanda left early the next morning to take Sheena for a vet appointment in Moose Lake, Minnesota. We were expecting to walk 17 miles and she would meet us at the end of the day, around 4:30 p.m. The sky was cloudy and hinted at rain as we began on the beach at Cornucopia, walking past the harbor and sailboats. We'd caught up to our circle and could continue east.

On the way to Meyers Beach Road, a young woman jogged past us. We recognized her from a couple days earlier when she had asked if we were the ones walking around the lake. This time Jessy Lemler invited us to have coffee or tea at her home up the road and we gladly accepted.

Jessy lives in a cozy old farmhouse that her husband, Bill, rebuilt over the past 15 years using recycled materials from other houses and barns. Jessy served us tea and grainy nutty rich chocolate bars. Her dog, Finnigan (black lab and blue heeler), pestered Mike to throw a ball. Mike obliged. A beautiful black-and-white cat wandered through the kitchen. Jessy said the cat is a good mouser, but she keeps him inside during the day so he doesn't kill birds (a lesson we wish more pet owners would learn).

Big gray chickens ranged in the yard, and a rooster crowed for reasons only he understood, as it was well past sunrise. In such a pastoral setting, we felt immediately comfortable. Jessy told us a little about herself. A student at the University of Wisconsin-Superior, she had been trying to start an environmental club on the campus. She wants to work in conservation, but she and Bill worry that they won't be able to stay in this place if she is to find work in her chosen field. Bill works as a teacher's aide in special education. We thanked her, took photos and continued on our way.

Apostle Islands National Lakeshore begins at Meyers Beach where a trail through a forest of maple, birch, fir and very old cedars goes to the sea caves. When we arrived, spring ephemerals bloomed all around us – spring beauty, dwarf ginseng, bellwort, wood anemone, black currant and honeysuckle. This is one of only four nationally designated lakeshores. Lake Superior has two of them, – the Apostle Islands National Lakeshore here and Pictured Rocks National Lakeshore, which we would visit in Michigan.

The sea caves appear both on the mainland shore and among the 22 islands of the Apostles archipelago. Battered by waves for 10,000 years and by constant freezing and thawing, portions of the sandstone cliffs have been carved into delicate arches and deep caverns with red pillars. The caves, seen from above, were impressive, but I had to keep calling Mike back – "You're too close to the edge" and "Don't get any closer." I sounded like a nagging mom, but these are seriously dangerous cliff edges. We'd been warned that often the ground at the edge is eroded, a condition not always visible from the top but that can result in a breakaway and a fall.

We took time out and sat facing an amphitheater of small caves as water surged in and gushed out. The sound effects soothed us. It was a perfect spot for a lunch stop, though we quickly became chilled and donned our fleece jackets. We continued on this upper trail until it took us down to a serene, empty beach. We walked until we could go no farther, then it was back up on top and bushwhacking through downfall to get to Sand Point Road to meet Amanda.

Bushwhacking was as bad as walking along a clay shoreline. We often had to climb over or under trees downed in windstorms. It was impossible to follow a straight shoreline path and often we had to veer inland to skirt the worst piles of blowdown. Beneath our feet, hidden branches grabbed and tripped us.

We finally reached the long, barely maintained old logging road where we were to meet Amanda. I was ready to quit and just wait for her, but Mike wanted to go see what the Sand River looked like.

"How far is it?" I asked.

"I don't know. I'll walk for a half hour and turn back."

"You mean we have to wait for another hour then?"

"I'll just walk for 15 minutes and turn back. Honk the horn when she gets here and then I'll come back."

"Yeah right," I mumbled. "You won't hear it." Mike doesn't wear a watch and too many times I sit and wait and wait and wait and wonder and then start to worry. Off he went and I got comfortable leaning against a big old birch on a little piece of land jutting out toward the lake. I took out my notebook and jotted

The most surprising litter? Balloons!
Release birds and butterflies instead.

down a few things and sketched
the view with a pen, wishing I
were a better artist and knew how
to indicate water. Mike returned
sooner than expected. What
he didn't tell me was that he'd
seen an old, lesser quality road
on the map and went to where
it intersected the shore in case
Amanda was waiting there. She
wasn't.

By 5 p.m. we started walking
out. The GPS showed the road
to be several miles long, but we
hadn't gone far when we saw a
pickup, followed by our car. Jim
Lynch was leading Amanda in
because she had found the road,
but was worried about the many ruts and holes. This proved that having a second
vehicle on the trip was important; there was no way the RV could have gone
down this path.

We gave Amanda a break from cooking and went to the Village Inn
in Cornucopia, where they serve good pub food. All three of us had our
computers on the table and were answering emails and posting on the website.
Cornucopia, like Herbster and Bayfield, has the feel of a small New England
fishing village, though only a few fish commercially these days.

Back at Little Sand Bay, Amanda and I continued to sleep in the RV; mice
really ruled the cabin, especially at night. One ran out from a behind bucket in
the bathroom while I was sitting there. I stomped my feet and it spun around
and disappeared. This place definitely could use a good mouser.

Another gray, chilly morning and my muscles were a bit sore. I'm always
stiff in the morning, so stretching helps. I thought about the toning of my
muscles during this walk and how I expected to lose 10 pounds – at least; overly
optimistic as it turned out.

By the time we left the Wilderness Inquiry cabin the skies had cleared and
the temperature was close to 55° Fahrenheit. The plan was to walk back to the
cabin, have lunch and continue walking into Red Cliff.

Amanda drove us back to the Sand River, where we walked the beach
as far as possible then climbed a steep bank – no clay this time – and started
bushwhacking through a forest of old hemlocks and white pines.

"Man, if we have to do this all the way to Little Sand Bay, we won't get there
till late afternoon," I thought. We had made only 3 miles in two hours. Jim Lynch
had told us about an old coastal trail that hadn't been maintained. We found it

and even though it was narrow, it had obviously been used by humans – a long, long time ago. We ran into piles of trees that were relatively easy to skirt, but then we encountered a stack of old trees that looked like someone had been playing a game with giant Pick Up Sticks. There was no way over or under them, so we had to angle far off course to get around them and back toward the cliff edge.

The trail ended above a beach near the old Hokenson Fishery at the Apostle Islands National Lakeshore marina. (For three decades, the fishery was run by the families of Eskel, Leo and Roy Hokenson and now is lakeshore heritage.)

The sun was shining and it was a warm walk back to the cabin where we had a lazy lunch on the back deck. As always, our meal was, let's say, "eclectic." I had leftovers (fried whitefish livers and baby potato cakes from the night before), plus beef jerky, sheep cream cheese and Diet Coke. Mike had red wine and a peanut butter sandwich, plus pita bread and some of the cream cheese. He worked on the computer uploading photos when Amanda arrived with news from the Red Cliff Band of Lake Superior Chippewa tribal office. The people there were sorry, but didn't know we were coming through on this day. We had gotten approval from the band last year to walk through the reservation, and Chairwoman Rose Gurnoe had said band members would be encouraged to walk with us, but the communications glitch meant that wouldn't happen.

Inertia often sets in after a leisurely lunch break, but the road waited. I wasn't looking forward to this afternoon though, because it would be a long dusty forested road with no lake access. At times like this, audio books became our diversion. After several long uphill stretches and 11 miles, my right big toe started to hurt. I have a large bunion that has never bothered me, but long distance hiking seemed to aggravate it.

Like most people, I get grumpy and whiny when I'm tired or sore or very hot and sweaty. The last two hadn't been a problem yet, but the others seemed common at the end of these first few days. Generally by the end of the day, Mike and I would be some distance apart, since I slowed down as the day went on. We would each be lost in our own thoughts or listening to books or music. I also tried to listen for birds in the forest and observe what was happening with the arrival of spring. I tried not to look at my watch and just focus on a distant point. For Mike, it was different. I knew he was hurting, too, but he just kept on going – such has been his personality and constitution from birth. I wished I could do the same, but I'm more like "normal" people.

Before we began this trip, I'd worried about encounters with dogs (not even counting Sheena). Early on we carried some capsicum spray (a kind of pepper spray), but after a while we left it behind. We are comfortable around most all kinds of dogs and Mike, with his height and deep voice, is good at exuding dominance when needed. Along this stretch of road, three dogs ran out of a yard and surrounded us. They appeared to be German shepherd/husky mixes and were barking, but we didn't feel threatened. With most dogs, we yell "Go home!" and they do. But before we said anything, a woman came over and herded them back into the yard. "They won't hurt you," she assured us, and we felt that was true.

Just before the small town of Red Cliff, where Amanda picked us up, a stunning fox, with a rich red coat and distinct white-and-black markings, crossed the road. It acted quite nonchalant, trotting up the highway and then casually turning into someone's yard.

We returned to the RV where Amanda heated up a yellow split pea soup her mom made. Joyce Hakala and Beth Blank were culinary godsends for us, making food and freezing it for us to heat up later. It simplified the preparation time and gave us great tasting, nutritious meals. We enjoyed the soup on this, our last night at the Sand Bay cabin. I was ready to move on.

It rained during the night and in the morning frozen raindrops clung to the car. When we got close to the Red Cliff administration building, we decided to stop to see Rose Gurnoe. She was in a meeting, so we met with Marvin Defoe, vice chairman of the band.

In many American Indian cultures, it is customary to give a gift of tobacco as a sign of respect and thanks when someone does you a favor or teaches you something. We have done this with Lakota people we know in South Dakota. We wanted to give the vice chairman tobacco for taking time to visit with us.

We asked Amanda to look for packages of tobacco to give as gifts to Ojibwe elders we might meet along the way. She came back from her hunt with a plastic bag full of TOPS roll-your-own cigarette packages. She had searched all over and was told by the ladies at the gas station that this was what people used.

We chatted with Marvin, and then Mike told me to give him some tobacco. In our relationships with the Lakota people, we always hand over the entire package, so I took one out of my pack and handed it to Marvin. There was an awkward moment, and I couldn't decide if he looked amused or offended.

He handed it back to me and said, "Open the cellophane and take it out."

I did this. Then he said to open the pack, which I did.

Finally he said, "Take out a pinch." He held out his left palm and told me to put the pinch of tobacco there.

"Don't you want the whole pouch?" I asked.

"I don't want to have to pray that much," he said, laughing. We joined him.

Mike asked if he'd be willing to give a statement on video about the lake and the Red Cliff people's relationship to it. Marvin said he would, and we went outside. He walked over to some trees, offered a prayer and the tobacco. Then he lit a cigarette, and we talked some more about what we were doing.

On the recording, Marvin first spoke in Ojibwe (some say "shinabay" – short for Anishinabe, as the Ojibwe or Chippewa people call themselves). When he finished, he explained that he'd given his Anishinabe name, his clan (Fish) and talked about how his ancestors had lived on this lake for 15,000 years, since the glaciers melted and filled it. He spoke about the four things we need to survive, just as he'd told his 8-year-old son the night before: food, air, water and love.

Marvin talked, too, about the division between the 153 bands around the lake (we had no idea there were so many) and how they need to come together to protect the lake, not be divided as they've been for generations, which he attributed to neocolonialism or greed for resources. To explain, he walked to an aspen and broke off a small twig, which he then broke into many pieces.

"You see this one twig? By itself, it is weak, but if I break it into more pieces – 153 pieces – you can hardly bend them. That is how we need to be."

It was an eloquent description and demonstration.

About then another man stuck his head out the door, and Marvin smiled and said loudly, "And I'm the best fisherman in Red Cliff."

He was taunting George Newago who finally came out. They both laughed and Marvin told him about our journey. He was much more vociferous than Marvin and immediately spoke about how the Indians never gave up mineral rights to the lake and so they should control the lake or at least have more say about what happens to it. He spoke knowledgeably about the Great Lakes Legacy Act, signed into law in 2002 to provide funding to clean up "areas of concern" around the Great Lakes. He also was adamant about Native rights.

Marvin told us, "You should put it on video."

George protested, "I don't want to be on YouTube."

"You're already on YouTube," Marvin reminded. George admitted that was true. Finally he consented and we recorded his views on Native mineral rights.

We spent nearly an hour with Marvin and would have gladly talked longer. We learned that he has built birch-bark canoes for 18 years, but lately has seen the big old birch trees dying. A change was coming to the earth, he said, a change that will make it hard for people to survive. Thanking Marvin for his time, we shook hands and went back to the highway, inspired by our talk with him.

Not much later, a car pulled up in front of us. An older woman rolled down the window and asked, "Are you the walkers?"

"Yup, that's us."

Sue Johnson had read about us in a newspaper and wanted to know if we were doing it to raise money for a cause.

"It's about fresh water," I told her, "but we do accept donations because we're self-funded."

She reached into her purse and handed me a roll of ones. "I don't know how much is there, but it's all I have right now." We thanked her sincerely and she drove on.

Bayfield was coming into view, and we were thrilled by the bright tulips and daffodils blooming along the way. At this point it struck me: I have just WALKED to Bayfield from Duluth. We've made the 1½-hour car ride dozens of times, but now we've walked it in seven days. I could actually grasp this, and yet it was hard to believe. It almost seemed more unbelievable than it would feel when we finished the entire 1,555-mile circle nearly five months later.

Just out of town, we passed a massive junkyard that spills out from a house to the edge of the road. A local business, this stuff is for sale, but it seems like hoarding. You could spend a whole day picking your way through it – amazing stuff sprinkled with hunks of driftwood and masses of rusting iron. It's the kind of place I enjoy exploring, but Mike wanted to get by it as fast as possible.

Bayfield is rightly called a "quaint" town, deliberately free of the blaring signage that can transform highway access through a town into an often-ugly commercial strip. Built on a hill, the town slopes down to and orients around the lake. It's the kind of place where walking from shop to shop to restaurant is natural. The waterfront in summer months hosts myriad sailboats – like the one on which we were married. We felt very much at home.

We had lunch at Maggie's, a popular restaurant in Bayfield filled with all manner of flamingos – plastic, glass, whatever. Mike – never one to miss an opportunity – handed out our surveys to people sitting nearby and we got about 10 filled out. I satisfied my craving for vegetables with a marinated Italian salad and Mike satisfied his never-ending desire for burgers with one of Maggie's best. Shortly after lunch, we started down the Brownfield Trail, an old railroad bed that goes to Port Superior. Running parallel to the shore, it provided a great view of the big bay. We met an older gentleman walking his little dog on the trail. He told us he worked on maintaining it.

"I saw a big tom turkey on the trail the other day," he reported with obvious pleasure. "It ran so fast down the trail."

Often these rail-to-trail conversions act as wildlife corridors, and people can connect to nature and find relief from the noise and stress of urban life (though Bayfield, population 440, is hardly urban life). It is a shame that the entire railroad grade wasn't preserved as a trail back in the '70s when there was a chance to do so. For whatever reason the state government didn't act on it and subsequently people bought up sections of property and built on it. Today there is so much private property along the old grade that it would be next to impossible to regain it as a public access.

The trail merged with the road as we got close to Port Superior. As we neared the marina, I reminded Mike that the sailboat we'd been married on and sailed for three summers had been sold and moved to this marina some years ago. It had been called the *Izmir,* and I decided to go in and ask at the charter office if they knew of it. No luck. Then we went next door to the marina office and I asked again. The woman at the counter hadn't heard of it, but she called out to her co-workers, "Ever heard of *Izmir*?"

One man who had been there a long time responded, "That was Dr. Tarhan's boat. Now it's called the *Doris E.* He sold it to one guy who let it run down; now new people own it and are trying to restore it.

"They put on bow thrusters," he continued. "People couldn't handle its length when coming into the slips. It's a lotta boat."

Mike, who captained the boat for five summers, agreed with him on that.

On the end of Dock 2, our old friend was looking the worse for wear. Her teak trim was all faded, but she had a solar panel on the back. It was good to know someone was taking care of her now. We spent our first three summers of married life on that boat and have memories to last a lifetime. Boats do take on personalities and hers was a good one.

Back on Highway 13, a gray minivan drove past and honked. We couldn't see the driver, but we waved anyway. It turned around and pulled over on the other side of the road. A woman and three kids got out. Carol Sowl, a teacher from the La Pointe elementary school on Madeline Island and one of Mike's former graduate students, crossed the road to us. We hugged, and she introduced the kids. We made a video of them because they had joined us just as we'd reached our landmark 100 miles. It was a great way to note the milepost.

Amanda, who had spent the day at the library putting photos on the website and getting it up to date, picked us up along the road just south of the

Bayfield Fish Hatchery and took us to the Old Rittenhouse Inn. Owners Jerry and Mary Phillips are long-time friends, all the way back to those sailing days in the late '80s. They have always been kind and generous and now they were providing us with a luxurious room for two nights.

We poured ourselves a glass of wine and sat at our computers. Julie, Jerry's sister who works at the Inn, came in and said a woman named Bridget Weber wanted to meet us. She was one of our Full Circle Facebook friends and asked if she could walk with us for a while. We welcomed her enthusiasm and invited her to join us the next day.

The kitchen was being remodeled at the Rittenhouse, a gorgeous Victorian era home converted to an inn. So we went back to Maggie's to celebrate Cinco de Mayo. Mike accosted other diners with a request to take our survey and all agreed. One man, sitting by himself, came from Austria – an American nuclear physicist based in Europe. He'd recently bought a sailboat and was in Washburn trying to get it ready for its first season. He and his wife plan to come in spring and fall to sail on it, and when he retires they will sail around the world. They will get good practice on Lake Superior, as Mike can tell them.

Later, Mike walked to the old courthouse building that serves as park headquarters for the Apostle Islands National Lakeshore. He gave the rangers information about the wolf signs and merlins we'd seen during our walk on park property. They had expressed interest in hearing about any unusual sightings we might encounter. A rainbow stretched across the sky over the lake as we walked around town after dinner. We both love the seaside atmosphere of this small community and have often dreamed of living here.

Back at the room I indulged my dream of a nice soak in a tub. Between the warm tub, the red wine and the quiet atmosphere of the wood-accented room, sleep wasn't hard to find.

This was it – my D-Day. The day we'd stand on the scale and the truth would be known. Part of our journey meant tracking our health, just as we were noting the particulars of the environment. I closed my eyes, stepped on the scale and repeated in my head – 142, 142, 142. When I looked down I couldn't believe it – 145.4! Could that be last night's filling dinner? That's almost a pound more than before we started. How was that possible? My blood pressure was 132/80 and heart rate 62, same as before. So all this effort hadn't made a whit of difference. I know muscle is supposed to weigh more than fat, but still, those numbers should go down on the scale. Mike weighed himself next and as would be the case throughout the trip, he saw a drop of 3 ½ pounds. Thus began my jealousy. Between his cheerful attitude and now this weight loss, my husband was starting to bug me.

We ate breakfast at the inn and Bridget showed up in time to observe some real senior moments. Just before leaving, Mike realized he didn't have the GPS. In and out of our room, he looked on every surface and dug through his pack. One more check in his backpack, and he discovered the GPS in a side pocket where it had slid under his water bottle.

Amanda dropped us where we'd left off on Highway 13 headed south, and we walked on the highway until we saw the old railroad grade to our left. It took us through private property, and when we cut through one yard we saw a vehicle in the driveway ahead. At this point, Bridget looked a bit uncertain about our route. Don't worry, I told her. "I call Mike the 'talking pathfinder' and send him ahead to negotiate with owners of property we cross."

A man got out of the car, and Mike called out, "Hello, I have a question."

"Just a minute," the man replied, "I have to get my granddaughter out of the car." He lifted a toddler out of her car seat and, with her standing next to him, turned his attention to us.

Mike explained what we were doing, but he already knew who we were. He'd seen us in an interview on Channel 21.

Dennis Kirchener had lived in this spot all his life. He and his wife now live in a condominium at Port Wing. In fact, they'd seen us the day before when we passed through the condo's parking lot and sat on a culvert for a phone interview.

Dennis told us it was no problem to go through his yard and the next one and said we'd come to a bridge over the Onion River and a big beach. At a beautiful stretch of smooth, sandy beach, we stopped to take photos of the river mouth and record data. I suggested we put Paddle in the stream. Paddle traveled in Mike's pack everyday, and we placed him in different locations to take photos for Amanda to post on our website under "Where is Paddle?" This helped us connect our journey to kids, including our own grandchildren.

Mike and I walked over to the stream edge with the little carving and suddenly I was sinking in quicksand. Mike, behind me, turned back when he saw what was happening, but I kept sinking.

"HELP!" I yelped as I watched my boots going under.

Mike came back, grabbed my hand and pulled me out. Both my feet were soaked – an embarrassing bummer. Naniboujou seemed to be having fun with me again. We decided to find a better spot to photograph Paddle.

We walked down the beach and stopped at a picnic table so I could wring out my socks. Taking off my pack, I set it down on the seat beside me. After putting my shoe back on, I donned my pack and we started out again.

Walking has its ups and downs, like here on the Red Cliff Reservation near Little Sand Bay.

On the beach were amazing sand sculptures, at least a dozen of different sizes. We called them "porcupine mounds" because sticks poked out the sides. We wondered who created this avant-garde art. It occurred to me we should record all the beach art we found. This was the first of many unexpected and fun creations we would encounter.

I felt for my small camera and discovered it was not in my pack's side pocket. I searched my pack, hoping it was in a different pocket. It wasn't. I realized it must have fallen out at the picnic table when I set my pack down.

Dejected, I said, "I'll go get it."

"No, your feet are sore," said Mike. "I'll go."

So he took off his pack and started back. I decided to do a 3-mile point count, but discovered the North/South index card was missing. In order to record which direction I was taking pictures of the shore and lake, I had made laminated index cards with one of the compass directions printed on each side. The photos would be worthless if we didn't know which direction we were pointing.

This had become "The Day of the Lost." To make matters worse, Bridget witnessed all of our embarrassing troubles. I'm sure she was thinking, "And these old people think they're going to walk all the way around the lake?"

Instead of sitting and waiting, she walked to the end of the beach to see if we could cross the Sioux River. The answer was no. Mike returned and, happily, had my camera. Going forward, we found the old railroad grade, but ran into a dead end at the river. So we returned to noisy 13, with cars and trucks too close. We came to a road that turned left, toward the lake and took it, hoping to reconnect with the railroad grade or an ATV trail. Finding neither, we continued on the road until we cut through a yard to the beach. Some old fishing sheds sat on the shore. Mike loves taking photos of historical structures. I was nervous about being there, and Bridget was nervous, too, but we followed along gamely.

I wanted to get out of yards, especially after we saw the "Bears will be shot" sign and a shot-up target practice sign lying on the ground. I told Mike as much, and we found the old railroad grade again. The trail seemed to end where a fence crossed it, but to our left someone was starting a lawnmower. I sent Talking Pathfinder to plead our case.

No need to plead. Rita Olson, owner of this big white house on the shore, said, "I've seen you millions of times on the television."

She shook our hands. "I thought you'd be skipping over the rocks down below." She gave us permission to pass through her place. Then she told us the place was for sale – $2.3 million. Tempting, but a little out of our range. Like us, her home and property are her retirement package.

Rita said it was "maybe 3 miles" to Washburn. We could hear but not see Houghton Falls, since it was in a steep rocky ravine. The beautiful trail wove through an aspen-maple forest, but wildlife was sparse. We saw only a thrush, a gray squirrel and a white-crowned sparrow.

When we got to Washburn, Amanda was waiting at Chequamegon Bookstore and Coffee Company on the main street. We put our packs in the car, so we could walk unencumbered for the final few miles out of town. Bridget stayed and waited for BART (Bay Area Rural Transit). An easygoing travel companion, she originally intended to go just part of the day with us, but ended up doing 13.3 miles. She said she saw much more than she anticipated and found spots she'd like to revisit (and some, I imagine, she would not).

We walked for another hour down some side roads and an ATV trail. Our goal was to reduce the distance to Ashland, since the forecast did not look good, calling for possible snow.

We had dinner that night at Jerry and Mary Phillips' home – a wonderful spring menu of fresh leeks, sautéed fern fronds, asparagus, mashed yams, spare ribs and couscous with leeks. A lovely fruit salad of apples, strawberries, spinach, watermelon, black walnuts and maple syrup dressing for dessert and a perfectly matched glass of pinot noir rounded out the meal.

We ate breakfast with Amanda and Jim Radford, our videographer. Jim came to shoot footage of us walking and wanted to show us how to upload videos to our computer. I was anxious to leave, since running a shuttle to our starting point always took extra time and rain was predicted to start at 10 a.m. Menacing clouds and a strong east wind already were in place. Jim agreed to shuttle us and Amanda left for the Mother's Day weekend.

We parked our car in the Walmart at the east end of Ashland. It was bitterly cold, with the wind at our backs. I tucked close to Mike's tall body, but I still look as though I'm freezing in our video. Light rain began to fall as we climbed into Jim's minivan and drove to our starting point just shy of 14 miles from our car. Raindrops changed to mist as we put on our rain pants for wind protection. The look on Jim's face as he waved and drove off seemed to say, "I'm sure glad it's them and not me out there walking today." Or maybe he actually said that.

We followed an ATV trail almost all the way to Highway 2, except for a detour onto a rural road that curved around the west side of the Northern Great Lakes Visitor Center. On the way, we had a phone call from reporter Mike Simonson of Wisconsin Public Radio in Superior and did a live interview with him. Heavier rain pelted us, and stopping to do data counts every 3 miles was just no fun. Our gloves were wet and our hands cold. The rain continued and our jackets lost their ability to keep us dry. Around noon we crossed a grassy field to the visitor center and some welcome relief.

Inside, Mike found a teacher from the Northwest Passage Expeditionary High School in Coon Rapids, Minnesota. Peter Wieczork and his seven students planned to camp for the weekend. They had been out the previous night and had gotten soaked, so they were hanging out at the center, hoping to stay dry – like us. The relatively new Northern Great Lakes Visitor Center, with its semi-circular floor-to-ceiling windows, walk-through exhibits and beautiful wood accents, is a great place to hang out and to learn about the lake, its watershed and wetlands. There are also nature trails on the property and a lookout on the top floor.

While our jackets dried, we ate our lunch. How nice it would be to just stay here the rest of the afternoon, I thought, but that wasn't going to happen. Reluctantly, we put on all of our semi-dry outer gear and headed east directly into what felt like gale-force winds. Cars and trucks roared by us in the two lanes going west on Highway 2 and very few moved over. We turned our backs to big trucks as they went by to avoid spray in our faces.

On our left, the lake churned muddy brown with white crests. Almost horizontal sheets of rain hit us, and even with our jacket hoods up we had to turn our faces away. It felt like being pelted by little ice balls. Sopping wet on the outside, we remained warm inside thanks to our fleece layers. The lakeside walkway took us away from the highway and we watched a pair of geese and five goslings wade into the rough water, oblivious to the storm. A killdeer skittered ahead of the waves. Earlier we had seen a green-backed heron fly out of a marsh. If birds can wonder, we, not as comfortably adapted to the weather, no doubt caused them to shake their feathered heads.

By 3 p.m., the rain took on a white tinge. Yes, snow in May. The closer we got to our end point, the damper and colder we felt. We shuffled into the parking lot at 3:45 p.m., never so grateful to see a Walmart. We had walked 13.3 miles, but surprisingly my feet and legs weren't as sore as other days. Walking grassy trails helped.

Even though hypothermia was a real possibility, neither of us ever thought, "Why the heck am I doing this?" But once again, I was very thankful that we decided against backpacking and tent camping for this adventure.

In the Walmart restroom, I peeled off my "rain pants," as they are euphemistically called. But then, nothing repels water after two hours of steady downpour. My polar fleece top was wet, as was my inner shirt and the tops and bottoms of my pants. To revive ourselves, we drove to the Black Cat Coffee Shop for hot drinks, and I treated myself to a slice of the zesty lime cheesecake. (Maybe this explains why I wasn't losing weight, you say?)

This was the Friday before Mother's Day and our scheduled weekend off to head home. We'd been walking nonstop for nine days and felt this would be a good time to take a break. We didn't know if this would make returning to the walk on Monday feel difficult; we looked forward to the at-home rest.

Up at 4 a.m. the following morning to leave for the Bad River reservation. A sliver of moon hung in the dawn sky, and there was a pink sunrise, which is pretty, but worrisome. (Red sky at night, sailor's delight; red sky in morning, sailor's warning.) There were predictions for rain in the afternoon.

We had arranged to meet Amanda at the casino owned by the Bad River Band of Lake Superior Chippewa at 7:40. Amanda wasn't there when we arrived, so we drove to the tribal administration building and found Bob Wilmer, the conservation officer for the band who would take us out to Long Island. With him was a man named John (we didn't get a last name), a trapper for the U.S. Department of Agriculture. Long Island is one of the few places on Lake Superior where the endangered piping plover still nests and part of the island is off-limits to anyone except the scientists studying them. Predators like coyotes and raccoons are their biggest threat, even on the island.

We had no cell phone reception and couldn't reach Amanda. Luckily, Bob and John were not in a rush. We decided to wait until 8:15.

We drove back to the casino parking lot, hoping to see the RV. Mike went into the post office, and I waited by the car, peering down the highway. Then the phone rang. The connection was bad, but I could tell by the number on the screen that it was Amanda.

"Where are you?" I said with some impatience.

"At casino" is all I heard. I didn't know if she was asking where we were or telling me where she was. We hadn't seen her on either side of the building and I started to wonder if there was another casino. Mike came out at 8:08. "There she is," he said, and there she was, walking across the parking lot toward us.

Driving quickly to meet Bob, we hopped onboard his boat and cruised down the Bad River. This river is a focal point for the reservation, and the band is fighting a proposed iron mine that threatens to pollute the river and harm wild rice beds. Bob watched for "deadheads" (submerged logs, not Grateful Dead fans). There are lots of deadheads in the spring, he said. A kingfisher sat along the shore, as did a mature bald eagle – the first of a dozen we'd see this day. Two spotted sandpipers flew in front of the boat – bare inches above the water – and as we caught up to them, they veered toward shore and kept pace with us. We were going 32 mph. We saw more sandpipers on the water's edge all day, usually in pairs.

The river was a foot low, so Bob had to be careful of shallows. The river mouth is a narrow channel and he slowly negotiated into the lake. We motored parallel to the island until he found a spot to beach the boat, and we jumped onto the sand. It was about 5 miles back to the river mouth, where he would pick us up, he said. Then he pushed off to drop the trapper farther up the island.

Immediately, we noted coyote tracks going both ways on the beach. The piping plovers face a big challenge. On this fine walking beach, we passed cabins on a higher ridge. On the other side of the island, we saw a huge shallow area filled with wild rice beds. I found an eagle feather lying on the beach and later gave it to Bob.

Giant driftwood trees lay on the beach, mostly parallel to the water. They reminded me of an elephant graveyard or of whalebones. The lake storms can be amazing and that's how they get pushed up so far, but I wondered if they came down the river or across the lake.

Besides the coyote tracks, we saw lots of otter tracks. Later we saw deer rushing out of the tree line to the water. One pranced and danced in the waves. It didn't go deep, but seemed to enjoy playing in the water, twisting and kicking its hind legs. A second deer stayed on the dry sand. They began to walk toward us, and we wondered how close they'd get. When they finally saw us, they shot back into the trees. It would seem animals can enjoy the beach as much as we humans.

Around 11 a.m., we reached the river mouth, sat on logs and ate lunch. We looked out at the lake, trying to spot Bob's boat. The sky had clouded over and the wind was building, along with the waves. The boat arrived around 11:15 to ferry us across the channel. By mid-afternoon, the waves had grown enough that we would not have been able to go out.

On the other side of Bad River, we found ATV tracks. They went all the way down to Joe Rose's campground. We also saw two eagle nests on this stretch. One adult wanted to land – it had food in its talons – but it kept swooping and soaring around and out and wouldn't go to the tree until we were well past it. Later another adult eagle landed in a white pine and screeched at us. There were a couple more big white pines nearby and I saw a nest in one and a human-built platform, used as an observation blind, in another one close to it. Farther down the beach, right next to the water, were three inflated mylar balloons and one deflated one, all tied together by ribbon – Mother's Day balloons. I picked them up and carried them to dispose of in the campground.

Melinda, a caretaker at the campground, was with two of her four little children. After every big windstorm, they find all kinds of stuff on the beach, including lots of balloons, she said. I commented on their good fortune to live in this place. She agreed, saying that they spend a lot of time swimming in the lake, sometimes as early as April and as late as October.

In the distance, we could see the point jutting into the lake. It didn't look good for walking – big tall clay banks. We decided to walk the beach as far as possible, then return the next day and start on the road. Amanda met us at the campground, then drove ahead to park on a bluff above the beach. She and Sheena came down the steep bank and all three of us trooped up the shore. We had to cross a couple of streams. On the clay slopes beside us, small rivulets seeped out, creating patterns – a series of miniature river deltas or perhaps more like moving glaciers or tree roots. Mike and Amanda couldn't stop taking photos.

As we climbed up to the car, I looked back. "Goodbye Wisconsin," I thought. "I loved your beaches, but hated your red clay."

Then we got into the car and drove back to the casino and the RV. After using the Internet service in the lodge lobby, we moved to the Saxon Harbor marina campground near the clay banks where we'd ended our day's walk.

By this time, it was cloudy and chilly. I rode in the RV with Amanda, and after negotiating some low-hanging branches on the road to the campground and a steep hill, we found a serene location, right next to the lake. The flocks of gulls whirling about the boats tied up in the marina, their calls mingling with the chiming of rigging against metal masts created the feeling of an ocean coast. We had walked 15 miles and reached another significant milestone. In the morning we would leave Wisconsin and enter Michigan.

**Who can ponder
the thoughts that have been gathered
where countless minds have wondered
by the lake?**
By the Lake, Jennifer Wells

After Thoughts
Point Samples

Mike:

Our first commitment was to take photos about every 3 miles along the shore noting GPS points and taking field notes. The photos were taken in the four cardinal directions – east, south, west and north – to serve as a visual record for a moment in time. We did 300 such point samples along the route. This kind of information gathering has never been done before around Lake Superior, as far as we found, and it can serve as a baseline for future studies. We have given the data to a number of academic institutions to archive so that in the future another adventurer or researcher can return to these locations and see just what has changed.

Each shore is different in terrain and climate conditions. On the south shore, hemlock and beech were dominant with a nice mix of forest types, substantially deciduous trees. There were also beautiful, healthy old white pines, very popular with bald eagles.

The large sand beaches that dominated this shoreline were usually backed up with a beach grass and the purple-flowered beach pea along with forest of pines, fir and spruce behind them. Paper birch, aspen, yellow birch and maple were common. The mountain ash grows to tree size here. In Minnesota, I am used to thinking of it as a shrub, but these were tall trees with high canopies mixed with the other native species.

Moving north into Ontario, we transitioned from the white pine/birch/cedar forest to the boreal black spruce forest between Lake Superior Provincial Park and Pukaskwa National Park. Here spruce became dominant and would stay with us across the northern reach of the lake. Sandy bays still had beach grass and beach pea, but the large areas of bedrock shore meant that lichens, mosses, butterwort and sundew patches were common.

Birdsfoot primrose and bladderwort were more common than butterwort and sundew from Gros Cap to Lake Superior Provincial Park. Three of these flowering plants (bladderwort, butterwort and sundew) share a unique niche. They are insectivorous, meaning they capture curious insects and extract nutrients from them after they die. On bare rocks and rock pool eco-communities, where there is no natural nutrition to provide energy for plant growth, this is an important evolution.

The pools forming along the Ontario shore are not like tide pools that are frequently replenished by the tidal flow of water. These pools do not get a regular cycle of filling and emptying. Instead, they begin the year with snowmelt and then evaporate unless replenished by rain or wave splash. This tenuous existence requires special adaptations. We found the normal realm of aquatic pond insects – water striders, whirligig beetles, water boatman and back swimmers, which have the ability to fly to another pool if one dries up.

It was in these pools in Lake Superior Provincial Park that we encountered the red nymphs (aquatic salamanders) who enjoyed the protection there from larger predators. Salamanders bury themselves and hibernate during winter, much like other amphibians.

Because this Ontario shore seemed to have a healthy moose population – though I never got to see one – and it was not overrun by white-tailed deer, we also found reproductive white cedar, young plants that would replace the ancient ones eventually. This is something missing in Minnesota, where the plague of deer has contributed to the decline of the moose and impacted the content of the forest flora. White pine, for example, has not been able to make a comeback from timber harvest because the deer favor the young seedlings.

From Nipigon south, the vegetation began to include more pines again. On Sibley Peninsula, the forest became similar to what we have in Minnesota, except on the exposed rocks and islands where arctic disjuncts (species from the last ice age) still reproduce and flower. A few of these also grow on the Susie Islands in Minnesota, near the border, and on the northernmost Minnesota shore, but nothing like the Ontario flora and its gorgeous array of plants like encrusted saxifrage with petite white blossoms (it also grows in the tip of Michigan's Keweenaw Peninsula), the purple six-petaled Arctic bramble and alpine bistort with its spike of flowers.

As we walked the Minnesota coastline, we moved into second and third growth forests with lots of birch and aspen. The birch was often in poor shape and there were no young white cedar because of the voracious white-tails. Some say the birch would have cycled out by now, replaced by pines, if the deer had not intervened. The mountain maple is browsed extensively by deer, too, but seems able to withstand the onslaught, while species like mountain ash are nipped back to the ground almost as soon as they have a season of growth. We found the Encampment Forest Reserve to be one of the last vestiges of the original shoreline vegetation.

Here's what we did every 3 miles throughout the trip when on the shore – took photos, marked GPS point locations and recorded flora and fauna.

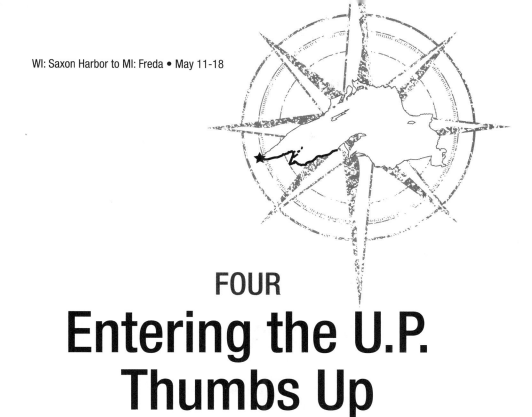

FOUR
Entering the U.P.
Thumbs Up

Perhaps the truth depends on a walk around the lake.
Wallace Stevens

Kate:

The next 51 days took us along the Michigan shore of Lake Superior.

We felt optimistic, having made it through Wisconsin in less than two weeks and knowing that the next several weeks meant walking the most-accessible portion of the lake's shore all the way to Sault Ste. Marie.

Still, there would be some challenges – anticipated and not – and we'd get the first inklings of what our bodies would endure for the next four months.

This first leg of the Michigan journey took us from Saxon Harbor at the Wisconsin-Michigan state line, around the 300-mile loop of the Keweenaw Peninsula to the entrance of the Huron Mountain Club, about 40 miles northwest of Marquette. On a map, Michigan looks like two askew mittens. On the top mitten – the Upper Peninsula – the "thumbs up" would be the Keweenaw. Many people living here refer to themselves as Yoopers – referencing the "U.P." and possibly started as a slam from those in the lower peninsula, but now proudly adopted by locals.

The people of the U.P. have good reason to feel slighted when it comes to the attitudes of their southern cousins. The state once produced a map that inexplicably did not show the U.P. Yoopers have their own name for those from the southern "mitten" – Trolls who live below the Mackinac Bridge, the

5-mile-long suspension bridge that links the two peninsulas – artificially, if not naturally – into one state.

We found most locals along this shore to be friendly, independent, often hardscrabble people who loved the lake and woods dearly enough to choose staying in place over seeking high-paying jobs in cities to the south. While there's a blend of those who come from a heritage of mining and extracting resources, with people who have moved here to be by the lake, the majority of people we met seemed to be concerned over the health of Lake Superior.

On May 11, we turned left on the road up from the Saxon Harbor Campground and entered Michigan. Not far beyond there, we also entered the Eastern Time zone for the next four months, through Michigan and Ontario.

The heavy gray sky carried a damp, chilly wind, raising goosebumps. We had dressed in layers, but once we turned the corner into Michigan, the wind stopped and we quickly warmed up, stripping off jackets, hats and gloves. Not able to walk the shoreline because of steep cliffs, we could only glimpse the lake between cabins as we walked along County Road 505. As we neared Little Girl Point at Oman Creek, we heard the roar of the waves. The rocky beach with white-capped waves rolling in looked for all purposes like the Atlantic Ocean.

The road took us past fragrant pink flowering apple trees and roadside ditches filled with cornflower blue forget-me-nots. These are delicate little flowers, yet their color was almost fluorescent against the greenery. (The week before, we encountered marsh marigolds in every wet spot.) Behind the apple trees, the paper birches' pale green leaves were just unfolding. Great, dark groves of hemlock, a coniferous tree uncommon west of Wisconsin, began to appear.

For lunch break, we chose a slope above a stream entering the lake and watched waves break into the mouth. All around us pin cherries, serviceberry, strawberry and dandelions bloomed. We frequently got lost in our thoughts and

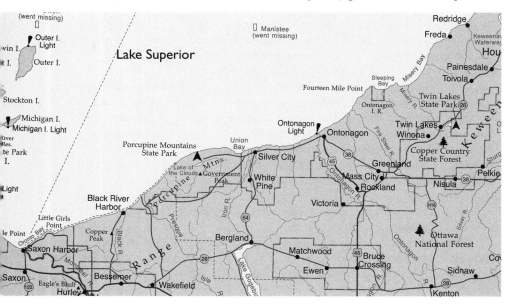

spent miles without a word between us. Other times, we chatted, often about our three children, four grandchildren and the grandchild on the way.

We had been pretty quiet on this stretch of asphalt when Mike, who usually walked on the flat dirt edge rather than ahead of or behind me, said, "I'm going to cross over."

Once on the other side of the road he suddenly stopped dead in his tracks, staring at the ground. A smile crept onto his face.

"You want any morels?"

I looked at him with disbelief. This was the right time of year for the wild delicacy, but in our years of hunting morels, we only found them in the woods, in the moist ground beside recently dead or dying trees. Yet here they were in the packed soil along the edge of the road!

Mike picked one, and we both nibbled on it. We did not see one other morel patch before or after this spot. Were the mushrooms calling to Mike? Or was it just an amazing coincidence? As lifelong naturalists, we are attuned to the proper location of plants and their normal blooming sequence, and these morels were definitely out of place.

Along this same stretch of road, a pair of small falcons, called merlins, provided entertainment. We heard them first and then saw one chasing a broad-winged hawk. A second merlin appeared, calling loudly, and the first came back to it. They landed in a tree near the road and squawked at us. We assumed they had a nest, since there were several big pines nearby.

Just beyond Little Girl Point, a speed walker caught up to us.

"Where are you headed?" she asked, with arms pumping up and down.

"We're walking around the lake."

"Oh," she said, not stopping. "So you're going all the way around? Do many people do that?"

"No."

"Are you Canadian?" she asked as she fast-shuffled ahead without waiting for an answer, and then added over her shoulder, "Good luck."

We looked at each other and shook our heads. We definitely were walking with purpose, but thank goodness Mike had time to find that gift of the morels, which we would never have seen on a power walk quite so determined as hers.

We ended the day at the western edge of Porcupine Mountains Wilderness State Park, following the North Country Trail, America's longest national scenic trail; it crosses seven states from North Dakota to New York. The trail leading into the park was an old logging road and even though it was early in the hiking season, the grass and ferns were thigh high. This trail system is maintained by volunteers with little funding so we weren't surprised to find old wheel tracks deeply rutted and places where the trail was completely washed out, creating shallow but steep ravines. Thick with ferns – ostrich, lady, oak, sensitive and bracken – the woods felt like a temperate rainforest.

Tired and muddy, we were happy when Amanda picked us up and drove us to the RV.

Union Bay campground in Porcupine Mountains Wilderness State Park brought back memories for Mike of many backpacking trips he led here.

The Porkies, so named because they look like a crouching porcupine from the water (the park says that the Ojibwe name for the hills is "skag"), are the backbone of the 60,000-acre park that features the spectacular Lake of the Clouds. There is an overlook at 1,350 feet above sea level and above that is the highest point of the park, Summit Peak, at 1,958 feet. Our trail, though, would be near Lake Superior, the park's lowest elevation at 602 feet above sea level.

Starting from Union Bay, we decided to walk westward (backward for us) along the 17-mile Lake Superior Trail to link back up with the North Country Trail before heading inland. In Michigan, we would often jump ahead and then backtrack to complete our full circle, sometimes to make a scheduled presentation and sometimes just because of logistics.

By walking to the west, we could head downhill at the beginning of the day and hopefully not have a steep climb at the end. This also would give our joints a chance to realign and take a break from the constant position of left foot-left leg lower than the right from walking east along the shore.

Immediately we were surrounded by towering old hemlocks. The park is known for its stands of virgin timber and 80 percent of it is designated as roadless wilderness, but the giant hemlocks take your breath away. Hemlocks are towering conifers with lacy needles. The gigantic old ones are our version of redwoods. We felt as if we were in the forest primeval, a place untouched by people. I decided that this day's walk was best described as "TREEmendous" because the trees left the most lasting impression.

We came out onto a rocky ridge with a forest of small, bent and gnarled oaks stunted by the lack of soil and exposure to the wind on these rocky heights. Surprisingly, much of the geology in this park replicates that of Isle Royale, some 70 miles across the water to the northeast. The rocks dip below the lake in a formation called a "syncline," essentially the bottom portion of a geologic fold, and come to the surface here and on Isle Royale.

Closer to the lake were a mix of old cedars and yellow birch, which grows up on what looks like legs because they always start on an old nurse log. They could have been models for the Ents, the walking, tree-like guardians of the forest from "Lord of the Rings." We saw no new generation of yellow birch, cedar or hemlock, only millions of maple saplings. In a way, we were walking through a forest of the "living dead." According to park naturalist Bob Wild, white-tailed deer yard up in the winter months in sections of the forest and are notorious for eating saplings and changing forest composition, but other factors like climate change influencing rainfall could also be involved.

One old, gnarled cedar caught our eye. It was close to the water, on the rocks and much larger than the well-known Spirit Little Cedar found along the shore near Grand Portage, Minnesota. This cedar's roots spread in all directions and were wedged under heavy, solid layers of bedrock and cobblestones. We left tobacco to honor its spirit and tenacity. It has withstood countless storms and has held its ground, while others have toppled. Of all living things, trees set the best example of perseverance, of living long and strong.

Trees were not the only impressive flora. In places, the entire forest floor was covered in trout lilies. Most were past bloom, but we spotted some of the lemon yellow flowers near the end of the trail. Their leaves are covered with green and maroon splotches. In the background the lake sparkled like a sapphire.

We were standing on a bridge over a gurgling stream when we heard voices and suddenly two big dogs came loping into view. Two men who followed appeared to be out on a day hike, since they weren't carrying packs of any sort. The dogs reached us first and the men yelled ahead not to worry, that they were friendly. We are dog lovers, but there is always some apprehension when you encounter unfamiliar animals.

As they approached, one said, "Aren't you the people on the cover of the Ashland paper? I just told my buddy, 'I think those are the people.'" We chatted about our adventure and learned that they regularly come to the park to exercise their dogs. We all agreed about the treasure that this park represented.

In talking about the lake, one of the young men told us about a grandfather who had been a lighthouse keeper in the Apostles. He said Lake Superior was in his "family's blood for 100 years." He would be the first of several who would share stories of their family's connection to the lake and how that seemed to have been encoded in their genes, even if they were no longer manning lighthouses.

We looked at each other and laughed as we walked away. It wasn't just their connection to the lake that was fascinating. It was the fact that our "fame" as walkers had found us in the middle of a 17-mile stretch of wilderness.

This day's hike was one of our longest to date and the last 5 miles were made more difficult by dirt ravines so steep, we had to sidestep down and traverse up. My legs and feet were hurting, but I recovered pretty quickly each night. Unfortunately the same wasn't true for Mike. I would wake up at night to Mike tossing, turning and whimpering from the pain in his knees. It wasn't noticeable during the day; he marched along, often faster than me in the afternoon. Each morning when I asked how he was doing, he'd say he felt OK, but I knew the lack of sound sleep would take its toll.

The next morning we awoke to rain and decided to shorten our day's mileage. I wore my old yellow Columbia rain jacket, figuring it would definitely keep me dry. And it might have if Tina Turner hadn't belted out "What You Get Is What You See" on my iPod. When Tina sings, it's no time to hunker down in your rain gear; I had to dance my way down the road. Mike had the video camera and filmed me from behind. When I saw the video later, it made me laugh.

Music in my ears always lifts my mood, so the rain really didn't bother me. If Mike needed an escape he listened to audiobooks. The wet conditions even came in handy when Mike discovered that he didn't have a pen (nor did I) to record information for our 3-mile point count. He picked up a stick, stuck it in some mud and used nature's drippy ink to scribble the coordinates on a piece of paper. Luckily we didn't have too many wet road days, but when we did, we would hug the shoulder when a car approached, not sure whether they would move over or not. Thankfully, most motorists were considerate.

On May 15 Amanda moved the RV to Ontonagon. This would be our pattern throughout the trip – a form of leapfrog. The RV would get parked in a community up ahead and then Amanda would shuttle us in the following days as we walked toward that location.

Finding a wireless connection was important, but not easy. In Ontonagon the only place that had wireless was the library, which was closed, but we drove there anyway and managed to pick it up in the parking lot. All three of us sat in the car, typing away, checking emails, Facebook and our website, while the car windows fogged up and hungry mosquitoes swarmed outside.

We ate dinner at Syl's because it advertised pasties (pronounced pass-tees). This is a U.P. specialty, like a pot pie you can hold in your hand. I ordered the mini-pasty and it was huge. This region of Michigan was settled by Welsh, Cornish and Finnish people who worked in the mines of the 19th century. With them they brought this meat-filled pastry. There are variations depending on the ethnic group, but generally it contains meat, potatoes, rutabagas or turnips and sometimes carrots. We found these pasties a bit dry – nothing a bottle of ketchup wouldn't have enhanced, sacrilegious as that may sound to some in the U.P.

After eating, Mike asked our teenage waitress if she'd be willing to fill out our questionnaire about people's attitudes and knowledge of the lake. She agreed and he handed out some to the kitchen help and owner, too. An older man at a nearby table asked about Amanda's camera. He was a former employee of the defunct paper plant and blamed environmentalists for the town's decline. He wanted to know if Mike was "one of them." Mike said he likes jobs, but environmentalists get a bad rap for bad decisions made by companies. The man said he didn't think he should do the survey because of his attitudes, but Mike said, "No, we want everyone's thoughts and opinions." And so he filled one out.

Ontonagon is one of many towns around the world that built its economy on an extractive industry and then as the resource declined, as it inevitably does, the local economy suffered. When the cost of mining became marginal, it coincided with public awareness of the environmental damage, and the copper plant closed. In Ontonagon, the White Pine mine was the last to close. In 1995, it was given a permit for in situ sulfuric acid leaching. Within a year others became aware of this environmentally damaging process, and in 1996 the permit was rescinded and the mine closed.

The next morning was cloudy and the wind was from the west at 20 to 30 mph, with gusts of 40 mph. The lake was riled up with big frothy waves rolling in and pounding the sand. We began 10.5 miles west of Ontonagon in these blustery conditions, and I was happy to walk on hard-packed sand. There were lots of streams, but the road paralleled the beach and often we were able to walk up to the bridges and then back down to the beach.

Near Ontonagon, we saw some Baird's sandpipers, a uncommon species, but one we saw often in Michigan.

52

We came to the Mountain View Lodges resort and asked owner Rick Varecha if we could cut through his place to the beach. We explained what we were doing and his wife, Jen, overheard us from the house. She came out and said, "I saw an article somewhere about you, in *Lake Superior Magazine*, I think." Their daughter came to meet us, too – a shy, homeschooled teen.

Rick had owned the resort for six years, spending a great deal of time and money upgrading the cabins. Then he warned us about bugs, asking, "What are you using to protect yourselves?" Before we knew it, he asked Jen to get a bottle of repellent, assuring us it was all natural, with no DEET. As we said thanks and goodbye, I told Rick I'd like to bring our grandkids back with us sometime.

"You'll be back," he assured me.

When we came around Sunset Point, as Rick called it, and onto a rocky shelf, we met a woman walking toward us.

"I bet you don't often see people walking on these rocks," I said.

She agreed. Her name was Kathy and she was getting ready to leave the cabin where she'd been staying. She had been coming to this small resort for 30 years. Like so many people we met on this walk, she'd spent a lifetime coming to the lake for recreation and rejuvenation.

This shoreline was a mix of sandy beach and shale ledges. These were mostly flat rocks, but we had to watch our footing. I tripped and stumbled a few times, but recovered before falling. One tumble could be a serious setback.

Our unusual beach find for the day was a green hockey helmet (no hockey player attached, thankfully). Near the mouth of the Mineral River the wooden planks of a shipwreck poked out of the water not far from the beach. This was the *Panama*, a bulk freighter that ran aground in a storm in 1906. It was the first of several wrecks to see along the Michigan shoreline – always a haunting sight.

Next to us the waves made a frizzing, sizzling sound as they swept over the sand. White bubbles like liquid lace fringed the edges. I played tag with some of the waves and managed to keep my feet dry, so when we came to one stream that wasn't too deep, we took off our boots and socks, rolled up our pants and walked across. It was numbingly cold, but it felt so good when we got back into warm socks and dry boots.

In Ontonagon we met Bruce Johanson, a reporter for the *Ontonagon Herald* newspaper and president of the Ontonagon Historical Society. A former teacher with a crewcut of gray hair, wire-rimmed glasses and a rich knowledge of local history, he took us through the restored Ontonagon Lighthouse, built in 1866 in a schoolhouse architectural style. The rooms are in near-original condition and artifacts reflect the lives of the lighthouse keepers. In an upstairs bedroom, Bruce pointed to an old sepia photo on a bedroom dresser. The man in it was missing his right arm. This was Thomas Stripe, a former keeper. A cannonball took his arm during one of the town's Fourth of July celebrations, when they regularly shot the old cannon as part of the festivities. The fuse was lit just as a friend of his stepped out of a saloon, "three sheets to the wind." Stripe saw the danger his friend was in and lunged to push him out of the way, but caught the 6-pound iron ball near his right shoulder. He was in his 30s when this happened, but managed to continue his duties at the lighthouse.

After the tour, Bruce interviewed us for the newspaper, and before we left we asked for advice about walking along the canal that fronts and divides the city. The lighthouse has become more and more removed from the lakeshore as sand has been deposited in front of the channelization. Behind are the now defunct Smurfit-Stone factory and a large, functioning power plant next to a mountain of black coal. Wanting to be helpful, Bruce told us we should be able to walk next to the channel to the marina parking area where Amanda could pick us up.

The next morning the lake was calm as we finished the last 5 miles to Ontonagon. Crossing the bridge over the Big Cranberry River, back down on the shore, we encountered lots of streams that we crossed by using logs, jumping over or removing our shoes and socks and wading through icy water. Up ahead we could see the channel of the Ontonagon River and the light at the end of the rock wall, but it seemed to get no closer.

There are numerous "camps" on the shoreline between Porcupine Mountain State Park and Ontonagon. We found no animal tracks, other than from dogs, and little bird life except for some shorebirds – spotted sandpipers, Baird's sandpiper and a willet, which is also a type of large sandpiper. Shortly before reaching the channel an adult eagle flew out at us calling, then flew back and landed on a big white pine where it had a nest.

Walking along the channel, it became apparent Bruce hadn't known about the chain link fence with the barbed wire on top and the padlock on the gate. Our only choice was to go over the top. Mike went first and then turned the camera on me as I stuck the toes of my shoes in the fencing and carefully lifted my shorter legs over the barbed wire. I expected to hear sirens at any moment. It felt like a prison break, but no flashing lights appeared and we tried to look confident and casual as we wandered off seeking Amanda.

In the afternoon she dropped us at the Fire Steel River so we could walk back to town. Soon we came to the Flint Steel River. The mouth wasn't terribly wide, but it looked deep. I told Mike there was no way we were crossing this, so we walked up the riverbank past one closed cottage and came to another house with people home. I sent "Talking Pathfinder" (my nickname for Mike) ahead as a man came out of the house and looked at us suspiciously.

"Can I help you with something?"

"I hope so," Mike said, "I have a strange request. My wife and I are walking around Lake Superior, and we're trying to stay close to the shore, but we've run into this river, and it seems too deep to wade across. I was wondering if you could ferry us across the river in your canoe."

He thought for just a moment and said, "Why don't you just take my canoe down there by the river. Take it across and pull it up on the sand on the other side and I'll get it later."

Mike said he didn't want to make more trouble for him.

He shook his head. "It's not a problem."

Then he paused and seemed to re-evaluate his offer.

"Actually, why don't you go back to the other cabin? There's a green canoe and you can take that across. My brother-in-law and I were just about to sit down to eat some dinner and we can go out this afternoon to retrieve it."

We chat here with a family on Misery Beach. Often people were curious about our walk.

He said we wouldn't have had trouble crossing the river a few days earlier before the rain and the massive west wind came and blew the sandbar away.

We dragged the green canoe to the river, paddled across and put it up high on the sand bank. We laughed and shook our heads as we thought about him generously offering a neighbor's canoe.

Next we met Gary Hauser walking down the beach with his dog, which looked like a Doberman. The lanky brown-and-tan pooch came up to us and I asked what breed she was. I didn't catch his response, though I did hear him say something about her age – 12, her lumps and her name – Greta. I patted the old dog's head while Mike and Gary talked. Still wondering about her breed, I asked once more, "So what breed is she?" Mike turned to me and snapped, "He's said it three times already – DOBERMAN!"

Maybe I had sand in my ears or I was daydreaming, but feeling sheepish, I said, "Oh, sorry, I didn't hear."

To complete the impression of us as kooks, Mike explained that we were headed for "Okinagon." I looked at him in disbelief and we both struggled to come up with Ontonagon. Gary, for his part, maybe because he was also of a "mature" age, took our confusion and floundering in stride. Who knows what he said to Greta after we left. We laughed about that episode for the rest of the day.

As we continued down the beach in the bright sunshine, mist rose in places; evaporation in front of our eyes. It was coming from pools of water trapped by the storm and from the sand as the sun heated it, reminding us of scenes from Yellowstone where hot springs send up wisps of smoke.

When we reached Four Mile Rock, we tried to walk the rock shelf, but that soon ended, so we turned around and climbed to the top of the cliff and began bushwhacking through thick and tall yew shrubs. I managed to trip and land in a comfortable heap in a cushion of soft needles, laughing at my clumsiness.

There were voices on the water below and we saw a man and two teenage girls in kayaks struggling to land on the rock shelf. We popped out of the woods and climbed down near them and thought they might be surprised to see two old folks carrying packs and walking sticks suddenly appear on this remote beach. Apparently their curiosity wasn't as great as ours, because they asked no questions as we greeted them. The waves were picking up and the dad was having trouble getting out of his kayak. Mike offered help, but he refused, probably to save face in front of the girls. We did wonder how they were going to get back into the kayaks and paddle out, but walked on, leaving them to their fate.

The next day we planned to walk out and back to the 14 Mile Lighthouse from the Fire Steel River because the topographic maps made it appear that there were only cliffs down to the waterline. I felt lethargic or less excited about the day's walk, maybe because it was going to be in and out. I hate going backwards – philosophically and literally. So even though it was a gorgeous day – bright sunshine and totally calm - the beach didn't thrill me as it usually does. Mike felt sluggish too, probably from lack of sleep.

We walked on a sandy beach until it ran out and we hit slate bedrock. As we neared Ten Mile Point we became more convinced we could make it without turning back. The fact that there were no waves gave us more surface to walk on. We were learning that a point does not really come to a point. We walked and walked, gradually changing angle, but never really making a right-hand turn. Footprints coming and going on the sand surprised us and we realized we weren't the only ones walking this beach. On the one hand it was nice to know that others were venturing off the beaten path, yet we felt somewhat miffed that we had to share this remote spot.

The patterns in the rocks continued to fascinate Mike. The sandstone and shale mix in this area is a brick red, and the flat rocks we walked on were divided into squares like tile with white grout-like filling. Hidden in the cliff face are lush little waterfalls and green grottoes, dripping with moss and algae. The water trickling through had turned the grotto walls black. I called them the hanging gardens of Lake Superior.

Spotted sandpipers accompanied us all along the shore, flitting and peeping at our approach. In the woods, black-throated green and parula warblers, least flycatchers, great crested flycatchers and American redstarts sang their hearts out. We got a really good look at a greater yellowlegs (shorebird) on the beach and watched a bald eagle being chased by a raven and a silent merlin coast overhead.

Finally rounding Ten Mile Point, we saw two people on the beach ahead of us. A man and a woman about our age were walking very slowly, as if looking for treasure. They, too, were headed for the lighthouse and had started at Ten Mile Road. They asked where we were going.

"To the Light." I said, "But we'd like to make it to Misery Bay. We're just not sure about the river."

We didn't know how to let Amanda know if we decided to change our plans because our cell phone wouldn't have coverage. The man, Robert, looked at his phone and said he had five bars and AT&T service, so Mike asked if we could use his phone, if we got to the light and decided to go on. Smiling, he said, "Sure, just don't take too long. I've only got 20,000 rollover minutes."

We agreed to meet at the light and moved on, quickly leaving them behind. Again, it seemed like the point went on and on; small points dissolving into more and more points, and we started making jokes about "Get to the point." "What's the point?" "I don't see the point." You get the point.

Soon the lighthouse appeared on our right in a small clearing surrounded by forest. It was a magnificent old brick ruin, with arched windows and thick walls. Behind it were an old collapsing brick outhouse, a solid-looking boathouse and a tall barn-like building. I heard blue jays, robins and goldfinch – all common around residences but not in the undeveloped portions of the shore. Considering the light was decommissioned in 1945 and destroyed by a careless fire started by a party in July 1984, I wondered why these birds continued to hang out here.

This was obviously a favorite party spot, accessible by boat, since we couldn't imagine anyone who was interested in spending a night drinking and tossing beer cans into a fire pit, then walking miles on a rugged shoreline.

The other couple still wasn't in sight, and Mike decided to walk back to find them and use their phone, since we'd decided to walk on from here. I sat on the rocks and waited, watching the water gracefully slip up and down. The lake was the calmest we'd seen yet, an amazing difference in mood from a few days ago. The sun beat down and the lack of wind made it one of our hottest days.

Mike returned having phoned Amanda. He had walked a half mile to reach the other couple, and when they hadn't appeared by the time we finished our lunch we figured they had given up. But then they appeared around the nearest point. You could see that Kris was not as excited about this exploration as Robert and she admitted she'd been about ready to give up and turn back. I took it as a sign that since we had met them with a working cell phone, we were meant to go on, rivers or not. As it turned out, we easily crossed the East and West Sleeping rivers by taking off our socks and shoes and wading across.

Misery Bay is a huge sandy bay. Ahead we heard and saw people by the river mouth, including Amanda and Sheena. We didn't ask, but it appeared that a young couple had seven or eight kids, toddler to pre-teen. They moved ahead of us and crossed the river. The dad walked out until the water was just at his knees and dived in! My feet and legs were getting numb just walking in the water.

They watched us cross the stream and come out of the water, then asked where we were headed. "Around the lake," Mike said. They stared at us two obviously old people and seemed impressed. When the older boys walked up, the mom said, "These people are walking all around the lake. Can you imagine?"

We covered 14.1 miles that day, and the mix of sand and hard flat rocks seemed to work better for my legs and feet than walking all day on sand. The lethargy from the morning had been washed away by the color in the rocks, the soothing sounds from the water, the bird song and variety of the terrain. I rewarded my feet with an Epsom salt soak after returning to the RV.

We drove both vehicles to the next spot, registered, parked, balanced the RV and plugged in. Because it was still early in the season, most of the state parks and RV campgrounds were sparsely populated. RV camping was something new for all of us, but we were grateful to have this vehicle to return to each day and to sleep in at night.

In the morning we walked from Misery Bay to Agate Beach where we met Amanda and ate our lunch. Looking at the map to Freda (an old mining town),

I plunge up to my knees in the lake just west of Freda, and heck yes, in May, Lake Superior is knee-numbingly cold.

Mike didn't think we could walk the shoreline, so we decided to drive ahead to scout the route. At an intersection with Highway 26, I said, "Let's stop at that restaurant (The Toivola) and ask someone there." Mike went in, but came back out shortly and told us to come in and see the place for ourselves. There was a long counter with vinyl-covered stools for eating and socializing, as well as a scattering of wooden tables and booths. It was the kind of diner commonly found in small rural towns of Wisconsin and Minnesota during the 1950s. Back outside, Mike asked, "Did you see the day's specials listed on the white board?"

"Bologna sandwich and egg salad sandwich."

Two days later we were still talking about the "specials" and decided that they had to have been made on Wonder Bread, topped with a leaf of head lettuce and dollop of Miracle Whip. Suddenly my childhood flashed into view and I said, "I think I need to buy some bologna and make one of those sandwiches."

Leaving the Toivola Restaurant, we searched in vain for a route to get us close to the lake. A blacktopped road took us into Freda. Expecting a ghost town, we found neat wooden houses and Freda Cliffs B&B, all situated next to the ruins of a mining plant. Freda and nearby Beacon Hill were company towns owned by Champion Mining Company. We parked next to a fence and picked our way down a steep slope to look at the shoreline. To our right were sheer red rock cliffs.

Looking left along the shoreline with my binoculars I thought it looked walkable, even though there were some cliffs, but today we would walk the road toward Houghton Channel. There were woods on either side and we looked at the trees and talked about how much we liked the diversity of textures, shapes and colors. Hemlock, quaking and large-toothed aspen, birch, maple, cedars and spruce were all pressed close together in myriad shades of green. We came upon some old apple trees with blossoms of oyster shell pink. All over the tree, bees and flies were doing their job as pollinators. I could have stood there all day just watching them.

Passing the Liminga (Redridge) cemetery, we detoured to check out the headstones, many with Finnish names. We often stopped by cemeteries to get a feeling for the people who settled the area and to see how different people remember and honor their dead.

Then it was just walk, walk, walk until Amanda passed us at 5 p.m. She and Mike looked at a map and couldn't figure out exactly where we were. A woman drove up and asked if we needed help. Mike went over with the map and she said, "You're a couple miles from the canal." We decided to have Amanda drop us off a mile or two up the dirt road and we'd walk the rest of the way to the canal.

When we got out, I asked Mike how much farther we had to walk and he said it would be another 3 miles. It was already 5 p.m., but I figured I could go another hour (our normal walking speed was around 3 mph). We reached the 3-mile mark and he looked at the GPS and said, "We just go down this hill and then turn left." By now my legs and feet were sore, and I was just putting one foot in front of the other. Even though Mike had his own pains, he somehow managed to get through the end of the day better than I did.

The car finally came into sight around 6:45 and Mike went off to take some photos of the channel. Ever exuberant, he said, "Aren't you excited that we made it? Don't you want to come and see it?" I barely mustered enough enthusiasm to say, "Yeah – I'm glad we made the channel," but my body stayed in the car.

It was chilly when we got up and loons were calling on Twin Lake, but the sun was shining and it looked like a good day to walk to Freda. Starting at Agate Beach, we walked over cobblestones and began the unknown portion of the hike. We rounded the first "point" and looked ahead to see another with a bay in between. Mike had estimated 8 to 10 miles and told Amanda it would take us four hours. On days like this Amanda either went into a town to find Internet service to update our website and Facebook page, or she worked in the car on her computer, entering data from our various research projects. She and Sheena would take breaks, too, so she could take photos and explore new locations.

The shoreline curved in and out and alternated between sand, cobblestones and nice flat shale bedrock. These remote bays were silent, except for the songs of countless warblers and other spring migrants, like the belted kingfishers who flew ahead, then looped back behind us, and landed on bare branches where they chattered at our approach. An immature eagle flew past, and out over the water. When three sandhill cranes suddenly appeared and flew overhead, I said to Mike, "That's Ogima Binesi Kwe, Matt and my brother John." It seemed appropriate to leave an offering of tobacco at their passing.

Walking on the mostly dry shale shelves was easy, except when your foot didn't land quite right. I stumbled once, and Mike saw it, reinforcing his worry about my falling. The partially submerged rocks were another story, tending to be slippery with algae and needing constant vigilance.

At one stop, Mike looked ahead and said, "Deer." I put up my binoculars and watched the pair. The one with antler buds waded into the water. I don't know if it was playing or getting rid of insects, but it skipped a bit before coming out. Then the second, smaller one joined the first and they walk toward us. Mike was waiting for that once-in-a-lifetime photo and I had my binoculars on them. When they got within a dozen feet of us the bigger one stopped, perked up its ears, stared straight at us, then both turned and ran into the shrubbery.

The rock ledges around the cliffs got smaller and mossier and our only option was to wade in the water around them. Mike went first and I waited for his OK before following. With one boot already wet, I decided "what the heck" and went in with both. I stepped as cautiously as possible, worried about the electronic equipment I carried.

We continued on and the water kept getting deeper (mid-thigh on me). We walked for longer stretches in it, our legs becoming painfully numb. This was the section I could not see when I made the pronouncement in Freda to Mike, "I think we can do it." Now he smiled smugly, knowing I could not whine or complain about this predicament.

Finally, we came to a spot where we could see no option other than deep water, so we scrambled up the cliff. Here the forest was fairly open with pretty yellow violets, ferns and lycopodium at our feet. We stumbled onto an old rutted logging road running parallel to the shore. Most of the ruts were filled with water, which was strange because the other parts of the forest that should have been wet were completely dry, especially for this time of year. There was also a big pile of garbage, old appliances and a grill next to the old road. We marveled at the trouble people will take to dump their garbage where it shouldn't be!

I fell a third time while we bushwhacked. I went down harder this time and got poked in the chest by a thick branch. I never fell or tripped this much in the past, and I didn't know if it was my age or lack of fitness. Maybe I wasn't picking up my feet enough. The only thing that really hurt was my ego.

At last we reached the beach before Freda, which was our first exposure to copper stamping sands. It was grayish in color where it was dry, but reddish brown where wet. It was not easy to walk on; even the wet edge was soft. Nothing grew on it. This lifeless quality is due to the arsenic in the sand. It is an awful legacy left by the mining companies and the whole place had an eerie feeling. We could not help wondering whether the arsenic was leaching into the lake.

A place like this makes us think about our grandparents and their grandparents. What did they worry about for their grandchildren's future? Perhaps they didn't think about it at all. What was important was leaving a material inheritance – money, property and land. They had cut the forests, built the dams and the factories – thinking they were making the world a better place for their offspring and descendants. And they had, but as grandparents of the 21st century we feel we must do what we can to prevent further damage to the environment and look for better ways of sourcing our energy and mineral needs. We are beneficiaries of our ancestors' labors, but aware of the costs of their actions. We have a responsibility to act differently and set better, conscientious examples of how to live more lightly on the earth. We hoped our walk would raise awareness about our freshwater resources and the choices we make.

**If you do not change direction,
you may end up where you are heading.**
Lau Tzu

After Thoughts

Local Food

Mike & Kate:

Sampling the local fare along the route was part of the discovery. Here are some examples of local foods, where we first tasted them and our two-cent review.

Wild Leek – Jerry and Mary Phillips House (Wisconsin) – Tender & Tasty

Fiddlehead Ferns – Jerry and Mary Phillips House (Wisconsin) - Ambrosia

Morel mushroom – Michigan – typically earthy

Wintergreen berries – Pictured Rocks/Michigan Shore – Teaberry gum flavor

Pasties –Michigan – Not spicy enough for our tastes

Sheep cream cheese – Wisconsin – strong flavor delicacy

Whitefish livers – Wisconsin – Kate says Yummy

Lake Trout – Michigan - nothing better than fresh from the Lake

Whitefish – Michigan – fresh is the best

Raspberries – Ontario – only ones we had we think made Mike ill – given to us by two guys in a car

Smoked whitefish – Knife River, MN – Kate likes more than Mike - wonderful except for fishy smelling fingers

Bannock – Bay Mills Pow Wow – a little greasy, but devoured them

Wild rice - Ontario – Comfort food for Mike

Maple syrup – Ontario (on the canoe trip) – nothing better

Blueberries – Ontario Lake Superior Provincial Park – Abundant and delicious

Local grass feed beef – Ontario - Tasty and an expensive treat (because of the drive to town)

Service berries – Sibley Peninsula – Kate's favorites

Poutine (French fries with mozzarella cheese and gravy) – Ontario – an acquired taste for us, but Amanda loved it

Butter tarts – Ontario - Decadent & Delish

FIVE
To the Tip & Back

A good traveler has no fixed plans
and is not intent on arriving.
Lao Tzu

Kate:

Mike and I stayed in a hotel in Houghton and the next morning found a fun little café, right next to the Cyberia Coffee Cafe, called Victoria's Kitchen. It served two eggs, herb fried potatoes and toast for $2.79! Part of the serendipity of this expedition was periodic visits to towns and cities, where we could meet people who live on the lake but don't make their living directly from it.

Back at the campground, Amanda visited with two fishing buddies camped near the RV. They talked fish for a while and told her they'd been to Agate Beach and collected a bunch of agates. They figured the name meant that all the rocks were agates, but their stuffed bags didn't include a single one. Over a cup of coffee, Amanda got out her rock book and showed them what they actually had.

McClain State Park, right on the shore of Lake Superior, was our next RV camp. The beach was just plain awful for walking. It was a sand/gravel/pebble mix and my feet seemed to go down and backward instead of propelling me forward. On top of the bad walking surface, I constantly had to dump pebbles out of my shoes. I fell behind Mike, who cruised ahead and never looked back until we got to the 3-mile waypoint. I caught up, saying, "I'm not stopping for anything." He was surprised. I told him his stride is that much longer. Plus, I realized that his feet are quite a bit larger than mine and maybe they were having a snowshoe effect. He didn't find this analogy especially flattering.

This shore showed serious erosion of the tall sand banks. Houses have been built on top and people have adopted drastic measures to keep them from falling. Some put up log retaining walls where the hill meets the beach to prevent more erosion. Someone dumped huge boulders down the bank. Where there were no houses, trees were falling over the edge. A number of birch trees stood on the beach, where they had managed to slide down the hill in an upright position. Wind and rain are in a constant battle with living things on this shore. We finished walking around 2 p.m. and went back to the hotel, where we changed clothes and went for an interview with the *Mining Gazette*.

This was our first major break since Mother's Day weekend and we looked forward to urban amenities. One of the first things I did was weigh myself with great anticipation, only to be sorely disappointed – only two ounces after walking 60 plus miles! "What *is* the deal?" I asked rhetorically to the universe. Mike had lost 11 pounds since we started, which just added to my sense of unfairness.

Houghton was our first mail pick-up from general delivery, so it was like Christmas after Amanda came bearing boxes and envelopes. In the evening we headed up to Michigan Tech where we gave a talk to a group of 20 people. This was our first presentation since we began the walk and it was nice to be able to talk about what we'd already done, instead of what we hoped to do.

The next morning we told Amanda to plan on picking us up on the road just past the Sand Hills Lighthouse in Ahmeek. It was a cloudy day with some sun poking through and a slight wind out of the east.

My spirits fell when we got out on the beach and saw that it was all gravel and cobblestone mix. There were a few sandy spots, a few side trails, some slanted sandstone and conglomerate rock, but way too much cobblestone. We even came to one place that you could only describe as Cobble Dunes – parallel rows of cobblestones several feet high.

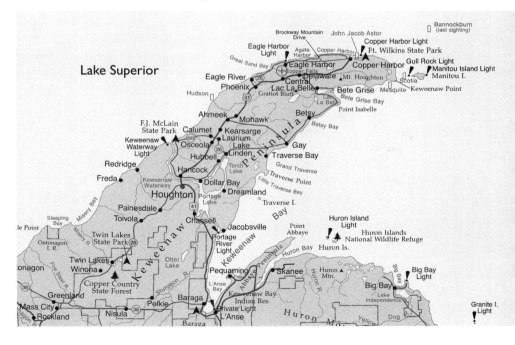

We passed some people at the beginning of our walk – an older couple cleaning their steps to the beach. He shouted out, "Are you the ones walking around the lake?"

"We are."

"Congratulations. You must be in better health than we are."

"We're trying to get there," we answered.

He told us that they spend the winters in Arizona and like to hike in the desert. Mike walked up to the steps to give them some questionnaires, but the wife looked concerned and tried to stop him by saying, "Don't come up here." But Mike went up on the first platform and gave the surveys to the man. The wife said, "This stuff has some kinds of chemicals in it. I'm trying to bring the wood back and it's not working."

Looking at the steps and the water of the lake just 20 yards away, we wondered why people don't see the connection of putting toxic chemicals on their decks or steps when it's obvious where it's headed. They wished us well, and we walked on, wondering how many people would hear and understand our message of protecting the lake.

We saw four water pipits on the shore in the morning and lots of deer tracks in the sand. The rest were human footprints, dog prints (most likely) and ATV tracks in blatant disregard for the big signs that said "Absolutely No Motorized Vehicles Beyond This Point," posted by the Michigan Nature Association. We saw these tracks on every surface and beach.

Crossing one stream took us into a desolate area with a field of dead tree stumps. The surface was all dark rust brown, which looked like stamping sands. And since there was next to nothing growing there, we figured it was another dumping site. Our GPS showed a trail and road nearby, but we couldn't find it, so it was back to bushwhacking and then onto an old logging road, more bushwhacking, and another road and still more bushwhacking until we got back to the lake. Now we were back to the cobblestones. By the end of 9 miles, my legs and feet were worn out and getting worse, which worried me when we had to walk over uneven boulders or volcanic rock. The variation in the rocks was striking in this Michigan Nature Association sanctuary.

We met an older woman with a German accent and her three long-haired Dachshunds. Mike asked her about 5 Mile Point and where it might be. She couldn't say for sure, but pointed out that we'd just come from Conservancy land and were now on a stretch of private property. She asked where we were headed and I told her, "Around the lake."

It took her a second to register and then she said, "You're walking around the whole lake? That's pretty cool." The houses on this bay and the next were massive, million-dollar structures, and apparently the beaches were well guarded because we saw no tire tracks.

The Sand Hills Lighthouse was an uninspiring yellow brick building, constructed in 1919, one of the last lighthouses built on Lake Superior. We walked past it and got onto a rocky beach of conglomerate formations and exposed beds. Mike was getting farther ahead of me and I was trying to place each foot carefully and watch where I was going, while he was nearly skipping.

We finally came to a huge flat, wide beach and I breathed a sigh of relief. The sky was completely cloudy by this time and every once in a while a strange, hot wind would blow across us. Mike spotted a solitary dunlin on the beach. It was an impressive shorebird with a very long slight down-curved black beak and a combination of reddish feathers on the back and black on the belly. It sat on the sand as we approached and did not fly away as we walked in an arc around it.

The beach ran out and we climbed up the dune onto a road where we passed another older couple walking with poles, too. They recognized us from the article in the Houghton paper, so we stopped and talked with them. They had lived on the shore for 12 years and the woman said, "I'm thankful every day."

My pace continued to drop as we walked up the road, and at 5:15 Mike called Amanda to make sure she knew where to find us. We were nearing Eagle River when a car came from behind and slowed down. The driver said, "You look like you could use a cold one." I laughed, and he added, "I've got a Gopher (Minnesotan) here who wants to buy you a beer," referring to the passenger. Mike, who was ahead of me, heard this offer and said, "That sounds good. We're headed to Eagle River." The man driving said, "It's only a quarter mile ahead."

Jim Williamson and Dick Parsons met us on the bridge by the falls. Amanda arrived and I rode to the bar with her, while Mike walked with Jim, a man of medium height, about our age, with a brown beard and glasses. After being "retired" by Pillsbury when he was 51, he and his wife came to Michigan for cross-country ski races. They found a secluded wooded lakeshore property, where they now have their home. He has become intrigued by the history of this small town and told Mike a little as they walked to the Fitzgerald Restaurant. The Eagle River Lighthouse is a private home and there is an effort among the townspeople to save the historic bridge that crosses the river into town. Like so many others we met, Jim said that when he travels, "The lake is always calling me back."

Dick was a big man with a thick crop of white hair. A former teacher and football coach, he and his wife moved here 12 years ago. A very friendly fellow, he seemed really amused by our undertaking. True to his offer on the road, he bought us all drinks.

At the other end of the bar, Amanda was sitting next to a man and woman who said they lived in Eagle River, but taught in Calumet. They saw the article in the paper, too, and wanted to

Dick Parsons, a friendly stranger, bought us a "cold one" at the Fitzgerald Restaurant in Eagle River.

know more about our project. Mike gave everyone questionnaires to fill out and when I explained why we were doing the walk – for grandkids, setting goals and fulfilling dreams – the woman pointed at the questionnaire and said, "But also to show them that you can and need to do things to bring about change."

The next day, we moved to Fort Wilkins State Park on the small inland Lake Fannie Hooe. The fort is well kept and staffed in the summer with re-enactors who demonstrate life in the old days.

We drove back to Eagle River to start the day's walk and passed the Jampot, a tiny retail shop belonging to the Order of St. John, Eastern Orthodox Abbey. Inside the Jampot we found one wall covered with shelves holding jams and jellies of every imaginable flavor. Mike felt he'd landed in heaven and struggled to choose. They make fruitcakes, fruit breads and regular bread, if you can even call freshly baked bread "regular." The smells alone carried us to the counter where we paid the man in black. We went away with lighter wallets, but euphoric smiles.

Walking on the sandy beach, we were greeted by spotted sandpipers. I now believe they are the most common shorebird on Lake Superior. I can't think of one day when we didn't see or hear them. They are shy and never let us get close, frustrating Mike's photographic efforts. We also noticed black flies during the morning's walk, but they seemed disabled by the temperatures, flying up and landing back on the sand.

When the beach ended at some cliffs, we went up steps back to the road. A young man across the street looked at us as we popped up over the top and stepped over a guardrail. As I took off my polar fleece jacket, he called out, "Are you the ones in the paper?"

"Yes."

"I've always wanted to take a motorcycle or drive around the lake."

"You should do it sometime."

"I have a friend who rode a bike around." He added, "I'll have to tell my wife that I saw you." Then he wished us luck.

We entertained ourselves on the road by looking at flowers. The striped coralroot was the most unusual and lilacs were starting to bloom. A little later an older couple in a pickup pulled into a driveway and got out. The woman said, "You're the ones walking around the lake. We saw it in last night's paper. I figured you'd be coming by this area on the weekend." The Olsons live in Cat Harbor. In 1989, they bought the property, surrounded by state land, and basically they have the bay and beach to themselves. We appreciated the sign near their house that said, "SLOW Grandparents At Play."

When we walked down to the beach in Cat Harbor, Mr. Olson followed and we asked about the water level. He figured it was about 2 feet lower than normal, but said he'd seen it like that many times over the years and it was typical for this time of year, but by July it would be back up. Mr. Olson had 21 years of observations to share, but with our 3-mile "point counts," we were documenting the level of the lake and other features on land, with photographs, GPS coordinates and notations on plant and animal life, so that 25, 50 or 100 years from now, someone can come back to these places and tell whether things really have changed, not just what one person remembers over a decade or two.

Next came the small bayside village of Eagle Harbor. We walked down the streets past neat, well-kept homes and imagined living on the pretty bay. Then an old hippie-looking, grey-bearded dude came out of a house, looked at us and asked, "Are you going to Canada?"

I replied, "Yes."

"It'll be a cold swim." He said, laughing at his wittiness. "I've got a canoe, but it only holds one person."

Black-throated green and parula warblers kept us company with their constant singing. When we sat on a guardrail to rest near birch trees, dragonflies began swooping all around and landing on the leaves. They must have just emerged from Lake Bailey to our right, which was surrounded by wetlands. This was a Nature Conservancy area. We kept seeing signs that said "Protected Area," but then we'd see a house and driveway. We found it very confusing.

Highway 26 is a narrow two-lane blacktop road and we hugged the sides as cars went by – some were polite and moved over, but many didn't and whizzed by apparently oblivious. After 12 miles, in order to divert my attention from my sore feet and legs, I put on my headphones and found that music is a very good painkiller. My discomfort evaporated and I walked easily for the next hour and 15 minutes until Amanda picked us up a few miles from Copper Harbor.

We took a detour from the shore near the tip of the Keweenaw Peninsula and drove up to Mount Brockway, one of the highest points on the peninsula, where the Copper Country Audubon Club (CCAC) and Laughing Whitefish Audubon Society (LWAS) resumed a spring migration hawk count for the first time since 1992.

Max, one of the counters, was standing in the nearly gale force wind watching the skies, yelling over the wind and struggling to keep his dark hair from blowing into his eyes. He had seen about 7,500 raptors since March 15, and the count continued until June 15 (the total ended up at 9,509). While we stood there three broad winged hawks passed just overhead. A group of ravens hung above us playing in the wind, barely moving their wings except to adjust the angle to the wind. The oak trees on top of this ridge, like the ones we saw in Porcupine Wilderness State Park, were stunted and twisted by the wind. We left Max with his eyes on the sky and drove back down to the shoreline.

The next day began with a humidity-induced haze and the temperature rose quickly, so that it was close to 80° F before noon. Happily, a kind east wind cooled us off. This was a road walking day, except for one short stretch through a Nature Conservancy area. The cobble beach and conglomerate bedrocks were covered with lichens and rare flowers, including butterwort – an insectivorous plant with blue flowers and slippery basal leaves that trap insects.

The black flies and mosquitoes appeared when we stopped for a point count, but otherwise left us alone. A completely silent flock of blue jays flew over twice. We wondered if they were on some kind of reconnaissance. Jays are rarely silent when in flocks. On the other hand, two very noisy ravens chased one another. We couldn't tell if it was play or an aggressive encounter, but one would occasionally flip over and reach out towards the other with its feet. These observations made the road less boring.

By the time we reached, Copper Harbor we were hot, sweaty and craving a cold drink. As we passed the Mariner Restaurant and Hotel, we looked up at its sign and saw in big black letters, "Welcome Full Circle Walkers." We were dumbstruck and had to stop to take a photo.

On the way into town a car had stopped and Lloyd Wescoat, a woman we met at our talk at Michigan Tech, greeted us. Owner of a bookstore in Copper Harbor called Grandpa's Barn, we had talked about our shared love of books. She knew we were trying to find a boat to take us around the tip of the Peninsula since there was no accessible shoreline, so she kindly made arrangements for a local guy to take us out in his boat.

Rich Jamsen's small cabin had a spray of bikes scattered around the yard. Rich, who is of small stature, was wearing greasy jeans and a sweaty baseball cap. He invited us in to listen to the NOAA report. It sounded pretty good for the next day, so we made plans to meet at 9 a.m. He said he'd take us out to the tip and back but didn't want to go around to the other side because of possible east-southeast winds. He told us he never sees anyone out there.

Before the day ended, we managed to explore the rugged and secluded Mary Macdonald Preserve at Horseshoe Harbor, giving us the last shoreline walking we could do on this side of the peninsula.

Captain Jamsen's small white fiberglass "tub" looked a like a child's replica of a tugboat, but was designed as a West Coast salmon trolling boat. A Copper Harbor Finn, Rich is part of a multigenerational fishing family. He first went out on the lake with his dad when he was around 9 years old, and started working on the boats at about 13 or 14. His family spent winters in Florida shrimping.

Rich retired from the Michigan Department of Natural Resources fisheries and lives in Marquette in winter. In summer, he lives in Copper Harbor, helps to run lighthouse tours and does odd jobs. He doesn't like crowds, snowmobiles or loud Harley-Davidsons, but likes to talk, though it was hard to hear over the roar of his engine. Besides sharing his family's history and pointing out good fishing spots, topics ranged from religion to his duty in the Vietnam War.

As we left the harbor, fog followed. Rich was cruising fairly close to shore, but the rock ledges began to fade in and out of view. There are shoals in this area and he kept an eye on the radar, as well as using his personal knowledge of the coast to guide us safely through the calm water. The fog got thicker the farther we went, so that by the time we neared the tip of the Peninsula you couldn't see anything except a smudge of sun through a cloud of white. There was no reason to go to the point in these conditions, so we turned around and wouldn't you know it, the fog drifted away and left a sky of blue. We returned to the harbor and thanked him for the ride. He accepted the $20 we offered to help pay for gas and said he'd give it to one of the organizations trying to protect the area. We liked that idea.

The day became increasingly warmer and more humid. We were sweating by the time we got back to the RV for a late lunch. Our next move was to drive to the other side of the peninsula to a small bay called Bete Grise (pronounced Beta Gree) where we connected with the Keweenaw shore again and found it 20 degrees cooler. The wide bay was a deep blue, except close to shore where the water was an odd yellow color. As far as we could see along the beach a strange yellow substance rolled in on the waves. I asked Mike, "Do you think it could be pollen?" And that was exactly it, a phenomenon that happens every year. A solid forest of conifers on the north end of the bay is positioned to send its pollen into the water. This was an unusually abundant year and suddenly the clogged sinuses we'd all been suffering from since coming onto the peninsula made a lot more sense.

As we got ready to start walking on the beach, a car drove past and the people looked at us curiously. The car made a U-turn, came back and Deb Filer rolled down the window and said, "Hi. I thought that was you."

Deb had contacted us through our website and offered to help us get across the Mendota Light boat channel. We walked to So Sweet Cottage as the sign identified their cabin: a simple, wooden, modern-looking home next to what is locally called "the Lagoon." This used to be a river, but it was channelized in 1867 to create a harbor.

We shared some cold beverages with Bob and Deb, both former teachers at Michigan Tech. Deb's youngest daughter, Jane, a college freshman, was home and out in the water with Daisy, a hyperactive young golden retriever. The couple has a home in Houghton, but spends as much time as possible at the cottage.

After our pleasant interlude, we got in their aluminum canoe, they got in a little kayak and we paddled toward the canal and the Mendota Lighthouse. Originally constructed in 1869, the light was decommissioned the next year because it was not needed for shipping. Then in 1895 a new lighthouse was established because the harbor had been giving shelter to boats in storms and the boaters recommended a light for safety.

Bob and Deb bid us farewell as we resumed walking a sandy beach, which soon gave way to sandstone. These were the most colorful rocks we had yet seen, unlike anything else along the shore. Red and yellow rock formations had been laid down in swirls and zig-zags, almost psychedelic in appearance. Some looked like desert sand paintings, while others looked like those spattered spin-art pictures you make at the State Fair. It really was a kaleidoscope of designs. Mike was beside himself with excitement over this geologic art gallery. He couldn't stop "oohing" and "aahing," saying, "Look at this one!"

Small waves curled in, and the sun was shining when we came across a semi-palmated plover. It had a dark neck and breast band, like the killdeer, but a unique pattern on the face. Amanda met us on the road as we walked past a big bog, with bog laurel and rosemary in bloom. Mike had never seen such an abundance of those plants in one place – more excitement and joy for the boy naturalist.

Mike drove the RV, with Amanda riding shotgun to evaluate his performance, since she was going home for a couple of weeks for family events. Friends and advisers Beth and Bill Blank would take over Amanda's driving and cooking duties. We parked the RV at the Tobacco River picnic area and Amanda drove us back to the starting point.

The breeze coming off the water washed over us with a soft, cool touch, and our eyes feasted on the rocks with their crazy, abstract patterns. Some were

Captain Rich Jamsen took us on his fishing boat up to the tip of the Keweenaw Peninsula.

speckled or had polka dots; others had inlays of red clay, surrounded by grey; some had a perfect bull's-eye or eyeball design.

Once again we appreciated our good fortune with the lower water level. Unless you get out of your car and walk down to the beach or the edge of the land above the beach, you would have no idea there was a treasure so nearby.

We had to climb under and over fallen trees on this walk, and sometimes the shelf of rock got very narrow or full of boulders. Immature and adult eagles were present all the way; more than we'd seen since the Wisconsin shore. Mike saw one adult splash down in the water, but couldn't tell if it caught a fish or was just cooling off. It perched at the top of a dead tree with wings hanging down and beak open. Below one such eagle perch we encountered a swarm of tiger swallowtail butterflies clustered in groups on the sand like parched pilgrims at an oasis, sucking down moisture or minerals. The nectar they sipped was white guano (bird poop) left by the eagles.

One of the most surprising wildlife sightings on our entire journey occurred as we walked this sandy beach. At my feet I spotted a tiny red creature that looked something like a lizard or skink. Mike recognized it as the larval form of a newt, known as an eft. It had an orangish belly and was about 4 inches long and very docile. It had been standing near the wave line and even though there were no streams close by, there was a bog through the forest and across the road. We've since learned that efts are slightly toxic and don't have many predators.

The surprises continued when Mike said excitedly, "A pileated woodpecker just flew out of that nest hole." I turned and saw a very large hole in the side of a birch tree facing the lake, right on the edge of the sand. We watched the bird fly around in the forest and return to the nest. How deep it must have been to hold an adult and babies.

Waves rolled in and swished back out and the forest edge came right up to the sandy beach, as we walked into Hermit Cove. Suddenly a white-haired elderly lady popped out from a front yard and said, "Are you the ones walking around the lake?"

Her equally white-haired husband came up behind her, "I said you'd probably be coming down this beach today. We read about you in the paper and we have some friends who told us about meeting you last weekend."

Ed and Dorothy Haajala have had their little cabin on this beach for 56 years. They built it with logs from the property and what they could afford over time. Now they spend six months here and six months in Copper City.

Dorothy said, "Won't you come up and have something cold to drink?"

Ed added, "Yah, we've got a good well, with really cold water."

It looked like Ed was preparing to take a sauna: shirt half-buttoned, a pair of white underwear peeking out of his jeans pocket and bare feet poking out of the pant legs. When we demurred, saying we didn't want to interrupt his sauna, he said, "Don't worry, I gotta wait for it to heat up."

We accepted, went up to their patio and sat on chairs chatting, sipping our glasses of water and swatting at the insects that appeared on our arrival.

We talked about the changes that had come to this beach in the five decades they'd been there. One was an increase in ATV traffic and I told Dorothy I liked the synthetic rope stretching from their "yard" down to the waterline. On it was a sign with an ATV in a red circle with a line through it.

Ed had the whip-thin shape of a lifelong athlete. He was once a cross-country ski racer and had done 19 of the American Birkebeiner races. He also used to swim from their place down to the point, "but I quit that in my 70s!" We had no idea exactly how old he was, but we're guessing in his late 80s. It seemed the sauna ritual was keeping him healthy, too.

Dorothy was excited to meet us and wanted to take some photos with the new digital camera her grandson had given them. First she took one with just Mike and me and then one with each of them in the picture. Smiling broadly she said, "Now I can show people that you were really here."

Wishing we could visit longer, we said thanks and got up to go. Ed said there was a sandstone point up ahead that we wouldn't be able to get around except by going on the land above.

"Don't worry," he said, "the owner is the constable for the township. He'll let you through. Just tell him Ed and Dorothy said you could do it."

We left the Haajalas in a high, happy mood.

Bill and Beth had arrived the evening before and parked their RV next to ours. In the morning they drove us out to our starting point. We chose not to walk the large stamping sands beach at Gay, Michigan, so that put us on the road. After crossing the Traverse River (boat channel) we hit the beach.

In some places our way was blocked by trees lying in the water, so we had to bushwhack through thick tangled forest and blow downs, slowing our progress considerably. As we approached the last bay we spied Bill and Beth. At the same time a lady in front of her cabin saw us and called out, "Are you the famous people?"

Without hesitation, I said, "Yes." And felt foolish for it right afterwards. Mike teased me almost immediately because it was so uncharacteristic, but I guess I was enjoying our bit of fame.

Mike said, "Well, we're walking around the lake."

She said, "I have to take your picture – do you mind?" Then her husband came out. Since retiring 12 years ago, Judy Spahn and Bruce Wolde have lived in the cabin on the beach for six months and the rest of the year in the

Bahamas. They said, "Come on up and let us give you something cold to drink." This was an offer Mike never turned down. We visited for a bit and discussed the Eastern bluebirds that had just returned to their property, and were late this year, Bruce said, as were the hummingbirds.

Bill and Beth had been walking down the beach in our direction. We joined them and walked back to their car, with storm clouds in the distance and thunder beginning to rumble. They drove us to the road junction (the shore was impassable ahead) where we put on raincoats and began the last 7 miles. Trucks roared by, spraying water as they passed. When it stopped raining, the sun came out and sunglasses went back on. After 17 miles both of us were hurting, but Mike somehow managed to keep his pain to himself. I was the one who whined.

Back at the Lake Linden Campground, we headed to the showers. Afterward, as we sat at the picnic table, a beautiful full moon rode in the pale blue sky and four sandhill cranes flew in low over our RV just as Bill and Beth came outside. I said, "Those four birds represent us on this short shared journey." We watched them fly across the lake, headed for a marshy area for the night.

Lake Linden is a small town with interesting architecture, including the Lindell Chocolate Shoppe, which is on the National Register of Historic Places. Someone told us they had fantastic ice cream, but we were looking for a place to have breakfast and an Internet connection. Just as we got to the corner, a woman put up a "breakfast all day" sign. The architectural details included ornate wooden booths that were installed in the early 1920s and lined the walls and center portion of the dining area. After eating a hearty bacon and eggs breakfast we drove to Hancock, over the bridge to Houghton and eastward to Sturgeon Slough directly across from where we had stopped the day before. We started walking as Bill and Beth drove the two RVs to Baraga State Park.

The sky was a brilliant blue, with just a few upper stratosphere cirrus clouds, a slight breeze and almost no humidity with temperatures in low 60s. That was the good part; the bad part was having to spend nearly the whole day walking on roads. First we walked out Portage Entry along the channel that divides the Keweenaw Peninsula. In the distance we could see a fishing boat on its way in. Bill and Beth had returned from the park and had scouted out some roads for us, but hadn't found any close to the lake. Mike walked out to the end of the channel to take photos while Bill, Beth and I waited for the fishing boat to pull up to the concrete wall. A man and a woman hopped out and began to unload big blue plastic crates filled with ice chips and shiny silver fish. I asked what they'd caught. "Lake trout," said the man.

"Do you ever sell from the boat?" I asked.

"Sure. You can buy one right now if you want."

I looked at Bill and Beth and asked, "Would you be interested in cooking some fish for dinner?" They agreed and bought us a freshly caught and filleted lake trout. The couple came in about every other day and sold most of their catch to local restaurants.

We started back out on the smaller gravel road to busy, noisy Highway 41. You can get on this road and drive to Miami (a fun road trip, but not for walkers). The sound and blowback from semis going by was overwhelming. We quickly learned to hang onto our hats when these behemoths approached. Even our headphones couldn't block out all the noise.

Mike was in a lot of pain, mainly his back. Without the beauty of the lake to distract him, the pain in his joints was more insistent. We did catch a glimpse of the lake through people's yards, but not enough to inspire us. It was May 27 and everyone was busy planting flowers and vegetables. We passed a garage sale and a place that sold Lake Superior greenstone jewelry. I really wanted to stop at both places, but Mike was ahead of me and wouldn't hear if I tried to get his attention.

A car went past and the guy waved. A few minutes later he came back, slowed down and asked Mike if we wanted a ride.

Mike said, "Can't do that – we're walking around the lake."

To which the guy replied, "Holy Wah!" That was a new one for us. We'd hear it again in Ontario.

We sat down in the shade of a grassy driveway to rest our feet. The cars and trucks were roaring by and I decided it would be a good video image – a dramatic contrast to our first day walking four weeks ago. Mike was hobbling by this time and not a happy adventurer. At 4:35 we stopped at a roadside park and our saviors appeared in their car. We got in, happy to be done with the day – 14.5 hard, hot road miles.

On May 29, after one month of the expedition, we were still standing and walking. At times our age-related short-term memory loss drove us crazy and made us late, like the morning we drove off and had to come back because Mike forgot his camera. Now we were on our way out to the top of the Abbaye (pronounced Abby) Peninsula. We thought we were going to have to walk back down a very long dirt road, but after walking out to the point and looking at the shoreline, we decided to give it a try. What we could see was a lot of flat sandstone shelves. Soon after we started, Mike realized he'd left the GPS by the

The shrine to Father Frederic Baraga, the "snowshoe priest," is south of the town named for him.

outhouse, so I stood around trying not to be frustrated, while he went back to get it. We talked about ways to help make sure he has everything before leaving. We could write a list of items, but where would we keep it so we'd see it?

There was barely a riffle on the surface of the lake. Many people had told us we wouldn't be able to walk this shoreline; we were happy to prove them wrong. We looked across the bay at the other shore and could see Hancock just beyond. Mirages caused by different air densities made images topsy-turvy, like the old-fashioned camera lens that turns things upside down.

It was Memorial Day weekend and people were out enjoying the beautiful weather. The first person we encountered was a young guy with a kayak and bike on the beach. We talked to him about the shoreline ahead and he said, "More 'camps' up that way." Here was another new word for us. In Minnesota people have "cabins" at the lake; in the U.P., people have "camps." We asked him if he knew what the shoreline was like and he described it as, "Kinda cliffy."

A little farther on, a man was on his riding lawnmower. When he saw us, he turned off his machine and called, "Where ya going?" We told him about our walk. "I read about you somewhere," he said. Dwayne Johnson tried to stop his little white poodle from yapping, so he could talk to us. "There are cliffs up ahead you can't get around. Go up on the road, past the place with the black gate and then there will be Coffee Lane that will take you back to shoreline." We thanked him for his help, walked across his lawn and out to the road.

Once we got back to the shore we came upon a group of people having a family reunion with cans of beer flashing in their hands. They also had a lot of big dogs, mostly husky types, and we hesitated before approaching. They saw us and grabbed the dogs, assuring us they were friendly. After telling them about our walk, one guy said, "It's a good thing you're doing it this year. Last year was really wet, but the lake was this low a couple years ago, too."

As we walked along we heard an eagle's high-pitched screech and saw a pair of adults. We assumed there was a nest in the nearby woods. The two circled and flew low over us and out over the water again and again, calling the whole time. We have never seen eagles act quite that agitated. We kept moving, but never saw a big white pine with a nest. Besides the eagles, tiger swallowtail butterflies kept us company all along this shoreline.

We ended up with wet boots where the rock ledge shrunk to a slippery, narrow ledge. The day was beginning to lose its pleasure as we found ourselves walking on small, cobble-like boulders. My feet were sliding this way and that and I could feel a blister forming on one of my toes.

Mike was ahead of me and the next thing I knew he was bent over and swearing. I rushed up and said, "Mike. What's wrong?" He shot back, "Shut up!" That stopped me short. I still couldn't tell what was wrong, though he was moaning and holding his head. So, I tried again, "What happened?"

"Just shut up!" he snapped.

So I did. I just stood there and waited, upset that there wasn't anything for me to do. I wasn't going to try to offer any more assistance, that's for sure.

Finally, he sat down on some rocks, regained his composure and said he was sorry for yelling at me, but he'd been walking with his eyes focused down on the rocks and didn't see the low tree branch aimed straight at his forehead. He walked right into it, saw stars and thought he might pass out. A combination of embarrassment and pain caused him to lash out at me, which really didn't make me feel much better. We got under way again, both of us walking in silence, and came upon another family that had been swimming. We were headed for Second Sand Beach and asked them if they knew how far it was. They said it would take us longer than the 40 minutes we had expected. They were right. It took us closer to an hour and 15 minutes. They offered to drive us, but we said no thanks and moved on down the miserable cobble shoreline.

The next day we started at Second Sand Bay under a sunny sky. Shifting to the road when the beach ran out, we walked to Pequaming, the site of an old Ford plant and where the first large-scale lumbering operation on Lake Superior took place. In 1923, the Hebards approached the Ford Company to purchase the mill, too. During its peak the sawmill provided wood for floorboards, truck boxes and panels for station wagons. When the Great Depression shut things down, Henry Ford experimented with a cooperative farm and used this social experiment as a model for his theories on self-reliance and education.

Mike wanted to take photos, so we walked past the campground and saw a man come out of the house on the hill where it said "Private Drive." Mike waved and went up closer to the old building for photos and to make a video.

A car drove down from the house, stopping near us. I thought they were going to ask something related to our walk, but the old guy driving yelled something I couldn't hear. I went closer, and obviously angry he said, "Can't you read the sign? That's private." I walked up to the sign, which said, "Our Boaters ONLY Past This Point" in big blue letters. Mike came over to hear what the man was saying.

"We have such a hard time keeping people out," he complained. His wife was sitting in the passenger seat, dressed impeccably with her silver hair perfectly coiffed. Mike told them we were walking around the lake and the man calmed down a bit and his wife said, "That's quite an undertaking. You've got a long ways to go." We agreed. Then they drove off and we walked toward the beach shaking our heads over the first grumpy person we'd met on the trip.

We understood the frustration he must have with nonmembers driving out on the pier, but we weren't boaters and the campground was open to the public so we weren't thinking it applied to us. There were no signs anywhere to explain the history of this site, which is a shame, but then I guess they don't want more people coming out to see it.

Following the shore, we came upon a small wetland with lots of songbirds. We were able to call in (making a "pishing" sound) a few red-eyed vireos, yellow warblers, a Wilson warbler (female) and a Baltimore oriole. The vireo and Wilson warbler were pecking at mass of tent caterpillars. "You go birds!" I cheered, It was the first time I'd seen birds eating these pests. We also saw lots of pieces of wood cut to all different sizes in the water, obvious leftovers from the days of the Ford plant. It seemed a shame that they couldn't be put to some use.

Bill and Beth picked us up around noon and we called it a day. Beth had read about an old Indian cemetery called the Pinery that she wanted to see. It was down a sandy road with forests all around and evidence of the 2009 forest fire. Some of the old spirit houses had burned as well. These low, rectangular "houses" are built of cedar shakes with different shaped holes in one end. This is where relatives leave an offering for the person who has passed on. Newer memorial headstones stood in some places. Spinning pinwheels adorned other graves. It was interesting and sad at the same time. Some of the names sounded Ojibwe, and some sounded Finnish.

We returned to Baraga State Park through the town of L'Anse (pronounced L'aunts) where we stopped at the Frostee Freeze to buy lunch and treat ourselves to a soft serve cone.

It rained slow and steady during most of the night, a gift for this parched land. Huron Point is down a long dirt forest road. This is a popular site for camper trailers and RVs. No people stirred, even though we could see smoke coming from one campfire. Under cloudy skies we set off walking back towards L'Anse on a sandy beach facing Huron Island. We stayed on the beach as long as possible, until we finally had to climb up to get around a bunch of steep cliffs. The forest was fairly open, making walking easy. We scared up a thrush of some kind, and found the nest at our feet – a tidy circle of grasses holding four eggs, still warm, elliptical in shape, and robin's egg blue. We quickly moved on, so mama could come back.

Our GPS showed a road we could access from the forest. Once we found it, we also spotted our first black bear. It was in someone's yard and seemed about the size of a yearling. It was moseying around, then turned and started to walk toward us.

"Shouldn't we say something?" I whispered to Mike as the bear waddled along looking at the ground for something to eat.

"No – don't say anything."

"But it's coming right at us."

"Let's just wait a little longer."

"Are you sure we shouldn't say something?" I whispered a bit more loudly when it was only 20 feet away. Then it looked up, did a double take, turned and bolted toward the woods.

We got back on the beach just as the sky had cleared. The color of the water was surrealistic shades of blue, with yellow bands (pollen) and reddish rocks.

While eating lunch on a broad beach looking out across the channel, we took off our shoes and socks and noticed that my tan line made me look like a bay horse with white socks. We gazed at the water, feeling the breeze and sun on our backs. All of a sudden Mike said, "Look" and pointed to the left. There were four little semi-palmated plovers coming our way on the wet sand. I wanted to grab my binoculars, but was afraid I would scare them away. They didn't seem concerned at all; some even veered our way to get a better look.

We continued on the beach to the Witz Marina, which is also the Skanee (pronounced Skay-knee) Harbor. Before reaching the marina we walked past a little red log cabin that was for sale and Mike said jokingly, "We could buy that one. That's the kind I like." It was very simple and small and had a great beach in front of it.

As we turned into the marina parking area, a group of four men in their 30s and 40s saw us coming and stared. I told Mike they were wondering, "What the heck are these old geezers doing?" They hailed us as we passed their trailer and one said, "I saw you over on Bayshore Road yesterday." Then another one offered us a cold beer and Mike walked over with his hand out.

They all lived in the vicinity of L'Anse. One man said this was "his" beach for the summer. They asked if we'd like to buy the place we'd just walked past. "Sure," we said.

"It's only a million dollars," one replied.

Ah yes. Little, simple cabins with million-dollar views.

We asked at the marina store for routes back to L'Anse, and the answer was "roads." But, oh, the lupines! Pink and purple spikes filled the roadside ditches. Each week brought us a different mass of blooming flowers.

We listened to audiobooks as we trekked down the asphalt, trying to stay in the shade. Catching a glimpse of the lake in a few places is just not the same as walking on the shore, but now the two large, pointed peninsulas were behind us and we would be heading east again with very different adventures ahead.

> In every out thrust headland, in every curving beach,
> in every grain of sand, there is the story of the earth.
> Rachel Carson

After Thoughts
Invasive Species

Mike:

During our walk, I taught an online graduate course in research for Hamline University, and one of most interesting questions was "What makes something invasive and why are invasive organisms automatically bad?"

My first thought is that we should ask the lake's indigenous populations about invasive species since in many ways the rest of us are all immigrants and we have done what other invasive species – plants, animals and micro-organisms do; we displaced the original inhabitants, limit the resources of the original inhabitants and change the habitat to favor the invasive species.

Luckily, some of the worst species were not observed along our path and we are pleased with that. Of course, we saw invasive species all over, but people forget that dandelion and burdock were originally brought in as garden plants and now there is no stopping them. Do we now refer to them as naturalized or do we continue to think of them as alien species? I am not sure what is right. Just as daisy and hawkweed color our fields in the summer and we enjoy the scene, we still recognize them as non-native species.

Species have long been introduced to the habitat over centuries of migrations of birds, animals and people. The beautiful purple, white and pink lupine that make the ditches so glorious also were brought here as were certain earthworms that actually may be affecting some northern forest growth.

Meanwhile, we have invented lots of new ways to transport invasive species (including viruses) quickly and in larger quantities than was historically possible. More travelers come from longer distances with "invaders" on the soles of our shoes, attached to our pants legs, in the seed packets and arriving through something we ordered on the Internet. We take them with us when we fly, drive, cruise and, yes, hike – usually without knowing it. They move across the barriers of ocean that kept our continents separated for so much of planetary history because of our transportation skills and options. Recreational fishing transports invaders – like the recently publicized fish virus causing bleeding and die-outs. Salties and lakers can also bring in or transport invasive species in ballast water. Even the locks and canals that allow access to the Great Lakes from the ocean allow invaders to swim into the upper lakes – like the sea lamprey.

As individuals, we might find something we like and want it to be ours, so we order plants and seeds from other places rather than choosing our native options. We saw spotted knapweed pushing out native plants in our sandy grasslands along the dunes and especially the roads in the Upper Peninsula of Michigan from Grand Marais to Bay Mills and again along Highway 17 in Ontario.

We saw purple loosestrife, thought to have arrived in ballast water, filling the mouth of a stream entering the lake near the old ore dock in Ashland, Wisconsin.

We found the plant blueweed (also called vipers Bugloss) in many places along the road, though not along the lakeshore, from Sault Ste. Marie, Ontario, to Grand Marais, Minnesota. It was especially prominent along the railroad tracks leading into Marathon, Ontario.

Along Highway 17, the invasive cane grass *Phragmites* dominated stretches of wetlands.

On a walk, it's harder to log invasive species that live in the water, but in Michigan on the Abbaye Peninsula, we saw a dead round-eyed goby washed up on the rocks and a rusty crayfish. But we know they are there. So what do we do? I am not sure we have a good answer. Personally you can buy local, plant local, enjoy the indigenous species. Take the proper care with your bait fish and your boat as you travel from lake to lake. Encourage regulations that protect the waters.

Is the lake truly a natural ecosystem anymore? We have to use weirs and chemicals to control lamprey and other species. There are experiments with the release of insects to control purple loosestrife (but aren't those insects invasive, too?). And then there is the choice of invasives we like. Think about the fish we enjoy in the lake – steelhead, salmon, smelt – none are native. We have put them there intentionally or accidentally, and now we actually manage some areas for their benefit.

Or consider the white-tailed deer. It is North American in origin, but prior to the cutting of the forest and the settlement of the shores, the white-tail was found more in southern Minnesota, Wisconsin and Michigan. Moose and caribou dominated the Lake Superior region (especially in Minnesota). We favored the deer because it is beautiful, easier to hunt and abundant. We also have a generation that made decisions based on the Disney movie "Bambi." In the Jonvik deeryard north of Lutsen, Minnesota, there was a point in the 1950s when the winter population of deer numbered more than 500 per square mile. (This was when wolves, which people had tried to eradicate, were at a low population ebb.) When the winter snows get deep on the inland area and the deer move to the shore, the number there can still exceed 125 per square mile. People like to feed deer, often causing them to cross the road and add to the traffic fatality rate – there are an average of 250 deer-car collisions along the 8-mile stretch of Highway 61 near there some winters.

Deer, as I mentioned earlier, have altered the natural forest cycle and they carry a brain worm not fatal to them, but that kills moose and caribou. So through biological warfare, so to speak, the smaller white-tail eliminated its competitors. Warmer climate has also stressed the moose, especially with an increase of tick infestations, and logging from the past removed the old-growth trees that caribou favored for their diet. Rolf Peterson, one of our advisors and a primary researcher in the five-decade-long Isle Royale moose and wolf study, asked us to look for moose and deer sign on our walk, especially in Michigan. Deer sign was everywhere in Minnesota, Wisconsin and Michigan. In Ontario, we found them up to the Goulais Peninsula and from Nipigon west to the international border.

Moose were not so abundant. In fact, I never saw one moose, only their tracks, which ranks as my number one disappointment of the trip. I did see tracks on the Abbaye Peninsula and at Bay Mills, but that was all in the United States. In Ontario, I saw tracks throughout the area where the white-tail was absent – not a coincidence, I suspect. However, we did walk in midday and saw the tracks in muddy areas near the road, not near the rocky shore. Amanda observed a cow and two calves in Lake Superior Provincial Park.

Not all invasive species are as easy to see as animals and plants. West Nile Virus traveled to our continent from Africa or the Mediterranean. It first appeared in the United States in 1999 in College Point (Queens), New York City when a sick air traveler was bitten by a mosquito that became the initial source for spreading the disease. It has since spread to most of North America. Transmitted by mosquitoes, it can be lethal to humans, but is much more lethal to the birds in the corvid (crow/jay) family.

One of my favorite birds is the whiskey jack, the camp robber or, less colorfully, the gray jay. A precocious bird, it taught us a lot about keeping our campsites in order. It epitomizes north country or high mountains, but I saw none on this trek. For the last few years, its prairie counterpart – the magpie – has been devastated by this virus. I wonder if it has affected the gray jay here. The entire corvid family has seen a population drop of 45 percent since 1999 and the Michigan Department of Natural Resources reported, "The impact of WNV on corvids in the U.S. is the greatest with between 50 and 90 percent of the reported avian cases being corvids."

We have to make choices. My choice would be to try to eliminate the spread of aggressive invasives as quickly as we can and then continue to monitor the overall health and ecology of the region. When I choose to plant my gardens, I'll think of native species.

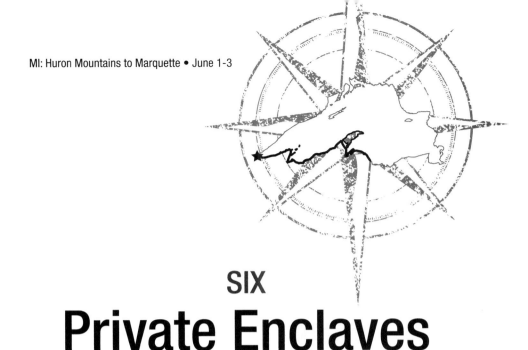

SIX
Private Enclaves

A lake is the landscape's most beautiful and expressive feature.
It is the earth's eye, looking into which the beholder
measures the depth of his own nature.
Henry David Thoreau

Kate:

Early in our planning the question was asked: "How do you plan to get around or through the Huron Mountain Club?"

For those of us who don't live in northern Michigan this question was a mystery. We had never even heard of this massive piece of private property familiarly known as HMC. But we quickly learned that it is a highly exclusive preserve for a limited number of families.

The Huron Mountain Club remains as shrouded in mystery as the mountains themselves are sometimes shrouded in smoky mists. HMC was formed in the late 1890s, encompassing some 13,000 acres of pristine forest lands. Membership has passed down through generations.

HMC has a long connection to the Huron Mountains Wildlife Federation, established in 1955 "to encourage and support scientific study of the living things, lands and waters of the Lake Superior region," as it says on the website. The foundation is located at Ives Lake within the club's property.

What we knew was that only members and employees are allowed on the property – so how would we proceed on that leg of our journey?

One of our Michigan advisers assured us that he knew some HMC members and was sure he could get us permission to cross the land. Later, through a Facebook contact, we had an even better connection. Niko Economides had been a guide at the club and knew people who still worked there. Niko was the key that unlocked the literal gate. He contacted the appropriate club officials and explained what we were doing and why we wanted to walk their shore. That we were doing research on the lake probably improved our chances. Permission was granted, and plans made to be guided across the property by a staff naturalist.

The lake was calm and a dusky light played upon it when we arrived at the campground from which we started the previous morning. Today we'd head east. Mike spotted a deer in the water on a long sandbar. I grabbed the video camera to film as it danced its way out of the water. In the marsh next to me, green frogs twanged, peepers peeped and birds sang. I caught some of those sounds on tape.

When I caught up to Mike, he was looking at a sanderling (another shorebird) at the edge of the Huron River. We took off our shoes and socks and walked barefoot until we came to rocks. Shoes on, we walked the rocks, then came to a spot where we had to get our feet wet. Shoes back off, then back on after drying our feet yet again.

We reached Little Huron River, where we thought we were to meet our guide Megan McDonald. She was to be our "keeper," in club parlance. I scoped the shore with my binoculars and saw two people by the rocks on the other side of the bay. They weren't moving, so we sat on a log and waited, periodically looking at the people. After a half hour, we threw a log across a narrow part of the stream, and Mike walked down the beach to see if they were waiting for us. I sat enjoying the peace and quiet, looking at the Huron Islands. When I looked again, the couple was gone, but Mike was still walking that way. A little while later, Mike was returning with the two people behind him. Very confusing. I stood up and put on my pack just when Mike turned and saw the people. Then he waved his poles at me, and I started across the stream.

Megan and Paul, one of the HMC security staff, introduced themselves. We learned later that they had been watching us, too, and thought I might be

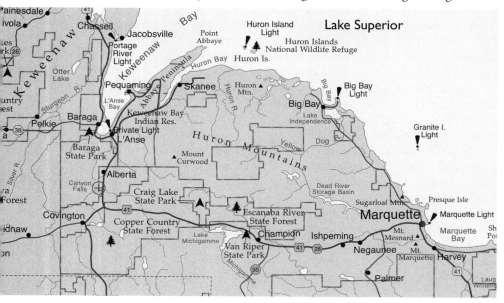

injured when they saw only Mike cross the river. Paul was wearing a tan uniform shirt and patrol cap with a brown HMC embroidered on it. He had driven Megan to this spot, but was not planning to hike with us, so he soon left and went back to his duties. Megan, a young woman in her 20s, had her long brown hair in a thick braid held back by a headscarf. Dark glasses hid her eyes, but her smile showed an easygoing personality. She wore a T-shirt, shorts, green backpack and running shoes. Later, I noticed some small flowers and stems had caught in the shoelaces and pointed it out to her. She said, "I know," and kept walking.

We moved from the beach to the cliff top because Paul had said there were too many sharp drops with no walking space along the water's edge. We pushed through brush and ferns and over downed trees. I fell once and got scratched on the thigh. A hidden branch rammed into Mike's calf. This was not fun, but we went on … and … on. Megan hadn't bushwhacked through this section, so it was new territory for her, too. Along the way, we startled another thrush from her nest with its four warm blue eggs. These nests are so well hidden in the undergrowth that you can't see them until you're almost on top of them.

Finally we reached the Flat Rock trailhead and found a nice spot for lunch with a picnic table next to the water. After eating, Mike interviewed Megan and learned that she had grown up in Duluth.

"The lake keeps me near it," she said. "Without it I don't feel connected. I go out to the lake and it puts everything in perspective. Every time I've left it, I've come back in less than a year."

Getting under way again, we walked on a beach and then a road until we came to River Cabin, our home for the evening. The HMC not only gave us permission to cross their property, but offered lodging for the night.

We put our packs down and relaxed before visiting the store to buy cold drinks. There were more miles to hike for the day, so I left my pack in the cabin, and Mike reduced the weight in his for our walk to the Salmon Trout River. Thick clouds and thunder rolled in the distance as we crossed the Pine River. It was low, with docks sitting several feet above the water and sandbars in the middle covered with vegetation. We judged the sky and decided to go for it. The trail took us through the coniferous woods to the edge of the massive red cliffs.

Without my backpack, I felt like I was flying. The thunder faded in the distance, but the clouds continued to ride low in the sky. The trail zigzagged along the edge of the cliff. When we peeked over the edge we saw massive rocks below the water's surface. We stepped carefully because so much was hidden by vegetation. Megan had been on this trail before, but it had since grown over. She saw the trail sign but missed the connection, and we walked a little more than a quarter-mile down an old road before turning back to link with the trail.

We started the afternoon hike at 3:10 p.m. and were still on the trail at 5 p.m., nowhere near the entrance gate where Bill and Beth were waiting. They had been given permission to stay with us in the cabin. Megan tried her handheld radio, but the reception was bad. She could hear the guards, but they couldn't hear her. She repeatedly called into the radio that we at "Stone Dock Road, send someone to get us." Finally we heard over the radio: "We'll send the support people (Bill and Beth) down the road to meet you."

We had logged a total of 19.8 miles – our longest day of the trip, and even though we were all tired and more than ready to quit, I didn't feel as tired as I expected. I think walking in the afternoon without my bigger pack was the biggest factor for this happy feeling. Mike actually felt good, too, which was a surprise considering the distance. But he would pay for it that night. For Megan, spending the entire day walking through the forest was a lark.

Back at the cabin, while the others sat down to relax and Beth prepared dinner, I snuck upstairs and happily sank into an old clawfoot tub filled with hot water and aromatherapy salts: my new definition of heaven on earth. We were in bed by 10:30, but as we feared, Mike's knee pain flared up, making sleep difficult, especially because he hadn't brought any of his medications from the RV.

Megan said we could have breakfast in the community dining room at 7:30. Because we were close to the lake it didn't really feel like we were in the "mountains." The five of us walked through the fresh, cool morning air to a small dining building just across from the River Cabin. As guests of the HMC we were offered a full menu, and we all ordered large omelets filled with veggies and cheese. We chatted with the kitchen staff and Megan about the wonderful food and how it would power us through our morning and into the afternoon.

One of the kitchen staff said some club members wanted to talk to us. Megan introduced Anne Manierre, a petite 86-year-old woman who came in and sat down with us. She wanted to know where we had walked – on the cliffs, roads or shore? She told us a story about some people who had nearly lost their dog over one of the cliff edges we'd walked past the day before. It was easy to picture such a near tragedy.

We also spoke with other members in the main dining room. Joining them at their table, they wanted to know how far we walked in a day, how many shoes we'd gone through, what was our favorite part of the trip; many of the same kinds of questions people all around the lake asked us. We were visiting before the arrival of the summer crowd, so we met only a handful of members, but they and the staff were all gracious and interested in our adventure.

The kitchen staff sent us away with fresh muffins for the road. We left the Huron Mountain Club having seen just a tiny fraction of the preserve, but having stayed as close to the shoreline as possible.

Next up was Big Bay, a small community about 25 miles north of Marquette, between Lake Superior and the 1,800-acre Lake Independence. On one side of the bay were steep red sandstone cliffs and on the other was a broad, wide sand beach sweeping out to a rocky point where Big Bay Lighthouse, now a private B&B, perches. That stretch of shoreline was inaccessible because of rock cliffs, so Bill drove us down the road to the site of the B&B and we walked back to town.

When we got back, we met up with 35 students, kindergarten through eighth grade, who had gathered on Squaw Bay Beach along with some local adults. Everyone sat on logs, and we were introduced by Kathy Wright, a local teacher, Northland College grad and student in 1991 at the Audubon Center where we'd worked.

The kids listened politely and with interest to Mike and me as we described our journey. Mike got them involved by having them come up one by one so he could position them so that eventually they collectively formed the outline of Lake Superior. Then they had a chance to ask questions.

"Why do you use ski poles?" "Have you been to Granot Loma?" (More on this later.) "What do you carry in your backpacks?"

As a thank-you, they gave us a T-shirt they'd decorated with 10 reasons why they love Lake Superior. Number 1 was "swimming." Number 10 was "watching the storms." Mike wore that shirt regularly during the trip and carried their love with us.

Later, we met up with Merrill and Bob Horswill, members of the Saux Head Point Owners Association. They had contacted us after learning about our walk through Facebook and offered to escort us across the shoreline, part of the association's 700 acres. Bob joined us on the bridge over the Iron River that afternoon. He had an air of dignity one associates with surgeons; a man who chose his words carefully and did not waste any on frivolous chatter.

Mike and I left our packs behind for the short 4-mile hike. Bob, wearing khaki pants, long-sleeve pullover, low-cut hiking shoes, a baseball cap and a camelback water pack, asked how fast we walked. "Around 2.6 to 2.8 miles per hour," I told him, forgetting that we walk faster unencumbered. Soon I noticed he panted while trying to talk. Then he stopped to take off his jacket.

Later I asked Mike our speed; the GPS read 3.4 mph. I apologized to Bob, but he was a good sport and made a strong effort to keep up. It was at times like this that we could tell our stamina had increased, because Bob, a retired orthopedic surgeon, used to be a cross-country competitor and still rides mountain bikes regularly. He and Merrill have a place on the shore and a home in Presque Isle, Wisconsin.

The wide old road made for easy walking, except for a few big mud puddles. As we neared the spot where the Blanks were to pick us up, Merrill drove up. "Just to see if you were leaving Bob behind," she said.

"They set a blistering pace!" Bob agreed a little later when the Blanks arrived and Beth asked, "How was your walk?"

Bob invited us home for a beer and we were greeted by Daisy, their shih tzu. We are fans of all dogs, yet partial to big ones. But this little white fluff ball was cute and friendly. Their

We stayed as guests in a cozy log cabin on the very private property of the Huron Mountain Club.

beautiful home featured lots of windows that brought in the wide blue expanse of Lake Superior.

Mike mentioned his knee pain to Bob, who could empathize since he also suffers from joint problems. He gave Mike medicine to help manage the pain. Later, while walking on the rocky shore by their home, Bob confided to me, "I don't think he's going to make it all the way."

Back at the RV, we had visitors, Jean and Jane Gertz, identical middle-aged twins with grey hair cut much like mine and wire rimmed glasses. They had been at the school program in Big Bay and came to buy T-shirts from us. They told us about growing up in the KeeVeenaw (the "Yooper way" to pronounce it, so they told us) with a dad who had been in the lighthouse service beginning in 1937 at a Life-Saving station in Whitefish. Subsequently he was assigned to Manitou Island, Gull Rock, Portage Entry and Sand Hill. He tried to stay in the Keweenaw so his family wouldn't have to move so much and took "bachelor" assignments because this allowed him to come home one week out of each month. Jane and Jean moved to Wisconsin near Lake Michigan for their careers, but came back to Lake Superior to live full time when they retired in 2005. When asked how they would define Lake Superior, Jane said, "Awesome." Jean added, "There are five great, but only one Superior."

We met Bob the next morning where we'd stopped walking the day before. He planned to walk with us to his property, then take us through Granot Loma's property. He knew the current owner and felt he could get permission.

Granot Loma was built for Louis "L.G." Kaufman, a financier involved in the building of the Empire State Building, who was born and raised in Marquette. The story goes that he was refused membership to the Huron Mountain Club and thumbed his nose at HMC by buying more than 5,000 acres, with nearly 4 miles of Lake Superior shore, to build his own compound with a fully functioning farm. The magnificent wood-and-stone structure, as big and luxurious as a five-

Granot Loma, a magnificent log "mansion" with a fascinating history, practically stands in water.

star hotel, became the Kaufmans' home. It took 22 architects and a few hundred workers – many of them local Finnish woodcraftsmen – eight years to build. In the summer of 2010 it was for sale for a mere $40 million.

The current owner was very gracious when the Horswills called. He gave us permission to drive in to see the lodge, something few people get to do. But before that, we had some walking to do – tackling a trail toward Bob's beach, which was mostly boulders. Mike started skipping ahead – bouncing from boulder to boulder – while Bob (who also has knee problems) and I picked our way forward. I like walking on the bigger boulders; it's fun trying to pick your way along. Finally, we caught up with Mike who was standing on some sand. I admonished him in a whisper, "You've got to slow down, especially when we're with others." Mike apologized, saying he didn't think he was going so fast. The joy of bouncing among boulders, he thought later, "might come from one of my personal rules – gravity is bad and the slower you go the more opportunity it has to take you down."

The stretch of sand was short-lived and then we were back on boulders. I found a perfectly round, pink granite baseball-size stone and picked it up. A keeper. Bob looked surprised. "You're kidding; you're going to carry that?"

"Yes," I said, putting it into my pack and thinking it didn't seem that heavy. A while later I spotted an unusual, larger dark rock. It looked like iron. I called Mike back to see it. This one was the size of a small bowling ball, weighing 10 pounds or more. "We really should take it back," I said, and Mike offered to put it in his pack. (Bob and I figured if nothing else, it would slow him down a bit. A belated revelation of how to pace Mike, but too late for any real effect.) We didn't have that much farther to go. It had to make Bob wonder about his prediction that Mike might not make it.

Merrill met us along the shore. "Boy, you made good time," she noted, to which Bob replied, "You should have seen Mike boulder hopping!"

We dropped our packs at their cabin and continued walking the beach. At one point, Merrill and I spotted a dark square head sticking out of the water. It was an otter. When it saw us, it turned and dove. We stood rooted, watching and waiting. The otter popped back up in time for Bob and Mike to see it, too. It dove again, but resurfaced a short way out. The Horswills had never seen one out there. It was our Full Circle totem – and our reminder of Mike's son, Matt – touching base with us.

Back at the cabin, we sampled Merrill's fresh-from-the-oven chocolate chip cookies. Bob suggested we have some of her homemade chili, so we followed dessert with a nice, nourishing black bean chili.

We couldn't hike through their neighbor's property, so we drove to Granot Loma, past the farm and some orchards. The gate was a work of modern art – all abstract metal designs in bright colors. After driving down a dirt trail, we came to the main lodge. Kaufman incorporated playful decorations in this three-story structure, like the stone ducks perched on the tops of the many chimneys. The front of a nearby building was made with bent pieces of wood that resembled a spider's web. Bob rang the doorbell of the main building, but no one answered. We knocked on the door to the kitchen, but still got no response.

We took photos of one another, then descended the concrete steps and ramp past the marina. The beach was short and ended in massive volcanic rocks, but Mike thought we might be able to climb up them to get around the point. We knew there was a road somewhere behind the line of trees, and I imagine Bob wondered why we didn't choose that route.

Scrambling up the black rocks, we soon got to a big gap that blocked our way. We bushwhacked to find a way, going through a forest of thick fir with tightly intertwined dead branches. Bob was tickled to find pretty twinflowers growing on a moss-covered boulder, but otherwise I suspected he was not having much fun. At one point Mike, in his usual enthralled way, chimed out, "I bet no one has ever been here!" Bob snorted. "Yeah, not even the animals are dumb enough to come through here."

We continued to follow Mike, who used the GPS to guide us over rocks and through brush toward "the road." Stopping briefly on a knob of earth covered with lichens and moss, where you could almost see the lake, Mike said with a beatific smile, "Isn't this a beautiful spot?" I agreed, but he didn't get much of a response from Bob. We finally broke through the vegetation, coming out onto the long-sought and long-promised road.

"That was really fun," Mike said.

Bob sat down to tie his shoe. With a look of disbelief, he said, "You're really weird."

"I've been told that before," Mike admitted.

Then Bob was laughing. "Maybe you need another poke in the head," he said, referring to the bump on Mike's forehead from running into the birch branch earlier.

"Maybe he's already been poked in the head too many times," I added, which made Bob laugh harder.

Continuing, we came to a heavily logged area, something Bob was discouraged to see. It was Granot Loma land, and the end of the logs were marked with colored paint indicating "Granot Loma " or with a number and "cords." If all those fireplaces in the house were used, it would take a big forest.

We remained fairly quiet on the rest of our walk. At the Little Garlic River, Bob called Merrill to pick him up. We walked down a driveway and back onto a beach where we could see the smokestacks in Marquette ahead. After Bob left, the rest of our walk was on the flat shelf rock with unusual designs. One in particular looked just like a landing strip, with a broad white line of rock stretching off into the water until we couldn't see it anymore.

We crossed a river and passed a number of college kids lying in the sun near Little Presque Isle, an island that is half volcanic rock and half sandstone. The water was so shallow, you could easily walk across to the island.

The next morning, June 4, we woke up to clouds and predictions of rain. Mike's knees hurt all night long, maybe because of the bushwhacking or perhaps because of the weather. We were also expecting to meet our videographer, Jim Radford, who now had a record of coming with the rain.

We left the campground and drove the car back to the spot where we stopped hiking the day before. It was fairly mild and very humid and almost as soon as we

We did many presentations, but only this once on a beach for elementary students at Big Bay.

started down the big hill, we felt sprinkles. We tried to stay on the shore, which entailed a lot of climbing up and over big smooth boulders and onto steep narrow trails until we reached a KEEP OUT sign. The rocks were getting slick with rain, so we headed up the hillside and found ourselves emerging onto busy Highway 550 on the outskirts of Marquette, just as the rain began to fall in earnest. I hadn't brought my rain jacket, but luckily we were able to call Amanda – back from her Minnesota break – and she found us. Cars and trucks rushed past, spraying water.

Jim Radford was waiting for us at Presque Isle Park, a beautiful cliffside peninsula park. Fox TV also wanted to interview us. Not looking our celebrity best – our hair, rain pants and jackets were soaked – we spoke to the reporter and Jim filmed us out on the rocky edge. Then we returned to the RV to change into dry clothes and grab some things to take with us to the Landmark Inn for two nights. This beautifully restored historic hotel was built in the 1930s. We thanked our lucky stars, our hot showers and soft bed ... and the Anderson Insurance Agency, one of our sponsors who made arrangements for us to stay two nights.

Amanda had an educational program to do at the Children's Museum at 6 p.m., while the Blanks, Mike and I were scheduled to sail on a schooner at 6 p.m. This Full Circle fundraiser was arranged by Niko Economides, who owns the boat, *Coaster II*, a 1930s-era, gaff-rigged wooden schooner. We met Niko through our Facebook site. A soft-spoken, big teddy bear of a man with thick curly brown hair and beard, he looks as Greek as his name indicates.

It was still misty when we walked down to the dock. It felt familiar to get on the Coaster II, which is basically the same size as the *Izmir*, the ketch on which we were married. The other passengers included Kathy Wright from Big Bay and her husband, Paul, and Michelle Halley and her husband, Gabe Gluesing. Our first mate was Niko's 17-year-old son Thanos, a stunning young man, with black curly hair, black eyes and a 6-foot-3 frame that did not fit well in the low-ceilinged galley. His mom is Egyptian and owns the popular Rubaiyat restaurant in town. She prepared the food for our sail – a delicious and appropriately warm cream of asparagus soup, focaccia bread and baklava for dessert.

A small wood-burning cook stove put out heat and warmed the soup in the front cabin, just behind the V-berth. It was a nice warm, cozy space, but it was hard to accept a wood-burning stove in a wooden boat.

Niko gave everyone a choice to sail or not. There was little wind, but we all agreed. "Let's go."

We set out with Mike at the helm, and he looked like he belonged there. I felt right at home going up and down the companionway and walking through the cabin. We got out of the harbor and raised the sails, but the wind continued to die as a fog rolled in. Soon we headed back. We returned to the hotel and went to the sixth-floor lounge with Bill and Beth for a hot toddy farewell drink, since they would head back to Minnesota in the morning. Through the rain-streaked windows the lights of the city came through in wavy lines. The warm room and snug booth, along with our hot drinks, wrapped us in a companionable embrace while we reflected on our shared adventures over the past 10 days.

Babycakes in Marquette is unlike any other bakery/coffee shop we know. Their specialty is giant muffins that taste like the richest butter cake you've ever had. The storefront is small, with only six or seven tables and a short counter, and people are always in line to order. Their other baked goods are also delicious, but nothing comes close to the muffins. It became our regular morning stop in Marquette for four wonderful days.

The Commons is a new community building near the Farmers Market downtown. We gave a presentation here to a packed crowd. At the end of the talk, we held a contest to win one of our *Grandparents Michigan Style* books. We posed a question from *National Geographic* magazine about water: How many gallons are used every day in the United States to irrigate golf courses? (The answer is 2 billion gallons). Peter Kaufman came closest. It turned out that he is a grandson of the L.G. Kaufman who created Granot Loma. After talking to him, he gave us his phone number and said to call, saying he could show us something we wouldn't see anywhere else around the lake. We were definitely intrigued.

We had another program that afternoon at the Moosewood Nature Center in Presque Isle Park. Three ladies and the center's naturalist were waiting for us – a small but enthusiastic group. It was wet and blustery, so we gathered under a picnic pavilion in the park. Mike put a map of the lake on the table and proceeded to tell them about the trip. The size of the group didn't matter to us – we wanted to share our story of the lake and fresh water. We hoped our message would ripple outward.

Walking back to town on the paved bike trail/walking path, a truck went by. Mike recognized Niko as the driver. He turned his truck, parked and started walking with us. He's been involved with the struggling nonprofit nature center and had hoped to attend our talk. A generous man, he was interested in making sure we were looked after. He walked a good ways with us, then said farewell.

Walking in a town has its own charm, and we were always entertained by looking at the variety of homes. Ridge Street in Marquette has some of the most elaborate old houses: Victorians with gingerbread detail, some painted like jewelry boxes, some with Mansard roofs. We assumed this was a community with lots of faithful churchgoers by the number of big old stone churches in the city.

The last presentation in Marquette was at a Unitarian Universalist Church on Sunday morning. This had been set up by Michelle Halley, who is the attorney and Lake Superior Project Manager for the National Wildlife Federation

We spoke to about 20 people for an hour and took questions after the potluck meal that followed the service. Michelle was leading the fight to prevent the Eagle Mine in the Yellow Plains area, where it is feared that the leaching of acid used to extract nickel may enter streams and ultimately the lake. There is serious concern about potential pollution entering the watershed, damaging sport fishing and the water supply. Like many others in this area, we fear that the desire for short-term profits and jobs generated by resource extraction clouds the potential long-term impacts that would cost more to fix than the profits justify.

We called Peter Kaufman after the service and accepted an invitation to his home. He and his wife, Audrey, have a magazine-worthy home on a rocky lakeshore. A large metal gate opened automatically to let us into their brick-paved driveway and landscaped grounds. Beautiful flowers and trees bloomed in the June sunshine. Their two little white teddy bears posing as dogs ran out to greet us. Like the Horswills' Daisy, these too were Shih Tzus. Was there some correlation with living on the lake and choosing this breed?

They have a natural rock marina, which is what Peter wanted to show us. They also have an incredible rock pool created by building a cement-stone wall on two sides of a natural indentation in the rock. They bring water from the lake for irrigating their grounds, which then runs down over the rocks into this pool. Peter, who owned a construction company, likes to build things. When we complimented him on the landscaping, he shared a favorite quote: "Landscaping is the cosmetics of architecture."

While we sat in their four-season porch, sipping wine and scotch and nibbling cheese, crackers and nuts, Peter talked about his grandfather and what he remembered of time spent at Granot Loma as a child. Outside, the ever-present deep royal blue lake sparkled, and curling white waves splashed against the rocks.

No matter what we may feel about their exclusivity, the large private inholdings we passed through these past six days have in fact preserved miles of shoreline from development and potential sources of pollution. These are shorelines that can be seen from the water and appear to be still wild and untouched for the most part. We are always happy to see land set aside and preserved, but we also hope that in the future, communities or government entities will ensure that the general public has adequate access to the lake, too.

I watched the ripples as I drifted away
The lake was deep, on this golden day
Lured by reflection, in this tranquil deep
I lost my mind, then I feel asleep.
Jon Coe

After Thoughts

Fresh Water on a Global Scale

Mike:

We aren't experts on fresh water around the globe, but since returning from the hike, we've become even more conscious about water issues worldwide. For example, we recently read about water shortages in the Fertile Crescent within Israel, Lebanon, Jordan, Syria and Iraq. Here, where agriculture began, people can't produce enough food to live. Climate change is a problem, but so is competition for water. International solutions are needed as solving one regional problem – like building a dam to produce electricity for Turkey, which might increase evaporation down stream – creates potentials for armed conflict.

In Tucson, we met with the water treatment education guide and learned how the wastewater is treated and injected – clean – back in to the aquifer to maintain a supply. Water managers project a gap between demand and supply may begin by 2020 – sooner or later. If growth continues in the city, this may become a critical problem, but try to tell a politician to suggest population limits for an area or to ration water.

In November 2010, Arizona started work on a new water pipeline through Nevada. Where do these arid states think they will get their water in the future? Is there enough political will to protect Lake Superior? There is a law in place that regulates and restricts removal of water from the Great Lakes basin, but will this be enough as demands grow?

We shouldn't be arrogant in believing Lake Superior is too big to harm. At one time the Aral Sea between Kazakhstan and Uzbekistan was the fourth largest lake in the world. A major diversion under the Soviet Union to irrigate cotton crops has shrunk the lake to one-third of its original surface area and it has lost 90 percent of its source water.

Can we be water wise? There are many simple and grand ways to save on water consumption, from shorter showers, waterless urinals and water-saver toilets to city systems that avoid overflows of sewage. If we think of the future generations, if we care about our grandchildren and their grandchildren, we do not have a choice. Fresh water is the basis of life. What we have is all we will ever have. We must take care of it.

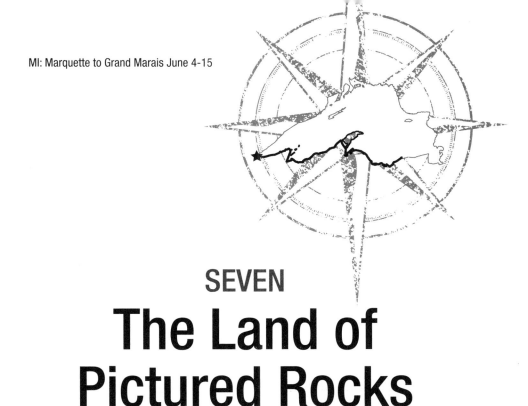

SEVEN

The Land of Pictured Rocks

Where does a wise man kick a pebble? On the beach.
Where does a wise man hide a leaf? In the forest.
G.K. Chesterton

Kate:

Walking out of Marquette, we followed the paved path to the Michigan Visitor Center on M-28. A woman was walking toward us. At first she stared and then asked what had become a pleasantly familiar question, which turned into the theme for the morning: "Are you the couple walking around the lake?"

She was Kim Nixon, one of our Facebook fans, another affirmation of the power of social networking. Our Facebook page, which started with people living around the lake, eventually expanded to include people around the world.

The smell of summer – sweet cut grass – filled the air as lawn mowers went back and forth across the park. The bike path took us by a big coal power plant and onto a road through South Beach Park with houses on one side and the lake on the other. A lady weeding her garden beds also asked if we were the people going around the lake. She came across the street to talk. How lucky you are, I told her, to live here. Her family had lived there for 50 years and just two years ago the railroad took out the tracks that ran on the side of the street where we were standing. When she and her husband moved to this place, no bank wanted to give them a loan; the neighborhood was considered unattractive and undesirable. Today she's probably sitting on a small fortune, with its proximity to the lake and the quiet cul-de-sac. Mostly modest working-class homes, the neighborhood also has larger, upscale ones, testifying to its desirability now. Much of the lake is quickly becoming "discovered" for its beauty.

Farther down the path, we came to a couple of bridges crossing a river. A woman on the old railroad bridge was talking on a cell phone. As we walked toward the river, she waved and came our way. Lynn Baldwin had seen us on the news. She'd love to do what we were doing, also with a SAG wagon – "none of this camping every night." Her biggest concern about the lake, she said, was the sulfide mining near Marquette and how sad that made her.

Just past the Michigan visitor center, we headed to the beach. A sign warned in great detail that this was a privately owned and maintained beach to the water's edge. It also warned that trespassers would be arrested. Knowing the law, upheld by the state's Supreme Court, that you can walk to the high water mark, we went ahead. We know that beachfront owners are probably trying to discourage people from camping or partying in front of their homes, but the waterline is public and we were just crossing. We hoped it would not cause complications.

Mike thought we should go back to the visitor center to ask about the beach, which normally I would suggest, but this time I said, "Let's just go for it."

After we passed a few houses, we heard a loud boom. I turned sharply, nervous that someone might be shooting at us. We didn't see anyone, and we walked on without problems.

The beach ended at the Chocolay River. It was wide and deep, except at the mouth, where waves washed over a rocky bottom. We could see the bridge and road not far away, so we tried to walk along the river to reach it, but a channel stopped us. We went for the water crossing.

I took off my socks and shoes, zipped off the lower pants legs and rolled my shorts up. The waves brought the water to the top of Mike's thighs and higher on me. It was a wide crossing with chilly water, and our legs were numb before we reached the other side.

This was not a good beach-walking day. Waves washed up at an angle and created a series of dunelike mounds on the sand. The slant, and the resultant up-and-down walking, made progress difficult. The other option was to walk

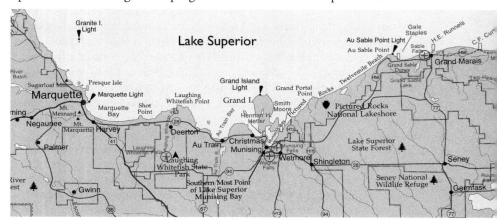

on the softer sand, which Mike chose to do. I veered back and forth from the steep, wet sand to the flat, soft sand – trying to find the best surface. My feet felt the ache quite early in the day.

We stopped for lunch on a log and were joined by a barking golden retriever. He ran down from a cabin and barked and barked. We mollified him with food, which stopped him only until the food ran out. Then he resumed barking. Eventually a young woman whistled for him, but he ignored her until she came out calling, "Sammy!" When he continued barking, she apologized, grabbed his collar and hauled him away. Less than 10 minutes later he was back – barking and looking for treats. It was both an entertaining and annoying lunch diversion.

Despite my aching feet, it was a gorgeous day. I loved looking at the water with my polarized sunglasses, enjoying the vast robin's egg blue sky, a navy blue line of water with a greenish-blue band next to it, and a final band of clear water. Sometimes I just couldn't believe the crystal clarity of Lake Superior.

We tried the road to give our feet a rest, but the noise of cars and trucks sent us back to the beach. At 10 miles, this was the longest continuous beach we'd walked. It also was the first beach I wasn't happy to be on, but it did cause me to reflect on that cliché: Live in the moment. "Stop the complaints," I reminded myself. "You're doing something you've dreamed of doing for years and you're only going to do it once." Surely I would see this beach this way only once in my life. The discomfort, though great at the moment, was indeed momentary. I tried to focus on "being" there and absorbing every aspect of this adventure and place. It did help – a good lesson for living each day.

Ahead of us rocks loomed and we decided to cut through a backyard to get by them. A chocolate Lab came barking and bounding over from next door, but we talked to him nicely and he went back home. When we reached the road, a woman came up the driveway with the Lab. She had on gardening gloves and looked like she was either checking out the mailbox or us.

Umbrellas still make the best rain gear of all, as I proved on this trail in Pictured Rocks.

Hi," we said.

"Where are you going?"

"Around the lake."

She was surprised, but enthusiastic. She and the Lab walked down the road with us. We told her we'd been through Marquette.

"I have a little shop there," she said.

"Oh yeah – what's its name?"

"Babycakes."

Our eyes lit up. "That's our favorite place!" Mike told her. "We've had breakfast there the last few days."

We chatted with Kim Danielson about the shop she's owned for 20 years. She asked what muffins we liked best and wondered if we'd like to take some with us.

"For sure!"

Kim said she'd call the shop and have them put aside three cherry and three blackberry muffins that we could pick up on Monday.

Once again we wondered whether this was another coincidence or the universe sending us positive connections. We walked away marveling at our good fortune, but I was almost limping by this point. I wanted to change my socks, so we stopped by a driveway. As I sat down on a rock, I felt the whoosh of wings go by me, but didn't see the bird. Mike looked up and saw a black-capped chickadee enter a hole in a very skinny birch trunk just above and to the right of my head. This was the second time we'd stopped right in front of a bird's nest cavity. For a couple of naturalists, this was like hitting the jackpot twice. Mike took some video and tried to take photos, but the parent bird didn't return. We began to worry that we were keeping her away from the nest. Mike had seen her carry in a grub and carry away a fecal sack, keeping her nest clean.

Walking the road back toward M-28 where Amanda would pick us up, we were charmed by an entire roadside ditch filled with blue-eyed grass. These tiny corn-blue flowers perched on long stems tickled us with pleasure.

Some mornings we just didn't feel like getting up, not because we didn't want to walk, but because we felt like being lazy. Luckily perhaps, the schedule didn't allow for this kind of behavior, especially on days when we'd be moving our base camp. This day, we were headed to Munising, 40 miles away, so the day was well advanced by the time we got to the Falling Rock Café. Owner Nancy Dwyer had offered us a place to stay in an apartment at the Falling Rock Lodge, which she and her husband also own and operate. The lodge is on Powell Lake in the Hiawatha National Forest. It was a long drive out of town, but after parking and plugging in the RV, we went back to Munising and back down the highway to our starting point for the day's walk.

A short stretch of beach and then it was on to M-28, right where the Sand River enters the lake. A couple across the stream saw us, and after we crossed the bridge, the woman came up her driveway to talk to us. The sign at the entry to their place said, "Tervetuloa." That's Finnish for "Welcome," Kathy Schuck told us. She'd heard about our walk, and said she was sorry she'd missed our talk in Marquette.

To the west the clouds had thickened and threatened rain, but we forged ahead, making good time. Not sure when or where we'd stop for lunch, I ate my bologna and mayo sandwich while walking. After 9 miles, we came to a wayside rest and stopped so that Mike could eat and rest. He lay down on the picnic table, while I changed socks and massaged my feet. Then we found old Highway M-28, which took us closer to the lake. We couldn't see what the shore was like because of the cabins along the road, so we stayed on it until we found a long sandy bay where we could walk easily next to the water.

A man was standing on the beach. Then he went up some steps and returned with a chair. "Are you walking around Lake Superior?" he asked.

"Yes."

"I thought you looked familiar," he said, explaining that he'd seen us on the news. Mark was 60 years old, retired and living with his wife in a small cabin on the beach. He walked with us a while and told us he'd been coming to this very place every year of his life. Rock River Beach Cottages used to operate along a big stretch of the beach. Now there are only a few cottages, but the place still had a functioning water wheel and actually sold power to the local electric company. A little bridge crossed over the Rock River and gave us a good view of the modest dam and waterfall. People still rent the cabins, but getting a reservation is tough. Most guests have been coming for decades and make reservations for the next year when they leave.

We walked past the cottages on the other side of the stream and down a dirt path until it ran out. Then we returned to the shore with its mix of rocks and sand. Doing more boulder walking actually felt good because I wasn't putting pressure on my sore heel and it stretched my foot in different ways. Unfortunately, Mike looked back to see how I was doing, lost his balance and went down. The rocks scored their first hit. He didn't hurt himself seriously, but his right knee and hand got banged up. Then raindrops began to fall, and it was time to meet Amanda on the road.

That evening we were to give a talk at the Falling Rock Café. This little café/store is an important gathering place for locals. It's filled with lots and lots of books, both new and used, and has unique handmade jewelry and art by local people. It also has Internet service. About 20 people attended, and one woman in the audience volunteered to make us some little notebooks like the Rite in the Rain, all-weather ones we used. It turned out that the Neenah Paper plant in town actually puts the special coating on the paper that Rite in the Rain uses.

Pictured Rocks National Lakeshore was a section of the hike we both looked forward to doing. Mike has backpacked it many times over the years, but I had only been out on the tour boat. We had been given tickets to go on the boat again and, with the sun shining and no wind, we couldn't pass up the opportunity. Plus Amanda had never been there before, so the tour would be fun for her. The boat was completely full – top and bottom. Adults filled the upper level and a sixth-grade class on a field trip from a school in Lapeer, a town near Flint in the Lower Peninsula, was below.

Mike and I sat in the front, but before long the sixth-graders bubbled up to the top and stood in the front of us. The captain came on the speaker and said all the kids had to have a seat or couldn't be on the top deck. We assumed someone complained about the blocked view. Some moved, but a lot didn't, so the captain got gruffer: "If the kids up top don't have seats, you can't be there, and if the chaperones don't take charge, I'm going to turn this boat around and go back."

After that threat (which sounded a lot like any dad on a family road trip), the students mostly found seats and got one more (perhaps overly zealous) warning before everything settled down. One chaperone told us that the 48 students and 11 adults had camped out the night before in the rain and leaky tents made for miserable campers by morning. Now everyone was smiling and enjoying the boat ride and sunshine.

A couple of East Indian people sat near us. I asked to interview them for their perspective on the lake. "When I came here and saw these (Great Lakes)," Niket Gandhi said, "I thought, 'These aren't lakes, these are seas.'"

The sun hit the rock walls as we turned back toward town, but in the west huge dark clouds were building. We returned to the lodge to get our gear and supplies, but while we were there, the storm hit – thunder, lightning, hail and major winds. There was a tornado warning for the county, so we stayed inside, worked on computers and waited for it to clear. Around 3:30 p.m. with some blue sky showing, we decided to head out. We drove west of town 13.3 miles, got out and started walking east on a pretty beach. Turns out that after a good hard rain, the sand is easier to walk on. I loved seeing the reflection of the clouds in the glistening wet sand right after the water washed the shore, then slipped away.

More birds were flying after the storm, mainly crows, ravens and gulls, but also a great blue heron that flew out over the lake. Right before we came to the Au Train River, I saw something in the water. Without my binoculars I wasn't quite sure what it was, but it looked like yet another Mylar balloon. Mike looked with his camera's telephoto lens and agreed. It was a balloon, the first we'd seen floating in the water. Earlier in the day, we'd seen a few others on land. Oddly, they continued to be among the most recurrent trash around the lake.

When we got to where the river emptied into the bay, we had to go on the roadway to cross. On the bridge, a group of preteen girls in bikinis saw us and when they spied Mike's camera, they made a show of jumping off, shrieking as they hit the water. After crossing, we saw the sign that said "No jumping or diving from the bridge." Oh well, considering the number of signs we'd been ignoring, we couldn't really criticize others for doing the same.

As we walked back to the lake on top of a big sand bank, swallows flew out from holes in the sandy cliffs fronting the river. The birds didn't go back in as long as we were near. The late afternoon sun shining on black clouds added sparkle to the tops of the lake's blue waves.

Jim Northup, superintendent of Pictured Rocks National Lakeshore, met us the next morning, informing us about park trails and detailing distances between places to link with Amanda. This was good news because we thought we'd have to backpack in and camp there. His suggestions meant several long mileage days, but that was better than days of carrying an extra heavy pack.

Our walk that day took us to the roadside town of Christmas, about 3 miles west of Munising. The founder of Christmas gave it that name after he retired from work as a local conservation officer and built a toy factory in 1939. The factory burned down a year or so after opening, but the town stuck with the name. All the street signs and most businesses have Christmas-themed names. A giant wooden cutout of Santa stands in front of Santa's Workshop store, an emporium that sells Christmas and gift items and is not far from the incongruous cutouts of the Old Woman in the Shoe and Peter, Peter, Pumpkin Eater.

We got permission to cut through Yule Log Resort to the beach, where a string of small, neat cabins sat by the shore. On the beach we found the most amazing purplish rocks. I thought they might be amethyst and Mike thought fluorite, but we were both wrong. They were slag washed up from an old foundry. They had wonderful patterns and swirls, like agates. One was completely blue. We kept bending to pick them up, but had to stop before our pockets burst.

We followed that beach as far as we could, then returned to the road at Ferry Landing. A small avenue off the main road took us past interesting houses and small shops that sold smoked fish. We stopped again at Falling Rock on our way through town and again bumped into Jim Northup. Mike interviewed him, and Jim put his description of Lake Superior into a single word we would hear often repeated on this trip: "Magic."

I didn't get out of town without buying some locally made items, including a pair of stone earrings made by Jim's wife, Phyllis, a talented watercolorist inspired by the shore rocks. I also bought beautiful old Munising wooden bowls, made at Munising Woodenware, which operated in town from 1911 to 1955. (The man who founded Christmas got leftover wood from this factory for his toy making.) The bowls are collector's items now, but still very functional. They're wonderful souvenirs, and every time we use them I remember Munising and the good people living there.

To finish our day, we drove to Miners Castle and walked to Sand Point. The trail took us through a verdant forest of maples, yellow birch, cedar and beech. Ostrich ferns brushed my shoulders. It felt like a rainforest. We heard and sometimes saw waterfalls pouring over the cliff, a long way down from the top. Plenty of boardwalk defined the way, which was good because where it was wet, it was black mud. Abundant birds sang in the trees and we were able to "pish" (our birder's call) warblers closer. A black-throated blue warbler hopped close enough to see without binoculars. It was a beautiful walk to end the day, though it was longer than we had anticipated - close to 15 miles total.

In the evening we had a drink with Nancy and Jeff Dwyer. They live in the house attached to the rental unit we were staying in. He works all week in Lansing, as an associate dean at Michigan State. It's his job that helps support the café, which opened in 2003. They both gave up jobs in Florida, came up here – he'd been here as a kid – and bought a cabin and then an old bar, which they fixed up and made into the café and bookstore.

During the night of June 11, Mike's legs bothered him badly; he constantly moaned and shifted. Feeling helpless, but exhausted, I went to the other bedroom to sleep. It seemed that Mike's pain was becoming increasingly bad at night and I wondered if Bob Horswill's prediction – "I don't think he'll make it" – would come true.

The next day was another moving day, and we needed to leave the cozy apartment so that the Dwyers could clean and prepare for weekend customers. We drove to the RV campground west of Munising. On the horizon we saw a mass of dark gray clouds headed our way, but decided to walk anyway and went back to Sand Point, where we'd left off the day before.

We noted a sign by a driveway that read "Home Again." I liked that name for a place. We'd been thinking about an appropriate name for our home in Willow River, and I was collecting ideas along the way.

Not long into our walk, the sprinkles started. On bad-weather days, we always seemed to match our start with the arrival of the rain. It continued to sprinkle as we reached the Munising Falls parking area, where we made a bathroom stop. I came out, put up my umbrella and waited for Mike … and waited and waited. I searched the area and yelled into the bathroom. He wasn't there. I called for him. No Mike. A nearby walkway led to a waterfall, and though he hadn't said anything about going there, I walked up the path, calling his name. Not seeing him or getting any response, I started back toward town. I didn't know whether to be worried or angry, but I was upset. I hate it when he just disappears; I blame it on his being an only child. He wanders off without considering the need to communicate. He is always apologetic – once I find him – but I know it will happen again. This was not a revelation from our trip around Lake Superior – this was an understanding from a quarter century of marriage.

I'd gotten to the street when he called me. He was back by the bathrooms and gave a little wave. When he caught up to me, I demanded, "Why didn't you let me know you were going someplace else?"

"Oh, sorry," came the slightly chagrined response. "I just walked up to see the waterfall. It was really nice, like Minnehaha Creek would be in a different setting."

We walked on in the rain, now falling steadily. Our feet were getting soaked, but our pants (above the knees), head and shoulders stayed dry. Good old-fashioned umbrellas – way better than so called raincoats. At the Neenah Paper Mill, I took a photo of Mike writing in his Rite-In-The-Rain notebook, our salute to the company involved in the notebook creation.

We walked to the Falling Rock to meet Amanda. Gregg Bruff, Pictured Rock's chief of heritage education and an old acquaintance of Mike's, met us in the café, where Mike interviewed him. He has been at Pictured Rocks for 22 years and has made Munising his home and "really dug in here."

"I liken the park to a grandmother's quilt." He explained. "This landscape is such a mosaic. Not only a natural mosaic, but a human mosaic with many, many layers of stories."

About the future, Gregg said, "My greatest concern is climate change … the surface water temperature is rising faster than air temperature, and the impact on Lake Superior's food web could be very, very dramatic."

Once again, we concluded that Pictured Rocks National Lakeshore is primo! We walked the loop from Little Beaver Lake campground to Miners Castle, going clockwise. It was overcast and cool the whole day – perfect. As soon as we stepped onto the trail, we were surrounded by a forest as rich and lush as any in

Olympic National Park. Water dripped off leaves, a winter wren sang its beautiful aria and in every direction flourished different shades of green. I especially loved the tender yellow-green new growth on the hemlock and fir branches. The moss at the base of the trees was thick and vibrant, renewed by the rain. Old trees leaning at odd angles became veritable gardens of lichen, moss and ferns. We longed to stop and just admire them, but we took pictures and moved on.

Low lying clouds escorted us in and out of fog most of the day. Fog is one reason for this forest composition, why beech trees and hemlock are common here but not on the Minnesota shore. In fact, the only place where hemlocks can be found in Minnesota is in a valley of the St. Louis River where competition with other species and moisture from fog allow a tiny population to exist. Historically this was true of a few other river valleys along the shore as well. Beech trunks rose straight up with smooth gray bark that reminded us of elephant legs. When wet, you can see that their bark is mottled with green, gray and black lichens. Very old yellow birches also stand with the beech, and sometimes I just had to lay my hand on their rough bark and hope some of their life force and tenacity would transfer to me. Reminiscent of the trail in the Porcupine Mountains, we are in awe of the trees once again.

Lakeshore Trail in Pictured Rocks is even better, if that's possible, because it rarely strays from the shore. Frequent openings in the foliage take your breath away by a sheer drop or a vista of sculpted caverns and arches. Unlike the Porkies, here we didn't find extremely steep ravines to climb. Most of the bigger hillsides had steps, natural or manmade, though they were above knee height for me.

This day, Spray Falls was shooting over the precipice thanks to the recent rains. Besides such waterworks, the streams ran brown with tannins, creating big clumps of bubbles in the eddies. Stemless pink lady's slippers were abundant. These are the same orchids that grow on our property. The delicate orchids still seem to hold their own here and we found a rare white lady's slipper – the first we'd ever seen. Bunchberry, a member of the dogwood family, produced the greatest floral abundance on this walk. Entire slopes had mass clusters of these white-flowered, low-growing woody plants clinging to their sides.

So far on our walk, we've gone through periods of floral abundance – from yellow marsh marigold, then to blue forget-me-nots, then yellow trout lily, then blue, pink or white lupines and now the small white bunchberry blossoms. What would be next?

Mike stopped by one log to photograph an orange mushroom growing on its side. He noted slugs, too. I didn't see any until I put on my glasses and looked closer. The log was crawling with slugs, all headed to the mushroom, it seemed. Some were already consuming it with slime exuding beneath their bodies. Some people would be grossed out; we found it fascinating. Then we videotaped it, mischievously hoping to show it to squeamish friends and audiences.

The day was turning out perfectly. We watched streams rushing toward the cliff edge, heard warblers singing nonstop and discovered orchids hiding beneath larger leaved plants.

We passed only four other groups of hikers on the trail. Three were overnight backpackers who hiked all the day before in the downpour and set up their tents in the rain. I did not envy their experience, but was grateful to see them out there enjoying our natural national treasure.

After the glorious day, Mike had another bad night, at least for half of it; tossing, turning and moaning. I talked to him a few times about how we could go on with him in such pain, but he just mumbled something that sounded like, "Don't worry," and fell asleep. The next morning I expressed concern for his lack of rest. He was surprised; he thought he'd had a good night's sleep.

We still had half of the park to hike and we tried to prepare for the demands that these long and isolated treks would require. For my own foot pain, I put new arch supports in my boots and hoped they would lessen the pain that always seemed to develop around 9 miles. They did feel good – at first. On the trail, the boardwalks were already almost dry and there was little to no moisture on the leaves. We started without rain jackets, and before long, we had to take off our fleece. The Lake Superior Trail headed east, and we met up with a dad and his two children, who had camped overnight and were on their way out. John teaches environmental subjects at Northern Michigan University in Marquette and said he's very familiar with what he called "Nature Deficit Disorder," which is why he's committed to getting Jack, 4½, and Colleen, 12, connected to the outdoors.

Moving on, the sky was a bit lighter, but fog covered much of the lake. The trail was well packed, but not hard and wet like yesterday. We planned to walk 15 miles (according to park literature) to Log Slide, but comparing the park map to the distance that we'd hiked the day before, 15 miles didn't seem right. It turned out to be 19 miles to Log Slide.

We stayed on the upper trail for most of the morning and came to Beaver Creek with its massive logjam. We'd never seen so many trees filling a streambed; many looked very old. The cause of the jam is not something we could figure out. It must have built up over many years with fallen dead trees from the highlands to be caught up in spring flows of the stream. We tried to imagine what the stream looked like during a gushing spring runoff with its massive load of timber.

Walking on the trail, Mike reminded me that we'd mostly be on unpredictable beaches from Grand Marais to Brimley and to enjoy this firmly comfortable, established trail while we could. When we left the trail for a beach that looked flat and wet enough to hold us, we half-slid down a steep sandy slope. The sun emerged at that point, along with a nice cool breeze blowing the misty fog over the water. Despite being warmer, the long sleeves and pants worked well to keep the bugs and flies off, if nothing else.

Numerous water seeps in the sand created openings filled with gravel. The beach sand stopped after a while, turning to rocks and gravel. We checked the GPS and saw it had stopped working at some point – always a frustrating discovery since mileage was important in gauging our day and when we'd take our regular measurements.

Here on Twelve Mile beach, there were no ATV tracks, rare so far in Michigan. There were not many tracks at all – a few boot prints, some canine tracks, deer hoof prints and bird tracks. We couldn't stay on the beach and cross Seven Mile Creek, so we climbed up the bank and ended up in a campsite; a good lunch spot, with sunshine and logs to sit on.

Resting on our log pew, I told Mike that it felt like we were in our church – it being Sunday, after all.

"I've been looking at that great old white pine in front of us," he said. "That makes good sense."

The leap from campsite to cathedral was not hard for me. I'm a pantheist; all of this creation around us is God, in my mind. So much mystery and beauty, how could it be anything else? It is nonjudgmental, it just is. Sitting there, I reveled in its glory and it lifted my soul as religion is supposed to do. I reflected on how I want to do all I can to protect this creation and make sure it remains as pristine for my grandchildren as it has been for me.

The philosophical, lofty notes lasted only a short time, though. Then I was on to something more basic. Lately, I'd been noticing a sour smell somewhere on my upper body, but I couldn't find it. So after lunch, I asked Mike for a favor, something you could only ask your spouse. "Could you smell me?"

He sniffed my hair, my chest and then I asked him to smell my back.

"Ewww!" he said, not very graciously. It was a lump on my back that I had noticed earlier, but had recently gotten sore and perhaps infected. Mike rubbed antibiotic/fungicide cream on me and suggested that I go to a doctor right away, I decided to try our medications and call our medical adviser, Dr. Dewey. On this, as on any extended travel, medical needs – even the little ones – might get tricky. This also points out why it is fabulous to have a spouse along for such a journey and why they are called "helpmates."

That accomplished, we left our lunch spot and saw a deer on the boardwalk by the beach. It looked at us with ears alert, then bounded off. White-tailed deer are definitely abundant.

We walked the narrow upper trail for a while with thimbleberry to our waists. On this section of the Lakeshore Trail, the ferns were mostly bracken, also called brake. They are tall with a rigid stalk topped by three fronds of lacy leaves. These fronds are parallel to the ground and not "flags" like those of the ostrich and lady ferns we had seen so much of in wetter landscapes. The number and variety of ferns on this walk were amazing, unlike anything we'd seen with all our years of visiting places for our guidebooks, like those for grandparents. Next we came into a stand of tall red pines and recognized that like the

Miners Castle once had two turrets, but one tumbled into the lake a few years ago.

The impressive sand "cliffs" at Grand Sable Dunes are easy to get down, challenging to get back up.

ferns, the forest types, too, were changing: beech and maples, yellow birch and hemlock, white pines and spruce and now, red pines.

We were making good time and stopped to rest at each campground. We noticed that some streams had wires across the water, near the bridges. Some also had solar panels near them. Then we saw a sign that explained these were lamprey weirs. The invasive sea lampreys are a scourge with which we were well familiar, though we couldn't see them. Sea lamprey had been noted in Lake Ontario since 1835, but creation of the Welland Canal allowed them to enter Lake Erie, where they were first discovered in 1921. They spread up the lakes from there, found in Lake Huron in 1932, Lake Michigan in 1936 and Lake Superior in 1938. An ancient jawless fish that resembles an eel and reaches about a foot in length, the lamprey has a round mouth filled with teeth and can attach to its prey for weeks. There are native lamprey and eel species, which are not a problem, but the hardy sea lamprey devastated fish populations already weakened by overfishing and habitat reduction. Until recently, Lake Superior did not have a naturally reproducing lake trout population because of that. Now, it does, and the lamprey are kept in check with chemical and physical controls. The story of this invader reminds us why there is such concern about the Asiatic carp at the doorway of the Great Lakes.

Walking along the trail to Hurricane River, we came out on a road under construction. We decided to stick to the road since the trail paralleled it. There was no work in progress on this Sunday and we seemed to be the only ones out hiking, until we encountered two middle-aged men with heavy backpacks hiking toward us. "Stay to the right," they told us when we stopped to chat. "There's a lot of mud ahead." And they were right.

We walked the service road to Au Sable Lighthouse, but strayed off-road to the beach to see shipwreck remains. The shallow sandstone shelf 1 mile out from shore is the site of a number of shipwrecks. Some ended in complete loss of the vessel and occasionally in lost lives. Other vessels were recovered to sail again. It was eerie to see pieces of wood lined up with big iron spikes sticking out, all neatly arranged in rows – the ship's ribs. After dozens of shipwrecks, the lighthouse was built in 1874. It helped, but did not eliminate, the dangers of this part of the "shipwreck coast" of Lake Superior.

When we reached the lighthouse, we encountered two young men near the buildings. One sat at a picnic table and greeted us. He and his companion were doing invasive species management for the park. We asked about the lighthouse. He said it had basically been rebuilt this past year and would soon reopen to the public. The grounds have two beautiful red-brick buildings with the white lighthouse in between them and smaller buildings scattered about.

Suddenly, the young man sitting down, asked, "Are you the ones walking around the lake?"

"Yes."

"No way!" he exclaimed. "We learned about you in training." Then with a smile, he added an assessment of our walk: "That's just plain crazy."

After wishing them well, we carried on to the last section of trail – the Log Slide. This well-known landmark is east of the lighthouse and west of Grand Marais and the Grand Sable Dunes. Story has it that this was the site where timber was sent down to the lake, using a massive dry log chute that sometimes caught fire from the friction of the logs going down. The chute is long gone. The steep dunes would be a major challenge. We had to climb an exhausting 290 feet uphill. This was especially hard on Mike, whose legs, feet and back had been bothering him all day. The view down the dunes was spectacular, a sight so rare and striking, it was hard to believe. Pausing for views helped break up the climb. We got to the top and shuffled our way to the parking lot, looking for Amanda. We had done 19 miles in 8.5 hours, one of our best times and longest distances.

After Amanda arrived, we drove into Grand Marais to have dinner at the Lake Superior Brewing Company, one of Mike's favorite microbreweries on the lake. As promised, I called Dr. Dewey to ask about the sore on my back. It sounded like a cyst or abscess, and he suggested it be cut, scooped out and then packed with gauze to let it heal from the bottom up. The cause of this unpleasant episode was a poorly handled excision of a plugged pore a month before our walk began. It had never healed properly.

Next morning, we returned to Marquette to get my back treated. I consoled myself that it wasn't a good morning for walking anyway; we couldn't see the sand dunes for all the fog. Urgent Care at the Marquette hospital confirmed Dr. Dewey's diagnosis. A young doctor examined me, then called in her adviser and they decided on a surgical procedure. The nurse admitting me had heard about our walk and said she was honored to meet me (which made me feel a bit better). The older doctor, too, chatted with me about our walk and had heard about it. Mini-celebrity still felt strange to me, but I appreciated their support.

The doctors, after giving me a shot of local anesthesia, got the opening big enough to heal and so Mike could pack it with gauze each day. Poor Mike would have the thankless task of daily dressing the wound, more than meeting his marital promise of "in sickness and in health." I felt sorry for him, but was glad I couldn't see the wound. About two weeks to heal completely, the doctors estimated, and it shouldn't stop our walking as long as it didn't get infected.

As a treat, we stopped at Babycakes. It was still cloudy as we drove back east to Grand Marais, but we could see blue sky ahead. By the time we reached town, it was sunny. We inquired at the Pictured Rocks National Lakeshore Visitor Center how far it was from the dunes, our last stopping point, to the campground. Only 6 miles, so we decided to go for it.

Back at the RV Amanda was battling a mini-flood. She had inadvertently left the sink faucet in the "on" position and then hooked up the water outside. When we got there, she was stressed, but had cleaned up all the water. She drove us to the Log Slide, and we headed down the dune. Perhaps younger, braver or dumber people might have done it more quickly, but as we headed down the steeply sloping sand with our walking poles, it felt like skiing down a hill covered in thick wet snow. Arriving safely at the base, we could look almost straight up at the amazing sandy clay slopes. It reminded us of the South Dakota badlands, especially the crevasses where a thick growth of trees and vegetation filled in the drainages. Gregg Bruff had told us to watch for rocks like Petoskey stones – a form of ancient coral. Mike found some quite soon. Since this is a national park, I curbed my rock-picking instincts and left the stones for future hikers to enjoy.

The only tracks on this shore were canine and deer. I wished we could see one of these animals going up or down the dune. We knew this was part of the hiking trail through the park, but found it hard to believe any backpacker would choose to go back up the slope we just came down. The beach was easy walking for about 3 miles and then it turned, abruptly, to a hiker's hell – all small cobbles and gravel for 3 miles. With every step, we slipped backward. Mike kept his pace, but not me. I just got grumpier, losing interest in the surroundings. Only the sound of the large rolling waves broke through my brooding. Sometimes they broke so loudly, they sounded like a volley of gunfire. At other times, they sizzled with a whisper, a rattle of small rocks – like a bag of marbles.

The night reflected the hard hike. Mike moaned, tossed, turned and kicked his legs for what felt like the whole night. At 3:40 a.m. (I checked my watch), I put on my headlamp to read. Mike woke up and asked me to rub his calves. That helped some; he went to sleep for the rest of the night. As I lay there awake, I wondered how long this could go on – Mike losing sleep and enduring the pain. I considered how I would manage the walk by myself. Mike would fight my striking off alone, but his legs were not getting better, even though he was losing weight. If we kept losing sleep, we'd both go downhill.

Clouds and sprinkles greeted us in the morning, and the forecast called for the same all day. We headed out anyway – we didn't have the luxury of being fair-weather walkers. We drove down H-58 to the place where Lake Superior State Forest campground ends. At the beach, we saw … aaaaaaargggh … rocks, cobbles and gravel. I had a new nemesis. We opted instead to walk on the beach grass, closer to the raised dune ledge. Amanda and Sheena went down to the water to look for the loons we'd heard calling. She found two, and we saw three more. We decided to call this "Loon Bay."

Walking west to let our legs realign, we ended up following a trail that skirted the campground. One young couple had a big windsurfing board on its side at their campsite. I asked if they were windsurfing on the lake.

"No," the young man said, "I'm using it as a paddleboard."

While I was talking to him, a man from the next campsite walked purposefully toward us. "Are you the two walking around the lake?" he asked.

When we said, "Yes," I could see out of the corner of my eye the young couple look at each other with surprise. It was fun to have them think of us as more than just another older couple on the beach.

The newcomer said that Betsy Lewis (a Facebook friend) had come to the campground asking if we'd passed by yet. Soon the young couple's Rottweiler, which had been growling at us, came over. I asked its name. "Tank," said the young woman, holding the dog by the collar. The older man was a high school cross-country track coach. It turned out the young woman had been in track at the same school and remembered him. He was from Charlesvoix and the couple was from Traverse City. Once again, a small world.

We proceeded on what turned out to be the North Country Trail along an excellent path, paralleling the lake. The rocky cobble shore continued as far as we could see, while the trail took us up and down some steep ancient sand dunes. The forest was predominantly jack pine with an understory of bracken ferns. When it started to sprinkle, I put up my umbrella. It never rained hard, but the vegetation got wet and so did our pants. We lost the trail for a while and made our way through the trees along the cliff edge. I had no desire to go to the beach, but we did go down when we came to some giant houses. We didn't feel comfortable walking through their yards. As soon as we passed the houses we climbed back up on the upper ledge and came to some steps in front of a place still being built.

We sat on the steps and ate our lunch. Close by, I could see dark flies swirling around the trees. We weren't sure what they were doing, but they weren't bothering us. "Just wait," Mike said. "These just hatched and aren't hungry yet." Every day without bugs is a good day.

We walked on, bushwhacking through forest and finally reaching a point where we saw the remains of a shipwreck on the beach below us. It was big, with a nearly complete hull partially buried in sand. Just on the other side of the point rested another shipwreck. Mike scrambled down to the beach and took photos. I stayed on top, working my way over and around tree blow downs. We came to one more house, and then the forest changed to sparse red pines and plenty of young jack pines. I saw blue marks on trees, the symbol of the North Country Trail, and yelled to Mike that I'd found the trail again. He came up and we followed it through a large forested region, sometimes close to the edge of the dunes, sometimes far inland. The multiple steep ups and downs were 80 to 90 feet in height. The climbs tested Mike's knees, and once again we were glad to have walking poles to take some pressure off our legs.

We followed this trail until it turned left along a road and we decided to keep going through the forest along the cliff. This worked until we ran into a spot too thick to traverse. Following old logging roads out, things got a little confusing. I wanted to turn on the roads that went toward the lake, thinking we'd catch H-58, but Mike looked at his GPS and said if we followed the line it showed, we'd get to H-58. It seemed counterintuitive – away from the lake was the wrong way. Finally we came to four roads. We took the road most traveled (sorry Robert Frost) and walked and walked and walked with no signs to indicate we were closer to the main road. After crossing the Sucker River, we re-encountered the North Country Trail, which finally did take us to H-58. We still had no idea how far we were from Grand Marais, until we came to a sign that indicated 2.5 miles to town. We'd already done a 12-mile point count before the Sucker River, so I knew that we were going to be far over our original mileage predicted for the day.

Mike's knees ached. By the time we got to town, I thought I should run ahead to get the car to pick him up, but he insisted on walking. At a store along the way, I bought frozen peas to put on his knees once we got back to the RV.

To prolong an already long and hard day, Mike still needed to check my back. The wound had bled some, or my sweat caused seepage. After my shower, Mike changed the packing. It made him lightheaded and it hurt me as he stuffed in the new gauze, but we got it done. Mike lay down afterward and put the pea packs on his knees. He braced his legs against the RV wall, shaking with pain. He took all the pills that he reasonably could and pulled the covers over his head to sleep. Surprisingly, he slept well all night. I woke up periodically and listened to the rain, happy I wasn't in a tent.

It was still raining in the morning. Someone suggested we try West Bay Diner for breakfast, and what an excellent choice. This classic dining-car diner was made in Pennsylvania in 1949. Over the years, it was sold and moved many times – mostly ending up in fields, sitting forlornly and deteriorating. Then Ellen Airgood and Rick Guth from Grand Marais, who had a restaurant in town, heard about it from a customer. They went to Rockford, Illinois, to see it. The diner was a wreck, but they saw its soul and hauled it across the Mackinac Bridge to this location. That was in 1996-97. After much remodeling, they attached the diner to a renovated old house and created a new classic.

We were very impressed with Ellen, a friendly woman who wrote *South of Superior*, a nationally acclaimed novel set in this area. The restaurant features a gift store with an eclectic collection. After a delicious breakfast of omelets, Belgian waffles and hash browns, we couldn't leave without buying postcards and a stout, old fashioned, white porcelain coffee cup, with West Bay Diner in red on its side.

The rain stopped by 9 a.m., once again verifying my grandmother's old saying: "Rain before 7, done by 11." We planned to move the RV to Muskellonge State Park and to meet with our Facebook friend Betsy Lewis, who wanted to walk with us. By noon, the sun was shining and we were on our way.

I have found that people go to the wilderness for many things,
but the most important of these is perspective. …
They go to the wilderness for the good of their souls.
We Need Wilderness, Sigurd Olson

After Thoughts

Logistics

Kate:

Many people are curious about the nitty-gritty logistics of undertaking a long walk without lots of amenities from Point A to Point B. Here are some answers for those "delicate" questions.

We did have clean clothes. We washed our laundry when needed in Laundromats in towns along the way – either at the end of a day or on a day when we had a bit of a break. Sometimes that was a good way to meet local people, as I found out in Marathon when I got the chance to chat about the lake with a man working there. We also found good laundry facilities in the campgrounds of the provincial parks throughout Ontario.

We each had two pair of shoes on the journey. Mine were more traditional style hiking boots – higher up on the ankle. Mike's were more like running or tennis shoes. When one pair got wet, we'd put them on a boot dryer overnight and wear the other pair. These lasted most of the trip, but we each got another pair of shoes or boots in Grand Marais, Minnesota, mainly because the soles of our shoes had lost a lot of their tread and weren't gripping the rocks as well. The shoes themselves were still in good shape.

Now the indelicate question of potty stops. While we were still in our planning stages for our walk – we were working on our *Grandparent Michigan Style* guidebook at the time – we met a man who said he said he'd like to walk around Lake Michigan, but what would he do if he had to use the bathroom? I remember thinking, how odd. That worry had never crossed my mind, and it never did prior to or during the trip. Having been backpackers and wilderness campers all our lives, this was just not an issue. We both learned to make use of wooded cover when necessary and carry a small trowel to dig a "cat hole" at others. The same was true on our walk around Lake Superior. We always used the bathrooms at the campgrounds before leaving and would make use of public restrooms or outhouses if they were available along our route. But truth be known, if need be, we would just move into sheltered areas, well away from the water.

Once in awhile through the book, you'll see that we are preparing for talks. We did 10 speeches along the way, all of them set up in advance: In Michigan at Marquette, Munising, and Brimley State Park; in Ontario at Naturally Superior Outfitters Lodge and at Lake Superior Provincial Park, both near Wawa, Sleeping Giant Provincial Park, and at Fort William Historical Park in Thunder Bay; and in Minnesota at East Bay Suites in Grand Marais, Cove Point Resort in Beaver Bay and Larsmont Cottages.

Making and receiving phone calls was also one of the logistical challenges. We knew in advance which services best could cover the full circle. We totally relied on our cell phones, but we had Verizon and Amanda had AT&T and that often caused problems because of our remote locations. Most days, we had trouble connecting with one another. She especially had trouble in Canada with her service. We saw some of the old-fashioned looking phone booths along the way, but never used them.

A necessary "member" of our team, our SAG wagon - a Support and Gear vehicle.

110

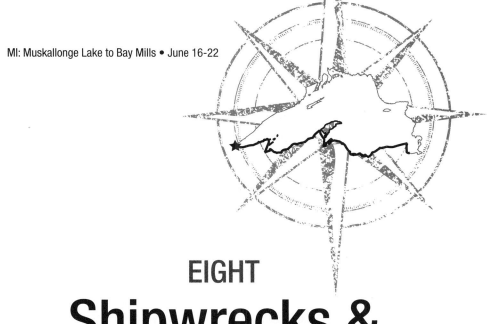

EIGHT

Shipwrecks & Sand Beaches

The real voyage of discovery
consists not in seeking new landscapes,
but in having new eyes.
Marcel Proust

Kate:

Driving along the sand road past the Lake Superior State Forest campground, we proceeded slowly through little ponds that formed in low-lying spots after the inundating rains. We held our breath as those "puddles" got deeper, wider and the water reached the bottom of the car doors.

We were headed for the state park on Muskallonge Lake. After a quick lunch in the RV, Betsy Lewis arrived and agreed to drive us in her four-wheel drive pickup truck back to our starting point. Betsy is a small woman with an outgoing personality who relishes conversation. As she drove slowly down the sandy road, she chatted about local and park history. She had been in the real estate business and knew a lot about the various roads going toward the lake and the streams we'd have to cross.

"You'll have to cross the Blind Sucker River, you know," she warned. "Are you ready to get wet?"

By now it was mid-afternoon, and we were eager to get walking. We were only supposed to cover 6 miles, but not knowing what lay ahead, we didn't want to delay. Besty decided to walk with us for a ways. The North Country

Trail was nearby, and I headed that way, but Betsy said, "Don't you want to walk down by the lake?"

We explained that soft sand, loose rocks and Mike's knee did not make a good combination, but she said, "Oh, it will be harder near the grassy area. We had all that rain, so the sand should be harder."

We were skeptical, but tried the beach, It was soft sand and loose rocks. Sporting only our lighter packs, we moved at a good clip. Betsy eventually moved away from the shore into softer sand and fell behind. When we stopped at an opening in the trees that looked like a trail, she caught up and said, somewhat out of breath, "I'd have to train to do a walk like this. I'm more used to meandering along, wearing my boots, sometimes walking in the water." She decided she would let us go on and she would return to her truck.

We connected to the North Country Trail soon after she left. It was a nice, narrow path following the edge of the beach. We moved quickly and made 3 miles in less than an hour. For some reason I had been thinking about the garter snake Mike saw on the boardwalk in Pictured Rocks, when not much later I heard some rustling in the vegetation to my left and saw the tail of a large garter snake slithering quickly across the path and under a log on the right. It was probably 2 feet long. Suddenly encountering a snake usually startles me, but seeing the tail end of this one was a naturalist's treat.

The sun shone bright, a cool breeze blew and the water took on a wonderful cerulean blue again, broken by rolling white waves. Finally, we came to the point on the trail where the river met the lake. There was a giant hollow log on the beach, and I couldn't resist crawling in. The river was shallow in places, and we waded across a riffle. The water hardly felt cold compared to our earlier Lake Superior wades. June 16 and already the inland waters were warming up.

The remaining 3 miles made for our easiest beach walk in some time, with long stretches of flat, wet sand. A large sandy bluff to our right appeared to be sliding into the lake. Betsy had told us that last winter part of the bluff

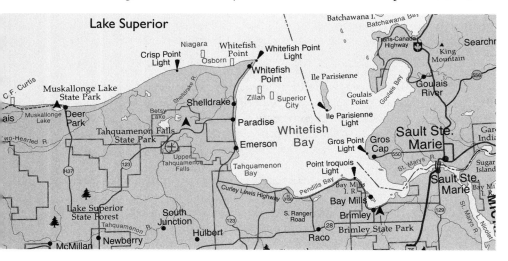

near the state park headquarters had collapsed, and the North Country Trail was moved back 20 feet. We did see trees with blue trail markers lying at the bottom of the bluff.

Mike spent the evening, as he often did, trying to figure out the next day's route. Finding access to roads for pick up and drop off and knowing which ones to choose became a big challenge, increasingly so as Mike's knees deteriorated. Not really knowing the terrain we'd encounter and the true distances between points, we worried about walking too far in a stretch. Already we were not as far along as we had planned, shortening our walking day to accommodate Mike's knees. Also, we had underestimated the time involved in moving the RV from place to place.

Mike had a restless night. His blood pressure readings were still high and my weight was still more than 140. But the day's positive note brought us to a most beautiful bay and beach between Big Two-Hearted River and Muskallonge Lake State Park, about 30 miles northwest from Newberry. Big Two-Hearted River is familiar to any fan of Ernest Hemingway, who used the name, if not the specific location, as part of his Nick Adams stories about the U.P.

We crossed the North Country Trail bridge over the East Branch of Two-Hearted River and watched an alder flycatcher "fly fishing" from a shrub – flying out on sorties to catch the insects and returning to its perch. The trail took us through the woods until we came to a big area of sand. From there, we walked along the beach to the river mouth, where we'd meet Amanda. The beach was a mix of hard-packed, wet sand, rocks and cobbles. Without the usual breeze off the lake, the heat was more noticeable. The mouth of the river was wide and rushing, but there was a walking bridge that we'd cross later. On this side of the river, we found our car, but no Amanda.

While waiting, we spotted an osprey overhead with a fish in its talons. We split a bottle of pop, then wrote a note for Amanda and set off across the bridge and down the beach. Before long the loose rocks became too annoying, so we cut back toward the trees to find the North Country Trail again. We also found Amanda and Sheena. They had angled back toward the woods, too. For a few miles they joined us on the shore, going up and down hills and angling back toward the beach. Sheena behaved perfectly when on the trail with us, keeping apace on her short little legs.

After lunch, Mike walked down to the sand, took off his socks and shoes and waded into the water until it covered his knees – a substitute for ice packs. Resuming our walk, we encountered one big dune after another. It was a challenging terrain, even toned as we were after weeks of walking.

At the top of one dune, Mike flushed a hermit thrush, a rather nondescript brownish bird with a white speckled breast. Near our feet we found a small round nest, made with long brown pine needles, holding four perfect turquoise blue eggs. Now we knew who made those other, similar nests we'd been seeing along the route.

Hill climbing is not my favorite thing, so we returned to the beach. Two animals shot out of the woods in front of us, headed to the lake. "Wolves!" was my first thought, but they were dogs. No human was in sight, but the golden retriever and boxer mix ran right into the water, playing and chasing one another. We suspected that they came from the cabin to our left. When the dogs came out of the water, they saw us and charged back up the hill. We tend to think the best of dogs and spoke gently to them, but the boxer got between Mike and me, taking a decidedly unfriendly posture. When Mike's friendly "Hi, Buddy" didn't work, he changed his tone, barking out in a loud, deep voice, "NO!" The dog turned away quickly, whimpering and running the other direction. Hardly the reaction we'd expected.

The dog looked at me as he shot past, and I felt a little sorry for him. Then the retriever started to whimper. The scene reminded me of cartoons in which a big bullying dog gets beaten up by a big mean cat. Despite my fears before our walk, we had very few encounters with strange or stray dogs. We had abandoned our can of bear spray some time ago.

The beach alternated between good sand and loose rocks. We veered from side to side, tracking the hardest surface. We passed a few people looking for agates (one older lady had a mound of rocks), and a couple of men were walking in the water. The location seemed remote and we wondered how they got there, though we didn't stop to chat.

Once again, we took a break so Mike could numb his knees in the cold lake. This time he took his poles and Paddle out for photos. Despite the waves washing to shore, the little boat headed for the open water. Perhaps that was its inner nature. Mike had to keep poking it with his pole to turn it toward shore. Paddle rolled in the surf, but in a nod to Mike's craftsmanship, it always righted itself. Mike wasn't sure if the kids who saw Paddle's photos online had as much fun as he had setting up the photo ops.

Walking along Lake Superior, you might think that you become immune to stunning vistas, but the water was especially memorable in this bay on this day. From the darkest blue on the horizon, the water was punctuated by little flecks of white on waves, and its hues progressed from turquoise to pale green to almost yellow and then platinum near the beach. We easily could just sit or stand here for hours watching the water curl in and spill onto the sand. This had to be the best beach on the lake, we thought at the time (a thought we'd revisit again and again). There was very little development because it bordered state-owned land.

As the afternoon wore on and the miles piled up, Mike wore out. He limped on his right leg. Already past 12 miles for the day, Grand Marais seemed to be moving away instead of getting closer. I put on my headphones to listen to "Africa Trek," the story of a French couple who walked 8,700 miles across that continent. I don't know why, but it distracted me from the soreness I'd started to feel and from the mounting heat in the full sun. Suddenly Mike veered left to a bluff and lots of trees.

"What are you doing?" I yelled.

He yelled back angrily, "LOOKING - FOR - SHADE."

I tried not to take offense at his sharp response. He was hot, hurting and just wanted today's walk to be over. To beat the heat, we climbed another bank, found the North Country Trail again and emerged onto an asphalt road just

Who could resist this hollow log near Blind Sucker River? Not me.

east of the state park. The total for the day was 14.4 miles, not our longest but one of our most wearing hikes. We stumbled back to the RV, where I weighed myself again – 138, a small victory!

Mike went to get ice cubes so we could have gin and tonics. He stuck ice cubes into his knee braces, too. Betsy Lewis brought vegetarian lasagna for dinner and Mike videotaped her as she talked about her love of the lake.

"I didn't know this at the time I moved up here, but Lake Superior has become a very good friend and I frequently talk about the beach as my studio. I try to get to the same locations over and over to see the change."

Betsy's art incorporates natural things, especially rocks that she finds on the beach. Then she photographs them as they change over time. She believes the lake brings out creativity in people. "I've built things on the beach and gone back to them a few days later and someone has built something similar near it and a few days later someone else has done something.

"Lake Superior is a place I go to find myself. It is safe and I feel very in touch with people and everyone on the planet because of the nature of water."

But like many of us, Betsy worries about the lake, too. "My biggest concern is that people take it for granted."

After the interview, Mike went to lie down. In my mind, I had begun to formulate Plan B and pondered when to talk to Mike about the possibility that he couldn't walk the whole way. I could walk roads alone or Amanda could join me for the shore or trail hiking. I didn't want to do it without him, but we had discussed that if one dropped out, the other would continue. We worried that the rugged parks in Ontario might require more serious backpacking and camping. One day Mike asked if I'd be OK doing fewer miles each day. I'd said yes, but I didn't want to prolong the walk into October.

By late evening, the beautiful clear sky blew away. To the west, clouds filled the horizon, threatening thunderstorms. The threat continued in the morning, though we would not be walking. We had a long drive to Tahquamenon Falls

State Park, a name we still can't pronounce right, though we are told it is Te-QUAW-men-in. We got the RV parked, ate lunch and packed smaller, lighter packs for the afternoon walk. The campground host said we could walk the shore of Tahquamenon Bay if the seiche wasn't a problem. A seiche is Lake Superior's answer to a tide. As barometric pressure pushes on one part of the lake, the water sloshes to the other side (like water in a tilting bowl) and drops or lowers several feet. One story has it that in 1834 a seiche on the easternmost tip of the lake, at Sault Ste. Marie, drained water from the St. Marys River long enough that people walked onto the river bed, and some nearly drowned when the water came rushing back.

There were no waves in the bay this day, and the whole shore was exposed due to a low water level. We soon discovered we'd have wet feet the whole way; the shore here was an extension of a vast wetland. This was a new experience, and we really enjoyed it. Unlike the deeper lake water, this water was warm, until we'd come to an icy cold spot with flowage from a nearby bog. We could see the cold spots coming – the water went from clear to deep reddish brown, tinted from tannins flowing out of the bog. When the sun went behind the clouds, obscuring the underwater terrain, my polarized sunglasses helped me to see through the water. Mike didn't have his sunglasses and struggled to find his footing whenever clouds blocked the sun. We walked far from shore, maybe 50 or 60 yards out, and still the water remained below our knees. Squish, squish, splash, splash – a delightful, very welcome 5-mile foot massage in the healing mud of Lake Superior.

Until this day, I'd never seen clam tracks. Some were long and curvy. Some even had a curlicue in the middle, like the clam got confused about which way to go. Others were a straight line ending with the clam buried halfway into the sand, resembling the head of some weird sea creature. Baby clams make tiny tracks. I also saw leeches stretching and contracting as they searched for a meal – one grabbed onto my foot, but I quickly dislodged it. Leeches are the ticks of the aquatic world, but I didn't find them nearly as gross as the angleworms we found clustered near some reedy water. I wondered aloud if they were escapees from fishermen. Mike suspected they were an aquatic worm. Either way, I was glad to get past them.

This turned out to be our day for wildlife watching. A log in the shallow water created a trough on either side teeming with tiny fish. I took the video camera to film them, and Mike herded them toward me. They swept onto and around my feet, creating a feather-light tickling sensation as they swam back and forth. Other schools skipped and zipped ahead of our feet as we splashed onward.

This felt like isolated wilderness, like we were finally seeing a place no one else had. It is so long and shallow that I doubt many people have been there. When we did wander onto sandy beaches, we saw huge, three-toed bird tracks. "Turkey," I thought, but that didn't make sense. It must be a great blue heron, I realized. Mike photographed the bird tracks near some bear tracks. I got the bear right, the heron wrong. Moments later, two sandhill cranes rose, calling, into the sky, the mystery of the tracks solved. Our totem birds flew in a circle, then away over the trees.

116

Farther up shore, the beach changed to cobbled rocks that stretched into the water. It got harder and harder to find footing on sand between the stones. We carefully picked our way to shore, put on our socks and shoes and entered the second phase of this day's walk: rock hopping (the easier kind, where you can step from rock to rock). Mike's footing was good, but he had to keep ducking underneath the cedar trees leaning out over the water. I had no such problems; occasionally, being short has its advantages.

The terrain had another change in store when the rocks gave way to wet, hard, flat sand. We were greeted by an immature bald eagle sitting on an exposed rock in the lake. It appeared to be drying its feathers after a bath. The road to the beach was closed, but we walked to it and saw three young people fishing on the bridge. We asked if they knew the name of this creek. "Naomikong," they said, but we knew that was farther ahead.

We reconnected with the North Country Trail on the other side of the bridge. The walking was fine, except for the sand flies, which had found us. It was nearing 5 p.m., when we expected to meet Amanda, but we went back to the beach to do our last point count of the day. Holding my arm out and looking through the camera lens, I looked ahead and could not believe my eyes. Gigantic, slender, slow-turning wind generators rose above the trees – the wind generators in Sault Ste. Marie, Ontario. We'd almost reached Canada! True, it was two days of walking to Whitefish Point and a day or so farther to the Soo, but we were excited to be so close to our halfway point.

At the Shallows parking lot, we went out to the road to get a cell phone signal, and Mike called Amanda. She had missed our meeting spot and had to turn around to come back. We explored the road while we waited, with the annoying flies buzzing around our heads and sweating bodies.

Unlike some, who march from Point A to Point B, we did on occasion let weather and lake conditions, and the necessity to get to scheduled talks, dictate our day's hike. So the next day, we had to drive 23 miles west to Little Lake Harbor for an 18-mile hike to fill in a missing portion. At the harbor, it looked like the only access was through a resort, so we drove down the narrow driveway past cabins until the road ended near shore. Mike turned the car around and started to get our stuff out when a man walked up from the last house. I knew I should wait for Mike to do the talking, but I blurted out, "Do you live here?"

"Yes."

"Can we go down to the beach from here?"

"No. People pay a lot to stay here and I can't have people coming through," he said, a stern look on his face.

"We just want to get down to the beach to walk."

"Sorry, no."

So much for my negotiating skills.

"Let me explain," Mike tried, and he proceeded to explain our mission.

"Unh huh," the man grunted, seeming to soften as Mike noted the number of miles we'd already walked and other details.

"I have a lot of people coming here today," the man said, indicating where we'd parked.

Ah, there was the rub. "We're just getting dropped off," Mike assured him.

"Oh, so the car isn't staying?"

"No."

He had a complete change of heart. "Well, then you can go down to the beach – there's a path."

Thank goodness once again for the negotiating talents of Talking Pathfinder.

As we got the last of our stuff out of the car, a minivan drove into the space. The driver rolled down the passenger window. "How's the hike going so far?" she asked.

We walked to the car. "Going good. How'd you hear about it?"

"Oh, I heard about it a year ago from Betsy Lewis."

We chatted and told her our plan to walk to Whitefish Point from here. It was a good 20 miles, she said before she left. Mike had calculated 18, but on this stretch of shore, the map numbers and his measuring technique rarely matched up. With this slight change of plans, we told Amanda to meet us at Crisp Point Lighthouse We'd travel light, get refreshments there and see how Mike's knee held up. The beach was good, really good – a broad, flat, hard packed surface for most of the way to Crisp Point. There were a few rocky places, but not enough to slow us down.

High cirrus clouds – the sign of a weather change – formed just before we reached Crisp Point. As we neared the lighthouse, we saw three people at the top. One waved at us and we waved back, thinking it was Amanda taking photos. Turned out, it was someone cleaning windows. Amanda was in the car working on her computer. The volunteer lighthouse keepers wanted to meet us, she said, just as a pleasant, big-bellied man came out. "I hear you're on a walk-about. Would you like a cup of coffee?" Mike accepted and I finished off a bottle of RC Cola Mike had opened earlier.

We still had 5 or 6 miles to get to Vermilion Point, which seemed like a good place to end the day. It was still another 10 miles to the tip of Whitefish Point and our original destination. We had good sand beach for walking, though in places big seeps (places where ground water drains from the sand and

A gentle stroll on the shallow edge of Tahquamenon Bay was Mike's favorite walking experience.

flows down the beach toward the lake) gave us wet places to avoid. Decaying organic matter gave the sand an iridescent sheen. The seeps also created neat patterns in the sand, like miniature examples of natural stream flows. Mike was in photo-taking heaven. He kept a steady pace all day, and our GPS indicated we were logging 3.1 mph.

We saw one mature bald eagle, the tracks of a canine and a deer in the sand, human footprints and one ATV track, but otherwise, it felt remote along the whole shore from Grand Marais to Whitefish.

At Vermilion Point Lighthouse, Amanda picked us up. We were grateful that the volunteer lighthouse keeper at Crisp Point explained how to find the road to Vermilion Point. Amanda found the road and got through some deep, soft sand in our low-riding car.

Driving into Paradise, we looked for access to the shore. The town reminded us of Christmas. There were a few nice motels and restaurants, a friendly general store, recreation businesses (boating, diving and such), but many places were either closed or in need of repair.

We hoped we could get to the shore at one of the hotels.

A woman walking through the parking lot saw us and said with a hint of suspicion, "Can I help you?"

"I hope so," said Mike. "We're walking around Lake Superior."

She looked unimpressed. "Uh hunh."

"And we were wondering if we could get down to your beach?"

"No, this is all private," she said, waving her hand at the cabins.

"Can you tell us where we might get to the beach?"

"Try the Community Center."

This wasn't feeling like Paradise.

Looking for the Community Center, we passed signs advertising fresh apple and blueberry pies, hot pasties and cinnamon rolls. Mike wanted to stop, but I chided, "How are you going to carry anything?"

"Oh. Right." Paradise lost for Mike.

Behind the Community Center, there was a slope to the beach. On a narrow strip of sand, we passed two couples sitting in front of their homes. "Hi," we offered tentatively. Everyone was friendly. Little streams entering the lake had wooden channels directing them, making it a challenge for crossing. We opted for the road.

Just short of Tahquamenon Falls State Park we stopped at a wayside rest. The sun had come back out, and troops of motorcyclists roared up and down the road. Just before we got ready to walk again, three trucks pulled up and a bunch of little kids and their young parents got out. As Mike was leaving the picnic table, one young man asked if we had hiked a lot of miles.

"Yeah, quite a few," Mike said.

"How many?"

"Oh, around 640."

The guy looked surprised, but jokingly asked, "What're doing? Walking around the lake?"

"Yup. Actually we are," Mike said, smiling.

After dinner, Mike and I drove back to Paradise to buy supplies. Mike also wanted to buy those pies he'd been dreaming about. An elderly woman named sold them from her home. She'd just taken two blueberry pies from the oven, and Mike triumphantly came away with one for the next morning's breakfast.

Looking for a Wi-Fi connection, we stopped outside Paradise Inn. I persuaded Mike to plead our case. The man at the desk invited us to come in and use the conference room, where we worked until our computers ran out of charge. This act of generosity proved that there was another side to Paradise after all.

Amanda gave a presentation in the state park starting at 9:30 p.m., and I went with her. We were driving to the group site where she would set up the PowerPoint projector, but before we'd gone 100 feet, two sandhill cranes strolled through the camp. Amanda grabbed Mike's camera and jumped out to get closer shots. The birds didn't even speed up, but a little later, one flew over, calling as it crossed the river. It landed in the tall grass on the other side. Then the second one flew and landed next to it. Eric, the park employee who helped Amanda get set up, said the pair had been coming every spring for about seven years. The adult cranes come to the campground to eat grass, but too often kids chase them, causing them to fly away. Apparently, they come back despite the harassment.

We awoke to sunshine after a night without knee pain for Mike – the first time in a long time. Mike credited the change with managing his medication during the day and carrying a lighter pack. That brought up the question of Ontario, and how he'd handle it, but I didn't push anything.

We returned to the Vermilion Point Lighthouse where we'd stopped the day before. This is also the 175-acre Vermilion Point Nature Preserve, where a huge wetland sits between the sand dunes and the lake. No wonder early settlers once grew cranberries here to sell. As we walked the dune top, we spotted someone, apparently a researcher, on the stony beach near an enclosure protecting a piping plover nest.

We had never seen the very small, pale plovers; they are one of North America's most endangered shorebirds. Past the researcher and nest area, we crossed through a grassy wet swale. To our right, we saw another wire-fenced nest enclosure protecting the birds from animal predators and people. Ahead near the water's edge, an adult plover skittered and weaved its way toward us. We came close enough for photos and video. For birders like ourselves, marking this bird on our "life list" was truly exciting. As if in celebration, our totem birds, a pair of sandhill cranes, lifted off and flew parallel to the lake, calling as they went. We came to the mouth of this vast wetland and stream complex and crossed it, still elated by our piping plover sighting.

The beach stretched ahead of us for 10 miles before reaching Whitefish Point. This was one of those days when my sunglasses made the world so much prettier. Forget rose colored glasses, I want to see the world through polarized lenses. The filter made all the colors more intense. On the downside, when I'd take the glasses off, for a few minutes everything seemed blah and lackluster until I readjusted to reality. With them on, the water was indescribable – about

Point Iroquois Lighthouse may have a ghost. It does have friendly visitors, one of whom recognized us.

as close to Caribbean blue as a northern lake can get. I never tired of looking at the water. Mike, who rarely wears sunglasses, prefers the real essence of the moment, and says he was equally enthralled with the reality of the sites (and sights).

Most of the beach was sand, the nice hard kind that is my version of heavenly walking. But nothing that good can last forever, and as we got closer to Whitefish Point, which from a distance looked like it had high banks with trees right to the water, we found a steel retaining wall and lots of limestone boulders. The waves were breaking right beneath our feet, so we climbed on top of the wall and walked on it until we had to go back down onto the rocks. Next we encountered downed trees, lots of big ones. We made the exhausting climbs over, under and around them. Finally, Whitefish Light came into view – along with lots of people picking rocks on the beach, the usual Lake Superior treasure hunters.

We met Amanda and Sheena, went into one of the stores for cold Cokes and fudge and ate lunch on the grass near the Great Lakes Shipwreck Museum. Inside the museum is the actual bell from the infamous 1975 wreck of the *Edmund Fitzgerald*. As mentioned earlier, this area is considered the "Shipwreck Coast" of Lake Superior and many ships have gone down near here. The *Fitz*, with the deaths of all 29 crew members, is the most tragic loss in modern memory.

Across from the Whitefish Point Bird Observatory. We talked to the three women working at the observatory, one of whom we'd met the year before on our scouting trip. We've visited this shop many times over the years, buying birding items, happy to add our dollars to support this nonprofit organization. Most of the research here focuses on the migration of raptors and shorebirds. This is one of three funneling points for such migrations around Lake Superior – the others are Hawk Ridge in Duluth, Minnesota, and Thunder Cape near Thunder Bay, Ontario. Unfortunately, I feel that many visitors to the lighthouse and shipwreck museum do not realize how much information this little shop just across the parking lot shares about bird life on the point. A white board posted out front is filled with daily sightings. The lighthouse is not the only lifesaver here. This point of land itself is critical to the survival of millions of birds that cross the water from Canada headed south each fall and returning each spring.

Back on the beach, we came to the Whitefish Point State Harbor, where fishermen were unrolling their nets and preparing to go out in their boat.

We stopped to talk. John, a member of the Bay Mills Band of Chippewa, volunteered to tell us how to cook "domers."

"You take a whitefish and scale it on the bottom and pin bone it – and then you add some butter, onions and garlic powder and wrap it up in double aluminum foil and put it on the coals. Wait seven to eight minutes and when the foil puffs up (domes), your fish is done." It all sounded good, except the "pin bone" part, which I didn't understand, but was too shy to ask. I think it's simply deboning. John had fished this bay for 21 years, like his grandfather before him. "It used to be everyone who lived on this bay was a fisherman," he said.

From there, we walked along the road until we found access to the beach and a nice long, curving bay with good sand. The water was calm on this side of the peninsula, which meant tons of sand flies. I had just taken off my long-sleeved shirt. Big mistake. My arms were instantly coated with the tiny pests. Not biters, they still are annoying on sweaty skin.

The next day – June 21, the official first day of summer – brought us to the 54th day of our journey and just 6 miles shy of Paradise (to finish this leg of our walk, that is).

The morning looked perfect for walking and we tackled those last miles first. We decided to stop at the Berry Patch restaurant after we'd finished. A Facebook friend had told us to stop there and say "hi" to Shirl.

I asked for Shirl and a blonde-haired woman came out from the back. When I explained how we came to be there, Shirl almost gushed and didn't stop for the next hour. She had read about us in the Marquette paper, she said. "I didn't think you'd stop by my place. I figured you'd pass by in the night or something."

Shirl calls everyone "Sweetheart," a term that certainly applies to her, too. She sat down and wanted to hear all about our trip, but we happily heard more about her life and work. She was a hoot, straight out of "A Prairie Home Companion," with her most wonderful, contagious, boisterous laugh. She works "370 days a year," she said, and can't take a day off ... except she'd be closing down to go to her granddaughter's wedding just to prove her family wrong. They've accused her of loving her work more than them.

Fifty years ago, Shirl and her husband honeymooned in Paradise (as many do, attracted by its name). She saw the bakery and decided one day that she wanted it to be hers. She talked to the woman who owned it. "Please let me know if it is ever for sale," she said.

When the owner turned 80, she contacted Shirl. Eight years ago Shirl got her wish. She obviously loves every minute of her work. Besides the pastries we bought, we peeked into the little attached gift shop, which is filled with lots of blueberry-themed items, appropriate because Paradise bills itself as "the Blueberry Capital of Michigan." Shirl buys hundreds of gallons of blueberries each summer from locals, and the staff makes jams, syrups and all manner of blueberry baked goods. She insisted on paying for our breakfast, then gave me a pair of socks (with blueberries on them) and Mike a mug. We feared if we didn't leave, she'd give away the store. So much generosity!

Amanda moved the RV to Brimley State Park along Whitefish Bay and about 17 miles from Sault Ste. Marie. We changed into our afternoon walking clothes. Mike had put Band-Aids on his toes in the morning. They were rubbing on his shoes; he wondered if his feet were getting bigger from all the walking.

We started the afternoon at Naomikong Point at Bay Mills. On the shore, countless insect exoskeletons lay in the sand between the rocks. We think they were mayflies. The sandy beach swept around a big bay, and we had to cross a few streams with shoes and socks off. At one stream, Mike decided to leave one shoe on to protect his Band-Aids. He hopped on one foot across the channel. The next one was too big for hopping. Both shoes came off.

We passed two couples sitting in beach chairs with two dogs next to them. They greeted us and one dog came down to check us out. "Don't worry about the dog, he just wants to walk with you," one of the women said.

"I don't think you'd want him to follow us all the way," said Mike, smiling.

"Where are you going?"

"We're walking around the lake."

The two women jumped up. "They ARE the two walking around the lake," they yelled, as if settling a bet.

They asked if we wanted anything to drink. I took a root beer and Mike took a real beer.

The couples were a brother and sister and their spouses – Chris and Chris King, and Pat and Thelma Godin. When Chris (the wife) found out we were staying at Brimley State Park, she offered us bed and showers at their place if we were interested. She and Pat were the siblings, and this was their family cabin. When they'd seen us coming, they decided we couldn't be those "walkers", because we didn't have big backpacks. They invited us up to sit in their Adirondack chairs, where we sipped our beverages, ate cherries, and talked about our trip and their history on the lake.

When they were kids they lived in the Sault and every summer their mom would pack up all the kids and head out to this tiny cabin, where they'd spend the next three months. Their dad came out on weekends.

Chris remembered that her mom seldom came down to the beach. "But one time we took this old boat out – Pat and I – to that sunken boat out there to go fishing for perch. My dad would make anchors out of coffee cans and cement so they were round and got stuck in the slats on the boat [wreck]… Mom walks out to the shore just in time to see him [Pat] jumping in because our anchor was stuck…It was no biggie to us, but she sure did not like it."

According to Thelma, "This was called Salt Point because there was a salt barge that went down on its way to the Soo. So I always thought [that sunken boat] was the salt barge, but I searched Grant's creek on the Internet and it said there was a Canadian schooner that went down here."

Chris has lived in California for 35 years and said, "When you grow up in Sault Ste. Marie the water becomes part of you. It's hard to leave….but it's a joy to come back and enjoy it for the summer. It's a part of your life. It's the place I come back to and I get grounded here."

While we visited, Thelma went in the cabin and called friends farther up the beach to let them know we were coming their way. I checked my watch and reminded Mike that we'd told Amanda to pick us up on the road at 5:10

p.m. so we said goodbye to our new friends and started back up the beach. The terrain changed from sand to boulders and a sandstone ledge, challenging and slippery, but pretty, too. Then a man and a black lab carrying a stick appeared. The dog dropped the stick. Mike picked it up and threw it.

"Now you own him," the man joked.

It turned out Pat Eagan was the "up-the-beach" friend of the Godins and the former owner of the Sault Ste. Marie *Evening News*. He wanted us to stop for crackers, cheese and wine, and though it was very tempting, we explained and apologized: We'd spent too much time with the Godins and had someone picking us up.

Before we left, Pat pointed to one of the small potholes in the nearby rocks and said he'd explained those potholes to some teenagers visiting last year.

"Oh," I interrupted, "you mean how the rocks form them." Thinking they formed when rocks get caught in one spot and the water spins them until they create a hole.

"No," said Pat. "These holes were made by Indian people, who used them for cooking. Rocks would be heated in a fire, and when they were hot enough they'd be dropped in the hole with the water until it boiled. Then fish were thrown in to cook." It was a good story and we left him on that note.

The RV was parked under a tree in Bay Mills Park, so the morning rain dripped off the leaves in a staccato beat. Mike had been looking at maps of Ontario with Amanda. Much of it was still a big mystery to us. What we didn't know is that it would bring the most exciting – and frightening – adventure of our whole trip. But that was still several weeks away.

I'd discovered that wearing a fanny pack was much better for my feet and legs, plus improved our speed, so I avoided the heavier pack as often as possible. Under thick clouds and a mist, we walked onto Bay Mills reservation. The Canadian shore, with its mysteries and uncertainties, got closer and closer. As we came around the point at Pendills Bay, we could see the lighthouse in the middle of the strait. It was amazing to see things on foot that we'd noted while traveling by car last year as we planned this journey. We could also see smoke rising from the steel plant in the Ontario Sault and the Point Iroquois Lighthouse sticking up above the trees.

The ubiquitous spotted sandpipers no longer ran ahead of us; they now popped silently out of the dune grass and flew away. There must have been nests about somewhere, but we failed to find any. As we walked, Mike talked about the birds we'd seen. Last year we'd spotted rare black terns, a species of concern in Michigan, on this shoreline, but we hadn't seen any on our walk. Not more than three minutes later a black tern flew past, headed eastward. A short while later, it turned and flew past us again, as if to show us it was real. I swear Mike conjured that bird by speaking its name. We didn't see any others.

We encountered rocks and cobbles for a stretch before reaching the Point Iroquois lighthouse. Mike's left foot and toes were very sore, and he said again that maybe his feet were flattening out. He also speculated that constant walking on sloping sand, with his left foot angled down, might be the culprit.

We finally reached the lighthouse around 3 p.m. Amanda was waiting for us in the parking lot. As we got into our car, a woman pulled in beside us. Were we the ones walking around the lake? Patricia Maas had been following us on Facebook and our website. A gray-haired woman about our age, she wished she could do what we were doing. She didn't think she'd make it, though, and her husband had physical limitations. Based on our Facebook posting, she figured we were in the area. We had a pleasant chat; one of many random, unexpected meetings that would make us feel good along our entire journey.

The wind in the wires made a tattletale sound
And a wave broke over the railing
And every man knew, as the captain did, too,
T'was the witch of November come stealing.
The Wreck of the Edmund Fitzgerald, Gordon Lightfoot

After Thoughts
Budgets

Mike:

The amount we budgeted came close to our actual costs of about $24,000. This budget was not just to cover our travel costs, but also to cover the continued expenses of our home, the basic maintenance, security, insurance, minimum electricity, etc. It is a truth: You cannot escape your bills by walking away from them (that is if you want to keep your home intact).

We were able to raise just less than $13,000 through sponsorships and multiple fundraisers before our walk began. It was less than we'd hoped. We also got in-kind support, such as free lodging and equipment, which probably totaled about $4,000 in value.

One of the important lessons for an undertaking like this is preplanning. Just like preparing for the days, miles and presentations we'd encounter along the way, our budgeting was thorough and we were lucky to avoid any major surprises. Maybe it is my accounting background, but things simply worked out as we had planned. The specific day hikes and surfaces could not be anticipated to that detail, but everything surrounding our daily adventures did. I believe that successful expeditions are often the product of the year before – the planning, the research, the attention to details.

Our major expenses, the ones for which we budgeted, were for our support driver Amanda), food, mileage for our SAG wagon RV, lodging and camping, and internet and phone services. We did not initially budget for a car, but that additional vehicle was necessary because the RV was too expensive to run for errands and for transporting us to and from hike sites. The big rig also could not get in to some of the places we had to be picked up because of the condition of the little roads and the forests that grew around and over them. The costs of the car, however, did not change our budget significantly because its mileage was so much more efficient than the RV.

Finally, medical expenses, like the visit to the hospital in Wawa, Ontario, and prescriptions were something of a surprise, but I considered those our "personal" expenses and not trip costs. But I did learn the hard way that our U.S. medical insurance has such a bad reputation for not paying in Canada that the hospital made us pay cash and then left it to us to try to get reimbursement from our own insurance – something that was only partially successful.

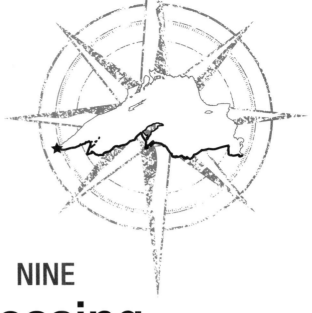

NINE
Crossing that Bridge

Oh may I go a-wandering
Until the day I die
Oh may I always laugh and sing
Beneath the clear blue sky
Happy Wanderer, Friedrich-Wilhelm Möller

Kate:

We drove to the Holiday Inn Express in Sault Ste. Marie that Anderson Insurance Agency had arranged for us. We exalted in the beautiful room and – hiking gods be praised – whirlpool. It was just what Mike and his back needed.

Our daughters Julie and Alyssa arrived that evening with our four grandchildren and son-in-law. The next three days would be a combination of rest (hardly, says Mike), relaxation and enjoying time with them.

They'd decided to walk across the International Bridge between Sault Ste. Marie, Michigan, and Sault Ste. Marie, Ontario, with us on June 26 – the one day the bridge is open to pedestrian traffic. We decided to make a visit into Canada a day early to explore. The waterfront in Sault, Ontario, has an excellent walking path and boardwalk. It leads to the Art Gallery of Algoma and its outdoor sculptures, perfect for climbing by 6- and 7-year-old boys (we hope this was OK) and attractive to waddling families of geese and gulls. The kids chased the gulls, and our grandson Matthew discovered feathers on the ground. That led to a contest to see who could gather the most – much like Grandma and Grandpa rock picking on a Lake Superior beach. A man carrying a camera took photos of the kids. He introduced himself as being with the *Sault Star* in Ontario, and he had actually been looking for us, which was fun, but he did not take the time to interview us. He must have been running late.

We hoped the break would be good for Mike, but that night he had pain in his legs, foot and back. In the morning, we met our kids in Soo Locks Park in the Michigan Sault and spent time exploring. The Soo Locks are an attraction for summer visitors – almost half a million each year – with boat tours through them and bleachers to watch the big "salties " (oceangoing vessels) and iron ore freighters and other "lakers" pass up lake or down. The locks on the U.S. side were built in 1855 and more than 8,000 vessels pass through them each shipping season. There currently are four locks – the Davis, Sabin, MacArthur and Poe. Looking at the huge freighters passing – some more than 1,000 feet long – it's hard to remember that the St. Marys River, the river rapids and their drop of about 21 feet from the level of Lake Superior to the lower lakes are the reason for the locks.

The river is the only natural outlet of Lake Superior, linking to Lake Huron. It is the first flow of water to the lower Great Lakes and emphasizes the "superior," or highest, position, of Lake Superior in the Great Lakes system. From the bridge, you can still see a section of the original rapids, where today's fishermen angle for whitefish in the same spots American Indians traditionally speared the same species. While industry saw the rapids as a transportation barrier, the native people recognized it as one of the best fishing locations on the lake.

The rapids sit between the small new Canadian lock (the original built in 1797, well before the U.S. locks, was destroyed during the War of 1812) and the huge U.S. locks, where industry connects to Lake Superior with cargos of ores, grains, coal and these days, wind turbines. It is this lock that allows Duluth to be the most interior "saltwater" port in the world – linking ocean vessels to the center of North America. The Canadian lock is surrounded by a park with historic buildings and nice walking trails.

The locks are a rather simple invention. Once a vessel is inside, massive doors close on both ends. To raise a ship up to Lake Superior, the natural flow

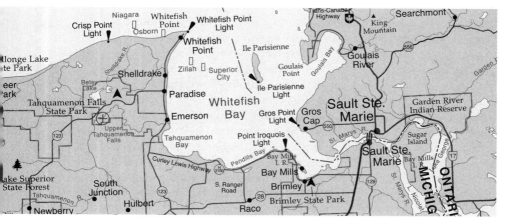

of water from the Big Lake is allowed to fill the lock and raise the vessel. In reverse, the water inside the lock is allowed to drain out until the ship lowers to the level of the St. Marys River and Lake Huron.

This is interesting because the river controls the level of the lake. As the continental glaciers melted, a variety of drainages were exposed around the lake. With each new one, the lake level adjusted to match the outlet. Eventually the St. Marys River became the lowest outlet, thereby establishing the level of Lake Superior.

Mike and I left our family to do a 2.3-mile walk from the hotel west to Sherman Park, a small shoreside park we'd found the previous year. Our grandsons Aren and Ryan were already enjoying the playground equipment when their older cousin Matthew arrived. Then they all went to the beach to play. Soon their socks and shoes were off and everyone, including Matthew's mom Julie, was wading. The water was so shallow, they could walk a long way out and still be mid-calf deep. Mike took off his socks and shoes and joined them. Eventually they waded to what looked like a small island, but turned out to be the remains of an old dock structure. Mike told the boys it was a shipwreck, eliciting squeals of delight. Then Grandpa showed them a fish skull. It had to be the teeth of a pirate skeleton, they decided, followed by even more squealing. Rain began to fall, the party on the beach ended and we headed back to the hotel.

Saturday morning, June 26, we gathered at the corner near the hotel and waited as a parade of people formed at the Norris Center just up the hill at Lake Superior State University. Everyone was preparing for the International Bridge Walk, held the last Saturday every June. The International Bridge, opened in 1962, is an almost 3-mile-long toll bridge between the U.S. and Canadian cities. Pedestrians are not allowed across the bridge except for this one event

The last Saturday of every June, people can walk across the International Bridge between the United States and Canada. About 1,500 walkers joined us (whether they knew of us or not).

each year. It was lucky for us – and a bit of good planning – that our walk coincided almost perfectly with this event. Otherwise, this stretch would have been in the car.

The main group of bridge walkers gathered in a parking lot and heard speeches and joined together to march toward the bridge. Instead we waited with our family and when we saw the festive group with a marching Chinese dragon and other families, we knew it was time to join the fun.

The sun came out, and it warmed up quickly. As the line of people passed, we jumped in and ran into Mike and Cheryl Landmark, our Ontario contacts from the Voyageur Trail Association. The kids did well, walking as fast as we did and staying close. Matthew spotted Ronald McDonald walking nearby and held his hand for a while, then asked him, "What do you think about Subway?"

"What? Never heard of it," Ronald replied. What a clown.

A woman was photographing people crossing the bridge. Mike stopped to talk to her. She was with a newspaper. Later, as we reached the middle of the bridge, she took photos of us and of our grandkids. "I've got to take a picture of this little munchkin," the photographer said, referring to Annalise. "She's just too cute." And she was, at least in this grandmother's opinion, in her red-and-white striped dress with her copper red curls falling around her head. Ronald McDonald pointed out that she had a nice shirt – just like his.

The crowd of Canadian and U.S. citizens was estimated to be around 1,500 and stretched nearly the whole length of one lane across the entire bridge, which is 2.8 miles long. The bridge walk began 24 years before 2010, and since we began our walk on our 24th anniversary, we thought this was significant.

There was not a lot of interaction between walkers, but everyone was smiling, laughing and having their own conversations, just as we were doing in our group. We took photos at the midpoint where we straddled the two countries and looked ahead and behind to see the streaming mass of people.

On the other side, we went through Canadian customs quickly and pleasantly. We picked up certificates saying we'd officially walked across the bridge and passed a band with kids wearing old-fashioned Navy uniforms playing marches. School buses waited to take people back over the bridge. It would be a long wait; cars and buses were backed up for as much of the bridge as we could see.

At U.S. customs, everyone had to get off the bus to be checked. We walked from there to the hotel. Our kids loaded up their cars, and after much going up and down to our room for forgotten items, everything finally got sorted out and off they went, we hoped with good memories of joining Grandpa and Grandma on their journey. We breathed a sigh of relief and satisfaction, then headed to the West Pier Drive-In, which sits almost under the bridge and is famous for its very good, very big hamburgers and fries. The reputation is well deserved.

We tried to relax for the remainder of the day, but I still needed to work on an article for *Lake Superior Magazine* about our time in Michigan. I struggled to condense 51 days into 1,200 words. We were chronicling our walk for the magazine. Tomorrow it was back to Brimley State Park to pick up the remaining portion of Michigan.

130

Rain started the next morning, and we checked the shore as best we could while driving along the road. We decided to go to the Dancing Crane Coffee Shop in Bay Mills for hot beverages and to use its Internet. We spent the entire afternoon there, dry and web connected.

The sky was cloudy the next morning when we started from the Point Iroquois Light. The wind blew hard from the northwest, and whitecaps covered the surface of the lake. The beach had some sand, but mostly rocks – the terrain for most of the 5-mile walk. Mike started slow, while I moved at a good clip. Looking back, I really could see the weight he'd lost and I tried not to be jealous. It's just easier for men to lose weight – I had to believe that.

We watched a big freighter pass. On this part of the lake, they seemed very near. Just beyond, the highlands of Ontario were topped by white clouds. A mama merganser and her nine babies rushed out into the water as we walked by on the beach. She dove sometimes, and when she popped up, most of the ducklings scurried ahead to catch up with her.

After the day's walk we stopped at the Dancing Crane and chatted with owners Cathy and Jim LeBlanc. Jim, a member of the Bay Mills tribe of Lake Superior Chippewa, recently found out he's of the crane clan – one reason for the coffee shop's name.

He reminisced about his childhood. "My mother would bring us here and she would look for stones and we would play by the lake. I spent a lot of time here when I was growing up."

Thinking about the even more distant past, he said, "I wish that I had been here a long time ago when it [the lake] was not messed up and the herring ran and the original fish – not the ones planted and introduced – were abundant."

Mike and I headed out at 3:30 p.m. and walked in sunshine! The wind had blown in a new weather system, which made for a comfortable walk back to the park

On June 29, we woke up and looked out the back window to watch three flickers – two adults and a young one – on the grass. They pecked around in the exposed dirt and then one adult ran over to poke food down the throat of the youngster. Then one adult flew into a tree while the baby and other adult continued to peck the ground. The baby seemed to understand that it was supposed to poke its beak into the dirt, but didn't seem to know what it was looking for.

This was our last day in Michigan and in the United States, as well as the two-month anniversary of our Full Circle Superior walk. We had 711 miles behind us. The day started much like our first day – blustery and cloudy, although a bit warmer. The wind was blowing 27 mph, which changed our plans for the day. We had wanted to walk through the water of the shallow bays to Sherman Park in Sault Ste. Marie, but 2-foot-tall rollers hit the shore, making it no longer shallow and considerably colder. So we drove to Birch Point Road near Brimley State Park and got onto the beach there. Turning right, we walked up to the point, where there was a range light (one of two lights that vessels align for navigation). On the other side of the point, there was still some sand beach, so we went that way, though we had to turn around eventually and retrace our steps. Whatever we gained going this way, though, could be deducted from our road walking later in the morning.

Gulls were soaring, drifting and hovering overhead. Big groups flew together, skimming the waves. They may have been feasting on a mayfly hatch. On our way back to the main beach, we passed some purple flowering beach peas, with their curling green tendrils, and shinleaf pyrola with its delicate white cuplike flowers spaced equally up the slender stem.

We wished for a passing freighter here. Because the point is so narrow, we imagined it would seem like you could reach out and touch the boats. No laker or saltie came and we continued on. Mike hadn't brought his poles with him, and he was limping. I loaned him one of my poles for support.

Walking back down the beach, we came to the home of Chris and Chris King, one of the couples we'd met at their cabin a week before. Their sailboat was pulled up on the beach. I paused, waiting for Mike to catch up. Chris (the wife) appeared in the doorway, waving us in. As we sipped coffee, she said this was going to be "a three-day blow." We believed her. She's lived on this stretch of lake all her life and knows its moods.

That afternoon, our walking route took us to a nature preserve recommended by the Kings. The map indicated the loop walk came close to Five Mile Road. I worried about having to bushwhack from the loop, but the trail took us right out to the road.

**Exercise is really important to me – it's therapeutic.
So if I'm ever feeling tense or stressed
or like I'm about to have a meltdown,
I'll put my iPod on and head to the gym
or out on a bike ride along Lake Michigan with the girls.**
Michelle Obama

TEN
Into the Wilderness

**With glowing hearts we see thee rise,
The true north strong and free!**
Oh Canada

Kate:

The last day of June 2010 was our "24B" anniversary (we had two marriage ceremonies in 1986), and it began our first full day in Ontario. We were excited about this Canadian leg of our journey and knew it might bring the most adventure. As it turned out, it had more adventure than either of us wanted.

The night before we struck out into Ontario was a bad one for Mike. He got up, went outside and was gone a long time. I was reading when he returned. He told me he'd walked around the campground three times. Instead of coming to bed, he decided to go sleep in the backseat of the car, since he didn't want to disturb my sleep or Amanda's by going in and out of the RV. When I got up the next morning, I found the car door open and Mike's sleeping bag sticking out with his legs in it. He said he slept OK – when he slept. I just didn't know how long he'd be able to go with these bad nights. Amanda was still sleeping when I got up. She, too, suffered a bad night and sounded congested.

We drove to the bridge and began our vehicle crossing into Ontario – having already crossed on foot during the International Bridge Walk. We had everything ready and were psychologically prepared to have the RV searched, but the customs person simply asked Mike, "Where are you from?" "Have any alcohol?" Mike said, "A couple bottles of wine," and started to say more, but the official said, "Any guns or firearms?"

"No," said Mike and we were waved through. He didn't even ask to see Sheena, who had her muzzle on so she couldn't bark or snarl at him.

Todd Starling, one of our young Canadian partners, met us at the Steamy Bean coffee shop and then drove ahead of us, leading the way to Pancake Bay. Todd is a former educational intern of the Audubon Center and he was one of the first to volunteer to help us during the Canadian portion of our trip. He and his wife, Carolyn, and baby Sierra live in Thunder Bay where he works at the Fort William Historic Site.

As we drove, I looked out the window at a seemingly impenetrable forest. The shore looked rocky or thick with wetland vegetation. "How are we going to do this shoreline?" both Mike and I were thinking. I figured we'd be walking a lot of roads.

We arrived at Pancake Bay Provincial Park right before Canada Day (July 1). This campground, like many in which we stayed, was on a strip sandwiched between Highway 17 and Lake Superior. We heard every truck roaring past. While Amanda set up the RV, Todd walked the beach with us. Immediately we noted lots of birds, a treat for these two birders.

Walking a trail that paralleled the beach, we were entertained by juvenile chickadees begging for food like all nestlings. A redstart male followed us a short way. Earlier I had seen and listened to a baby cedar waxwing flutter its wings and cry and cry for a parent to feed it in the branches of a tree behind the RV. Our first Canadian bald eagle flew up in front of us near some cedar trees and older birch trunks. A female merganser swam with her oversized brood – there had to be 20 ducklings. Not far away a second female swam with a few young, and a third with none. I guessed the one without any ducklings conveniently dropped hers off with the other ladies, saying, "I'll be right back." Yeah, right. The baby ducks were almost as big as the female and the whole group was

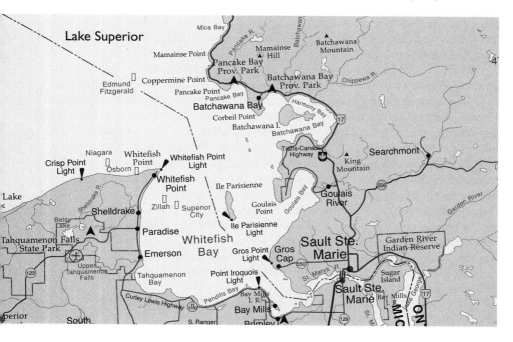

Paddle poses by a picture of a slightly bigger canoe on the menu at the Voyageurs' Lodge in Batchawana Bay.

preening, the youngsters standing up to flap their not-yet-full-size wings.

We walked the trail until it came out on the beach, then followed it out to a point, which led, naturally, to another point. Sand quickly turned to gravel and rocks, rocks and more rocks. Along the way, we passed a cabin that had the most amazing little outbuilding with two doors. Each had a rounded portal, one normal size and the other a miniature door, as if for children or gnomes. The whole place was obviously made by a craftsman with great attention to detail.

We went as far as we could, then returned to the campground on Pancake Bay. The beach could just as well be in the Caribbean – white sand and cerulean-colored water. It is a beach made for children.

Todd left us to return to Thunder Bay, and, with Amanda, we went to the Voyageur Lodge and Cook House, a restaurant-motel complex alongside Highway 17 on Batchawana Bay. It was recommended by one of our Facebook friends. The interior features log walls, Voyageur regalia and art. The menu offered Canadian and some voyageur choices. Mike had the tourtiere (French meat pie) with baked beans, excellent coleslaw, French fries and bannock. I had the bannock, too, which usually is a type of fry bread, but in this case was more like a biscuit – a delicious one at that. Amanda ordered the poutine – the Quebeçois way of eating French fries with gravy and semi-melted cheese curds on them (an acquired taste, in my opinion).

That night as we lay in bed, I reflected on the 24 years since our marriage on the sailboat at the dock on Madeline Island. What a life (and adventure) we've had together; two very lucky people who found each other at the right moment in their lives and made it work. Another dream come true.

The next morning was perfectly sunny and calm. The waves curled onto the beach. We walked as far as we could and came to a river with a narrow channel that was over our waists and decided not to get soaked, so we turned back. A merlin – a small falcon with a reddish brown-striped chest – made itself known, first by calling, then flying out in the open. We saw so many merlins along this lake, they seem as much a part of the landscape as the white pines and the eagles.

After lunch, the handle on the RV's side door stopped working. Something inside the latch had given way, and Mike spent a great deal of time trying to fix it. The only way to enter the RV was by climbing through the driver or passenger doors, then over the seats. Not too bad for me or Amanda, but a big challenge for Mike.

While driving, we happened upon Salzburger Hof Resort on the other side of the Batchawana Peninsula. The Bavarian-styled lodge and restaurant perches on a bluff overlooking the lake. It has a quiet, European feel. Ann Elsigan, the owner, is from Austria. Mike asked her permission to walk on the property. We walked the rocky beach as far as we could, then moved onto the road until we reached Highway 17 and the Voyageur Lodge.

A middle-aged man with dark hair and glasses was sweeping the patio and greeting everyone who came in. Frank O'Connor owns the lodge, along with his wife, Gail. Mike told Frank that we were walking around Lake Superior.

"I just read about you in the *Superior Outdoors* magazine," Frank said, "and some lady stopped by to ask if 'the walkers' had been by."

Frank gave us an enthusiastic, "Oh, right on!" as we explained what we were doing and why. Then with a "Wait a minute," he went inside the restaurant and returned with two of the Lodge's logo polo shirts.

When we thanked him, he added, "I'd like to buy you breakfast tomorrow if you're coming by this way." How could we turn that offer down?

We told him we were finishing our walk along Batchawana Bay.

"So you're walking the shore, past all the cottagers?" he said, some wonder in his voice.

"Yup."

"Oh, right on."

Back at the park, we headed to the showers. We'd like to publicly thank the Ontario provincial parks for their clean, efficient "comfort stations," including a great system of timed showers. You push a button, and the water comes out, already warm. It stays on for more than enough minutes and, hopefully, results in less wasting of water.

That evening Mike decided to sleep in the car again. He was afraid he'd cause too much commotion trying to get past Amanda's bed if he needed to go out during the night. So he moved everything over in the back of the car, blew up his air mattress and spread his sleeping bag.

Sleeping in the car didn't alleviate his knee pain, but he was up and ready to go in the morning as we headed to the Voyageur to take advantage of Frank's breakfast offer. When our coffees arrived, we found a spoon stuck in each. We assumed this was because most Canadians put cream, sugar or both in their coffee. These small differences tickled and intrigued us, pointing out again that while Lake Superior unites us, each region is distinct.

The Voyageur has a gift shop, where I found a traditional-looking red woven wool voyageur sash for Mike to wear on our upcoming canoe trip. Mike had been telling our waitress about our walk. A man, his two grown sons and two little grandsons were sitting at a table near us. As they left, the older man, who looked to be about our age and who had overheard our conversation, said, "Good luck with your trip."

"Thanks," Mike said.

Then he looked at Mike and asked. "How're the knees?"

"They're getting crankier," Mike said.

The guy tapped his own. "New ones. The best thing I've ever done."

After breakfast, we drove back to the Sault to run errands, then started walking through town. Our route took us through working-class neighborhoods, with the big Essar Steel Algoma mill looming behind them. Smokestacks rose above the mill emitting a stream of steam or smoke. A new filtering system, with a capacity of 940,000 cubic feet per minute of gas flow, was installed in 2010. It removes 120 tons of particulate annually, so despite the busy mill, we were breathing newly cleansed air. The neighborhood homes were neat and tidy, some with absolutely gorgeous flower gardens. We called to one woman in her yard about how much we admired her flowers. She called back that her husband got the credit. I was sure I heard her say that they'd won prizes for them. We made a point of complimenting gardens we liked whenever we saw people in their yards.

Our neighborhood route finally ran out, and we had to semi-bushwhack our way through grass and brush behind a house to get to Highway 550 – the route we'd follow all the way to Gros Cap. The housing gradually gave way to a country setting. The walking became a tad uncomfortable – it was a very warm day, and there was no shade on this road.

As we walked against oncoming traffic, a car drove by on the other side of the road and the guy yelled out at us, "F… you!"

I couldn't believe it. It actually made me jump a little inside – such a rude, strange thing to say to two people walking along the road. It was also a rare negative incident for us on this trip. I still do not know what caused the outburst, since we weren't blocking his way.

We realized before too long that we wouldn't make it all the way to Gros Cap on this day. Mike had tried to measure the distance on the map using his fingers, but there had been no scale for mileage. The lake was not visible, but we could easily see the dark volcanic rock of the bluff lands. My feet were sore again, and Mike, despite his own aches, was making much better time than me. He'd bought an ankle brace, picked up some new thinner socks and was taking new medication – all of which seemed to help.

We were up early the next day to take the RV to get the door repaired. The mechanics looked at it and estimated a 15-minute fix. It took 45 minutes, but was still a quick fix.

When we went to pay, our Visa card wouldn't work. We'd had a similar problem the day before and Mike had called our bank and was told it would be corrected. The problem was the anti-theft protection; it apparently decided someone had stolen our card and fled to Canada. To add to the problem, with less than ideal phone communications, Mike had gotten cut off twice talking to the bank. Now this was the Fourth of July weekend, which meant no service until Tuesday. Luckily we had another card, which we had not intended to use.

Just admiring my inukshuk – one of many I left along the roadsides, railroad tracks and beaches on our journey.

137

We made a stop to get propane for the RV, only to discover that only two places on the Ontario shore could provide it – Sault Ste. Marie and Thunder Bay. Due to a recent explosion at a propane vendor in Toronto, the government closed all area propane distributors except these two.

Finally we made it back to Gros Cap and Mike Landmark's home. We had met Mike, who is president of the Voyageur Trail Association, the year before during our scouting trip. He was a vital connection to the Voyageur Trail we'd be walking. Mike was washing his truck when we walked up his driveway. "I expected to see you yesterday," he said.

We explained our stops and errands and asked for advice on how to get to Red Rock Road, where we wanted to start walking. Mike volunteered to take us and drove us through the Prince Township Wind Farm to our starting point.

We walked down Lakeshore Drive, passing lots of cottages. At the end of the road, we picked up the Voyageur Trail, which paralleled the beach, but walked out onto the big rocks instead. They made for better hiking than the humid, buggy woods. It was just a matter of watching your step going from one large rock to the next. We also found shale and sandstone shelves on which to walk.

For a lunch stop, we sat on a rock outcrop with the wind blowing on us, and watched the small waves chopping onto the beach. Besides a good picnic spot, the flat rocks were ideal for building inukshuks – stone figures on the side of the highway that show the way. Mike built a fairly big one, and I decided to make a small one on a rock outcrop sticking out over the shelf below.

I have to admit I liked mine better, especially the nice round stone I chose for its head. Mine wasn't terribly stable, but as we walked away, I looked back a couple times and could see the two inukshuks marking the point. Mike still insists that his was the best.

Eventually we had to go back into the woods, despite the humidity and insects. At first the trail was well maintained, but when it turned and led up a steep grade, it looked more like a washed-out mountain streambed than a trail. I huffed and puffed my way up. We discovered very quickly that this portion of the trail, named for one of the founders, Tom Allison, had a lot of wet boggy areas. We tried stepping around them, looking for more solid surfaces without much luck. At one spot, Mike stepped down and his right foot sunk to the knee. He managed to extricate his foot without losing his shoe, but carried an extra layer of gooey muck for the rest of the hike. Up and down we went, and every down was wet and muddy.

As we started the climb I could hear a faint sound that I couldn't identify. It was a soft, rhythmic and not unpleasant swoosh. As we got closer to the sound, I realized it came from the turning blades of the wind generators on top of the ridge. We emerged into the opening where some generators stood above us; it was an amazing futuristic sight with the gigantic pure white pillars, each with three long arms whooshing in an enormous circle. I love that these giant sculptures are creating clean energy on this wind farm in the forest. Mike Landmark told us that there are 126 turbines that together produce enough electricity for all of Sault Ste. Marie, Ontario.

After each wind generator clearing, we would re-enter the woods. In one, Mike said he really wanted to see a moose. His sentence barely ended when he slammed to a stop and loudly whispered, "Bear!"

His unexpected outburst scared me, and I looked to where he was pointing, ready to respond. No need. I saw the streak of a black bear, running through the woods ahead of us. Mike had heard it "huff" before it took off.

We were following the blue trail marks that kept going on and on. I began to wonder if this is where the phrase "Where in the blue blazes" comes from. Our GPS device, out of satellite range, didn't register the first mile. We figured we'd logged 7 miles since starting and wondered how much more lay ahead.

The trail passed an overlook where we could see Lake Superior and across to the Michigan shore. We got a good view of Round Island and the shore where we'd walked last week. Could it really have been just a week? Time and distances were losing meaning for us.

When we found our way down to the lake, Mike walked into the water to wash the mud off his shoes and to soak his knees. I knew they must be causing him pain; it was even hard on my knees walking down the long, steep slope. Just that morning as we were driving to the Sault, he gave himself only a 30 percent chance of finishing our walk. Mike says I said, "Don't say that" – so he didn't say it again.

The next morning, July 4, gave us something to celebrate. Mike had gotten a good night's sleep. He awoke rested and happy about it.

On our way to the Goulais (GOO-lay) Peninsula and Bay, we drove down one road until it dead-ended, and stopped to ask a woman for directions. She suggested we talk to the man of the house. He told us the whole bay was walkable, although, he added, Goulais River was probably waist deep and there was the shallower Cranberry Creek we'd also have to cross.

We estimated that we'd be walking about 4.5 miles to the spot around the bay where Amanda could meet us. We told her to be there in 1.5 hours. We started in front of a cottage at the end of Kelly Creek Road, where the shore began with very manageable rocks. We passed a house where a man and woman had just come in from kayaking. We told them what we were doing and asked about the shore. They thought it would be accessible.

Soon, though, the loose rock turned into bigger, sloping bedrock, going right down into the water. We decided to get our feet wet, so we slid into the water and made our way gripping the wet rocks as best we could. In some places, we just couldn't go around them; they were too steep. We realized we'd have to go over the top and past cabins.

Mike was already on the top of the rock when he told me to take the steps built from the shore to a cabin up above. When I got to the top, I saw an old truck parked down the walkway, but the cabin looked closed, with the shades drawn. When I got to the front of it, I couldn't see Mike. He called to me, and I yelled back, "How do I get there?" The woods were really thick.

"Go next to the cabin," Mike called. That's when I heard a thump from inside the cabin.

"Hello," a man's voice called out.

"Hello," I answered.

"Hello," the man said again.

Mike called to him, "Hello! My wife and I are walking around the lake and need to get down to the shoreline and would like permission to go down to it."

The disembodied voice said, "You can't walk the shoreline. It's all rocks, and then it's all private land."

Mike asked nicely again.

"You can't walk the shoreline," the man kept saying.

Finally Mike said, "OK then. I guess we'll go down here and then find a way out to the road. Thanks."

We never saw the man. He sounded quite old, and we probably woke him up. This was the last grumpy person we'd encounter on our entire trip.

We found more negotiable rocks on the beach and kept walking. Ahead we could see more bedrock sticking out into the water. Up ahead a man was working in his garage near the beach. I told Mike in a loud whisper, "Ask him about the shore and what's allowed."

Mike greeted him and said, "I need some advice."

"I can give it for free," the smiling man replied.

He told us there were places where the rocks were a challenge, but then we'd get to a sandy beach. We asked about permission to cross private land. He thought most people would be fine with it. We went on feeling a bit better about walking this shore.

On a rocky cobble beach, we saw a family near the shore. We stopped to talk to the man and woman, who were with their son-in-law and grandson. Next we went up on a slippery slope of bedrock and when we came back down to the beach, we encountered another man. His cabin was in a cozy little inlet. He saw us, and we asked for permission to go up on the high rock. "For sure," he said.

Through vegetation and back down, we came upon a couple of middle-aged women who had been out swimming. They were surprised to see us come over the rocks, but they were friendly. We had to wonder what people said when we left, after suddenly appearing out of nowhere.

At the next rocks, we decided to stay at the waterline. It was tricky; waves splashed us, and the rocks beneath the water were slippery. Mike made a good recovery after slipping down a small angled rock. We again appreciated the trekking poles, though I wished they had rubber tips. Finally the rocks came to an end, and we found ourselves in a broad, shallow sandy bay. It was a good day to be in the water and lots of people had flocked to the lake. Temperatures were close to 90° F and the humidity high. The water was so shallow it remained only hip-level on people standing hundreds of yards from shore. Behind us, the wind generators stood tall on the ridge – a very cool, otherworldly vision.

We walked for 2 miles through bathtub-warm water, except for one deeper stretch that was dark with tannin. This led us to the Goulais River, where we met Amanda after about three hours of mixed terrain. She drove us down the Goulais Mission Road for our afternoon walk, which would be on a mix of First Nations and private land.

Along the way, we passed groups of people. Most gave a friendly "Hi" or waved. Some commented on the nice weather or day; some asked where we were going. We received three offers of water and a place to stop. The first invitation came from four families having a reunion. They asked us to join them at the table and offered us bottled water and fruit. The cantaloupe and cherries were irresistible. A large man about our age became their unofficial spokesman. His parents had built this cottage, as the Canadians called cabins, back in the 1960s, when they could drink water right out of the bay. "You definitely can't do that anymore," he said. The water was warmer and shallower now, he added, pointing to an old waterline that indicated the lake was once a good 3 feet higher.

At the next cottage, a woman sat on her deck. When she saw us, she said something I couldn't hear. Mike stopped to talk as she came down to us.

"What a great adventure!" she said when we told her our mission. She, too, commented about the lowering lake level. She'd seen it drop several feet in the 16 years she'd been there.

Just as elsewhere around the lake, lots of the people we met this day said, "I read about you in the Sault paper" or in the online SooToday.com. One man said, "Congratulations."

We were happy that they took vicarious pleasure in our adventure.

The shore changed to a cattail wetland, which we negotiated without any trouble, but the farther we went, the muckier the bottom got. Just before another wetland, my feet were sinking into gray gloppy mud. I told Mike that we needed to go out to the road. A woman was sunbathing at a nearby cottage, and Mike had already asked permission to cross her lawn. Then he asked if we could go out to the road through their place, and he explained what we were doing. She said she'd read about us and offered a cold bottle of water to take along. "Sure," we agreed gratefully.

On the road, I used the bottle to cool my neck, arms and legs. Many cars passed us, but only one slowed down. The man rolled down his window to warn us about bears in the area. Mike thanked him, not mentioning that we'd actually like to see one.

It was late afternoon when Amanda picked us up and we drove to Chi-we-kwe-don, which means "Big Bay" in Ojibwe. Two groups of people had told us not to miss this fish-and-chips place owned by a First Nation family. The husband catches the fish, and his wife and other female relatives cook it. The menu is quite extensive, but why would you order anything other than fish?

The unassuming, funky little roadside eatery was crowded on this hot Sunday evening. The menu board said: "Sorry Whitefish for dinner." We guessed that meant there wasn't any pickerel – the Canadian preferred name for walleye – but there was trout, too, which Mike ordered. Amanda and I got the whitefish. The wait was long, but worth it. The fish was excellent and complemented by fresh coleslaw and fries. It was a good Fourth of July feast.

The next morning was still cloudy and muggy and our walk began at the dead end of Four Seasons Road. We held to the road for much of the morning, and both immediately felt the boredom of road walking.

Half way into the walk – at Batchawana Bay – Mike finally found Lake Superior. Men.

"This is mind-numbing," Mike complained. I agreed, but then thought, "Wrong attitude." I reminded myself of a modified version of my road philosophy: "I'm only going to get this day once in my life, and I should enjoy it to the fullest even if it is sticky and humid." I felt better almost immediately. I mean, I could be headed to an office somewhere. I was still trying to learn to live in the moment.

We made good time – about 3.4 mph – and saw some beautiful monarchs and other butterflies. Part of the reason we made better time was because Mike had left his camera in the car. We met Amanda and Sheena walking down the road toward us about 6.5 miles into the day. She'd already done a good check of distance and shore access for the afternoon walk. There didn't seem to be any public access to the lake, she said, just empty lots waiting for buyers and development. We were surprised that so far we'd found far less public access on the Canadian shore than in the United States.

In the afternoon, a sandy trail led us through shrubby vegetation, then out to an open, rocky shoreline. There we met a pair of sandhill cranes; maybe the same pair we'd seen earlier in the day across the Goulais River in some wetlands. They were very close, and Mike got good photos, having picked up his camera at lunch. They moved ahead of us, going the same direction, so we trailed them until they grew annoyed and took off, flying over the trees complaining the whole way.

When we met him, Ray Alton was sitting on his beach watching his grandsons Peter, Mitchell and Trent play in the sand and on their kayak. We asked him about the shore ahead. He didn't think it would pose any problems, but asked if we had any maps. Then he went into his cabin and came back with a satellite image of the whole peninsula. It even showed where the famed *Edmund Fitzgerald* went down – not far from here.

Ray asked how old we were.

"64," said Mike, and Ray said he was, too.

When I said, "60," Ray said, "Oh, just a young chick."

We thanked him for his help, and as we walked away, he asked if he could take a picture. No one would believe him otherwise, he said. We also asked to take one of him and his grandsons.

This shore was easy walking, with lots of flat sandstone and shale, almost like pavement. We met a man named George with a strong German accent who asked if we wanted a cold Coke.

George moved from Cologne, Germany, to Canada in 1997 and bought this property. At that time, the water was much higher and Ontario gave him permission to dredge a small channel from his beach toward the water. More and more people on this shore were doing the same. We finished our Cokes as sweat beaded on our foreheads and ran down our backs from sitting in the sun, too far from the rocks to get a breeze. When I stood up and thanked him, saying we had to get going, George told us to be careful and to "watch out for the wildlife."

Not too far from George's place, around a rocky point, we did encounter an animal, but it was the friendly dog of Bill Semeniuk. As we were explaining our walk around the lake to Bill, his wife, Laurie, came out of the house. Would we like to come in for coffee, she asked, and we explained that we'd just had a Coke with their neighbor.

"Well, how about a muffin? I just took some out of the oven." She brought out two in a baggie. We ate them, still warm, at the end of the day's walk.

Mike thought we should go onto the road when we reached about 12 miles because we weren't sure where Amanda would meet us. Soon after we started road walking, though, he felt it in his knees.

We stopped at the Voyageur Lodge on our way back to the Pancake Bay Provincial Park. Frank came out to visit. Because we'd been using our laptops with his wireless web service, a customer had teased him: "What are you running now, Frank, an Internet café?"

Frank explained what we were doing and how we needed to keep up to date with our web followers. We expressed again our appreciation for his generosity and his willingness to let us occupy the patio during our time in Batchawana Bay.

In the morning, I could hear the rain dripping on the roof when the light began to show through the windows. With clouds all around and high humidity, we drove beyond the Batchawana River, put on our rain pants and jackets and started walking on Highway 17. The trucks and cars sent up spray, and luckily we found an ATV trail next to the road.

When the rain stopped, we'd heat up and take off our rain jackets. Then it would start to rain again. I put up my umbrella, my preferred means of staying dry, but the gusts created by the passing semis proved challenging. I'd hold the umbrella tighter and try to angle it so it wouldn't turn inside out. Up and over a hill or two, we came to a beach, where there was too much vegetation to walk, and where lots of flowers bloomed. Mike commented about how much more interesting this entire walk had been for us because we recognize (at least he does) all the flowers and birds. This knowledge engaged our minds and filled them with colorful memories.

As the rain began to fall harder, we switched to the other side of the road to see the waterfalls on the Chippewa River. I held the umbrella over Mike's head while he took pictures. There was supposed to be a historical marker next to the bridge, noting the halfway point in the Trans Canada Highway, but the plaque had been removed from the stone structure.

At the end of the day's walk, Mike and I decided to get a room at the Lake Shore Salzburger Hof Resort. It would be more comfortable since his cousin Lois Woodman and her husband, Tom, were due to arrive for a visit. Our room proved ideal for visitors, with a couch, coffee table, big chair and ottoman, as well as a table and compact kitchen.

After Tom and Lois arrived, all five of us went to the resort's restaurant and enjoyed the quiet European feel and delicious meal, compliments of Tom. The menu offered wonderful German-style food – sauerbraten, goulash with sides of red cabbage, schnitzel, spaetzle and cabbage rolls.

That night was a bad one, again, for Mike. It almost turned into a complete catastrophe when he decided to go out to the car to get some pills. It was completely dark in the room and I told him to use my headlamp.

"No, I don't want to disturb you any more than I have," he said just moments before the loud crash.

"Mike?!" I yelled. "What happened?"

I scrambled to find the light switch next to the bed. He was on the floor when I flipped the switch. I rushed over to where he sat with his back against a corner of a closet. He'd stepped on his plastic box of medicine and had fallen. I examined his back. It had a long red welt.

"Where does it hurt?" I asked. "Your back ... knee?"

He got up on his own and didn't appear to have any permanent damage – though he bears a faint scar to this day. I wanted to say "I told you so" about the light but didn't. What an ignominious way it would have been to end our walk – by falling in the dark in a motel room. As Mike says, it all reveals the tenuous situation we were in, where a twisted ankle, a fall, or so many things could have ended our dream.

Tom and Lois returned before noon the next day, and we visited out on the lawn. The fog was just lifting, revealing the vast blue lake in front of us. They live in South Carolina and had never been to the Ontario side of Lake Superior. They were awed by the view and by the fact that we were walking around this majestic lake. They knew we had to continue walking, so after our slow morning, we bushwhacked down to the shore and found a mix of rocks, cobbles and sand. There was no breeze and the humidity weighed on us.

We walked past several groups of people and chatted a bit about our walk.

One said, "Congratulations," and another asked if we'd like something to drink. These seemed to be the most consistent responses to news of our journey.

Since we'd just started walking, we thought we'd better keep going and asked the man about the shore ahead. We could see another outcrop blocking the way. It was too steep, the man said, suggesting that we go back to the road and cut down on the other side. We walked to the outcrop, though, and when we looked around the "corner," it appeared do-able, so we went on. We were only making about 2 mph, which was typical for this kind of terrain. Our walking speed varied depending on the surfaces and their angles, but we considered 2 mph to be slow.

At one spot, the cabins sat very close to the water, and a couple was sitting right in front of their place.

Mike called out a hello.

"Are you the ones …?" the man asked the now familiar question.

"Yes."

"Would you like something to drink – a cold soda, water or something?"

We'd split one, I said, and, of course, he brought out two. John and Cathy Phillips lived in Sault Ste. Marie, Ontario, but this cottage had been in John's family since 1959. He spent his childhood summers here. "This feels like home." We inquired about changes he'd seen here and he mentioned how Canada geese and eagles are more common now.

Back on the road at that point, it was hot and noisy, as expected.

We crossed over a stream when Amanda drove up to take us back to the Salzburger Hof. Tom and Lois were there in their RV and we were only too happy to sit in the shade with them and have happy hour with nice cold drinks.

Rain fell during the night and early morning; I listened to it and fell back asleep.

Mike felt stiff all over and had a numb left foot and sore knees. Not a good way to start the day. The sun emerged when we finally got under way to finish the Goulais Peninsula. This shore was a polyglot of rocks – conglomerate, granite, schist, lava and sandstone, all shapes and sizes, so it wasn't fast walking.

The first family we encountered on the sandy beach had two little dogs.

"So are you just out exercising?" the man said.

"Oh yeah," I started, and then in unison, we said, "We're walking around the lake."

"Really?" came the response. I always loved the expression on people's faces – first confused, then astonished when the recognition of what we'd said sunk in.

Up the beach, a younger man and a couple of women sat on the sand with some small children. One woman kept asking where we started. I kept saying "Duluth," but she couldn't hear me. She got up and came closer, repeating, "Where did you start?"

"Duluth."

Stunned shock showed on her face, and then, "Right on!"

We hadn't heard this expression for decades, but it was becoming so common in Ontario that we'd started using it, too. As we walked away, the man said, "Nice meeting youse" – an accent familiar on almost all sides of the Big Water.

We met more big dogs on this walk – the kind that made us nervous.

One a big chocolate lab was on the beach with a little girl, and Mike said, "Call your dog." It was already coming toward us, barking loudly. The little girl called, "Emma!" but Emma ignored her. The dog, in defense mode with a child to protect, kept barking around us. Another little boy came out and called, too, but to no avail.

Mike started saying, "NO, Emma" in his most authoritative voice. The dog would hesitate, but then resume barking. Eventually, we managed to get by and Emma lost interest when we were far enough away from her territory and her young charges.

At another place a dog ran out after us. The adults called it back, but again, the dog kept coming. It finally stopped at its jetty. The last dog of the day was a Doberman pinscher on a long chain at another jetty. Thankfully, the man there came out and held her close. He told us she was friendly, but the big thick chain and her Doberman looks made us wonder.

We came to a cement walkway that paralleled the water and crossed over a beach. A family was out front and Mike hailed them asking if we could go up on their steps.

"No problem," said the younger man. He was with an elderly man, both standing by their garage. We told them of our trip. The elderly man smiled shyly but never spoke. We asked about the terrain ahead and whether people would mind us crossing their property.

He didn't see a problem and mentioned about the high-water mark being the legal boundary. He asked us if we wanted something to drink. I said, "No thanks. We need to keep going." Mike would have said yes.

We climbed up and down, over and around big piles of rock jetties that separated one cottage from the next; very slow going. Then we came around one and popped out onto a small sand beach, where a woman was picking up rocks. Mike asked if we could cross. She smiled. "Sure."

Then Mike explained what we were doing.

"Do you want to have something cold to drink?" Sheila Mount asked enthusiastically.

"Yes!" Mike blurted out before I could stop him. I said we'd share a soda.

The woman's adult daughter was sitting on the steps of the cottage with a cute little toddler. "Oh no, you can each have one," she said. I can rarely finish a can of pop in one sitting.

"Do you want some fruit?"

"No, no. We're fine, really."

"What kind of soda? Dr. Pepper, Fresca?" They came with straws in them.

"Are you sure you don't want some fruit? How about a sandwich?"

"No, really, we're fine."

The daughter, Alexis, had gone in the cottage and came out with a serving plate overflowing with watermelon, grapes and blueberries. Their generosity could not be declined.

It gave us time to chat with Sheila about her cabin, which she bought in 1982. We told her what a great spot she had. Modestly, she said if she had a sand beach, it would indeed be a "million-dollar place." Despite the stone shore, it is nice, she added, and she can watch the moon rise over the hills beyond the bay and the cars passing on Highway 17. Alexis, who is a teacher in Fort Francis, sat nearby with her little boy Gavin. Before we left, Sheila asked to take our photo. Then we took one of her with Alexis and Gavin. She hugged us, and as we were leaving asked, "Are you sure you don't want a sandwich? We have lunch meat."

We managed to get away sans sandwiches – people can still be amazingly generous to strangers. We walked a little farther, going up, around and through stretches of marshy, mushy rush vegetation. We crossed on lawns to avoid the muck and finally left the shore at a spot where it was completely washed out. It had been roped off, and in the water there was a mishmash of plastic sheets, mesh, ropes, rocks and anything else that could be used, all unsuccessfully, to contain the mud from washing into the lake.

We ended the day back on the highway, having finally finished the Goulais Peninsula. Looking back, we could say the peninsula began at the Goulais River and it required all of three days and parts of two to get around its 40+-mile shoreline. Its size is deceptive because the south side forms a big hook, which lengthens the distance to be covered.

The peninsula was completed, but Mike's back and neck were in pain. I tried massaging them that night and kept at it until I heard his breathing change and he was asleep. It reminded me of rocking a baby to sleep and gingerly putting them in the crib. As soon as you stop, they wake up. After determining that Mike was finally asleep, I didn't want to move or turn. I feared that I would wake him. Slowly, very, very slowly, I moved my legs and arms from around him. He turned onto his side, but fell back asleep, so I slowly turned onto my side and eventually fell asleep, too.

The next morning was gorgeous, sunny and cool – a perfect walking day. Time to move the RV. We stopped at the Agawa Crafts mall to fill up the gas tank. Here was another blast from the past, as refreshing as "Right on!" It was a full service station. A couple of teenagers pumped the gas, asked how much we wanted, checked the oil and washed the windshield. We were loving Ontario.

> Just as the wave cannot exist for itself,
> but is ever a part of the heaving surface of the ocean:
> so must I never live my life for itself,
> but always in the experience which is going on around me.
> Albert Schweitzer

After Thoughts
Questions

Mike:

After we completed the journey, the questions people ask most often are: 1) What was your favorite place? 2) What was your toughest day? and 3) What did you learn?

The first of these questions is the hardest to answer. When we were walking, the answer often depended on where we were when we were asked. Our experiences were so strong and fresh that whatever happened in the last week or two was always the most prominent in our minds. My favorite place usually was some place we'd been recently; I had so many favorites. Some that stand out still, though, were Beth and Bill Blank's home, where the view out their windows, the food on the table and their friendship made it a favorite stop on our journey. One of Kate's favorite places on Lake Superior is Amnicon Bay on Madeline Island, though we didn't hike there on this circle. It shows that you must find your own favorites around the lake – and we are certain that, like us, you will find many "favorites."

The second question probably came through in the previous chapters. Kate struggling in the red clay along the Wisconsin coast and falling there remained among the toughest sections for her, and it occurred in just our first days. For me, the days in Michigan when my knees hurt so much I wondered whether I could continue were tough and disheartening.

Throughout the book, we share our ailments and aches that might have been obstacles to our success, but pain, by itself is not enough to stop you when you have a dream. Our commitment to the cause, the accomplishment of completion, to sharing the experience with another person allowed us to follow – and achieve – our special dream.

As for what we learned, our learning curve was constant and happily positive. We found the benefit of consistent exercise (though Kate will say she still feels she deserved to lose more weight). We loved Lake Superior before we started our walk and became even more enamored with it as we discovered the diversity in rock and scenery that inspired us daily. People became part of the lake's wonderful rich tapestry of story, personality and generosity that made the expedition extra-special. We did see problems for the lake and its environment that need addressing, but we also reveled in a freshwater body from which you can still dip a cup and drink in places. The overall quality of Lake Superior needs to be celebrated when compared to so many other natural areas and Great Lakes. It also needs to be preserved.

Here are some other questions:

Place you'd most like to return to: Kate – the smooth "whale back" rocks at Marathon, Ontario; Mike – Pictured Rocks National Lakeshore

Most secluded: Pukaskwa National Park

Prettiest view of the lake: Impossible to pick!

Firmest sand beach for walking: Just depended on the wave action from day to day or if it had rained.

Rockiest shoreline: A tie between Pukaskwa National Park and the Minnesota shoreline.

Most difficult shoreline stretch to cross: Mike – stamping sand beaches south of Freda; Kate – gravel beach and cobble dunes walking back to McLain State Park, Michigan.

Best bay for swimming: Hidden and nearly closed bays on the canoe trip through Pukaskwa National Park.

Hardest physical day: The 17-mile walk through Porcupine Wilderness State Park, Michigan.

Most wildlife present: Sleeping Giant Provincial Park (black bear, deer and wolves – not seen by us, but by others).

Strongest sense of place: Bayfield, Wisconsin.

Densest vegetative cover: Tip of the Keweenaw Peninsula.

Lowest ebb emotionally: Kate – tumbling down the Wisconsin clay bank early in the trip; Mike – the day before the beginning of the canoe trip when I was so sick.

Highest point emotionally: When we walked onto the Canal Park sidewalk and looked up to see all the people above waiting and waving to us on our last day.

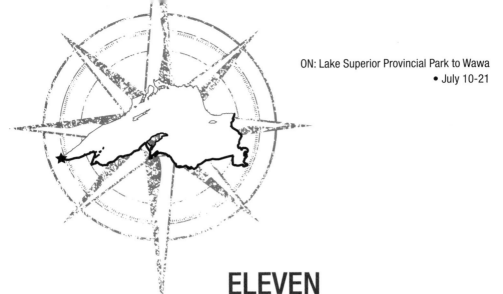

ELEVEN

Dragons & Michipeshu

His shoes were cut by rocks of the mountains
and he stood ankle deep in mud and moss of swamps.
A curve, just ahead, lured him miles.
The Mesmeric Mountain, Stephen Crane

Kate:

The drive after Pancake Bay to Lake Superior Provincial Park is spectacular. Truly wild. "It's almost scary, it seems so impenetrable," Mike said. It must have been a difficult journey for the earliest people, when there were no roads.

Highway 17 hugs the shore all the way along the jut of land that curves into the lake and then back up into the provincial park interrupted only by the small community of Montreal River Harbour. This is not a community in the usual sense of stores and a single focal point. Instead, it is a string of small cabins and a group of neighbors along the rocky coastline of Lake Superior adjacent to the Montreal River, which forms the small harbor and includes a hydroelectric dam. A combination post office, gas station, diner and another motel and diner constitute the business district, while small roads lead to clusters of cabins (camps).

When we got to Lake Superior Provincial Park, we went to the visitor center, which has wonderful displays incorporating art and historical photos of the park area. A young naturalist was sitting at a table outside, set up with lichens and mosses, one of Mike's favorite subjects. Annabelle, a tall young

150

woman with a blond ponytail, knew a lot about them, but Mike knew them all. She was excited to meet someone as passionate about these primitive plants as she. I went inside to look at the map of the park, while Mike talked to the park staff about our scheduled presentation. A young woman behind the counter showed me the Coastal Hiking Trail and explained the distances of the various sections and potential pick-up spots.

A new day with a clear sky, cool breeze, no humidity and waves washing onto the rocks made perfect walking conditions. The shoreline surface of volcanic rock or loose rock was easy for us to negotiate, until it got steep. Beautiful orange, green and white lichens grew on the sides and in the cracks, and delicate flowers stuck out of tiny crevices. How can you not feel invigorated in such a place?

Unfortunately, it was also at this point in the trip that Mike began to notice his vision getting worse. The eye with the torn retina seemed to be less clear, affecting his depth perception. We would learn later in the year that during the walk, Mike's vision declined from 20/20 to 20/50.

Staying close to the shore on a steep cobble beach, a dog heard us and ran out, barking, to meet us. An older woman came down some steps of a house after the dog, but the combination of wind and waves made it hard to hear what she was saying. I went to ask her where we were in relation to Ellen Van Laar's place.

The lady said the dog, Blackie, was friendly. When I told her we were walking around the lake, she said it was "a nice day for that." She was from Germany and said it was too bad her husband wasn't there; he spoke English better. I tried to find out the walking conditions around the next point, but all I could understand was something about cliffs, brush "and zen zere is zee street." We decided the shore route might not be the best choice. I told her who we were looking for, and she said, "Ah yah, Ellen of zee Black Forest."

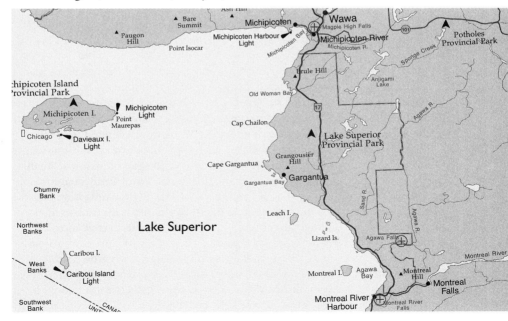

151

Ellen Van Laar is an artist we met through Facebook who had invited us to stop at the home she shares with her husband, Dan Bisson. Ellen is originally from Michigan, but moved to Canada in 1997. She has a degree in design and art, is a musician and gives music lessons. We turned down a driveway off of Highway 17 and walked into a grassy open area. A sign read: "Dan and Ellen." A woman about our age with a long grey braid down her back and a broad, welcoming smile walked over. Ellen invited us inside the house and asked if we'd like some wine. Hanging on the walls were her wonderful, colorful paintings – flamboyant, playful and mystical oils of the lake, many incorporating images of dragons.

We were looking at a map on a table when Dan came in. He's about our age, too, with a thick mop of white hair. He had a strong handshake with hands roughened by years of working outdoors. Ellen suggested we go in a bright, sun-filled room that looked out onto the lake and to a small island just offshore. She asked if we preferred appetizers or dessert. Neither, we said, we were just fine, but she brought out a dish with crackers and some sushi-type appetizers anyway. Hospitality continued to be superior on all sides of the lake.

After chatting some about our backgrounds and our walk, she got up and said, "I'll make us some salad."

"No," we said in unison. "We really can't stay because we're supposed to get picked up on the road at 6:45."

"Well," she said, "we'll go with you – show you the way on the shore or on our trails."

Before moving here, Ellen had spent years visiting and hiking trails from Pukaskwa National Park on down, even through crown land, where few people ever go. Old Highway 17 can still be found in places. It used to run much closer to the water than the current road, but you have to know where to find it.

Ellen put on her shoes, and we set out from the front yard. The house has been renovated and pieced together by Dan from a number of smaller buildings. He also built a very attractive wooden deck that looks old and nautical, with corner posts rescued from wood washed up on the beach.

We walked the shoreline rocks, then cut up into the woods to another trail. Dan told us the most amazing story about how he made a "dragon" for his three grandsons. Taking the bones of moose and arranging them in a cave on the island offshore, he created mystery, magic and an adventure they will never forget.

We listened attentively as he the tale. "Courage, honor and truth – these three words were carved on the three wooden swords the grandkids found by the dragon, slain by three young brothers in ancient times. Many knights had tried to kill the dragon with their own might and metal swords, but the dragon prevailed. The old wizard (a friend in costume) told the three grandkids this story, and they found the evidence on the island through the use of an ancient scroll and map, evidence – wooden swords, a dragon skeleton, a beautiful rose-quartz crystal heart – broken into three pieces. Our grandkids used this evidence to prove to their school classmates (during show and tell) that dragons do indeed exist."

The dragon had been dismantled some years ago, but Dan still had the skull in his garage, and later Mike would record the story and the skull on video.

152

We walked past some small round holes; like caves in the rock, Dan had stories for all of them. Two small caves next to each other were "eyes." Dan hid a treasure chest there and marked it with a raven's feather at the entrance. What incredible fun fantasies he has made with his grandkids. They're teenagers now, but still unaware, we think, of the true magician.

We skirted steep edges, walking over nearly submerged rocks and ended up on a high rock that gave us a view of the highway. Down we went back onto another gravelly beach, then up to the road. Ellen invited us to return Monday night for a potluck party. With such kindred spirits, it was all too easy to accept.

Amanda met us a few minutes later on the road. On the drive back to the Park we passed a sign for Twilight Taters, a small box-like building that served food from a limited menu. The second word in the title, though, is the real focus of fast food in Ontario – French fries. We decided to have dinner at this local eatery. Inside was a note: "Go to office." The Twilight Resort has a few cabins and a campground, and Mike found the proprietor, who came over and made us juicy burgers and fresh French fries.

At 2 a.m. I woke up and tried to hold still so I wouldn't wake Mike, who seemed to be sleeping soundly. Then I realized he wasn't in bed. I hadn't heard him get up and go out, but figured he was probably in the car. I lay awake wondering, until finally I put on my headlamp and read until 3 a.m. Then I put on warmer clothes, took my headlamp and went outside. As expected he was in his sleeping bag in the back seat and didn't turn when I shone the light in and looked at him. As long as I was up, I took a trip to the bathrooms and came back enjoying the clear, starry night. Once back inside I decided to work on finishing the previous day's journal.

After a while I heard the car door opening and closing, then the RV door opened and Mike came in, asking why I was awake. We both managed sleep,

No, not Hemingway in the Keys, just Mike, Amanda and Sheena at Twilight Taters, Montreal Harbour.

153

but mine was disturbed by a weird bad dream – something to do with yelling at an evil, frightening woman. I was agitated, muttering and whimpering. Mike heard me, turned over and put his arm around me, stopping the dream.

Mike got up first and went outside. Then Amanda went out. I worried that we'd ruined her sleep. "Good morning," Mike greeted her, but she just shook her head and rushed off to the bathrooms.

I took Sheena out for her morning walk. She wanted to go toward the lake, but there were people camped behind us, so I stopped her. A woman there looked up. "Are you Kate?" she said. It was Megan from Naturally Superior Adventures, and she informed me that our upcoming Voyageur canoe trip was now full, which meant that 10 people had signed up to join us on the 10-day journey around the Pukaskwa Peninsula. The last time we had talked to her, we were still short three people, which would have meant that the cost would not be covered and we would have had a harder time paddling the big canoe.

Back at the RV, I told Mike about Megan's good news. Amanda came back from the bathrooms, looking wan. She'd been hit with some sort of intestinal upset. I felt badly for her, but glad we weren't the cause of keeping her awake during the night.

We began our day on black and reddish volcanic rock – some broken up and flat, others slanted and jutting out into the water. Amanda and Sheena joined us for the first half hour. Along the way, we passed a cedar tree with the most unusual bird excavations we'd seen. They looked like those made by a pileated woodpecker, but these multiple large holes were rectangular, with almost squared corners. We also encountered unfamiliar rocks, gray or red with micro-columns in them, so that on the surface they looked like they had measles or pimples. The whole area we were walking had this formation. The little bumps were feldspar crystals that had been exposed as the surrounding rocks weathered away.

We climbed up and down sharp ridges and came to a section where the rock dropped straight into the water. We tried to inch our way around it, but it looked like we might need to get our feet wet. Then my left foot slipped in and I was sitting on the edge with both feet in the water, making the question moot. Mike ended up getting his feet wet, too. There just weren't any more places to step. But the water wasn't cold anymore, and we had gotten used to walking in wet boots.

After these rocks, we walked along a broad, beautiful sandy beach with some cabins behind it. Some women were sunbathing on lounge chairs, but I don't think they even saw us walk past. We marveled at such perfect sand and water after that rocky shore – talk about a multi-million dollar location. The closest community – Mamainse – was around the bay where it met Highway 17. After crossing more rocks, we found ourselves on an equally beautiful and even bigger sand beach. This seemed to be public land because a bunch of tents were set up along the back near the trees. As we got closer, a barking dog came toward us. Two women sitting under a tarp told us not to worry, it was friendly.

I asked how they got down to this beach and they said on a path from the old highway. They'd been there a week and hated the thought of leaving. It was an amazing remote spot and apparently free to campers, but we did wonder about disposal of waste – human and otherwise. There were no facilities of any kind.

We climbed more rocks, found an easier sand route, then returned to more rocks until we came to another nice sandy beach with an array of tents. People played in the water, and as we approached, their brindled bulldog started barking. From the water, a woman yelled that the dog was friendly, but she came out to grab it. The next dog charged, barking, from another campsite. Mike again used his forceful "NO!" and that held it off until the owner yelled for its return.

The next beach brought us close to the road, where our car was parked. We found Amanda and Sheena on a rocky island just offshore at the point where there was open water, rocks and another island. It had taken us more than two hours to cover three miles of shore. In and out of beautiful hidden inlets and bays, with very little forward progress, I was getting antsy to get miles behind us. For Mike, these slow spots were some of his favorites.

After a quick lunch by the car, we were on the road and met a couple of bicyclists – two men from Halifax, Nova Scotia. They were fixing a flat tire. We told them about our walk. They'd met another man walking across Canada in segments, and this year he was crossing Thunder Bay. The 69-year-old was stopping at homes, asking to camp along the way. These fellows said that he'd been robbed. Someone took his small pack with his money, camera and journals. To add insult to injury, they'd thrown his journals into the lake. He'd recovered them and was trying to dry the pages. We found this very sad and were grateful that our experiences so far had been overwhelmingly pleasant.

By the time Amanda got us, we were dragging. We stopped at the Lake Superior Provincial Park Visitor Centre, and I bought a beautiful, handmade patchwork bag with the horned lynx stitched on the front. Michipeshu, a manitou or a spirit, lives in the lake, according to Ojibwe tradition. It can be malevolent to those who do not show proper respect. It was a nice souvenir, made by local artist Heather Sinnott, who we would meet a few days later.

After the visitor center, we made the hour-long drive to Wawa to check out the farmer's market. If I'd known it was going to be a 100-mile round trip and that the market wouldn't have any vegetables left for sale, we probably wouldn't have gone. But I was desperate for fresh produce and that seemed like our best shot. It was a pretty summer evening, though, and we made the most of our drive by buying beef from a local farmer and groceries from a store in town. I love looking in grocery stores in other countries; there are always different, unique and interesting things to try. We loaded up on canned wild rice, maple sugar spread, barbequed rib-flavored potato chips, and the English toffees that Mike loves.

Back on the street we found a connection with the Internet in front of the Municipal and Police Building. We'd become the Internet version of storm chasers, seeking out and tracking down wireless eddies around the lake to keep in communication with our Facebook fans, as well as friends and family.

The next morning brought cloudy, muggy weather and looked like it could rain. We set out on the road near Mamainse and got glimpses of the lake as we walked. Mike entertained himself noting flowers in bloom and rock formations next to the road. Ravens called, and gulls and turkey vultures flew around us. At first, I couldn't figure out why there were so many gulls, but then I remembered there was a landfill nearby.

Trucks and cars blew past us, most pulling over if they had room. A herd of motorcycles roared by on the other side of the road. Later, as we came down a hill to the overlook, two Honda Goldwings passed us. We commented on how quiet they were. Each carried two people, and on the last motorcycle, the woman riding behind the man turned, waved and called, "Hi!" as they passed. She seemed extra friendly. As we got closer to the overlook, a man and woman started walking our way – the motorcyclists we'd seen earlier.

"Looks like we're going to have a showdown," joked Mike.

"Maybe they're looking for a place to go down to the lake," I speculated.

But no, they came to see us. Roxie and Clint Mattson had met us in Port Wing, Wisconsin, back in May near the beginning of our walk. They were from Maple, Wisconsin, and Roxie bubbled with excitement. When they decided to do this trip around the lake with their friends, Larry and Barb Riedasch, finding us had been one of her hopes. It was sheer luck and coincidence – something we encountered frequently on our walk. We visited awhile before parting ways. Of course, they'd be completing their circle of the lake long before we would.

Later that day, we passed a beautiful little inland lake with water lilies growing across one end and a loon swimming in the middle. Even with the trucks roaring by our backs, it was a tranquil scene. We went up and down several very long hills and caught glimpses of Lake Superior, but mostly it was woods, rocks and roadside vegetation. We finished before 3 p.m., and since we were near Twilight Taters, we stopped for cold drinks and a couple butter tartlets. The owner, who now knew what we were doing, mentioned the long-distance walker who had been robbed. We'd just missed the unfortunate man by a couple days. It sounded like his walk had gone from bad to worse – he'd gotten hit by a car just a few days before as he was coming out of a driveway. Not surprisingly, he was discouraged and ready to quit for this year. Again, we thanked our lucky stars – or whatever was aiding us – for not having similar experiences.

Back at the RV, Mike wanted to cook the steaks from Wawa on the site grill. Thunder rumbled in the distance and I fretted he wouldn't get the fire going before it started to rain.

"Don't worry," came the typical Mike response. His initial attempts produced more smoke than fire, but I found additional wood scraps, and finally he fanned them into flames – just as raindrops began to fall.

The steaks were on top of some aluminum foil he'd put on the grill. While flipping them, one fell on the ground.

"That one's yours," I told him.

He picked it up and said defensively. "Don't you think I've eaten meat that has fallen on the ground before?"

The rain increased and I went inside, but first handed my purple umbrella to Mike, who continued tending the fire. The steaks turned out great, and the rain continued to fall.

After dinner, Mike lamented about the one thing he missed most in the evenings – a comfortable chair in which to sit and read. Sitting in the car just didn't do it, and he couldn't read in bed, without falling asleep. Strange, the things one misses.

The rain stopped in the night, and it felt warmer in the morning. We started out east from the road next to our campsite toward Highway 17. The fog had come off the lake and made for a misty sky and cool temperatures. The clouds were magnificent – huge and blindingly white against a deep blue sky (prettier with my polarized glasses, of course), piling up above the hills and forests.

Every day as we walked near the road, we watched for moose. Signs along the highway warned of moose on the road, and that's one reason I never wanted to drive this highway at night. We saw a great blue heron fly up from one of the wet areas, which we scanned for moose, but all we found were whitened bones in a ditch. A scapula on the edge of the road caught Mike's eye. "I'm taking this with me," he said. "It may be the closest I get to a moose."

We spotted beautiful flowers in the wet ditch - bog orchids and sundews; fascinating carnivorous plants with delicate dew-tipped spikes.

This day we also heard several birds we hadn't yet heard in Ontario, including a broad-winged hawk and a least flycatcher. The white-throated sparrows were still singing, as were the vireos and winter wrens. We could tell that the nesting season was coming to an end, though. It was getting noticeably quieter. We had seen many monarch butterflies flitting from flower to flower, and, sadly, many lying on the side of the road, victims of car collisions.

A gurgling little stream ran beside the road, and when no cars or trucks were going by, we could hear the water trickling over the rocks. Not even bicyclists would notice this gentle sound; you have to be on foot to pick up on these subtle sounds and sights. We passed a couple of more beautiful inland lakes. It was strange to think of them sitting as much as 400 to 500 feet above Lake Superior.

We had chosen to walk clockwise this day, thinking we'd walk up fewer hills, but Mike had me write down the distances on our drive back to the park. It was pretty even. We walked downhill 2.5 miles and uphill 2.3 miles. One downhill was at a 7 percent grade and offered a breathtaking view of the vast blue lake, shimmering under the sun. Sweeping down to the water's edge were dark green coniferous forests. It was the most show-stopping view we'd seen on the Canadian shore. I wish everyone could see the lake from this spot at least once.

At one point, a broad-winged hawk called and I saw it soaring overhead. A passing trucker must have wondered what I was craning my neck to see. While I watched, the hawk ejected a string of white guano. I've seen lots of little birds poop when they take off to fly, but this was the first time I'd seen a raptor do it. Mike said now I could be like the Northland College students and put it on my "shit list" – yes, the list of birds they'd seen poop in flight. Mike explained that since the discharge has a scent, birds like to leave it behind when in flight, so as not to attract predators.

We ended up back at Twilight Taters. A couple of bikes were parked there, and we guessed they belonged to the people who passed Mike coming down one of the steep hills.

The Twilight Resort seemed to be a stopping off point for a lot of adventurers: bikers, walkers and, today, some paddlers, too.

A group of teenage boys camped near the bathrooms and we went over to talk to them. They were from a camp near Algonquin National Park, out on a 50-day canoe trip. One of the two leaders, a 25-year-old, had been going to this camp since he was 7. This trip was designed for young guys like him, who were approaching the age where they could become leaders, too. All were nice-looking, pleasant guys. When asked their thoughts on Lake Superior, we got exclamations of "Beautiful!" and "Incredible!"

Mike decided to interview the two bicyclists, who turned out to be French Canadian. This was their second bike trip across this stretch of Canada. Réal Fournier and Linda Gaudette are both artists. Réal tried to explain his art to me and about his gallery in Calgary, Alberta. Several times, he mentioned his "treaty" art. I pondered what "treaty" he had made or was part of; he did not seem to be from a First Nation. Then it dawned on me, he was saying "3D." Ah, language barriers. That made more sense, although I've never heard of an artist who paints with oil in 3D. He said it took him more than 20 years to perfect the technique; he uses 3D glasses when painting. Having made this trip before, they said that having the lake on their right provided them with inspiration and rejuvenation.

This encounter reminded us of all the artists we'd met on the trip: Ellen Van Laar, Betsy Lewis, Gregg Bruff and Phyllis Northup. The lake seems to draws creativity from people. Indeed, I felt the urge to draw or paint when I was near it, and wished I could take a watercolor class that Heather Sinnott was teaching at Lake Superior Provincial Park, but this year the walk took precedence.

Back at the park, we showered, changed and headed back to Ellen's for the potluck party. Amanda decided not to go, feeling that she needed to prepare for the two children's programs she would be doing at the park. Driving back to Ellen's and checking the mileage, we saw that we had covered 20 miles.

At Ellen's home, we met Marcos, an older man from Colombia; Enn, a wild-haired guy from the area; Robin, his activist wife; Sheila, another artist who makes beautiful glass jewelry; plus Larry, Stan, Shasta and Eunice. Having visited with Ellen and Dan, it was the interesting, eclectic group we would expect for their party.

The sun was shining and a cool breeze blew in from the lake. The potluck included lots of salads (heaven for me) and perfectly grilled burgers (heaven for Mike). As we got ready to leave, Ellen plied us with three containers of salads and pasta. She also gave us one of her framed paintings of Lake Superior and a birthday calendar that features a number of her paintings. On our drive back to the park, Mike marveled again about all the great people we had met on this journey and throughout our married life. We hoped that other walker – the one who had been robbed – had many good experiences to make up for the bad.

The next steps for us were along the trails within the park. The first leg would take us from Sinclair Cove back to the visitor center. Suzy, a park employee, estimated it would take us four-plus hours, and she was right. We started by visiting the pictographs at Agawa Bay. They are found on a smooth cliff with the lapping lake right beside them. It's a difficult, steep and rocky trail down to the pictographs, and across a sloped, smooth rock to get out close to them. These ancient paintings are estimated to be 100 to 400 years old. (Some of the earliest artifacts found within the park date to 500 B.C., when ancient people gathered near the shores in summer.) A park employee is posted at the site to answer questions and keep an eye on visitors who go out to the pictographs and might need help if they fall in. I'm serious. There's a life ring tied to the fence, and ropes hanging down in the water so people can pull themselves out. We found it amazing that people are allowed to walk out to the paintings and potentially even touch them (though that is forbidden).

As we walked down to the pictograph site, a couple of peregrine falcons flew overhead. The adult female perched on a branch on the cliff above the paintings, as if guarding this ancient place. The paintings are clear, strange and offer more questions than answers. One looks like a horned dragon and is Michipeshu.

Once we got on the official Coastal Trail beside Lake Superior, we found it even more challenging than anticipated. Almost immediately we scrabbled up and through wedged rocks, with big overhangs and narrow crevasses. Sometimes we had to stop and look over the edge to see how to get down. Often we'd sit down and carefully place our feet on the lip of a rock beneath us. I worried for Mike because of all the deep knee bending to negotiate these cliffs. We both wondered aloud how someone wearing a full pack could complete this trail.

We stepped off one rock face to a flurry of feathers and feet — a small covey of spruce grouse, females and juveniles. After the initial shock of seeing us, they settled down and didn't seem particularly afraid as I videotaped them.

One of the hardest parts of this walk was passing by all the blueberries. We both stopped occasionally to pick some, but a person with the time could fill a bucket without moving a foot. The raspberries were also ripe and thick, but Mike is more of a fan than I. There are too many seeds for me, and too much effort for the reward.

The trail took us down to the rocky shore once again, to big boulders and wobbly rocks, across which we carefully picked our way.

Finally we turned onto more of a forest trail; flatter and covered with pine needles for a time until we were back on lake level. Then it turned toward the road and took us to the bridge over the Agawa River. Beyond the bridge, the shore became the dreaded loose gravel, so I was happy to be on a more compacted trail. The sun shone brightly on the water and a little wind picked up. Mike's shirt was soaked with sweat early on, and he had to put his camera into his pack because it was fogging up next to his body.

After about five hours of hiking, we had a lovely evening, calm and basically no bugs, with the Big Lake spread before us. How lucky we are, we thought.

The next day we took the trail from Sinclair Cove and walked northeast.

This trail turned out to be even more difficult and challenging than the previous one. It was sunny, but still and humid. Soon we were both sweating heavily. Amanda and Sheena followed us through narrow rock passageways covered in moss and up some steep climbs before returning to the RV. We all lost the trail at the top of one outcrop and had to search back and forth for it, because some of the blue trail markers were in hard-to-see places. Climbing made my heart pound and my head feel light. Despite being in pretty good shape by this time, I'd have to stop at the top and bend over to wait for a normal pulse.

Around noon, Mike wanted to take a break when we came to a nice, big, flat outcrop beside the water. In it were pools holding aquatic creatures. Mike pointed out fish, then said, "Wait a minute. That's a newt." Sure enough, it had four legs, a long tail and fringed gill-head. We looked at other pools and found more of them. We also found tadpoles, water striders and mini-rock gardens with sundew and butterwort flowers sprouting from the cracks.

In his excitement to take photos, Mike's foot slipped on a rock and he slid into a pool. His camera didn't get wet, but everything else did. The pools were thick with algae that had an unpleasant smell, so Mike went farther down the rocks, stripped off his clothes and submerged himself in the cold lake. When he came out, he stretched out au naturel on piece of warm rock like an amphibian seeking heat. I took a photo of him lying there, reflected in a pool below, and was pleasantly surprised with the artistic result. (It's not one we share often.)

After lunch, we continued back up into the woods, climbing steeper slopes, then down and out to big boulder beaches. Surrounded by absolutely gorgeous scenery, we eventually found our thoughts turning from the beauty to our feet as we cautiously stepped from boulder to boulder.

A mature bald eagle flew out from the trees and over the lake, headed in the same direction as us. Later, when we stopped to "pish" (call) some songbirds, a gull flew toward the trail, squawking loudly. It banked suddenly and at the same moment came the whoosh, whoosh of large wings. An eagle, possibly the same one we'd seen earlier, flew away with the gull right on its tail. It had been sitting in a pine just a short ways ahead of us and that gull saw it long before we did.

Heat and the stress on our joints were wearing us out. The only bright spot in late afternoon were the plentiful blueberries right next to the trail. We stopped to grab as many as our hands could hold. An incredible bounty, but we sampled so little.

The trail came to a sandy beach, where I shucked my socks and shoes to cross a small stream. Mike's feet were already wet, so he just walked through. I went on, carrying my boots until the sand got too hot, then sat down to put my socks and shoes back on while Mike kept walking. Up ahead we could see two motorboats and some people in the water. I was thinking, "Mike should ask them if they would sell us something cold to drink," when I noticed him drinking something from a can. The three middle-aged men and one woman talked animatedly with Mike; who was gulping a Coors Light, enjoying it simply because it was wet and cold. They offered me one, but, not being a big beer drinker, I just had a sip of Mike's. Then the woman offered me bottled water.

John and Carol Miners, Dale Davieaux and Pat Parker were locals. John's grandfather once operated a commercial fishery and some cabins on the island across from the pictographs. They told us we still had quite a ways to go to reach the Sand River.

Three hours later we reached the Sand River, where a family with three kids was playing in waves that had developed in the past hour. The warm river water was dark, rusty brown from tannin and it flowed out a long way into the lake, carrying the color in a plume with it. Even the waves rolling in felt warm; this seemed very strange for Lake Superior. We heard later from Jim Radford that the *Star Tribune* had reported Lake Superior was registering 59° F down to 50 feet, a temperature you'd expect in mid-August, not mid-July.

Just before Katherine Cove, we passed Bathtub Island. It's almost connected to the main beach by sand and people were swimming there, too. We walked to the road and reached the parking lot where Amanda met us after 8 exhausting, but inspiring, miles. Mike's knees took a beating, and they weren't shy about letting him know it.

These day hikes convinced us that we could never have managed a backpacking and camping circle of the lake. The extra weight would further stress Mike's back and knees (and hips) and I would be overwhelmed on the climbs. Two young men we met who were backpacking even expressed surprise at the difficult terrain.

Mike stopped trying to sleep in the car, and some of our Facebook friends sent "remote Reiki" treatments. At this point, any offers of help were appreciated.

The morning broke cloudy and dark, but we decided to walk to Gargantua Harbour and back. (Gargantua, pronounced gar-GON-twa, is named for a giant in the stories by French author François Rabelais.) A park person had told us it would take eight hours round trip, but another person said there were old logging roads most of the way, so we weren't quite sure what to expect.

We drove 14 kilometers (about 8 miles) down the rocky and narrow road to the hiking trailhead. When we began walking, the sprinkles had stopped, but it was still cloudy. I brought both my rain jacket and umbrella; Mike put on his bigger backpack.

Amanda and Sheena walked with us down to Gargantua Harbour, a large natural harbor at the end of the Gargantua River. Both are named for Gargantua, a giant in French literature.

After reaching the harbor, Mike and I split off to go to Warp Bay and beyond. The trail was an old logging road, and we made good time. It felt great to be moving at 3 miles an hour, even if there were a few climbs. Unfortunately, the trail wasn't next to the shore, but mostly in the woods. Along the way we did see interesting flora and fauna, including toads that may have been boreal toads, each having a noticeable white stripe down its back. We crossed wet patches and at one small bridge we encountered a cluster of the largest bright yellow-capped amanita mushrooms either of us had ever seen. They were the size of salad plates. Mike thought of them as trolls guarding the bridge, but a bear must also have been on guard – we saw its fresh-looking paw prints in the mud.

When we reached the Warp Bay sign, we decided to continue on to Indian Harbour, which involved more climbing. There we found a woody part of the trail with no sandy beach for sitting, so we kept going toward Chalfant Cove – the end point of the Coastal Trail. On a rocky slope in the trail, we found an exposed rock face and decided to eat lunch there so we could look out onto a beautiful expanse of water and islands. The sun had come out, and a deep blue sky surrounded us. After eating, we continued to Chalfant Cove.

A bald eagle flying over one of the outer islands landed at the top of the very tallest pine. Its white head and tail were like beacons. We also encountered boreal chickadees, identifiable by their chirruping sound and brown plumage, different from your run-of-the-mill black-capped chickadees. After hearing a

Almost all Lake Superior Provincial Park trails were rocky, most up steep stoney inclines through the woods, but and this one, much easier, on the shore.

cheeping, like a woodpecker alarm call, a woodcock suddenly flew up and away from the ground just ahead of Mike.

As we got back to the split in the trail and Gargantua Harbour, Mike stopped and signaled for me to be quiet and to back up. I wondered what great animal had finally appeared. He signaled for his camera and I spotted the snowshoe hare – all brown, with short ears and immense hind feet. Mike got one picture, but when he moved, the hare took off. We walked down to a campsite off this trail and found a sandy spot with picnic tables and fire pit and water out in the bay. Once again, Mike shushed me and motioned me over. This time it was a fisher under a picnic table in a stand of trees. Mike tried to take photos, but when he moved closer, the fisher looked up and scurried away.

Picking up our gear, we started up the trail once again and met Amanda at a campsite picnic table as we walked the last kilometer back. These campsites were right on the secluded sandy beach, with a bay and an island out in front that you could paddle to on a calm day.

"Guess what I saw?" Amanda beamed.

"Oh no, you didn't?"

Yes, she did. She'd seen a moose with two calves across the water at Gargantua Harbour, where we'd split from her. They were grazing by the water. She took photos, but they were too far away. Still she *saw* moose. We had seen moose droppings on our walk; not much of a consolation prize.

Back at camp, Lin and Walt Pomeroy, old friends of Mike's, stopped by the RV while we were at the showers. Walt had worked for National Audubon and Lin at Northland College. They signed up to go on the canoe trip with us and were camping in the park, exploring this area. They came to our program that evening at the visitor center and later we went to their tent site to share drinks and conversation. A gorgeous quarter moon hung low in the fading blue sky. Once the mosquitoes started hunting, we said good night and headed back to the RV. It was 10:45 p.m. when we left and we were pleasantly shocked to see light still in the sky. You have to love the long northern summer days.

That night, Mike slept well. The "remote Reiki" must have been working. The next day we moved to Rabbit Blanket Lake and another campground in Lake Superior Provincial Park. Rabbit Blanket is a popular lake name in the north country, and we wondered if it comes from a traditional story of Fox and Rabbit (similar stories have been told about other animals). In this version, Fox showed Rabbit how to fish by sticking his tail through a hole in the ice. (Fox was jealous of Rabbit's long tail.) Rabbit stuck his tail in the lake and overnight the water froze with his tail in it. Poor Rabbit had no choice but to leave part of his tail. His descendants have had short tails ever since. That might be the etymology of Rabbit Blanket, or it might simply have to do with a blanket made of rabbit fur.

After getting our site picked out and the RV hooked up, Mike, Amanda and I got in the car and drove to Wawa to check at the post office for mail, get on the Internet at the library, and pick up supplies. We checked the miles on the way. I knew we'd have to walk the road part of the way the next day, and the forecast for the next few days called for rain.

Wawa was an important junction along the fur trade route. Economically, the region had been part of the fur trade of the 1600s, then forestry and mining, with gold first discovered in 1896. Most recently, diamonds have been discovered (mainly industrial grade). Today the town has more than 3,000 people and like so many of the communities, especially on this side of the lake, faces serious challenges to broaden its economic base. Wawa means "goose" in Ojibwe, and there is a giant statue of a Canada goose at the visitor center at the entrance to town, about a mile off Highway 17 along Highway 101.

We bought postcards and Mike picked up some more pills and creams for his aching back and knees. Before leaving town we made the all-important stop at Tim Horton's to pick up some breakfast treats. We had found the Boston cream bismarks irresistible.

On the way back to the park, Amanda dropped Mike and me by Henry Lake and we began walking to the campground. It was still cloudy, and we brought rain gear just in case … which meant that the sun was out by the time we reached Old Woman Bay.

We passed several pretty lakes and wetlands and searched in vain for sign of moose. Mike purposely left his camera in the car, thinking that would guarantee he'd see one. (The rain gear worked with the rain, after all.) We did see a pair of wood ducks and an osprey, new on our Canadian birding list. A peregrine falcon flew over the road near Old Woman Bay with something in its talons, but it was too far to see even with my binoculars. Mike speculated it might be a duck. We also came upon a huge number of northern green orchids in the ditch.

Walking on the road, there were many big hills to negotiate. Huge cliffs kept us away from the lakeshore. Most semi-trucks nicely moved over the centerline when they could, but one SUV pulling a boat nearly clipped us on a bridge. They could easily have pulled to the middle; no one else was on the road.

A short time later, slogging up yet another hill, a car slowed down as it approached. When it came even with us, the window rolled down and a young man said, "Fellow travelers, would you like some Amish raspberries? They're good, but I've eaten my fill."

"Sure, thanks!" we said gratefully, as he handed over a quart box about half full of berries.

Wishing us a good day, the two men in the car drove off and we walked on. Once again we thought about the kindness of strangers. (In retrospect, we suspect a bacteria on the berries that Mike so loves may have laid him low a few days later. Still, a generous gesture.)

Walking the road, we saw quite a few bicyclists. Almost all were headed east, taking advantage of the prevailing westerly tail wind. Most traveled in groups, and most were men. We admired their ambition and adventurousness, but have no desire to circle the lake on a bike. The narrowness of the shoulder and amount of traffic on this transcontinental highway was just too scary for us.

At first light the next morning, a Swainson thrush started singing. We'd never heard such a chorus; it woke both of us. There were clouds in the sky, but some blue, too. I felt confident it would be good weather. We drove a few miles to the parking lot for the Orphan Lake Trailhead, and Lin and Walt were waiting for us. They'd talked about joining us on this stretch, but we weren't certain they would make it. We had been told that the hill, called Bald Head, was the steepest on the entire Coastal Trail. Both Mike and I felt apprehensive about it, plus we'd be traversing a lot of boulder beaches. I anticipated a tough day. We found that most people who chose to walk with us walked a lot slower, but Mike's body was saying go slower anyway.

Neither Lin nor Walt had brought hiking shoes, not intending to do any hikes. Mike had his extra pair along, so Walt tried them and they fit. Lin, on the other hand, had to wear her regular running shoes. They weren't sure if they would go the whole distance to Katherine Cove, but were willing to give it a shot.

The trail wasn't that steep going up to and beyond Orphan Lake and soon we spied Lake Superior. On this day, unlike the first two on the trail, we walked on a pine needle-cushioned forest path, with some rocky but manageable climbs. We'd count it an easy trail. As we walked, we talked with Lin and Walt about the National Audubon Society treks they'd led, including one to the Falkland Islands. At one point I spotted just below us a partially submerged rock that looked like a giant elephant seal. The top end of the gray rock resembled the seal's head. The "body" was creased, like the skin on these sea mammals. Walt and Lin agreed with my interpretation, then told us how the two of them wandered onto a Falklands beach with more than 100 real sea lions.

At the top of the trail on Bald Head, we admiring the amazing view from high above the lake. The day was perfect – sunny, cool, with a fairly strong wind, while large, white-capped waves broke on the rocks below. We ate our lunch with this perfect view spread before us. From there, the trail entered the woods, but we often veered down to the boulder beaches. One charming little cove with a white sand beach about 2.5 miles from Katherine Cove had a great campsite. Carrying a full backpack here would be a challenge, though, especially balancing on the boulders. Walt had slipped earlier on a rock that rolled beneath his feet. He smacked his right leg, but assured us he was OK. More importantly, his camera was OK. Walt loves photography and once owned a gallery in Bayfield.

Mike, feeling much perkier after lunch, was doing his usual skip ahead on the boulders. He claims he doesn't trust gravity and so doesn't want to stay in one spot too long. Coming down off a high rock, his foot slipped and he rolled one ankle. We so easily, with one misstep, could seriously hurt ourselves on these rocks. For Mike, though, this was "the most beautiful walk of the trip."

With our destination in view, we diverged from the cairn-marked trail and improvised over and around rocks wet and slippery with algae. Eventually, we reached Katherine Cove where people played in the waves that rolled and broke on shore. One group rode an air mattress in and out on the curling waves. The water's colors again mesmerized us, ranging from cobalt to royal to aqua blue.

We'd hiked 6.5 hours, but we all felt invigorated. We'd recommend this day's hike to anyone coming to the park. Amanda met us at Katherine Cove and we loaded everyone in the car for the ride back to Orphan Lake, where we said our "see ya laters." It had been great fun to share that shore with a pair of similar-minded nature lovers.

Back at the campground Mike was already into his nighttime agonies. Anytime he'd lie down, his right knee and hip would develop sharp shooting pains. Maybe it was because the muscles were starting to relax, or there was nothing to distract him from the pain. In addition, his sciatic nerve would cause his left calf to spasm into Charlie horse cramps, his left ankle would feel stiff and sore, and he would get a burning sensation in both feet.

Mike spent the night in the car, but according to him, didn't really sleep. I saw him around 9 a.m. and he looked horrible. I'd slept pretty well in the RV but felt guilty that he'd had yet another miserable night. It was getting extremely old for both of us. Mike so enjoyed bouncing over all the rocks and hills the day before, but he ended up paying for it. He also felt nauseous this morning, maybe from all the pills he'd been taking.

The sky, which had been fairly clear, got progressively more cloudy as we set off for Orphan Lake and our last hike along the Coastal Trail. We decided we'd hike in and go toward Gargantua Harbour as far as we could, then retrace our route to see some of the shore and cover the miles needed without walking the road. Amanda and Sheena joined us on this stretch.

Mike walked much slower than normal, but that was OK. We went back to the cobblestone beach that we'd crossed yesterday and headed to what turned out to be the Bald Head River. I swear the map in the parking lot showed the trail crossing the river and assumed there'd be a bridge. There wasn't. The river mouth looked deep and rocky, so it was an easy decision to wear boots through it. Mike went first and found the shallowest route – just over our knees. Amanda carried Sheena. We squished up onto the other side and looked for the trail, but found no blue markers or cairn. Climbing onto a big outcrop, we started walking and soon spotted the marker to our right near some campsites.

Next we walked over a boulder-strewn beach, smooth slanting rocks, and a cobble beach. Occasionally the trail went into the woods, but sometimes it didn't seem much better than walking on the rocky shore.

In one narrow spot hemmed in by tall rock walls, a bird shot out next to my right shoulder. Just below eye level was a perfect phoebe nest – a moss and pine needle cup attached to the rock with ferns hanging over it. Tiny babies nestled inside with fluffy feathers on their heads, big bulging closed eyes and pin feathers on their rudimentary wings. They all peeped. We paused only a moment then kept moving, so the mother could return. We've observed phoebes, sparrow-sized gray-and-white flycatchers, feeding along the south shore.

We were nearing the 3-mile mark, but lost the trail when we went out onto some rocks closer to the water. Someone had made a cairn-looking pile of stones, but it did not indicate the trail.

"Let's eat lunch here anyway," I said finally. Mike sat there for a bit, looking beat. I ate my tortilla sandwich, and then walked ahead without my fanny pack to look for the trail. No luck.

We backtracked and began circling to pick up the trail. It had to go farther up the rock ridge, and that's where we found it. We had missed it by angling to our left instead of seeing the marker higher and to the right. Up, up, up we went, encountering mucky trail conditions. Finally, the path returned to a boulder beach. At 3.25 miles, Mike was feeling so poorly, I said, "Let's just go back."

We turned and retraced our steps, but remembered halfway up the trail that we hadn't "spotted" (pushed the button on our SPOT unit satellite tracker to mark our endpoint). Mike said he'd go back. I said, "No way, I'll go." Thankfully, Amanda said, "Let me go." She shrugged off her pack and trotted to the beach.

Before long we reached Bald Head River and did the wet walk again. On the other side, we noticed what looked like a trail paralleling the river. We took that and sure enough came to a sign indicating the Coastal Trail and pointed to a wooden bridge crossing the river and the Orphan Lake Trail, up the hill. Oh well, the water wasn't cold, really, and having wet boots didn't affect our progress.

We heard waterfalls as we moved up the trail, but couldn't see them from our side of the river. A little farther and we were at a steep, sheer rock face with bird guano splashed around a ledge. With my binoculars, I could see a large stick nest above the whitewash. Some very large bird had nested there – too big for peregrines. Would bald eagles use a cliff face, or maybe turkey vultures? Mike didn't even look at it with my binoculars; his right eye was too fuzzy.

The trail went uphill until we came even with Orphan Lake, and then we had to climb some more. Mike was parched and felt feverish. Back at the RV, I suggested he sit in the car with the seat reclined and try to sleep. He tried, but it didn't work well. He tried lying in the back seat, but had to keep the door open because he was too warm otherwise.

After dinner, Mike went back to the car and I started to go through our clothes and stuff to see what to send back to Minnesota with Amanda and what to take with us on the canoe trip.

Later in the evening, after Mike went to sleep in the RV, I was working on the day's notes when a loon made its tremolo call, one heard most in flight, but this loon kept doing it over and over. I assumed it was on Rabbit Blanket Lake. The howl of the wolf and the call of the loon epitomize the Northland for us.

Mike managed to sleep almost 12 uninterrupted hours. In the morning we drove to the Kinniwabi International Cuisine restaurant outside Wawa and parked our car there (with permission). Then Amanda drove us back down the road to our starting point for the day. We said goodbye as she and Sheena headed back to Minnesota for a two-week break.

It was sunny and slightly breezy as we started toward Wawa. Interesting wavy rocks on one side of the road and a wonderful family of loons on a lake kept us entertained. The two young loons were half covered with brown down and half with new adult feathers. The adult loons peered into the water and dived for food. It occurred to me that these same loons would soon go south to the Gulf of Mexico, where I feared they would be exposed to the oil from the recent BP spill.

A pick-up truck stopped; it was a couple from Michigan who camped across from us at the Lake Superior Provincial Park. They had seen us walking far from each other and had asked at our presentation: "Do you ever walk together?" A big semi truck rumbled up from behind, so our chat was short, but it was a nice pick-me-up to see people who knew and appreciated what we were doing.

As we got closer to Michipicoten River, dark clouds began to fill the northwestern sky. We made it to the restaurant in sunshine, got in the car and drove to High Falls Motel and Cabins. They advertised Internet and mini-kitchens, two things we wanted. The small resort has a nice cluster of little log cabins, neat and tidy, with all the amenities, including (praise be) tubs. Owners Zenn and Anna are Polish, warm and accommodating. They told us how they had upgraded the property and made it more energy efficient since buying it three years ago. Zenn did all the work himself.

After getting settled into our new space and carrying our gear inside, we went to Wawa to the post office. Happily we had two packages from Rhea Kontos, our Gabel walking pole supplier. She had sent new carbide tips and rubber "paws," which would come in very handy for the rest of the hike.

We drove to Naturally Superior Adventures just outside of town. Owner David Wells invited us to hang out and eat there the next day. We accepted then returned to Kinniwabi International Cuisine to celebrate 900 miles walked. A chilly wind made deck dining unappealing, though it was a beautiful evening. David Ayoung and his family came from Trinidad and opened the restaurant 12 years ago. The menu presents a mouthwatering mix of Trinidadian, Chinese and European (German/Czech) cuisine. I ordered the spicy Trinidad pork and Mike had the raspberry chicken. Both came with rice and veggies. One word: excellent, including the beef vegetable soup first course and the sweet, chewy white dinner rolls. A glass of wine, and we couldn't have been happier.

It's so easy to forget that you're in a foreign country on the north side of the lake (the people are the same friendly folk), but small things occasionally remind you. When I went to a bank in Wawa the next day to get fresh Canadian $5 bills for our twin grandsons' birthday, I needed to present two forms of ID. Not something you encounter when making change at home, of course.

Back at the motel, Lin Pomeroy had called. Her sister had died of cancer. They'd visited her before coming to Ontario and had intended to see her again when they returned, but now they needed to go home for the funeral. They could not come on the canoe trip.

Later in the afternoon, we returned to Naturally Superior's lodge for dinner. The lodge is on a point next to Lake Superior and it was a lovely evening for people to sit on deck chairs out front. We were 12 for dinner, sitting at tables arranged into a large square in the main room closest to the water – a delicious meal with delightful company.

Most dinner guests were staying at the lodge, taking kayak lessons or going on trips with the staff.

That evening, back at the motel, Mike felt increasingly ill. He developed diarrhea and was alternately feverish and chilled. He suffered all night with stomach pain and other symptoms.

By morning, I was thinking about the day's walk we'd planned from Naturally Superior to Sandy Beach. I told Mike that I should meet our guide for that stretch. He agreed, without much argument, so I knew he truly was sick. At 8:30 a.m., I called Vaughn Chauvin. Our long canoe trip was only two days away. At my urging, Mike promised to call our medical advisor Dr. Dan Dewey.

I met up with Vaughn and Megan by the equipment shed at Naturally Superior Adventures.

"You're missing the other half," Megan noted.

I explained Mike's condition and said I still wanted to do the walk. Then she told me that she was arranging for a boat to pick up Walt and Lin halfway through the canoe trip. That way they would be able to participate for at least a portion of the trip before leaving for the funeral.

Megan and I followed Vaughn to Sandy Beach, where he left his car and rode back with us to Naturally Superior. Then he and I started walking. Vaughn's family lives on this bay, and he spent much of his childhood exploring the shore. We traveled over beaches, up slopes to a dirt road and back to his home. Vaughn is a pharmacy student in Toronto. His dad, a dentist, and his mom, a retired teacher, live in a lovely home not far from the beach. Unfortunately, a new neighbor had cut down the trees next to them in order to build a house at the top of the hill. Even with the rock walls terraced down the slope, the Chauvins still worried that the soil would wash away, and possibly their property as well.

Vaughn's mom, Marney, joined us. We went onto the beach to a great rock outcrop. This property belongs to the parents of Annabelle (the lichen-loving naturalist). I did a point count and hit the Spot unit to record the location. It was the first time I'd done it without Mike. It was strange to walk without him, but my two companions kept the conversation going. We ended at Sandy Beach, and Marney shared an uplifting story about the high school students who saved and restored the beach, which had been badly degraded.

"I had a wonderful group of students who worked on the restoration of this beach," she said. She added that historically it had always been a popular spot for both locals and well-known personalities like Glen Gould [pianist] and A.Y. Jackson [artist], but it was being loved to death.

"Around 1998 we noticed that lots of recreational vehicles were driving all over the dunes, destroying the grass and changing the landscape. First my students and I came and put up snow fences to direct the traffic."

They partnered with agencies and blocked the vehicles, then began transplanting native grasses in the fall. The result is a beach that looks like it has never been touched. More recently a boardwalk, parking lot and kiosk with informational signs has been added. We found this so inspiring; evidence that a small group could have a significant impact on the health of the lakeshore.

They drove me back to my car, and I returned to the cabin. Mike was still in bed with medicine bottles all over the table. He'd had an email conversation with Dr. Dewey, who suggested he take the antibiotics we'd brought along.

I insisted we see a doctor in town. With the canoe trip looming, we couldn't take any chances. Mike was weak and, after helping him get dressed, we drove to the Wawa Medical Centre.

Because Canadian hospitals have had trouble getting payment from American insurance companies, the hospital needed pay up front with a credit card. It would be $375 for the emergency care, not including doctor or lab fees.

Mike looked at me and said, "That's too much."

"You just spent $300 getting the computer fixed," I retorted. "You have to do this for yourself." In the end, the charges were much less than we would have paid at home.

A nurse advised Mike to see a doctor, and he agreed. Another nurse took his blood pressure – 111 over 66, very low for Mike. Then a blood test and a urine sample. Mike lay down on the examining table, and we began our wait. An hour later, the lab tests indicated the blood work was all good, but we still had not seen the doctor. Mike fell asleep reading a magazine. Then the power went off. Dark storm clouds had gathered and rain began as we arrived. Soon a generator kicked in and lights came back on. All over northern Ontario, the power had gone off, but not because of weather. It had to do with the hydropower generation.

I asked about the doctor. The nurse assured me he knew about us. We got to the hospital around 2 p.m. and didn't see the doctor until 5:30 p.m. Mike had said if he didn't show by 6, we were leaving. There was only one doctor for the emergency room and clinic. Since we really weren't an emergency, he took care of his clinic appointments first. A short, fit man with gray hair, the doctor reminded me of Minnesota's former Congressman Jim Oberstar. Friendly and apologetic about the wait, he felt Mike's stomach, asked questions and decided it was probably a bacterial infection. He advised Mike to continue taking antibiotics.

When we returned to the High Falls cabins, Mike got back into bed. I microwaved tomato soup, which he ate. That seemed to give him a boost. He drank Powerade to replenish lost electrolytes. By bedtime, he was feeling better.

Mike slept all night long and didn't get up once – hallelujah. When he did get up, he felt much better. The room, however, was a disaster. It looked like a bomb had gone off, and we had yet to pack for our 10-day canoe trip.

I emptied the car, then gradually put bags and boxes back into it. After lunch we drove to Naturally Superior. We knew seven of the 10 trip companions. Besides Walt and Lin Pomeroy, Beth Oehler was a former Northland College student and Audubon staff person. She had invited her younger brother John, whom we had not met before. Duane Johnson had taken a course at the Audubon Center from Mike back in the 1980s. There also was Lisa Cassioppi, another former Northland College student, and Cindy and Harry Carlson, our friends and neighbors from Sturgeon Lake. We had yet to meet Jane and Gerald Wichtman, who learned about the trip from a newspaper article and knew of the Audubon Center because they had donated a van to it in the early 2000s.

Our lead guide, Chris Tompkins, introduced himself and Nic Olner, the assistant guide. Both looked to be buff, capable young men. The two, aged 22 and 18 respectively, would guide a group ranging in age from early 40s to 80 – with more than 100 years of outdoors and canoe experience between us all!

At 2 p.m., we gathered around the 36-foot Voyageur canoe for practice. The paddles were much longer and skinnier than regular canoe paddles. In this huge canoe you sit up higher, and the combined effort of all paddlers is needed.

A gorgeous puffy-clouded blue sky and little wind greeted us on the beach, where we gathered around a picnic table to examine charts. Then we headed to the water's edge, where a 600-pound canoe waited for us to grab the sides and lift as one to put it in the water. We climbed in two abreast and were instructed on commands. Chris, in the back, was the *gouvernant*; Nick in front was the *avant*.

You can imagine moving a boat this size and weight. Fully loaded, it would be more challenging. Yet on this test run, on smooth water, we paddled effortlessly. Before long Chris inquired about the time. I told him and he said we were "rocketing" along. My question was this: How long can we keep it up? When you're sitting two to a seat, you can't switch sides. Our short paddle took us up to a pretty waterfall where we turned back toward the Lodge.

Later at a rudimentary orientation, the two showed us the maps and pointed out where we'd try to stay. Chris talked about toilet practices – basically how to dig a cat hole using the trowel kept in a stuff sack – heretofore known as the "poop" bag. They gave us our dry bags, in which to pack all our gear and shared two-person tents.

Before dinner, people gathered on the rocks below the lodge. The lake was nearly calm and the sun still warm. In the dining area, the sun beat through the windows, heating the space. We ended the day with a talk about our walk to a room full of guests and local community members. Even with two windows and the door open, we were all sweating. The huge windows turned the dining room into a greenhouse. After the program, we asked people to fill out our survey, and we made plans for our departure the next morning. Earlier when I had been talking to Chris about the weather for the week, he said it didn't look "too bad."

"Oh," I said, "I'd heard that there might be rain in the first couple days."

He looked confused for a moment, then said, "I wasn't talking about rain. I was talking about the wind."

"Oh," I said. "Yeah, I guess that would be important, too." I didn't realize just how important.

> It starts with a step and then another step and then another
> that add up like taps on a drum to a rhythm, the rhythm of walking.
> The most obvious and the most obscure thing in the world,
> this walking that wanders so readily into religion,
> philosophy, landscape, urban policy, anatomy, allegory and heartbreak.
> Wanderlust, Rebecca Solnit

After Thoughts

Streams

Mike:

Our primary concern for streams had been how to get across them. We waded many, or sometimes stopped our trek on one side one day and began the next day on the other side. We also canoed across two, walked over many on bridges and crossed on numerous logs. Some stretches of shore had more rivers flowing into the lake than others. The Amnicon to Brule River section of Wisconsin and the Porcupine Mountains to Ontonagon in Michigan presented the most concentrated stretches of rivers and streams to cross. These were also the earliest in our walk and still probably had spring runoff.

During low water stages, these streams can become isolated from the lake by sandbars in late summer. Water level fluctuations need constant review. Consistently low levels, whether from climate changes or other diversions, might inhibit streams and rivers from bringing nutrients to the lake or from giving access to spawning game fish.

We did our best to provide meaningful information on this topic by measuring the width and depth of streams we crossed, their GPS position and the time and date we crossed them. These can be matched with lake levels by research scientists and perhaps projections can be made about any potential low water threats.

TWELVE

Voyageur Adventure

**We voyageurs
We work the waves
We ply the waters
We relish each other
And seek safe harbor**
Jacinta T. Carlson

Kate:

It was July 23, time to push off on our canoe trip. But Mike had another bad night – his knees this time, from standing during our talk.

"Good grief," I thought. "How will he be able to walk after the canoe trip?"

When we got up, Mike felt pretty good, but he still had some hot and cold flashes. After an 8 a.m. breakfast, everyone packed their gear into waterproof stuff sacks. We watched Nic and Chris carry two extremely heavy wooden boxes and a cooler case to the canoe. After it was loaded, we heaved the canoe into the water and climbed in. I had tobacco and gave it to anyone who wanted to offer it to Michipeshu. No use taking chances; we wanted to be respectful.

Then we shoved off, saying "au revoir" to the people on shore. Mike called this canoe trip as our hike equivalent of a portage. Instead of switching from water to land, we were doing the opposite. Traveling by water was the only way to undertake this portion of our trip and remain by the lakeshore. Otherwise we'd be away from the shore on the highway far inland for nearly two weeks

172

around Pukaswka National Park. The distance would be less than 7 percent of the total and each campsite provided a section of shoreline to hike and explore.

With flat calm water, we made good progress. There was talk and laughter and clacking of paddles, but we soon discovered how difficult it would be to paddle on the same side of the canoe for long periods. Sitting two to a seat, we couldn't switch sides with our paddles when we got tired, as you can in a normal canoe. Harry and I were in one of the narrower seats near the bow, and kept hitting elbows. On both sides of the canoe, paddlers were splashing the people in front of them. A well-oiled machine, we were not.

As we followed the shore, we paused by Michipicoten Harbour, where our guides told us about a trap-rock open pit quarry proposed for this site by the U.S. company that now owns it. It had once been an industrial dock area used for iron ore and coal shipping. The idea of an open pit mining operation that would allow removal of millions of tons of rock, crushed for road aggregate across North America, disturbs many people living on this shore. They have been fighting to stop it and the damage it would cause both visually and potentially to area waters.

Paddling again, we enjoyed groups of loons singing to us and observed plenty of intriguing rocks to entertain the geology buffs in the group. The lunch stop brought relief to stretch both arms and legs. Our guides chose a place with smooth, water-sculpted rocks to sit on and a river with a nearby waterfall.

I brought out the woven red wool voyageur sash I'd bought at the Voyageur's Lodge and Cookhouse in Batchawana Bay and gave it to Mike to wear. He tied it around his waist, but came back from the woods wearing it around his neck – continental style. He looked debonair with his new orange paddling shirt and the silver pendant necklace I'd given to him a few days earlier.

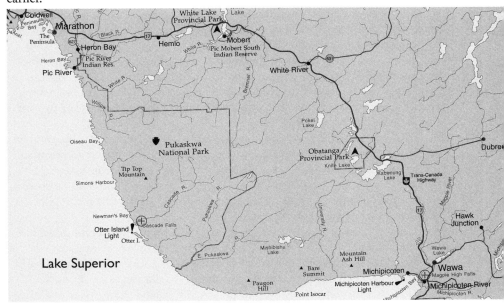

The wind picked up as we paddled out. Cindy called it a "walleye chop" – a Minnesota colloquialism meaning just enough roughed up water to make walleye fishing good.

She was sitting next to me now, having switched places with Harry. She and Nic bantered back and forth, but then she said, pointing ahead, "I'm not going to talk until we get to that rock." She dramatically clamped her mouth shut. Almost immediately the waves grew bigger, splashing over the side and bow. Our paddling was unsynchronized. All the paddles were banging against one another, making Chris' job at the back of the canoe even harder. We watched nervously as whitecaps grew on top of the waves. Finally Chris told everyone on the right to stop paddling and on the left to keep it up. The canoe turned toward a small beach, riding in on the surf.

We pulled up on the beach and Chris climbed a rock, trying to get a weather report on his communications radio. Having no luck, he asked to use Mike's little NOAA radio and together they clambered to the top of a big rock. When they came down, Chris said because of the wind, we'd stay put for the night. It was already mid-afternoon and Dog River (our original destination for the night) was still 13 kilometers (7.8 miles) away.

A water trip on Lake Superior always requires flexibility in schedules as the weather dictates. That sometimes can mean putting up in a safe place for several days to wait out bad winds or storms. We suspected this would be a shorter interlude.

This broad, sandy beach offered protection thanks to the large rocks on either end. Setting up tents was quite a circus, this being our first night. The dome-style tents assembled easily, once you got the hang of them, but this first time out prompted many amusing mutters of "Where does this pole go?" and "How does this rain fly work?"

Chris made a tarp shelter for cooking and hanging out. Lisa went for a walk, and what would become our daily happy hour began. Mike broke out his single malt scotch and John got out his bourbon.

Dinner set a high bar for future meals – Thai chicken peanut stir-fry with rice and veggies. Enjoying a glass of red wine with dinner seemed a civilizing touch out here in the wild. It's one we would all look forward to each evening. After dinner, we sat like satiated seals and watched the clouds breaking up and the waves rolling in.

This would be the most social part of our journey. Mike had some trouble adjusting to the constant presence of other people. He had grown accustomed to just the two of us spending our days in semi-seclusion, talking at times, but being lost in our own thoughts and observations at others. The fact that these were people we enjoyed being around made it easier, and our own tent allowed us to have alone time when we needed it.

Chris warned us that he'd be getting up at 4 a.m. to check conditions. If it was a go, he'd make coffee and wake everyone by 5 to be under way at 6.

After dinner, I walked out to a rock point away from camp. From this beautiful spot, I could survey the distant shores of Lake Superior Provincial Park and try to comprehend that we had actually walked those shores and hills.

I returned to camp with the sun going down and a warm light spreading across the water.

The balloon count continued. We found five on this beach and one in the woods. They would be scattered throughout this remote stretch of shoreline. Amazing how far pollution could travel.

To my surprise, Mike seemed to have had a good night. His knees hurt at first, but the pills worked. I got pretty comfortable with my new sleeping bag and air mattress, but the sound of the waves kept waking me. They still sounded big. I looked at my watch: 4:20 a.m. I wondered what Chris had decided, then thought, "No point in worrying" and went back to sleep. The next thing I knew Chris was "knocking" on our tent. Mike admitted later that his eye continued to deteriorate, his knees, hips and back made sleep difficult … and he still felt the effects of the intestinal virus. He hid it all well.

The waves had calmed, so we slammed down some coffee, loaded the canoe and paddled a couple hours before landing for breakfast. Mike and I were in the tight second seat and only too happy to get out at the mouth of the Dog River. On the sand and cobble beach with the river flowing out at the far end, Chris and Nic prepared scrambled egg burritos with salsa – just barely enough for us hungry voyageurs.

This day, Lin Pomeroy got to wear the voyageur sash. Since we knew that she and Walt would only be with us for the first five days of the trip, I wanted to make sure they each got a chance to be the Voyageur before they left. Belatedly, I made a new rule: Whoever wore the sash got to eat first. Unfortunately for Mike, that perk came after he'd had his sash day. By 10 a.m. we were back in the canoe for a long day's paddle. We made good time until early afternoon.

Dark clouds gathered after our breakfast stop, but by the time we beached for lunch, the sun had reappeared. It generated a boatload of smiles (as did lunch) and we sprawled on the rocks like shipwrecked, but contented, sailors. Gerald demonstrated an amazing ability to fall asleep moments after lying down, a talent he employed throughout the trip.

After lunch, we started in relatively flat water, then paddled past a protective point of land. Boom! The wind drove right in our face. Waves coming from the west swelled from hundreds of miles of fetch – the stretch of open water on which they built up. Jane and John, sitting in the middle, changed places. Many of us stopped paddling to watch the waves until Chris yelled, "Keep paddling!" We already felt tired from the 18 miles we'd just paddled - we certainly didn't need a headwind and big waves for the last 7 miles of the day.

I was sitting right behind the bow seat occupied by Nic, our 18-year-old assistant guide. Both of us were catching buckets of water in our laps; Nic cursed each one.

"We need to paddle hard and fast with each big swell," I said. Those in the back didn't seem to realize how much water was coming in. I hoped someone was bailing, but that seemed unlikely. Almost every inch of space was occupied by gear or people's legs and feet.

Having made up yesterday's lost miles, we made it to our destination - Floating Heart Bay and its soft sand beach with a small river outlet. Mike and I struggled to climb out on legs that had been immobile for hours. Our shoulders and arms complained, but I stopped listening to them once the first fly bit me. I slapped at my leg, while stumbling up the beach carrying our dry bags. More flies, hungry flies, moved in. Mike stood in one place, trying to maintain his balance, while others lifted out gear. The sun came out in full force soon after we got the tents up. Even the heat inside them was better than being eaten alive by flies outside. Later, a breeze came up and allowed us to venture out.

When we got together to eat, our exhaustion and pain made sense; we'd paddled 41 kilometers (25.5 miles). Meanwhile, despite being surrounded by fresh water, I'd failed to drink enough, which led to a serious headache. We ate dinner sitting in a circle. Chris brought over driftwood and built a small fire. A pleasant post-dinner chat followed until everyone wandered off to the tents.

The third day started with blue skies and fresh wild blueberry pancakes. Moods ran high since we knew it was only 7 miles to our next campsite.

Mike and I got the seat at the back of the canoe, just in front of Chris. It was like riding in first class; we had more room than we knew what to do with. Getting in was a new challenge, though. The back paddlers stood in deeper water when pushing off. I didn't jump quite fast enough and ended up with soaked shorts. We paddled out just as the fog rolled in. The rocks to our right floated in and out of view. Gulls perched on top like sentries and flew sorties over us. Moving at a good 4 miles per hour, our spirits soared. Today would be a breeze.

Then the wind and waves built and our pace slowed. From my drier place in the back, I did get some guilty pleasure watching the big waves hit the bow.

Chris grunted with the effort of trying to keep the canoe on a straight path. It didn't help that everyone occasionally stopped paddling to rest aching arms. The confused seas pounded us and we were losing steam. At a little more than 6 miles into the day, Chris turned into a beautiful sandy cove. We all breathed a sigh of relief. We landed and got out to stretch sore muscles and briefly explore. Thick tall marram (native beach grass) grew on the shore.

Whenever we landed, Nic would jump out to guide the canoe. This time he lost his footing and fell under our paddles. He came up sputtering ... and laughing.

Both of our guides were interesting young men. Nic had been in foster care almost since birth. Being in the wilderness and on the water gave him reasons to smile. A few years earlier, he had gotten in trouble with the law. Heading down a dangerous path, good fortune stepped into his life in the form of a young woman. Nic talked about Jenn Upton, a former guide at Naturally Superior Adventures, with near adoration. She met him in a mandatory program he was attending and introduced him to kayaking and the outdoors. His new life goal was to work with young people in outdoor settings.

Chris was much more reserved and had a deep voice not congruent with his slight, muscular frame. Chris was just four years older than Nic. We were glad they were both young; the rest of us were old enough to be their parents or grandparents.

We were a mile short of our day's goal and it was still afternoon, but it was decided that this would be our camp for the night. Everyone spread out. We pitched our tent next to a little channel separated from the main cove, which was called, ominously, Le Petite Mort – "the little death." The channel, created by low lake levels, proved a much better place to swim than the lake, being both protected and warmer.

After a picnic lunch, several of us walked to a Pukaskwa pit that Chris found as he scouted out this beach. These are ancient Indian sites, the purpose of which is not fully understood. They date to a time when the lake was at a much higher level. Today, the sites are large expanses of broken rock covered with green, gray and pink lichens. The forest grows around them, but the rocks are piled so deep that no trees can take root among them. They appear as large openings on the shore. As we entered this spot, we came upon a large round circle of stones at least three high, with a hole in the middle.

Though it cannot be confirmed, it seemed to be a ceremonial site. Some speculate that these places were used for vision quests. I could sense the spirits of those long-ago people.

Ruins of another kind were just behind our beach – a tumbled down fishing shack and a tall fireplace from a 1920s cabin. These made the inscription etched on the rock next to our tent even more mysterious. It said: "Frank Kucinich – Nov. 1920." Who spent time and effort to carve that? The old cabin site also had the remains of an outhouse where the "thunderbox" (outhouse without walls) was located.

The afternoon was spent lounging and swimming. Then like sleepy seals, we migrated to the hot black rocks down on the beach – a built-in spa treatment for sore muscles. Mike, Harry, Cindy and I were hanging out there when Nic and Chris showed up to ask who wanted to "jump off these cool rocks into the lake."

Lisa was nearby when I asked, "How cold is the water?" Warm, they assured us.

"How high are the rocks?" "Not too high," said Nic. Lisa and I decided to check them out.

We watched Chris and Nic jump a few times from a rock ledge. We chose a lower ledge. There were some rocks at water level, and we'd need to leap far out to avoid them. At the count of three, all four of us jumped.

An exhilarating rush, plunging into … water that was not cold! All four heads popped up at the same time. The boys whooped with delight. Having seen our success, Lin, who'd come over to watch, leaped in after us.

Besides having fun, I'd gained a little respect, it seemed. "I never would have expected Kate to do it," Nic said later, "but she was like, 'How high is it? OK, I'll go.'"

Tweaking the image of a grandmother with this teenager gave me pleasure, but one jump was enough for me and I swam back to shore. We left the boys and Lisa still jumping and yelping with each leap and went back to the black rocks. It was on one of these that Cindy used a small piece of chalky rock to write a bit of ephemeral poetry (found at the beginning of this chapter.)

Mike took this picture from our canoe of another voyageur canoe heading out.

While we savored happy hour, our guides struggled to get one of the Coleman stoves working. Mike gave them our Littlbug, a wood-burning stove, and it helped save the day and dinner. This wonderful little stove was given to us before the trip by its creator, Kent Hering. Designed to concentrate the heat of a small twig fire, it works amazingly well.

Lisa was the official "voyageur" on this day, so she got to go first for food. After dinner she conveyed the sash to Duane with great ceremony. "At first it seemed kind of silly," John admitted, "but now it seems really appropriate."

Cindy and Harry sat in the canoe. Harry couldn't sit easily on the ground – at 80 he was our group elder. Gerald joined them, and the rest of us sat on the ground in a circle. After dinner we shared stories about other trips and adventures, but as it got cooler we drifted off to our tents. On the lake, whitecaps frequently topped the waves, while behind us the yellow orb of moon crept higher.

Sitting on the shore of this vast inland freshwater sea in the dying light of the day brought reflections to the surface. This timeless, seemingly limitless space invited us to think about the scope of our enterprise, the opportunity to undertake this kind of once-in-a lifetime adventure.....and it felt wonderful.

The third day out, we watched the sun come up over the trees, and after a Romper Room "bend and stretch" routine with Miss Betty (aka Cindy), we loaded up and pushed off. The lake remained blissfully calm for the hour of our breakfast stop. At times like this, Chris relaxed in the stern, and we would hear him singing softly to himself.

Several loons came into view, and then a couple kayaks. One kayaker used to work at Naturally Superior and she was spending the summer paddling the Ontario shore. Her beautiful, blond-haired mom had joined her for five days. Their broad smiles reflected their pure joy of being together on the lake.

Chris wanted to get ahead of schedule because of the winds we'd been fighting. The kayakers told us we weren't far from the Pukaskwa River (the boundary of Pukaskwa National Park). Be careful of "the rollers," they cautioned. This was one canoe I definitely didn't want to roll.

We passed a high bluff and heard a peregrine falcon's call. Chris said they nested there and, as if on cue, the adult flew toward us. Cackling, it flew right over the canoe, then returned to perch on the rocks. The baby made a racket not far away. The moment seemed timeless. All along this shore, we felt we were seeing the world as the voyageurs had, completely wild and rugged.

We landed on a small, cobbled beach with a steeply angled bank. This was the eastern boundary of the park. Chris gathered everyone together and officially welcomed us to Pukaskwa National Park, and we cheered. This wasn't the best camping site, too many rocks, so we pushed back through the curling waves and paddled a short distance until we came to a sandy beach – the longest yet. The day was cloudless, with little wind, and fair-skinned John sought shelter among some scrawny evergreens with a tarp shelter. He named this campsite, appropriately, Little Shade Bay.

Mike took his Crazy Creek folding camp chair and sat under our tent's rain fly, which he draped over logs. It was shady and cool – a good place to hang out. Beth and Walt soon joined us. Then Walt said, "Look, there are four kayaks coming."

When they got close, I heard them say to Mike, "We heard about you. Your reputation precedes you ... Are one of you walking around the lake?"

"Yup. That's us."

The group was from Wawa. We didn't know at the time, but we'd be meeting them again ... at least Mike would meet one of them again – the doctor from the local hospital.

After a dinner of veggie burritos, I suggested we hold a contest to see what we could construct with the massive amounts of driftwood on this beach. I'd been inspired by the various forms of beach art we'd seen on our walk. Response was lukewarm ... until I started dragging logs to one spot. Gradually others joined in, and soon it was a group effort. The result was a dragon-looking creature as tall as me.

Cindy had been searching for heart-shaped rocks on this trip and she had an uncanny ability to find them everywhere. During the afternoon she had written a prose poem that she wanted to recite, especially since this was the last night all 14 of us would be together.

How to Find Heart-shaped Stones

Start out wanting to find a heart-shaped stone
and don't let yourself be distracted by other shapes or colors
or the particular gleam of a stone that's wet.
It will dry and go dull.
They all do.

Go where the better stones are,
and don't waste precious time and energy
where it is obvious they are unlikely.

Scan the surface, of course, but don't give up if the search becomes tedious,
as it often does.

Don't expect it to be presented to you –
expect to discover it,
to find one part sticking out amongst the others –
the pointy bottom or the right lobe, for example.
If it says "HEART" to you, go after it,
pick it up,
take it in your hand and decide.

Remember
there is no naturally occurring heart-shaped stone.
It is shaped by chip and roll,
friction and resistance.
It is hidden among the other stones until the day it is revealed
to you,
because
you were the one who hoped for it,
found it,
claimed it,
took it to yourself.

As natural a selection as ever there was.

Cindy would also spontaneously start singing at different times of day. Sometimes we'd join in; other times she serenaded us. Once while in the canoe, she made up a song about Michipicoten Island (off to our left) to the tune of "Little Boxes" sung by Pete Seeger. She dedicated it to Duane and Walt, who she said "have been complaining for days that all they see is this island in one form or another." Many a time as we plowed through the waves, we'd glance over our left shoulders at the Island and wonder if we were making any headway at all.

In the evening, Chris built another small beach fire, and we sat in a circle and talked and laughed and teased one another. The sun set behind the trees, and the mosquitoes came out. Gradually everyone left the circle except for Lin and me. We talked about her sister and the funeral she would be attending. She described the difficult treatment for the cancer that ultimately took her sister's life. I told her about my youngest brother, John, who died of cancer in 2009, and who was one of the people to whom we were dedicating our walk. It was a comfort to share the sadness of losing loved ones too young to that cruel disease.

At 3 a.m., Mike sat up to take pills, which roused me. A huge bright planet glowed in the southern sky, east of the full moon. I had to open the screen door to make sure it wasn't a UFO, which allowed the mosquitoes drooling impatiently on the other side to stream in.

Between mosquitoes biting me, worry over wind and waves, and feeling too warm and sticky, I didn't sleep much. The day began with the sun shining and waves crashing onto the beach. We pushed the canoe out a little ways and pretty soon the breakers were coming in over the stern. I started bailing, and then Chris joined me.

"You're going to have to paddle real good this morning," he announced.

I'd moved up one seat and sat next to John. A big wooden box pressed into my knee. Walt, sitting behind me, often stopped to take pictures or chat. Meanwhile Chris grunted and strained to keep the canoe aimed toward a far point. Swells rolled in at 4 to 5 feet. The canoe would rise up as waves slid beneath us. We kept far from shore for two reasons: One, to cut the distance, and two, to stay away from the waves that bounced off of land, which created even more confused seas. At times, when the wind kicked up, I'd think, "Please, Michipeshu, give us a break."

We reached the rocky point we'd been aiming at for 13 kilometers (about 8 miles) from where we started. When we slipped behind some big rock islands, a tail wind drove us. Finally able to take a break, I switched places with John. Chris rested a bit, and we all leisurely looked at the scenery. Suddenly Chris realized that he'd misjudged the distance. We were already at Otter Island! This is where the boat would pick up Lin and Walt.

We put the canoe into shore on a mix of pink and black granite cobbles. Since we were a couple hours early, Chris suggested a leisurely paddle to explore some nearby islands. No one said anything; they just started to wander off in different directions. Walt disappeared into the woods and came back holding the prize – an old lichen-covered caribou antler - the only sign we'd see of the small herd on this island portion of Pukaskwa National Park.

Eventually Chris got us back in the canoe and we paddled down the shore until we came to a passage between two islands and into Dave's Cove. We were alone except for a single powerboat anchored in the middle of the cove. As the canoe drifted into a quiet, tree-lined bay, I can say, in retrospect, that I felt a sense of unease. This island didn't feel as welcoming as our other beaches and campsites.

Otter Island, a speck of rock and forest, sits just off the mainland. A functioning lighthouse and former keeper's house perches at its high point. We landed near the white clapboard sided and red trimmed two-story assistant lighthouse keeper's house. There have been no resident lighthouse keepers for years, and the houses are now available only for emergency use by boaters.

Chris thought this would be the best place to wait for Walt and Lin's boat. Before long a small, round man from the anchored motorboat came over in his dinghy to chat. Bernie Clein was spending the summer cruising the Ontario shore. Weather forecasts didn't look good for the next two days, he told us. Big winds and waves were predicted to build all afternoon. Chris decided we would overnight on the island.

Everyone had gone up the narrow trail to the lighthouse, and on the way Cindy and I stuck our heads in the back door of the old wooden house by the concrete pier. The smells of must and mildew were overpowering.

Up at the lighthouse – a classic white-and-red-topped tower – we had great views to the east, south and west. The two nearby buildings were a concrete powerhouse and a second keeper's house – smaller, but newer looking than the one in the cove. It was unlocked and didn't smell as bad as the other. There was no electricity or water, but it was shelter from the windstorm buffeting the island and lake.

The area around the lighthouse was thick with spruce and fir trees, lots of sphagnum moss, lichens covering hidden crevasses, and cliffs. A wooden boardwalk got us safely from house to trail.

Mike and I sat on the rocks by the lighthouse for a while, pondering this turn of events. We were wind bound. Even though we weren't the leaders of this trip, we felt responsible for people's happiness, probably as a result of having led so many trips like this over the years. We went back down the trail, which was narrow and rocky with some downed trees. I found Cindy sitting by herself on the concrete pier, obviously angry. When Cindy complained about no place to stay, Chris said, "You can stay in a stinky house or you can find a place to put up a tent."

"The house up above really isn't that bad," I told her, and then gathered our gear.

"Let's get our stuff and move up there," Harry said.

"I'm waiting for the final decision," Cindy responded.

"This is the final decision," said Harry. Nerves were obviously fraying.

Nearby, Walt and Lin grew more and more anxious about their boat's arrival. The waves, still out of the west, weren't getting any smaller. I couldn't imagine how distraught Lin would be if she missed her sister's funeral. Chris went out with Bernie to his boat and with his radio was able to make a phone call. The boat was on its way, he reported. We all breathed a sigh of relief.

The trail up to the lighthouse included wooden steps, as well as roots and rocks underfoot. Loaded with our gear, it was slow going. Chris made lunch on the pier, but in the process hit his bare toe on a metal spike sticking out of a wood block. He was bandaging it when we came down for lunch. Ominous vibes seem to permeate this place. The hot, humid atmosphere in the windless cove didn't improve moods.

The chartered boat finally came into view. We'd all been joking about getting a "cold one" from any boaters we encountered. Bernie had already been approached on the matter. He had ice, he said, but no alcohol. Keith, the charter boat owner, answered our prayers. Without us even asking, he carried out a cooler and opened it like a true treasure chest. Everyone cheered at the sight of the glistening brown bottles of cold beer. Then it was time to say goodbye to Lin and Walt with hugs all around.

Big white clouds filled the sky, and it looked like rain, even though the forecast called mainly for wind and waves. Our crew was scattered, mostly reading or writing. Nic was in and out of the house near the light and found a place to jump off the rocks into the water.

I was sitting beneath a helicopter pad when I heard a peregrine's call. One shot out from the direction of the lighthouse, then banked and vanished over the trees behind me. I went back to writing, but when I stood up to get a new pen, I saw Chris, Beth and John all standing and looking out at some rocks off shore where gulls hung out. This is where the peregrine had gone to hunt.

We watched it chase one gull and attempt a dive, but it didn't connect. Lisa appeared and announced dinner would soon be ready. We all headed down to the cove.

Mike was still feeling slightly nauseous after eating. He'd used all of his antibiotics, so we hoped they worked. His legs were hurting, so he climbed into his sleeping bag. Out in the living room, the younger crew was noisily playing cribbage. Everyone planned to sleep in the house, except for Duane who had set up his tent next to the house. Finally around 8:30 p.m., when the light was fading, I went out one more time to "water the bushes." When I got back, Beth and Nic were brushing their teeth on the edge of the boardwalk. I wished them a good night.

It was around 10 p.m. and there was still some ambient light, but I fell asleep. Our sleeping bags were on the floor, since the mattresses didn't look all that appealing.

THUNK.

The sound woke me. At first, I thought someone fell out of bed. Another, louder sound followed. Mike heard it, too. At first, it sounded like hysterical laughter – Nic's. Then it seemed more crying and hysterics. I grabbed some clothes to throw on. Other people moved around in the living area, talking frantically. The horrible sound continued.

Down the hall, I found Chris with his headlamp on.

"What's happened?" I asked.

"Nic fell," he said, then was out the door to retrieve the first aid kit at the canoe.

"Put this under his leg," I heard.

The scene was a chaotic, surreal sight of headlamps flashing off the walls and stunned faces. On the floor was Nic. One quick glance showed a bloody face and disheveled clothes. Cindy and Lisa were kneeling next to him trying to offer comfort.

"He's been wandering all night, trying to get back here," Beth said. The thought filled me with horror and nausea; my watch read 4:40 a.m. I went back to our room and told Mike.

Shortly, I returned to kitchen area with our solar water bottle, which has internal illumination, to help provide a little more light. When I set it on the counter, I got a better look at Nic, sitting on the floor, with his legs stretched out in front of him. His face was covered with cuts and dirt, which Cindy delicately tried to clean with a washcloth. I knelt down by his left shoulder. He was not screaming anymore, but occasionally would start to hyperventilate and we'd try to calm him down.

Putting my arm behind his back, I inhaled the smell of fear, blood and the essence of loam and fir branches that he must have pushed through to reach the house. It was a smell that planted itself in my brain.

"I'm sorry, I'm so sorry," Nic repeated, turning to me and to Cindy. It was an accident, we kept telling him. "You didn't do anything wrong."

Chris returned with his first aid kit and started to unpack it. He mixed a saline solution to irrigate Nic's ankle wound, which was a mass of blood, dirt and bits of green vegetation. As soon as Nic realized what Chris was going to do, his panic rose.

"No, Chris, don't do it! Don't touch it! DON'T!"

But the wound had to be irrigated, in order to clean it and to assess the damage. Nic launched into horrible screaming and swearing. Most of us rarely find ourselves in situations where people are in excruciating pain, and we don't know how we'll react. All I could do was close my eyes and squeeze his hand. My mouth was dry and my heart was racing.

Finally, calmer after the irrigation, Nic said, "Will my knee be OK?"

We didn't know, but we assured him it would. Sports, especially football, were bright spots for Nic, the one socially acceptable activity where he could shine and receive approval and admiration. At the time we didn't know that he'd broken his kneecap, but his left leg was a mess. The knee was badly swollen.

Cindy, who had been gently wiping the blood from his face and softly cradling him against her side, asked someone to spell her. I thought I heard her say, "I have to go throw up." The fresh air revived her and she came back and resumed her care – gentle, tender and consoling.

Nic had on shorts and a T-shirt. "We've got to cover him up," I said, thinking of shock. We put his fleece jacket over his chest. Lisa found a sheet to put over his legs. Cindy was on his right side acting like a human radiator.

"I'm so sleepy," he kept saying. "I just want to go to sleep." But we had to keep him awake; we didn't know if he had a concussion, but strongly suspected so.

It was amazing, I told Nic, how he found his way back. "I was just going to brush my teeth," he said several times.

It broke our hearts to know how hard and long he'd been trying to get back to the camp. He'd been calling for help, crawling and dragging his left leg. Drops of blood on the cement walkway leading to the house tracked his slow progress. We couldn't find where they started, but apparently he had crawled up from the ravine. He'd been out there for at least six hours. We assumed it had rained because the rocks were slick and his clothes were damp.

Nic's terrible pain continued, and so did the screaming. I asked John to take my spot, then I walked over to Mike, who was near the front door with Harry and Beth. I put my arms around him, needing his solid warmth to still my trembling limbs. At his advice, I went to find something warmer to wear. Back in our room, we both sat staring at the window, willing daylight to arrive. It was 4:50 a.m. and the moon was still the only source of light.

From the other room, we knew Chris was still trying to clean Nic's wounds and stop the bleeding. Nic's screams continued. "You're hurting me Chris. STOP! Don't!" I finally had to cover my ears. No matter how many first aid courses I've taken, I was not prepared for hearing such pain.

Daylight finally arrived and the screaming stopped. We went to see what we could do next. Chris had pushed the 911 and Help on his SPOT unit at about 5 a.m. He asked us to do the same to make sure someone got the message. Then he and Mike put both of the SPOT units on the nearest helicopter platform, where we hoped help would arrive.

184

Mike & Kate

Our family crew: Alyssa, Aren, Kate, Annalise, Matthew (in Mike's lap) with arm on Ryan and Kate's mom, Ann Crowley at Canal Park Lodge before leaving.

Kate grins and bears near Thunder Bay

Mike's inner bunny with mullein ears

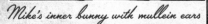

Holding a 'swamp candle' & Grandma and Annalise

Front: Duane Johnson, Mike & Kate; standing: Lisa Cassioppi, Gerald Wichmann, Jane Wichmann, Harry Carlson, Cindy Carlson, Lin Pomeroy, Walt Pomeroy, John Oehler; back: Beth Oehler, Chris Tompkins and Nic Olner.

Wisconsin Shores

A pack check near Port Wing

Sea caves in the Apostle Islands National Lakeshore

Commercial fishing in Bayfield and a stroll along the sandy beach by Cornucopia.

We take a lunch break above the sea caves. • Clay and sloping trees become Kate's nemeses. • Paddle and an Indian pipe plant. • Spring storm waves in Superior.

Michigan Shores

Pollen turns the water yellow at Bete Gris. • Waterwalking in the Keweenaw. • An interior arch collapse in Pictured Rocks National Lakeshore.

A local fellow told us it was clear passage but that included a fence climb near Ontonagon. • The tree challenge at Little Traverse Bay.

Keeping our feet dry north of
Ontonagon. • A formation at Pictured
Rocks. • Taking a break on the way to
the Fourteen Mile Point Lighthouse.

Ontario Shores

Exposed Canadian Shield in Lake Superior Provencial Park. · A tenacious tree on Goulais Peninsula. · Carefully inching toward the pictographs at Agawa Bay.

Yes, Ontario trails are like this vertical challenge on Casque Isle Trail. • A wet shore walk between Gros Cap and Goulais Bay. • Nature reclaims the tracks. • Big rocks between Red Rock and Hurkett.

Minnesota Shores

Hammo guides us through the Slade property near the Caribou River. • A bundled-up Kate on our first day out. • A Lake Walk island view southwest of Judge CR Magney State Park. • The north and south piers in Duluth.

Kate picks her way along the cobblestones at Grand Portage Bay. · The familiar, friendly welcome of Duluth's arched icon — the Aerial Lift Bridge.

Rocks & Sands

Water ripples the sand on this beach while gray slate dotted an Ontario shore. Spotting rocks that churned the imagination is part of the joy of beach walking. We found a target, an alien footprint and an underwater landing strip.

Polished by glaciers · The
pictographs at Agawa Bay show
the Horned Lynx called Michipeshu
and other intriguing images.

Kate clears the path
on an Ontario beach.
· Who was watching
whom on the beach in
Michigna's Keweenaw
Peninsula?

Flora

Varieties of fungus
flourished in the forests
around the Big Lake. ·
A fritillary settles on a
Joe Pye weed. · Edible
roadside attractions —
raspberries.

Black-eyed susans. · A monarch butterfly on a hawkweed and lakeside hawkweed and fireweed near Rossport, Ontario. · A Lake Superior Provincial Park wild rock garden of sundew and butterort — both carnivorous.

Fauna

Black burnian warbler • spruce grouse • a spectacular buck taking a dip on Siblely Peninsula.

From the top and clockwise: a green frog, a red eft, a red squirrel, that swimming deer (see facing page), a garter snake, hermit thrush eggs and a sandhill crane.

People

Crossing the International Bridge between the Sault Ste. Maries. • Our SAG wagon team, Amanda Hakala and Sheena. • Artist Ellen Van Laar of Ontario with her distinctive artwork.

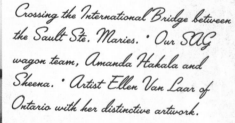

Bill & Beth Blank with Kate in Michigan. • Our grandchild Annalise with her dad Tray Carlson on the International Bridge Walk

By now Nic's head was bandaged. His right eye was a big black smudge. His legs were covered, but the bottom of his left foot was exposed with a bandage on it and blood around it. He was awake and responsive; he could wiggle his toes, which we took for a good sign.

Mike and I went down to the canoe to get cookies and roust Bernie in his boat to call for help and to call Naturally Superior Adventures. We moved very cautiously because the trail was slippery, and we didn't want to add to the day's drama.

In the cove, the wind blasted through the channel opening. Bernie's boat was shut tight. We tried yelling, but didn't get a response. We'd have to wait until he woke. It was 6:30 a.m. when I got the cookies from the food box and walked back up to the camp. Mike waited to get Bernie's attention.

When Mike got on Bernie's boat, they discovered that the satellite phone got a signal only once every hour for a total of 15 minutes. Thus frustrating hours of trying to get help began. First, Mike contacted Naturally Superior, thinking the people there could make all the necessary calls. But the primary staff was off campus and a teenage housekeeper took the call. She told Mike to call 911. "No, you have to get in touch with someone and get the message out," he told her. Then the connection went dead.

Bernie had moved his boat to the opposite side of the bay to get the best reception. When the next signal came through, Mike called the police, who said to call the Coast Guard. He called them and, once again, the call ended abruptly. An hour later, he got the Coast Guard again and they said he had to call the National Park because they had received our signal. Finally, he was able to get some information to Pukaskwa National Park personnel and began to

describe the wounds but they only heard about the broken ankle and then it cut out. By this time Mike thought he should to go back and see what was needed at the house – he just hoped the rescue was now on its way. Back on shore Mike walked to a high point to see if help was on the way, but he could see neither boat nor helicopter in the distance. Park staff tried their rescue boat first, but encountered 9- to 12-foot waves and had to turn back. Finally a helicopter was called into service.

Rugged cliff shores made the "water portage" necessary on this part of our "walk."

"I smell chocolate chip cookies," Nic said when I returned to the house.

We all laughed. That had to be very good sign. He didn't get cookies, but we gave him water and electrolytes. He was mostly lucid, repeatedly saying, "When are those paramedics going to get here?" and "I wish they'd get here."

"They're not coming," he finally decided. We assured him they were on the way. The sky was totally clear, but the wind blew hard and the waves grew huge.

Nic was sitting up, draped in the red sash Beth had bestowed on him, making him our voyageur for the day. Cindy and Chris, on either side of Nic, made sure he didn't fall asleep. Each time he closed his eyes for a few minutes, they'd urge, "Nic, wake up," or "Nic, say 'Boo.'" Sometime Chris would whistle loudly. "I'm up man!" Nic would say. Or simply repeat, "Boo!"

Then he surprised us with a joke. "What did the one strawberry say to the other strawberry? … If you weren't so fresh we wouldn't be in this jam."

Everyone laughed and felt more optimistic.

I brought out the Crazy Creek camp chairs for Cindy and Chris. They had been sitting on the hard linoleum floor for hours. Lisa arrived with freshly made coffee. "Anyone want Scotch in theirs?" I asked.

"Yes," said Chris. I gave him a good splash; he needed it. I did too, and put a splash in my cup. It was nearly 9 a.m. When would the rescuers arrive?

Standing outside with Duane, John and Harry, three peregrines shot over the tops of the trees. One flew out and hung above us, silhouetted against a deep, deep blue sky. We wondered aloud how they could do that in a wind of 20 knots or more.

Inside, Nic was lying on the floor, resting. We still woke him up periodically. When Chris and I sat with him, we somehow got talking about tattoos. That woke Nic up. He animatedly talked about getting his first at age 13 with a friend – the Patriots banner on the inside of his bicep. His goal was to make his arm a sleeve of tattoos.

When Cindy returned, Nic said, "They're not coming for me."

Many times he said, "I'm so sorry. It was such a stupid thing to fall."

Then he said, "I don't want to leave you guys."

We didn't want him to leave either, but this was one very, very lucky kid, I thought. It was a miracle that he was sitting there alive.

I was back in our room when Cindy said, "Listen, I think I hear something." From the bathroom window I could hear a helicopter.

"They're coming for you, Nic!" I announced and went outside. The copter came into view high over the trees, flew past us and circled around the island. When I went inside to tell them, Nic started to cry. Cindy told him to keep crying and that she intended to cry when he left.

As soon as the copter set down, three men jumped out. In the house, we filled them in on the details, and they evaluated Nic's injuries. Cindy got up and walked quickly back to her room, making good on her promise. I followed her. "He's going to be fine," I said, putting my arms around her. "We gave him the best treatment possible."

"I know, but I just feel so bad for him being a motherless child," she said with tears streaming down her face.

"He must have someone who cares for him to have turned out so well," I replied.

Mike was over by the helicopter talking to the pilot and I joined them. The message they'd received said Nic just had a broken ankle. They weren't expecting anything more serious. They were from Pukaskwa National Park; two in dark blue jumpsuits with "Initial Attack" on the back were firefighters. One of them came from the lower level of the house carrying two 2-by-4 boards. Grabbing a chain saw out of the helicopter, he put on protective gear and proceeded to cut splints.

They carried Nic in a seated, legs-out position. He had a neck brace on and was holding it on either side. We all stood by as they put him in the helicopter. Then the lead ranger called Chris aside and spoke quietly to him. Chris called us together. Did we want to continue the trip with him as our guide? "Of course," we told him. We had complete confidence in Chris, though I wondered if our reduced crew could provide enough paddle power. With Lin and Walt gone and now Nic, we were down to 11 people. Could we cover the distance with wind and waves out of the west? The lake was 20 degrees warmer than usual for this time of year and warmer water means bigger waves. No one else shared my worries; everyone else felt we could do it.

Before the helicopter left, the park ranger asked us again if we felt OK to go on. We did.

"You can call us if you change your mind," he said. I laughed at that, explaining we had no way to communicate except through Bernie in the cove.

We filed back to the helicopter to say goodbye to Nic. "Enjoy the ride," I told him. He managed a wan smile. Everyone had a kind word for him.

The blades began to rotate as we drew away. Soon the whine of the engine increased, and they soared away with Nic at the window, waving with his left hand.

"You did good, Chris," I told him as we watched them go. He turned, put his arms around me and hugged me tightly. He had handled a tense, desperate situation with great competence and calm.

With the crisis past, people started talking about breakfast. It was 10:30 a.m. and we all trekked downhill to the cove as Chris offered to make eggs. We sat down on the pier, then Chris said something about making coffee and disappeared up the trail. At 11:30, Beth and Lisa went to see if he was okay. Soon they all came back down. Chris had changed clothes and, not surprisingly, needed some moments alone. Our breakfast turned into a delicious lunch.

Bernie came over in his dinghy and wanted to know what had happened. We filled him in, but before he left, I asked if we could use his sat phone again. I wanted to get a message to our family and neighbor Dick, in case they got a 911 signal message or help message. (Our unit did send an alert to our contacts, it turns out.) We got satellite coverage and my mom answered on the second ring. I tried to deliver the message quickly. Then I asked Chris if he wanted to call Naturally Superior Adventures, but he said he'd already reported everything.

After lunch and the call, most of us went up for a nap. Mike tried sleeping with his legs propped up on the bed. John tried to sleep after he'd cleaned up bloody newspapers and such on the floor. People seemed to be doing really well considering the emotional roller coaster we'd been on. We were all relieved that Nic was in good medical hands.

All day the seas built up, crashing in huge white sprays and gushing over the off shore rocks. The water became a deep navy blue, and the swells were dangerously big for any small boat. We ate dinner outside on the concrete walk – too many flies and bad memories inside. Then we sat around, talked and laughed, a therapeutic reaction. We raised our wine glasses before dinner to Nic and Chris. Beth suggested we go out and brush our teeth together in honor of Nic. We didn't, but it was the sort of black humor that often develops after a traumatic event and helps to break the tension.

The next day, the seventh of this paddle, marked three months on our walk, even though we were not walking at the moment. Cindy and Harry were packed and ready to go by 6:30 a.m. Cindy hoped to get going before the wind picked up, but even as we carried things down the hill, the ever-present wind was building.

By 9 a.m., whitecaps topped the waves. As the others had finished carrying things, I offered to sweep and straighten up. It was eerie being there alone. Nic's cries haunted this place now. I felt the drama unfold again and was all too happy to close the doors on La Maison Blanc Avec Rouge (as Cindy had christened it) and to leave Otter Island behind. To me, it will always be a haunted island. Others before us had left business cards. I tore a page from my little notebook and left a message, "Be cautious when going into the woods, because crevasses and cliffs are hidden everywhere."

Back at the dock, I learned that Bernie had gone. I was sorry I hadn't been there to thank him. After breakfast, we got the big boxes in the canoe, and Chris went up to look at the lake again from that vantage point. "Whaddya think?" someone asked after we'd waited silently for a moment. It didn't look good, Chris said. After we finished loading up, he added, we'd cross to Cascade Falls and to see what happened.

Next we had to find someone to take Nic's place, someone who could set the pace and jump out to land us safely. That ruled out most of us.

"OK, Duane, you do it," Chris appointed him. Duane was a good paddler and agile, though close to our age.

After paddling out a little way – then back to retrieve a daypack left behind – we turned toward the channel past the protection of the island and felt the full force of the wind and waves. Cascade Falls was across the channel from the island and the waves broke on our left side. Chris worked hard to keep us headed straight despite the rollers. We could see waterfalls tumbling down the face of the rocks at the base of a cobble beach. We pulled in close to the rock wall on a small sandy landing spot, disembarked and walked to the waterfalls.

Three kayakers landed soon after we did: two women, one man and a dog small enough to ride in the cockpit. The woman asked if we knew about Bill Mason's cabin back in the woods, then told us how to find it. Bill Mason, a Canadian legend considered the godfather of canoeing in the country, also produced the "Paddle to the Sea" film. Apparently the cabin was one of his favorite spots. It turned out to be a tiny, roofless log structure about the size of a tent.

The forecast for the next day had the same bluster as today's, according to the kayak woman. Chris briefly talked about pushing the Help button on the SPOT so a boat could be sent for us, as the park ranger had suggested when they took Nic. Then he directed us to set up camp, and we searched for a sandy spot among the cobbles.

After lunch, Cindy, Jane, Beth and I took a cooking pot next to the waterfall for a private shampoo party. The water felt cold, but invigorating. It was great: just us girls in our shorts and bras, the sun shining down and the wind blowing us dry.

"You know," Cindy said, "the thing about trips like this is you learn how little you need to live with, but for me, feeling clean is important and having a toilet to sit on, even the thunder box, is something I really appreciate."

Later I was in my tent writing when I heard Beth and Lisa inventing games with rocks on the beach. They'd tried bocce ball with the round rocks, but they wouldn't roll in the sand. Next they started throwing rocks at another rock, scoring points if they hit it. All the men were in the tents sleeping, except Duane, who was reading, and John, sleeping in the shade.

I joined Beth and Lisa. We took turns trying to hit the rock. We modified the game for our version of HORSE, which in this case was ROCK. Beth, the rock queen, won most often. Then we switched to STICK. We stuck a beaver-chewed driftwood, about 4 inches long, into the sand and braced by rocks. Then we tried to knock it down. If you knocked the stick completely down, you won. I'm proud to say, I was the stick queen.

I started throwing rocks at a log floating in the water close to shore. Our grandson Matthew came to mind; how he loved this kind of activity. He would be screaming, "Get 'em! Shoot 'em!" I told the others this as we all tried to pelt the log. The thought sent Cindy into hysterics until she said, "Oh, I'm going to pee." All of us roared even more, which didn't help Cindy's situation. By now, the four of us were bent over, holding our sides with tears coming out of our eyes. Cindy, when she could talk again, said the thought of all our careful game rules tossed aside to "kill" the log struck her as some weirdly hilarious version of *Lord of the Flies.*

After regaining our composure, we made little piles of rocks and Stonehenge creations. Later Beth said it was the best happy hour she's ever had. Cindy, too, admitted she hadn't laughed that hard since college. Maybe it was just a delayed reaction to the traumatic events and near tragedy of the day before. Through all the screams and laughter, the guys never budged. I went to the tent to drink my last little Bacardi Breeze. I savored every sip and shared it with Mike. Then he invited everyone to our tiki bar, aka our tent, to share some Scotch.

By 5:20 a.m. the next day, we started packing under clear skies with a chill in the air. Loons called as we shoved off at 6:50. It started to get windy, but amazingly the wind stayed at our back. It was our first full-morning paddle with wind and waves behind us. After a quick stop on a small sandy beach around 8:30 for breakfast, we paddled until 11 a.m., still running with the wind.

We made another landing at White Gravel River to explore. Some of us walked down the shore, others up the river. Mike was botanizing with a group when they spotted a young garter snake. At the shore, I found Cindy and Harry looking for heart rocks. Out on the lake I could see whitecaps beginning to form. Later, as we pushed off, I tried to hop in butt first, but (or butt) missed. I tripped and half fell into the water. The sunny day dried me quickly; no harm done. We turned the canoe north and entered the wavy main waters.

The whitecaps continued to build, and though the waves weren't over a meter, they were big enough to lift and push us forward. Chris used all of his 175 pounds to steer the big boat full of big people. He turned the canoe toward what looked like a large inlet, but turned into a large, deep cove with a fabulous white sand beach backed by forest. Fisherman's Cove was about the prettiest spot we'd seen. The water was Caribbean clear lapping over a sandy bottom.

"We're staying here," Chris announced. The waves were too big for us to continue, plus we were back on schedule, so no need to push. I picked a tent site with shade on two sides, but facing the bay for breeze. Later in the afternoon, sitting on rocks in the shade with all the women, I asked Lisa to tell me about the night with Nic.

John had heard and seen Nic first. When she awoke out of a solid slumber, she saw a figure in the doorway. The sound reminded her of Nic's laughter, but it momentarily scared her. Then Beth and Cindy came out. Nic had been standing near the doorway, waiting and saying, "My ankle, my ankle, I've hurt my ankle."

Chris woke up and put his headlamp on to shed some light. John only had a small flashlight, but they could see Nic's ankle was badly damaged. The right side of his face and his right eye were also bloody; the eye was swelling. John said that when he shone his flashlight at Nic, he almost went into shock himself. Cindy and John (though neither remembers the other being there) got on either side of Nic and helped him into the house while he cried hysterically. Beth got a sleeping pad for him to sit on, and they got him leaning against the kitchen cabinets. They weren't sure where his leg was cut, but it bled a lot. When the paramedics moved him, there still was a pool of blood on the bag.

It was hard to talk about that night, but it helped to hear people's different memories. Our conversation roamed, and we watched as Mike and Duane reappeared from the trail. Mike walked straight into the lake with his shorts and shirt on; Duane ran into the lake in his black Speedos. Chris woke up, got Mike and the two of them came down the beach toward our "women's camp." Gerald was sleeping in his tent. Harry had gotten up from the ground and moved into his tent. John was sleeping somewhere. If you've ever wondered about life for shipwrecked sailors on deserted isles, there you have it. We relaxed the rest of the day and through the night.

At 6 a.m., Chris "knocked" on the tent. I hated to wake Mike, since he was finally sleeping, but it looked like we were going to leave early again. Mike got out his green solar/crank weather radio to hear the morning report. We resembled scenes I've seen of people during a World War II blackout gathered around the old Motorola radio for news of the world. The weather report produced by Environment Canada is in both French and English. The forecast sounded reasonable, so we loaded up and set off. The water was completely calm in the cove. As we reached open water, Mike announced that we'd reached 1,000 miles on our walk. Everyone stopped paddling and lifted their water bottles in a toast. Duane documented the moment with a photo of everyone from his place in the bow.

Then we got into open water waves. They weren't whitecaps yet, but the swells lifted us up and down. Chris was working hard. We made good time with the running seas, but Chris turned us into a hidden bay and beach to take a break. Here in Fish Harbour, we saw two kayaks, a tent and campfire. A white-haired man appeared from the trees and came to talk to us.

Kim Ransom and his wife, Leslie, live in Marathon, Ontario. Their son was one of the guys in the rescue crew that came for Nic. We learned he had been airlifted to Thunder Bay, because his injuries warranted the larger hospital. They also described the team's shock when they saw Nic, having just expected a broken ankle. This discussion may have been too much for Chris; he walked away down the beach.

We all headed out on a nature walk. The trail took us through a lush forest with moss-covered rocks, lichens and ferns everywhere. Mike loves to look at mushrooms and small plants, so he shared what he knew about the growth on the rocks and the forest floor. When we got back, Chris was sipping coffee at the Ransoms' campsite. We waited at the canoe until he finished, then we took off again. Chris wanted to reach our scheduled night campsite, but I questioned that once we got on the big water. Between the whitecaps and bigger swells, Chris was waging war with the canoe. A pair of kayaks appeared up ahead. Mike and I wondered if they might be the two young Minnesota men, Lucas Will and Greg Petry, who we'd met before leaving on our walk. They had undertaken a trip they called "Superior Dream" to kayak around the lake. "Kate and Mike?" one of them yelled. We couldn't stop to chat, but Mike wished them well.

The Ransoms had told Chris that the Willow River campsite, where we intended to stay, was closed. Park staff were working on it, but Chris still turned the canoe into this big bay. The wind and waves disappeared as we paddled toward a wide sandy beach. Chris wasn't sure if we would stay there. First he needed to check with the First Nation crew working on campsites, the trail and a suspension bridge over the river.

After listening to the radio and talking to the work crew, Chris made the call to stay. While we set up our tents, the Ransoms paddled in. It was another afternoon of idleness. Cindy and Beth went to sit in the shade to read and write. I soon joined them. Mike entertained himself by making beach-grass twine. He braided 27 feet of it. It looked nice, but it wasn't very strong, as he and Gerald found out when their tug of war ended with broken twine and Gerald on his back. The work crew found Mike's twining fascinating and they had a good conversation about First Nations in the area.

As the afternoon wore on, we played a game with a large baseball-size, round black rock – another castaways' diversion. Before our game, Beth put the three remaining wine bottles in a cleaning bucket with water to chill. When happy hour began, we cheerfully drank the last vino of the trip.

Earlier the Ransoms had issued an invitation to roast marshmallows at their place, so after dinner, Jane, Gerald and I wandered over. Kim is a tall man and Leslie is small, about my height and close to the same age, but with an enviable girlish figure. They enjoy a comfortable retirement and do a lot of biking and kayaking in the summer.

As we toasted our marshmallows, Kim talked about the lake being 20° F warmer than it should be for this time of year. "It's scary. You see how the lake is out there right now?" he said, referring to the calm surface. "That's how it should be in July. There could be 10 days in a row like this." The waves for this time of year were an anomaly, he was saying. And this summer they had seen people playing and swimming in the water; normally Leslie could hardly bear to get wet.

The next morning was supposed to be our last in the canoe, and anticipation rose with us in the morning. We loaded up and left by 7:20 a.m., after our last bend and stretch routine. A pair of loons called in the distance as a parting gift.

As we paddled out of the bay, I was already apprehensive; I could feel the wind building. When we got past the outer rock, swells rose and whitecaps loomed ahead. The waves were coming from behind, but angled so they to hit our side. The swells got bigger and though none broke over the bow, they were close and dumped water in the back of the canoe. That's when Chris decided to turn around. Everyone's spirit dropped as they paddled halfheartedly back to the beach.

Lindsey Moses, one of the Ojibwe (or Ojibwa as it is in Canada) park workers, saw us come back. He came over to take our photo and chat. The 59-year-old said that 50 to 75 percent of the Pic River people his age speak the Anishinabe language. His grandchildren were learning it in school and from grandparents; a much different situation than in many Ojibwe communities on the U.S. side. While Mike talked with Lindsey about Indian language and culture, the rest of us sat on the beach and stared at the lake, wondering what would happen next. Chris listened to Mike's weather radio, then got his SPOT unit and pushed Help. He had reached his limit with this weather and the large canoe. We were under the impression that Keith (the man who had picked up Walt and Lin in his boat) would be able to come get us, and Naturally Superior Adventures would handle retrieving the canoe.

The maintenance guys had a radio Chris could use to contact the park staff to make sure they knew we needed help to get out. Chris relayed the message, so our hopes were up.

Mike, Chris and Gerald visited with the park employees and came back carrying bulging plastic bags filled with chicken, bratwurst, potatoes, cheese, meat sticks, juice, bagels, cereal and bacon. When Mike realized the work crew was leaving, he knew they had a treasure in food. Chris didn't think we needed it, but who knew how long we would really be here? Mike was thrilled with the haul and talked about how long we could stay now. There was a distinct lack of enthusiasm among the others. "We've got to get out of here today," John kept saying. Most everyone except us had schedules to keep and jobs waiting. This was the day they expected to end the trip.

Suddenly a white boat appeared from behind the rocks. It looked official, but it didn't look big enough to carry all of us. It headed toward the river mouth, where the water was deeper and the park crew waited. They got onboard with their gear and took off. Not long after that, Keith's aluminum boat appeared from behind the rock outcrop. Again our hopes rose. Chris thought the boat would pick up some kayakers, then come back for us, but he and Gerald went over to talk to Keith about the plans. After conversing, Keith reversed his boat. He couldn't take us because he couldn't tow the canoe. There were going to be some unhappy campers with that news. Chris decided to wait to see if the lake would calm down later in the day or by tomorrow morning. The radio forecast didn't sound good for either option.

This would test the group's true cohesion and cooperation. Emotions were high, and though we still had enough food for days, people were psychologically done with the trip. It was hard to keep a dark cloud from forming. Chris tried. He put up a tarp in the Ransoms' campsite, which still had a fire going in its pit, and cooked a tasty lunch.

Good food always lifts spirits, but a long afternoon and evening weighed on our minds. The stress of the past few days was causing Chris to withdraw. The group dynamics grew more complicated. Mike, who has led groups on adventures for more than 30 years, recognized the strain. When the park boat returned to pick up the last of the workers, Mike gave them three written messages: have Naturally Superior Adventures send the shuttle this afternoon, in case we made it in today; have it stay overnight if we don't; and send a rescue boat tomorrow if the winds remain bad.

After lunch, I went for a hike with Mike along the rocky shore on the left side of the bay. We met Duane, and he walked with us out to the end of the rock point, where we found a survey marker. From here, we could feel the full force of the wind and see the waves and whitecaps below us. The sun was shining, so the wind felt good, but the waves were too big to paddle. We made our way across sloping rock faces and boulder beaches and took off our shoes and socks to wade across the mouth of the river, which was narrow and thigh-deep.

Keith's boat returned. Mike, Gerald and Duane went to talk to him. Chris had walked over that way earlier. The rest of us watched from

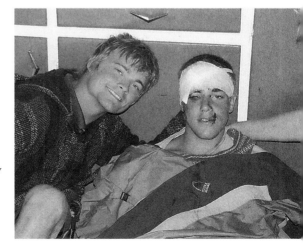

Guides Chris Tompkins and Nic Olner await the helicopter rescue.

the beach, speculating on what would happen. As the boat backed up, Mike and Duane walked back toward us, while Gerald watched from shore. I joked that Chris had gotten on board to leave. Turned out it wasn't a joke. He was on the boat! In order to get reception to call Naturally Superior he needed to go a mile out into the lake. With Chris gone, everyone's frustrations and angst came out.

Mike tried to offer options. He wanted a consensus of what the group wanted. We decided to tell Chris we preferred to leave tonight, but if we couldn't, we wanted a pick-up at 9 a.m. tomorrow if we couldn't paddle. We had our decision set, but Chris already had a decision when the boat dropped him off. The answer: "Wait and see."

Chris had been told to see if we could paddle out tonight or tomorrow morning. If not, he could push the help button in the morning. This seemed too open-ended and did not sit well with the group. They wanted the pick-up in place right now.

It was time for dinner and sadly there would be no happy hour tonight, when we most needed it. We had finished the wine the night before. (Note to future expeditions: Always keep a spare bottle of wine for emergencies.) Mike happily cooked the bratwurst on the fire pit, plus two cans of baked beans and hot dogs. There were four buns and 10 brats. The group of 11 decided Chris needed a whole brat – and it became something of an issue with the testy crew. Mike offered to cut up a few brats so everyone got some and Chris could have a whole one. Beth and Cindy volunteered to give up theirs. Mike said it wasn't necessary. "But Chris has to have a whole one," Cindy countered. He would, Mike tried to explain, but somehow it didn't come out right. Cindy smacked her plate down. "I don't want any," she said and stomped away. (Note to Mike: Let people be generous if they want to be.)

Chris shared news of Nic. His kneecap was broken and he needed knee surgery. His head was OK and there was no word on his ankle. Chris reported that Naturally Superior Adventures called everyone's emergency contacts to let them know of our delayed return.

Delays due to being wind bound on this big lake are not at all surprising, though there did seem to be an inordinate amount of wind on this journey. All of the participants had been told by Naturally Superior in the pre-trip documents that this sort of thing could happen, but we are a people conditioned to having things work out our way or having someone fix problems like this. It was an unfortunate situation, but one that couldn't be avoided.

We set up our tents on the beach not far from where we stayed the previous night. Chris walked off to watch the water from the rocky point. A group went to play a rock and stick game. I didn't feel like socializing and sat at the tent near Mike. The most disappointing thing was to have the trip end on a less-than-positive note. It had been challenging, but people would have felt good if we had been able to paddle in today. More than any other time on our trip, I realized that Lake Superior makes the rules.

Chris came back. He planned to get up at 4 a.m. to check the lake and wind. If it looked like a go, he'd make coffee and wake us. If not, he'd let us sleep and would push the HELP button for a pick-up. All night, I heard the wind gusting.

The next morning, I lay awake in the tent, listening to the waves roll into our little bay. Somehow they sound so much louder when you can't see them. Mike got up at 6:30 a.m. to get coffee. I came out shortly after that. Both Duane and John told me we were going to go.

The sky was solid gray, and the lake looked even darker. I couldn't see any whitecaps, but I'd lost faith in our ability to get out. Others staggered out of their tents and headed to the coffee and tortillas with peanut butter and jelly. We took everything down and put it into bags for the canoe. I looked at Mike and asked where his necklace was, the one with Lake Superior etched into it that I had given him before the trip began. He looked back with a blank stare. I hadn't seen it in the tent as I had other mornings. We took the tent out of the bag and each stuck our head inside to look for it. No luck. I wasn't sure I'd seen it on him yesterday. We both felt sick about losing the necklace. Not that it was terribly expensive, but it already had sentimental value. All I could think was that somewhere in that great sandy beach a necklace was waiting for a new owner. Still, I wasn't ready to give up. I returned to our tent site. Standing there, I turned, looking in the four directions. On the sand not far from my feet was the black leather string with the silver pendant. I called to Mike, then thanked Michipeshu for any help it had given. The day seemed brighter and our chances better.

When we were about to get in the canoe to push off, Chris said he needed to say something: If anyone felt at all uncomfortable when out on the water, tell him. It was very important. I was uncomfortable already, but didn't say anything. With no objections, we pushed out for the last time from the Willow River campsite and turned our bow toward the big water. Swells began before we even got out of the bay. The wind was coming off the land for the first time; it was a good change. The swells, it turned out, were left over from the previous day's wind and they weren't too high. There were no whitecaps, but every two or three waves lifted the canoe up.

Cindy started singing. "It's boys, it's boys, it's boys that make the world go round. It's boys, it's boys, it's boys that make the world go round. … Oh rolling over the ocean, rolling over the sea, rolling over the ocean and the deep blue sea, oh, rolling …"

She got through two verses before stopping. Usually Cindy's singing lifted my spirits, but I was too anxious. Up ahead I saw large white marks. They were not whitecaps, but large boulders sticking partially out of the water. The waves bashing against them made the white splash. Five kilometers into the paddle, I was feeling more confident we could make it.

As we neared the end of a drink break, the bow of another voyageur canoe suddenly appeared, flying the North West Fur Company flag from the stern. An older, gray bearded man appeared to be gouvernant. Their canoe splashed into the big waves (which had grown whitecaps). We couldn't imagine how they made any headway. They paddled into the distance from which we'd just come.

We reached Hattie's Cove at 10 a.m. and cheered when we hit the beach.

"Free, free at last!" Harry said as he stood up. Naturally Superior staff were there to meet us and offer us plates covered with sliced cantaloupe, oranges and cookies. Owner Dave Wells appeared, cheerfully telling us how he'd been looking at his watch for the last three days. Many in our group responded positively. We unloaded our gear. By way of thank you, I gave my Crazy Creek chair to Chris, who seemed sincerely touched by the gift.

After the canoe was unloaded, Dave directed us to haul it up on the beach, turn it over and put it on the rack over a trailer. He was itching to get the thing delivered to the next group who was starting in Rossport and going to Red Rock. Whether this was the normal procedure at the end of a trip with this boat we didn't know, but the staff couldn't do it by themselves.

Gerald and Jane had their minivan delivered at Hattie Cove, so they loaded up their stuff. We all said our goodbyes. Mike drove Naturally Superior's 15-passenger van and Chris drove a pick-up truck with an extra-long trailer attached. It was a long ride back to Wawa on Highway 17; I was so thankful we didn't have to walk that stretch – our obligation paddled away. At White River, our group bought us cold A&W root beers. This town is the home of Winnie the Pooh, and we took photos under the statue of the pudgy yellow bear. The original female cub, named Winnipeg, was acquired by a British soldier and eventually ended up in the London zoo. It was here that author A.A. Milne and his son, Christopher Robin, first encountered the bear, which would become the inspiration for the storybook classic.

Back at Naturally Superior Adventures, we scattered to unload our gear and get our cars. Then we ate a delicious lunch of soup, grilled cheese sandwiches and a great corn/bean salad. I pigged out. Mike and I headed to the Mystic Isles Motel after everyone left.

Would we do a trip in another Voyageur canoe on Lake Superior? No. Are we glad we did it on this trip around the lake? Definitely.

During a very challenging 11 days, we were surrounded by great people and amazing scenery. We experienced the lake as the toughest voyageurs did in the past, with only our muscles to propel us. We understand much better now the absolute power of the lake. We adjust to its demands; it does not adjust to our schedules. Only this kind of trip could humble us that way. Along the route, we dipped our drinking bottles and cups into the lake and drank freely of the cold, clear water. This was the most wonderful lesson of all – clean fresh water still exists on this continent. In drinking from it, we affirm the need to keep it always so.

The journey of a thousand miles begins with a single step.
Lao Tzu

After Thoughts
Climate & Lake Levels

Mike:

Traveling around Lake Superior was easier for us in 2010 than it might have been in other years. We faced a minimum of bad weather days, the insects were never maddening and we knew that if we could get to the shore, we could legally walk to the "normal high water" line without trespassing. This becomes more difficult when the normal high water line is half way up a cliff, but for most of Wisconsin, Michigan and up to Montreal Harbour in Ontario, this fact made life much easier for us.

Our low-water benefit was also the bane of some Ontario shoreline property owners – in many places their docks were so far from water that you could walk to the end of some and jump onto bare, dry rock. This was especially apparent in 2010 on the Goulais Peninsula, where we found the breakwaters, docks, boat launches and boat houses many meters from the water's edge.

It was also obvious that this was not a one-year event. To compensate, the Ontario Ministry of Natural Resources had allowed some cabin owners to create channels to get their boats in and out.

In fact, as it turned out, 2010 was a recovery year from low-water levels. Minnesota Sea Grant reported: "In 2010, Lake Superior's water level has returned to its pre-2006 level. From 1998 to 2007, however, lake levels dropped steadily until they reached near-record lows in 2007."

In 2007 Minnesota Sea Grant published a story in its newsletter that put a lot of perspective on the lake levels, saying that "Since 1998, Lake Superior has slipped to the shallower side of average."

The article, credited to the Sea Grant staff, pointed to two main reasons for the lower water level: Less precipitation and more evaporation.

In 2007, precipitation had been short by about 6 inches across the Lake Superior Basin, the article continued. Since the winter was also warmer than average, Lake Superior was left without much ice cover. Although Lake Superior rarely ices completely over, when it has little or no ice cover in winter, it is susceptible to mass evaporation – a consequence of such a large surface area. As the article pointed out: "Contrary to what one might guess, Lake Superior evaporates fastest from October to February when dry cold air from Canada moves over the warmer surface of the lake soaking up water like a sponge. The ice works like a lid on the big Superior jar and when it is left open, the liquid meets the air and the air moves it out of the basin. When the lake looks like it is boiling in the winter time, it is the action of water changing to vapor and is normal up to a point."

The article further pointed out that "for at least the last 150 years, Lake Superior has lost and gained massive amounts of water (on the order of 20 cubic miles) while maintaining a remarkably even water level, varying only about four feet." That has been changing and water levels have reached record lows – this despite the additional water being diverted into Lake Superior from two Ontario dams, stealing essentially from Hudson Bay. Since 2007, the conditions have not changed appreciably– the U.S. Army Corps of Engineers in 2011 said the lake was 9 inches below 2010 and the winter of 2011-12 was abnormally dry and warm by most anyone's standards.

The term watershed describes the area where water collects and moves into another water body – whether a lake or river system. For a body as large as Lake Superior, we might anticipate a gigantic catchment basin, but in fact it has a very narrow feeder area of about 50 miles from its shores.

Dr. Rich Axler at the Natural Resource Research Institute, the University of Minnesota Duluth, explains how to judge the size of a watershed by measuring the total watershed, water area to lake area ratio (Aw:Ao). According to Axler, Lake Superior has a ratio of 2.6 compared to Lake Michigan at 3.0, Lake Huron at 3.2, Lake Erie at 4.0 and Lake Ontario at 4.4." So despite it having the largest surface area – and more water than all of the other Great Lakes combined, Lake Superior's watershed is relatively small.

John Flesher, an environmental writer for The Associated Press, in 2007 wrote, "Preliminary data show Superior's average water level in September dipped four centimeters beneath the previous low for that month reached in 1926."

As we traveled around the lake, people would say, "the lake always fluctuates, it will come back," but, in fact, Flesher noted in that article that the "lake has plummeted over the past year and has dipped beneath its long-term average level for a decade – the longest such period in its known history."

We were not in a position to measure the lake level on our walk, but we could observe what the lake looked like. In some places, it was quite disturbing. Low water level affects so much more than whether a landowner's dock reaches the water. Even big industry, like maritime traffic, can be affected by lower water levels. Losing an inch of depth can mean tens of thousands of tons of lost cargo capacity in a year. As Sea Grant reported: "a one-inch (2.5 cm) water level drop can mean over 250 tons of coal will be left on the dock when a thousand-footer weighs anchor. A two-foot drop means that upwards of 6,000 tons, approximately 10 percent of a thousand-footer's capacity, will be left behind. Hydro-power plants, like those by the Soo Locks, also run at a diminished capacity with less water."

On a smaller, but culturally significant scale, wild rice and fish spawning can be affected. To Ojibwe tribes around Lake Superior, wild rice (manoomin) is "the food that grows on water" and that fulfilled a prophecy of where they would find a home in their migration from the east. The Bad River Band of Lake Superior Chippewa, for the first time in its history, canceled its rice harvest in 2007 because the low-water levels reduced the rice crop.

Water levels are not the only concerns. The natural fisheries of the lake are impacted by many factors, including toxins entering the bays from industry discharged before regulations curtailed pollution. Those toxins remain for decades in the water or soil – and in the fish. Reduced water levels concentrate the toxins. As the water warms, too, we fear fish spawning might be affected by toxicity and temperature. These factors, coupled with the history of overfishing and the arrival of the predatory sea lamprey, already strain some fish species, like the great sturgeon, which can live to more than 100 years and grow to more than 5 feet. Meanwhile, the wetlands needed for fish production were so dry on our trip that we walked through many of them without getting our feet wet. This is also habitat for birds, turtles and other wetland species. Wetlands are natural filters, but they cannot filter the water if the water does not reach the plants.

Our concerns are for the indigenous people of the lake, the resident land owners and recreationists, the fish, the quality of the water, the economy and the natural landscape. The argument over global climate change is getting old and in many ways it is foolish. Whether from "natural" or "artificial" causes, we can observe changes. There is no reason not to take action to reduce our impact where we can. We need to prevent damage to our fresh water and our air. We need to think about the future and not debate whether humans can create a change in the climate. If nothing else, we should agree that we can change a regional environment just as we can create a Chernobyl melt-down, a BP oil spill in the Gulf of Mexico, Hungarian toxic sludge flows and Bhopal plant explosions.

We fiercely believe we should put the future of our grandchildren and the planet we will leave them as first in our priorities. Starting with the care and keeping of Lake Superior is a wonderful way to begin.

THIRTEEN
True North

To say that Lake Superior is the greatest of the Great Lakes is to say much, but it draws no picture of the vastness of this haughty queen of fresh water.
Pretty Tall Water Here, Shipwrecks and Survival, W. Ratigan

Kate:

This stretch of the hike we call True North. We've driven around the lake a few times, but this east-west section from Marathon to Nipigon never made the impression that it did as we walked it. We reached the pinnacle of the lake's north, the top of the wolf's head if you like. Once this portion was completed, we would be traveling only south.

We started this stretch with a trip to seek medical help. We decided to go to the Wawa hospital to get steroid shots in Mike's knees. He was told not to do much walking for the next 24 hours, so we spent the rest of the day taking it easy at the motel, catching up on emails and doing other computer tasks. I made another visit to the grocery store and bought a container of spreadable maple sugar. When I asked the young checkout guy about its uses, he declared it "awesome," especially on crepes. I also found a bottle of sauce to mix with avocados for making guacamole. That was awesome, too. We ate it with chips and salsa as we watched an old 1960s film starring Michael Caine. It felt absolutely decadent.

Driving back to Pukaskwa National Park the next day, we were again grateful that we didn't have to walk the highway all the way from Wawa. Amanda was at the park visitor center when we arrived, and the RV was parked in the campground. Amanda told us that our friends Dan Bisson and Ellen Van Laar had stopped by. They were camped just around the corner. Dan invited us to share dinner, which included a big pickerel (the Canadian term for walleye)

216

that Ellen had caught. Sitting at a picnic table, we savored a few bites of the excellent fried fish, salad and fire-cooked potatoes when raindrops began to fall. We quickly loaded everything in the car and returned to the RV, where we ate and talked until after 9 p.m., when the rain finally let up.

The next morning, it was mostly cloudy and looked like more rain. We packed umbrellas and rain jackets and hefted our daypacks, which felt unusually heavy. Mike estimated the day's trek at 12 to 15 miles, but we were both feeling confident and ready to walk again after nearly two weeks of paddling. Amanda dropped us in Marathon, and we began our walk back to Pukaskwa.

Starting at the post office, we walked residential streets until we came to Pebble Beach. What the Canadians call pebbles, we would call bowling balls, given the size of the stones on this beach. Big, noisy waves lapped the shore, as the water glistened a gorgeous aquamarine. It wasn't easy walking, but pleasing to the eye and tempting, too. As avid rock pickers, we wanted to pocket these great round and oval stones in soft pinks and grays. But the thought of carrying an extra 10 pounds all day in a backpack tempered our desires.

We climbed a slope through vegetation and the smell transported me right back to Nic's accident. Labrador tea – he must have lain in, or pushed through, a lot of it. I clearly recalled the scent, and it gave me a moment's shudder before we moved on.

At the top of the path, we surveyed the rocks we most love – beautiful, sensuous rocks, smooth and curved like the backs of whales sliding into the water. In the deep blue August sky, puffy cumulus clouds coasted above the lake. The roaring waves crashed and splashed onto the shore.

We continued farther down the shore as Mike assured me there would be another path back up to the railroad track. I was skeptical, but we did find one and took it. Running parallel to the lake, it brought us back to another bay. Mike's GPS showed the road and railroad to our left. He found a path used by off-road vehicles, and we followed it to a gravel road. Another path through the brush brought us out on the railroad track.

We quickly discovered that walking on the track ain't easy. Ties are not spaced for any normal human's stride.

The rocks surrounding the tracks were chunky and pointed. I tried in vain to find flatter places alongside the tracks. Sometimes a wide avenue of vegetation made for easy walking, but it didn't last long.

Lunch was enjoyed on a nice outcrop of rock alongside the track, covered in bearberry with bright red berries and dark green leaves embracing the stone. A family of chickadees came down to investigate, but otherwise it was just a peaceful spot to eat.

Our ears were tuned for any distant train sounds, but the dull roar from the lake made it difficult. When I finally heard a new sound and realized it was a train, we hustled off the track. The engine came around the bend, and the engineer saw us and blew his horn. I couldn't see if he was smiling or scowling, but it was one long, loud freight train.

By now Mike was limping, and we stopped to rest more often. We only had one walking pole each. I hadn't brought both of mine because I thought if it rained, I'd need one hand for an umbrella. After we got off the track and onto the road, I gave Mike my pole. This day convinced us that walking train tracks was novel and sort of fun, but we wouldn't choose it for long distances.

We passed Heron Bay. At the end of it was a big cement factory. Sitting down, we did a point count (part of our continuing surveys) and let Mike rest his legs. Next we heard some loud engine noise and up popped two ATVs with guys wearing reflective work vests and helmets. They drove up as we were starting to stand.

"What're you doing?" they asked.

"Walking." Mike said and then asked if they knew where the Voyageur Trail was.

They said they'd just driven up from it, "but it's a long ways yet."

"Oh yeah, how far?"

"Gotta be a good kilometer yet!"

Then we told them we were walking to Pukaskwa. They looked at us in friendly disbelief. They were doing brush cutting and trail work for a gold mining company. A geologist bought up the mineral rights to a bunch of land and had plans to sink a mine into the rock under the water of the bay. It sounded like a bad idea to us, but we kept that opinion to ourselves. They said it was still a few years away before anything would be done.

A little farther on, a yellow vehicle approached us on one of the tracks.

"OK, now we're going to get busted," I thought.

As it slowed down, I prepared for a lecture, but the guy just leaned out and said, "There's a train coming on that track in about 10 minutes."

We thanked him as he went past, followed by 10 to 15 similar work cars. They were mostly open air and used for rail maintenance. We waved at them and smiled. A pair of ravens trailed the last of the work vehicles, squawking and flying back and forth.

We stopped to talk to a pickup truck full of railroad employees. The guy driving asked if we'd been "up fishing."

"No. We're walking around the lake."

"Holy wah!" he said (or something like that). Then he looked at us and almost involuntarily started, "And you aren't …"

"Young?" I finished for him.

"Yeah," he said, a little sheepishly.

By the time we got to the crossing, Mike had to stop every 50 feet, lean on his poles and try to bend his knee. My feet and hips were feeling sore, too, so we were both slowing down. The "water portage" may have affected us after all. Mike thought it was still 6 miles to the park. With the clouds getting thicker, and sprinkles beginning to fall, we made it to store on the Pic River First Nation. We ducked in and asked the owner if we could bring in a couple of the chairs from the porch.

"Sure," he said. He and a woman were chatting at a table at the far end of the building. I bought a Nestle's turtle ice cream bar; nirvana. Mike got a Diet Pepsi. The man asked more questions and we told them about our walk.

"God bless you," the lady said.

Outside it was pouring. While we waited for the rain to stop, another Pic River man came in. It was John, one of the park crew who Mike met at the Willow River beach on our canoe voyage. Recognizing Mike after a moment, John asked how we were doing. Soon his son came in carrying John's grandson, a darling chubby baby.

The rain let up, and we set out again, with 3 or 4 miles to go. It was agony for Mike.

Girls came by on bikes and slowed down to ask, "Are you Mike and Kate?" One worked at Pukaskwa and had helped on our survey forms. They told us we had about 3 more kilometers to the visitor center.

At the Pic River, we took another break. Since the rain had stopped, it had turned into a beautiful day for sitting outside, even on the curb of a bridge. And we'd take any excuse to stop and rest our aching legs.

As we reached the RV, the GPS said 15 miles exactly. We both collapsed onto the picnic table bench. Obviously, this had been overly ambitious for our first day walking again. But even with the discomforts, we were happy to be back observing the shore with our feet on the ground.

I waddled down to the showers and couldn't figure out how to turn them on. It had the same push button as others, but nothing happened when I pushed it. Three preteen girls were using one other shower. I tried three more with no luck and asked for help. The girls went in, pushed the button harder and it came on. Duh!

I had brought along a plastic pan and foot-soaking salts and filled it after the shower. A couple arrived to do dishes while I was sitting there.

"Long hike today?" the woman asked.

"Yeah, really long – 15 miles." Then I figured I needed to translate to kilometers and paused to do the math in my head. "Ah, 25 kilometers. We walked from Marathon."

When I came back from the shower, Mike was on the bed moaning, shaking and quaking. He tried a variety of positions, none comfortable. He finally fell asleep around 9 p.m. and slept nearly 10 hours, a new record. There was no way to figure out this problem of pain at night. He could rarely sleep on his side, so he was left with his back or stomach.

The next morning on our way to Marathon, we stopped at the Pic River First Nation office. The Ojibway of the Pic River are an extension of trade settlements here for thousands of years. By water from here, native people and later traders would reach James Bay and, ultimately, Hudson Bay. According to the First Nation's website history, fur trading with the French started here in the 1700s, and a permanent post was set up by 1792. The river is also the halfway point for paddlers crossing along the northern shore of Lake Superior.

At the office, we discovered the chief and manager were both on holiday, but we met the financial officer and others. We explained what we were doing and mentioned meeting the gold miner guys. They seemed to know about them. Nothing could happen, the officer said, without the First Nation's approval. That made us feel better. Before we drove away, a young woman came rushing out. She gave each of us a keychain with the Pic River name. It was a friendly gesture and would be a reminder of the people whose traditional lands we'd been crossing.

The next stop was on the Voyageur Trail at Marathon, which is a dead end, but we decided to follow it and double back to cover that area. The day brought sunshine, a few clouds and just enough wind for comfortable walking. We started on a smooth sand beach, then took a trail through the woods to a smaller bay. The shore ahead appeared to have steep slopes. We decided to try it since we were accomplished rock and cliff walkers by now.

We got across one stretch of rock and Mike heard his name being called. He thought it was me, but it was Amanda. She and Sheena had taken another trail out to the rocks. At one spot, it was hard to tell what was around the corner so Mike went ahead to look. He came back and had to act as human steps, letting Amanda and me use his shoulder and thigh to brace ourselves as we inched down from a high rock ledge. These severely slanted rocks had large crystals in them, making it much easier to get a grip with the rough soles of our boots.

Once around the point, we were back on rounded, gradually sloping rocks – those "whale-back" rocks I love. We spotted yellow and orange in the leaves of the mountain ash and birch. It seemed awfully early for leaf changes, but Mike pointed out that we were at the most northern section of our journey. I wondered how much the change had to do with the dryness and heat of the summer.

A small semi-palmated sandpiper stood motionless on the rock, barely moving as we walked past it. Bird calls were diminishing daily. We were hearing the drawn-out call of white-throated sparrows a week ago, but now they were absent. A winter wren at the campsite and some mergansers in the water were other notable bird sightings.

The smooth rocks we traversed were polished by glaciers many thousands of years ago. I sat down on the sun-warmed surface and noticed an area chipped or flaked away, exposing the "raw" rock before it had been polished. I imagined this gradual slope of rock on a rainy day and what a great slide it would make, though probably more fun in my imagination than in reality.

After Amanda and Sheena turned back to get the car, we continued along the shore rather than on the gravel road. It looked easy, but we didn't see all the inlets, which kept going farther back and taking more time.

A lot of lime green algae grew on the rocks – a definite indicator of warmer water with organic matter in it. On the far side of the bay was a decommissioned pulp and paper mill, the reason that the bay is loaded with mercury and is a Lake Superior Binational Forum Area of Concern. The sparkling blue water masks the toxicity. Luckily the bay has a fairly small opening, so the water does not flush easily into the Big Lake.

At a deep inlet, we veered to the gravel road, then to a train track, finally switching to dirt roads and back streets as we got close to Marathon. On the main street near the library, we saw Amanda and Sheena. She had been driving around looking for us and was going to the phone booth to try calling.

After lunch Mike and Amanda went to the library to work on the Internet. I went to the Laundromat. I sat inside, while I waited for the clothes to dry. A gentleman working on the lights commented on the nice day and mentioned how it had been foggy in the mornings. We talked about the lake. He'd come from Edmonton, where the water is swampy. He'd lived in Marathon for 20 years now and could still go down to the lake and be astounded by the clear water. We talked about the temperatures. He told me that the bay hadn't frozen the previous winter. It even rained in January.

Around 6 p.m. Amanda dropped us off on Highway 17. We walked next to a little stream – Mink Creek – that paralleled the road, still hoping to get a glimpse of a moose. When we reached the car, Mike decided to drive ahead to see how far it was to Neys Provincial Park, where we'd be walking the next day.

Outside the Neys store, a beautiful husky was parked near the door. A young man came out and started to get its leash. "Beautiful dog," I said and asked if he skijored with it. No, he hadn't tried it, and the dog was getting less interested in pulling as it got older. He asked if we were the ones walking. He'd been talking to Mike inside the store. He, his wife and baby were paddling a canoe on rivers and lakes across Canada. They had been doing it in a sequence of years. Last year he got cancer and had to take a break. They had stopped at Neys because they had gotten wind-bound – something we were now familiar with thanks to our own canoe trip. I can't begin to imagine canoeing across Lake Superior with a baby less than a year old. He told Mike the mosquitoes had been horrible farther west, and the baby had been bitten badly. (In 2011 we heard from some Canadian friends that they had resumed their quest with their 18-month-old son).

At Neys the next morning, we started our trek on the beach toward the Volcano Trail.

Neys Provincial Park, located between Marathon and Terrace Bay, juts out into Lake Superior and includes Pic Island. The park features sub-arctic plant life and a caribou herd. Used as a prison camp for captured German soldiers during World War II, today the park's visitor center has a good exhibit describing that piece of history.

Neys' beach was like others we saw with a huge amount of fine-wood material dried on the beach and floating in the water, making it look black and

The rocks near Marathon are among our favorites because they look like the backs of whales.

soupy. We crossed a few streams, then got to the trail for the geology walk, where there were long, sloping rocks with a unique formation of syenite, a course-grained igneous rock. These rare rocks evolve from a specific mixing of the magma that occurs when it comes to the surface. It's easy to see the gouges in the rock created by boulders dragged over the bedrock at the bottom of the glaciers. There were parallel lines of these scrapings, now smoothed and rounded by water and waves. Signs describing the geology extended about a kilometer down the shore. These rocks had different textures and patterns from others we'd seen, including some large, chunky, angular boulders that we had to clamber over. Mike was in heaven, exclaiming over various formations and explaining what the signs also described. He thought it was the best geologic trail he'd ever walked.

We found a sign for the Voyageur Trail and got onto a forest path. It weaved back out onto the rocks, then returned to the forest, crossing the streams. Then we were back on the beach. It was already after 3 p.m. and we decided to do the last stretch of beach the next day.

The next morning, Mike and I walked the beach out to the Little Pic River. At the mouth, an osprey soared overhead, circling before flying off. Then it returned, tucked its wings in and plunged into the water. It came up with a fish. When the osprey flew to a far tree-covered hill, we thought that was the last of it, but it returned to look for another fish.

The day was perfect: Blue, blue sky, white cottony clouds and a slight breeze. We started walking near Little Fox Lake, where we found the invasive species, purple loosestrife, growing along the edge. When you think of invasive species, you think of something ugly, which purple loosestrife is not. Unfortunately, even these pretty flowers devastate the landscapes they invade because they do not fit into the natural balance. They've degraded our wetlands and native plant populations since they arrived in North America in the 19th century, probably in ballast water from European ships.

The variety of rock exposures, lakes, cliffs, and forests made the next two hours of walking pleasant. We met Amanda on the road and took a break in the car with socks and shoes off and legs elevated.

After finishing our day's walk, we headed to Rossport, a lovely little town on the Schreiber Channel. I could easily live here – at least in summer. It resembles a small seaside fishing village, with houses clustered on a slope that drops down to the water's edge. Flower gardens are abundant and, except for the freight trains that pass through, it has a quiet, idyllic mood. Scattered offshore is a cluster of forested, hilly islands, ideal protection for people who want to sea kayak on Lake Superior, but don't want the thrill or risk of being exposed to the whims of the Big Lake. At the Rossport Inn, we met Ned Basher, who allowed us to stay in one of the little cabins Friday night for free. Chris Tompkins (our lead guide or gouvernant from the canoe trip) was at the outfitting shop, not far from the water. We had warned him we would be coming to visit, so we got out snacks and beverages, and Chris brought down cold bottles of beer to share.

The next morning was sunny and felt like it would be warm. The only breeze came from semis blowing past on the highway. We found more purple loosestrife, and Mike noted its location for our invasive species survey. The high-pitched screech of a couple broad-winged hawks caught our attention. One circled around and around. Mike was entertained by all the good rock exposures, including some quartz with flecks of a mineral like gold.

We crossed over the Steel River, where a new bridge was being built, then walked up a long hill to a shady spot for lunch. Around 1 p.m. the phone rang. Mike Simonson from Wisconsin Public Radio in Superior called for an interview. My Mike sat down on the side of the road and talked, then I got on and told the story of Otter Island. Mike Simonson was a regular radio contact on our walk. We appreciated the effort he made to keep track of us for his listeners.

Before we got to Jackfish Lake at the base of a long downhill slope, we passed a gravel driveway and a red pickup with the front door open. As we passed the truck, the man asked, "Where you headed?"

"We're going to Duluth," I said, which brought the usual surprised look.

His name was Bo. After I explained what we were doing, he said, "You're getting fit." Mike's knees weren't, I replied, but at least he'd lost a lot of weight. Mike ended his phone conversation and got into a discussion with Bo, who was from a First Nation in Nipigon, but also from the Grand Portage Band of Ojibwe in Minnesota. Bo worked for a construction company building the new bridge and was waiting for a delivery of steel.

At the bottom of a hill with a 400-foot descent, we approached the two little motels across from Jackfish Lake, which is really a long narrow bay of Lake Superior. We decided to make a pit stop, but there was no public bathroom in the motel with the café. Amanda met us and since the car needed gas, we drove to Terrace Bay to take care of both needs.

Back at Neys Provincial Park where we were staying, we took showers and ate dinner at the picnic table. The Can-Op store was nearby, so Mike and I went there and spent the next hour and 45 minutes connected to the Internet. Outside a thick fog had rolled in, and Mike decided to walk the 2.4 miles back to the campsite – in his sandals. Big mistake, or so I tried to suggest, but he said he'd be fine. I drove back to the campground at 10 p.m. (an hour later) and Mike was just arriving.

Near Terrace Bay, the next morning, we found a path off the road that took us by houses and into an area that looked like the old downtown with a series of shops connected to one another under a small overhang roof. The town itself didn't come into existence until 1947 and now has about 1,700 people. Forestry has historically been its main industry. On our walk through Terrace Bay, we saw many backyards with clotheslines. It was one of the most visible differences we saw in Ontario. They were ubiquitous and it was amazing to me that so many people still dry clothes this way – ecological and economical. Along this northern shore of Lake Superior, people lived in smaller houses and worked hard to keep their yards neat, tidy and attractive. Flower gardens abounded. The longer we were in Ontario, the more we understood Canada as truly a different culture, though we share a language, a continent and, in this case, a lake. Our two months walk here reaffirmed our positive feelings toward their way of life and friendliness.

At the Terrace Bay Visitor Centre, we found Amanda. Since it was lunchtime, we headed to the Drifter's Roadhouse, a place recommended by Gerald and Jane from the canoe trip. It was dark inside, with ceiling fans spinning. In true Canadian style, the entry display case held hockey shirts with the names of Gordy Howe and Bobby Orr.

We were expecting Tobias Tan, our volunteer webmaster, to arrive that evening. He planned to spend a week with us. In 2009, Tobias took a January interim course that Mike taught on wolf and lynx ecology for the Audubon Center. Tobias, originally from Singapore, was truly inspired by his experiences along the shores of Lake Superior. He is a genius in many academic subjects and is especially talented in computer technology.

Tobias offered to create and maintain our website – a gift we could never repay. Now, as a student at the University in Edmonton, he made arrangements to fly to Thunder Bay, where Todd Starling generously agreed to pick him up and deliver him to us. They arrived later in the afternoon, with Todd's wife, Carolyn (another former student of Mike's), their baby, Sierra, and dog, Teva. We'd be having a lot of company for the next few days.

The next day it was nearly 11 a.m. by the time we got to the Aguasabon Campground near the Aguasabon River falls and gorge. Todd and Carolyn were already setting up their tent at their river site. Ours was close to the road and driveway, but also close to the bathrooms. We were ready to leave, but Todd and Carolyn still needed to make lunches and get their baby ready.

We still seemed to have the uncanny ability of starting to walk just as the rains come down. This day was no exception. Not too far along the road, the skies opened up. Todd, though disappointed, decided not to join us. It was too complicated – and too wet – to bring the baby. They would hang out and relax at the campground.

The falls and gorge were impressive, even in low water. The Casque Isles Trail, wide and grassy, ended at a beach. It became a narrow footpath with lots of vegetation and rocks. As we emerged on a small sandy bay, it stopped raining long enough for us to sit on a log and eat our sandwiches. Then the rain picked up. We moved back into the woods, continuing to another bay with a beach of loose, wet boulders. Walking on a wet rocky surface was new for Mike and me, but for Tobias, walking on any boulders was completely new. Mike and I moved along a bit slower than normal, but still faster than Tobias and Amanda. (Admittedly, it felt good to keep up – even slightly ahead – with younger people.)

The rain let up, and we came to a number of broad beach terraces of old rock just like those in Pukaskwa Park – more Pukaskwa pits. An abundance of fat, sweet blueberries slowed us down, but eventually the trail traveled through a couple more secluded, sandy bays and more boulder-strewn beaches. Up and down rocky forest trails, we marched single file. At one spot, we had to climb down a hand-built wooden ladder. Amanda did it one handed with Sheena gripped in her other arm.

The forest was lush with fern and moss. Tobias rattled off their Latin names. A single white-throated sparrow cheeped at us. We walked to the sandy beach, but this would take us to some cabins, so we bushwhacked back to the trail, which was wide enough for an ATV.

At camp, Todd prepared dinner. They generously brought several boxes of fresh vegetables. In the RV, Mike was kneeling on the bed, which was more comfortable for him than lying down. Soon we headed to dinner and found sautéed zucchini, plus salmon and potatoes cooked in foil.

By now, Sheena the rat terrier had accepted Mike and me into her family. Tobias was a different matter. Even Amanda had a hard time restraining her whenever Tobias came into the RV. Not much bigger than a large cat, she has the soul of a Doberman pincher.

It rained hard during the night and the morning fog was soupy thick. Change of plans – we decided to go to Terrace Bay to wait until the fog cleared. Then we would walk the road beyond Rossport and save the Casque Isle Trail and shore for nicer weather.

Tobias Tan negotiates the railroad ties – spaced specifically to keep walkers off, Mike insists.

I was sitting in the car at the Terrace Bay Visitor Centre and library when a young man arrived with a fully-loaded bike. He set about putting together his single burner stove on the picnic table. I got out and asked about his bike ride. Cory had nearly orange hair and freckles scattered across his face. His friend, Andrew, a tall fellow with curly black hair and, not surprisingly, muscular thighs, had a smile that exuded self-confidence, bordering on cockiness. They were from California and had been riding since June, starting from Maine. Few bikers ride east to west into the prevailing headwinds. These two intended to board a train in Winnipeg for Jasper, Alberta, where they would continue biking to the west coast of Canada, then down to California. They'd camped – illegally – in town overnight and had to get up early so as not to be caught. The thick fog had delayed their start.

After lunch, the fog lifted and the sun broke through the clouds. We headed to the Rainbow Falls/Rossport campground and chose a site close to the lake and away from Highway 17. Back to Lakeshore Drive, we started walking. There was little wind, lots of humidity, and it felt close to 90° F.

The second home we passed had a barking golden retriever and two people sitting on a deck. Joe and Kathy were friendly, interested in what we were doing and helpful, telling us about possible alternative road routes past Rossport.

On the shore, we negotiated a mix of cobbles, boulders and smooth rock shelves and were soon sweating. I took off my shirt, dipped it into the lake and put it back on. Once I survived the initial shock of cold water, it felt good whenever a breeze blew. Mike took off half his clothes and lowered himself into the lake. It made me shiver just to watch. Despite the heat, the lake here remained chilly.

We met up with Amanda close to our campground. Tobias had kept busy in camp and opted out of the day's first section. He asked what the second part would be like. As often happens, we didn't know, but we knew we'd walk it regardless. Tobias decided to join us.

For 2½ hours, we traveled over and around rocks. After 4 miles, it was taking a toll on Mike's knees. We passed many people swimming in the lake and felt the same urge, but settled for scooping water into our caps and dumping them over our heads.

Once in Rossport I told Mike he shouldn't walk any farther, but I could keep going. I knew just how much he was hurting when he agreed to my suggestion. So I got out my iPod, took the GPS unit and walked out of town for the last 2 miles of the day, a stretch of highway with a long uphill grade. Cars and trucks didn't seem to be moving over for one woman walker as they had done for two of us. Then I met Mike walking uphill. "Dammit," I thought. "I told him I'd walk, so he could give his knees a rest." When I told him as much, he said, "I'm cooling off," then, "I could feel my legs stiffening up, so I needed to stretch them." Not good excuses. Amanda walked up behind him and said, "I told you so."

We drove back to the park and took nice hot showers and ate dinner. I weighed in today and was back to 138.3 pounds. Mike weighed less than 200. No fair! Mike had taken a slug of pills and was lying crosswise on the bed with his feet up. I worked at the picnic table with my computer, and Tobias was at the back of the RV getting some things out of the back. All of a sudden, he said, "Whoa."

"What's the problem?" I asked.

"Something just fell," he said. It was the plywood board beneath the mattress on which Mike was lying.

Amanda looked at it, upset. I knew she was concerned about making sure the RV returned to her mom in good condition. The screws apparently had given out. I suggested bracing it with something. Amanda thought it would be better to screw it back together. But first we'd have to take the mattress off. It turned into a tiff between us as we each held to our own best solution. We continued to disagree, with tempers rising until Mike calmed things down by saying he would figure out what to do.

This may have been a good distraction; his back had been killing him. Mike found a park employee who cut a piece of 2-by-4 to use as a brace. Amanda and I settled down after that. After living in close quarters for three months, some tension was no surprise.

The next morning came with clouds and the threat of rain. Again, it wasn't a good day for the Casque Isles Trail. We were back to road walking and leapfrogged along the route, covering it all eventually. Tobias put on his headphones, because he didn't like the roar of cars and trucks on the highway. Mike and I walked along, talking, he moving a bit slower than usual. It started to sprinkle, then sprinkles turned to rain. I put up my umbrella, and Mike put on his raincoat. Our Granite Gear backpacks had handy built-in rain covers.

On one very long hill, the trucks lumbered by and had to gear down to make the climb. They crept along barely faster than we did.

The rain stopped before we got to the Pays Plat First Nation, where Mike spotted some good amethyst veins in a rock face beside the road. This reserve seemed quite small; there was a store on one side of the road, houses on the other and a small wooden church across the Pays Plat River with a modest cemetery spotted with plain white wooden crosses. A sign said Mass was offered the first Sunday of every month.

Tobias, an avid geocacher, knew from his GPS of a geocache up a side road. He veered off, and Mike and I stayed on the main highway. We were headed uphill again, and the rain returned. Amanda met us with the car, and we climbed in to eat our sandwiches.

Mike found another amethyst vein and we stopped to look before resuming our walk. Tobias hoofed it up the hill to catch up. He'd found the cache, but it was empty. He got ahead of Mike and me, though soon we found him on the other side of the road, crouched under a rock overhang, trying to stay dry. Mike offered Tobias his umbrella, which he gladly took. The rain got heavier and vehicles that didn't move over sprayed us with water.

We walked through a canyon of rock that didn't give us much wiggle room for passing vehicles. As we reached the end of the rock walls and emerged into the open, a fog rolled up from the lake and over the highway. Now the drivers couldn't see us until they were almost upon us. A couple of semi trucks got close, then made quick lane changes. Our red-and-purple umbrellas, and Mike's orange shirt, may have helped make us visible.

The GPS unit started failing during this walk. According to the unit, we made our usual 3 miles in an hour, and then 15 minutes later had gained 11 miles. Impossible. Mike figured were walking 3.5 miles per hour. So when we reached 12 miles, by his GPS, we wondered why we didn't see Amanda. If the GPS was right, we should have been able to see the car. We started to worry that something had happened. Mike didn't have his phone, so we couldn't call her. We kept walking and the next time we looked the GPS indicated we'd gone 14 miles. By the time we found Amanda, it read 15 miles – 3 miles farther than we'd agree to meet. We reset the car odometer and checked the mileage on our way back. The GPS was wrong, a disturbing development, since we depend on it so much each day. Luckily Mike had his own unit, but we preferred the newer one.

That evening Mike and I would stay at the Rossport Inn, where owner Ned Basher walked with us to Cabin 7. He had several cozy little white and red cabins, newer than the 1884 main lodge. They are just big enough for a metal-frame queen-size bed, a writing table and bathroom. We love them.

We each took a shower and had a glass of wine. Mike did an interview with Bob Carter from WTIP radio in Grand Marais, Minnesota. We had dinner at the inn, always a treat since Shelagh, Ned's wife, is the chef and serves a heavenly trout Hemingway. Mike chose sirloin steak, saying this would be our splurge night. Eavesdropping on the tables near us, we determined the guests were fellow Minnesotans. The couples to our left were from Shakopee, riding motorcycles around the lake. The couple came from Rochester, who had been kayaking the Schreiber Channel for three days. Later in the meal, they asked Mike what most surprised him about on this trip. Not seeing any moose, Mike said.

"That's because the wolf population has gotten so big," one man said. Mike told him ticks and summer heat were more likely to blame.

Ned explained that his business has been way down. Over the years he's gone from having 100 percent of the Rossport tourist business to a small share. There are now three or four bed-and-breakfast inns and guesthouses. These places all have TVs, Internet and other amenities. All he has, said Ned, are these "funky little cabins" and the bedrooms upstairs in the inn with shared bathrooms. Ned and Shelagh love the Inn and have put blood, sweat and tears into its remodeling/restoration work. We'd hate to see it go away.

That night, three freight trains went by before 8 p.m. and more later, but even with their horns blowing and cabin shaking, we managed a good night's rest. We loved our "funky little cabin."

We woke to a sunny, cheerful August morning. Ned came by announcing coffee was on, so Mike got up. I lazily stayed a bit longer. By the time I arrived, Mike was in the lobby overseeing the four motorcyclists as they filled out our survey. Breakfast wasn't being served, but Shelagh still wanted to make some for us – an offer we couldn't refuse.

Shelagh spends 12 hours a day in the kitchen. She asked what we wanted, and we both chose eggs, home fries, bacon, toast, coffee and juice. Ned joined us later. He'd been working on installing a wood stove upstairs.

It was noon by the time we left the inn. The sun was still shining, and the weather to the west looked good. I suggested we tackle the Casque Isle Trail section that we'd been putting off because of rain. Tobias had developed a blister on his big toe from yesterday, so he decided to stay back.

We began at Schreiber's cobblestone beach. Tobias wanted to look for a geocache, which he found pretty quickly, returning triumphant and happy with his "treasure." We started up the trail, expecting a 7- to 8-mile walk. The guidebook said it would take five to six hours, which would indicate a longer trail. And it was likely to have challenges that would slow us down.

Almost immediately, we encountered water and newly formed streams with mini-waterfalls from the previous day's rain. Soon we came to a wooded section with a huge puddle in the middle of the path. "What the heck," said Mike, stepping right into it. I followed suit. Before long the trail turned into a stream, with water coursing over the stones and our boots. Water spilled from one ledge to the next. At a larger stream, a sign read: Bridge 650 meters up. We continued to the small wooden walkway built across the flow. Pretty waterfalls cascaded above and below us. Big green darner dragonflies swept up and down the stream. The trail had a steep grade, shifting down after the stream, and then we were in the forest again. Weaving up and down, the trail took us to the lake a few times, once to a place called Twin Harbors with two nearly identical inlets.

Seeing the inlets reminded me that it was the sixth birthday of our twin grandsons. While Mike lay down in the sun on an outcrop, I called them on our cell phone. Wishing them "Happy birthday," I tried to explain where we were; hard to know how much they understood. The kids had visited with us at the midpoint of the trip and could see where we were on the website, including our "Where is paddle?" section for children.

The trail returned to rock outcrops exposed to the sun and covered with blueberry shrubs heavy with fruit. Some leaves had already turned scarlet, but the berries were perfect. We bent down, scooped as many as we could in our hands, then poured them into our mouths.

Up another hill and perched high above the Big Lake, a mid-sized inland lake showed lots of beaver activity – stumps with teeth marks on the ends and piles of sticks and branches in the water. We were setting a good pace, but as we came down the slope toward Lake Superior, I slipped on a rock. Falling face first, my throat hit against one of my walking poles while my knee pressed against the other. Mike, ahead of me, didn't see what happened and couldn't hear when I called out. I was shaken up and muddy. After standing and ascertaining there was no major damage, except to my ego, I rejoined Mike on the rocks next to the water. We didn't notice the cut on my arm until Tobias saw the blood later in the day. A couple of days later I noticed soreness on my left side, between my waist and armpit, whenever I took a big breath, coughed or hiccupped. There was a big bruise on my left hip and I realized that when I fell, I must have landed on the pole on my left side and bruised my muscles or ribs. It was a painful reminder that one misstep or one slippery rock could bring about serious consequences.

Out on the rocky shore, Mike said, "It sure would be nice to stay on the rocks for a while." He got his wish. The trail, marked by white-painted arrows on the rocks, followed the water line. A lot of it was smooth, volcanic rock, but there were broken up boulders, too. One section was so black and fresh-looking, you'd swear lava flowed there just a few years earlier.

We passed Flint Island, part of the Schreiber Channel Provincial Park, and then went back into the woods, crossed a few more streams and climbed a steep bank to a railroad track. By this time, it was 5:30 p.m. (we started at 1:10). We had to cross the tracks to get back to Highway 17, but our little map offered few details. We were beginning to get nervous because of the time and uncertainty. After some additional steep hills, Mike's knee started to complain. We headed for an overlook and just hoped it wasn't a dead end. A panoramic view from the top revealed ... Amanda and Tobias ahead. But there were more hills to climb and more muck through which to slog. Our anticipated 7.8 miles turned out to be 10.9;. a big difference when you are hiking those last 3.1 miles.

Later in the evening, a man stopped by the RV to say he'd read about our hike. He couldn't believe we were staying in the same campground. Joe was from lower Michigan, where he had an apple farm. He and his wife were traveling around the lake, and he just wanted us to know how impressed he was by what we were doing.

August 15, Tobias' 22nd birthday, was blustery, with a strong wind coming from the west up the Schreiber Channel. Low clouds blew overhead, too. It was (as Snoopy might say) a dark and stormy morning to the east. That day we moved the RV to the Birchwood campground, just past Nipigon. This place also had a restaurant that served fresh baked pies – a bad choice for pie lovers, if you were so foolish as to be trying to diet.

Mike and I got dropped off on the road and started out with swallows and a bald eagle overhead riding the wind. The swallows appeared to be catching insects, which made sense since it was pretty humid. The weather was unsettled – sunshine, then thick clouds, then a rain squall, and the whole cycle repeated. Rain jacket and hat on, sunglasses on, no off, no on, hat and jacket off and back and forth and back and forth.

We came to the Little Cypress River, which seemed like a strange name for a river in the north country, not far from tiny Gurney. (It was probably the only thing "not far" from Gurney.) I glimpsed a sign on a tree that said "Brook Trout" and something about "one fish over 22," though I didn't find out what that meant. (The world record brook trout was caught near here: a 14.5-pound, 31-inch trout landed by Dr. W.J. Cook in 1915 on the Nipigon River.) This river, more like a stream, was rocky, and with so little water this summer that we couldn't imagine catching fish in it. We took our snack break beside another section of the Cypress River. That's when the rain let loose. We quickly put on our rain gear and stood under a tree (there was no lightning). When the rain stopped, we resumed walking, followed by that same sun, cloud, rain regimen.

As we walked up one hill, in partial sunshine, a silver SUV pulled over on the other side of the road. A woman got out and quickly crossed toward us. I took off my sunglasses to see if I recognized her, but didn't.

"Are you the Superior walking couple?" she asked. She hardly seemed ready for a north woods day – neatly coiffed blonde hair with very pink lipstick and very black eye make up, wearing a closely fitted skirt with a loosely-strung line of pearls around her neck. Maria was a friend of Ken Storms, whom we'd met in April. Ken had invited us to his cabin on Nicol Island near Rossport, but the timing was such that we couldn't take him up on the offer.

Maria lived in Toronto. I asked if she gets to her place on Nicol Island often.

"Oh, yes, about every week!" she said. She was flying back to Toronto that day (that explained the city dress) and planned to return Friday. She wished us well, got back into her car and sped off toward Thunder Bay.

Normally walking the road doesn't offer much in the way of mysteries, but on this afternoon at a rock cut there was a black stencil of a trilobite (a classic Cambrian fossil). Mike had to check it out. The rocks were either limestone or dolomite and probably did have fossils in them. It was evident from the crushed and cracked stones that someone had been working on top of the rocks.

By late afternoon, I really wanted to be done for the day. The weather remained fickle and we faced a long uphill before we'd meet Amanda at a picnic area. I pushed forward, head down, until I saw her coming down toward us. She made us both happy when she said she'd moved the car to a nearby entry road on the highway. No last hill today. Hallelujah! We barely closed the car doors when the heavens opened up with a real downpour.

As we drove back toward Nipigon, the sun came out. Amanda reminded us that it was Tobias' birthday and that he really loved fish and chips. We didn't know of any place in Nipigon that sold this fare, but the Nipigon Drive-In was famous for its burgers. We got him a fish burger and poutine. Mike and I got burgers and a small poutine to share, and Amanda got a big poutine with smoked meat in it. This was the best poutine we'd had on the trip. Poutine is not really French fries, though it is potatoes shaped like fries, slathered with gravy and mozzarella cheese curds, a Canadian comfort food.

Back at the RV, we gave Tobias his food, some small gifts and a cookies-and-cream ice cream dessert that Amanda had purchased for him. Pleased with all the attention, Tobias said he'd never really had a birthday party. Another Lake Superior first for him.

It was mid-August (the 16th to be exact) and it rained during the night. As I listened to rain pelt the roof, I remembered my grandmother's saying: "Rain before 7, done by 11." I could

Nipigon recently developed a Paddle-to-the-Sea themed park, so, naturally, we brought our Paddle.

only hope. When we got up, the rain had stopped, although there were still lots of clouds and a sharp wind. After pie for breakfast (I told you it was a dangerous campsite), we headed for our starting point: Kama Hill. Yet another provincial park, Kama Hill features purple-red mudstone, an unusual rock formed during the Proterozoic Era, 2.5 billion years ago, according to park information.

Under cloudy skies and with a strong headwind, a group of ravens soared just beyond the cliff edge. On the other side of the road, a car stopped and a man crossed over, asking, "Are you the ones walking around the lake?"

Randy and his wife, Wendy, hailed from Duluth and had read about us in newspaper articles. Randy spotted us on the road and told Wendy, "That has to be them." We chatted for a little while, but Randy was obviously cold in the gusting wind without any jacket. Before this friendly fellow returned to his car, we asked him to take a photo of the four of us – Mike, Amanda, Tobias and me – with beautiful Kama Bay and the islands in the background.

We continued and at one point, Mike found a remnant of old Highway 17. We followed it until it disappeared into the forest. You could still see some of the white line, but plants were making inroads and the winter snow, rain and freezing was breaking up the old surface.

We had lunch on rocks above the road, then climbed down to continue on our way, thinking we had about 6 miles to go. Strong headwinds pounded us, then a rain squall hit, strong enough to require jackets and hats, but lasting less than five minutes. Then the sun returned. If ever the joke about "Don't like the weather, wait five minutes" applied to a location, Lake Superior is it.

Near one bay, a loon called. We also heard flickers across the road, and several ravens. Merlins, those small falcons, perched at the top of a spruce and yelled down at us. This was the soundtrack as we reached the 2,000 kilometer mark on the hike. Tobias thought this a noteworthy moment (it's also slightly more than 1,200 miles), so Mike took a photo of him and me spelling out, sort of, 2000 with our fingers. A bit farther on the road, we reached the northernmost point of Lake Superior. It was too far off the road to get directly down to the lake, but we hit our Spot unit and recorded the coordinates – N49 01 008 W088 01 74. This was the first time our GPS had recorded the 49th parallel. It was all south from here on out. It was a memorable August 16.

At the end of the day we drove back to Nipigon to pick up mail. There was nothing for us. Throughout the trip we would check the general delivery at post offices in the bigger towns. Though most of our communication came through emails, we still needed some supplies, bills and checks mailed to us. Back at the RV, Mike grilled hamburgers at the picnic table, using the umbrella technique since it was raining. Amanda gave all of us stone necklaces to commemorate our milestone day (she was generous with gifts throughout the trip.) Besides reaching 2,000 kilometers, we also reached 2,000 friends on Facebook. Tobias said we'd gotten thousands of individual hits on our website, too. Since getting people to be aware of Lake Superior's attributes and challenges was one of our goals, this was great news.

Another damp, gray, chilly morning. Around 10 a.m., we loaded up and drove to our drop-off point. Rain had been predicted, but by then the sky had cleared to a mix of sun and clouds with, naturally, a major headwind. Gusts of 25 mph made walking an isometric exercise. As we approached Nipigon, a white-tailed deer ran across the road - the first we'd seen on the Ontario shore.

One way I entertained myself on highway treks was by judging the cars, trucks and RVs – ranking them on a hand signal scale. If the vehicle's wheels touched the centerline, showing some effort to avoid us, they got an index finger wave. If they got completely on the center, they got a two-finger wave. If they crossed completely into the other lane, they got a full hand wave. Those that didn't move over at all got – no, not what you're thinking – a scowl and shake of the head.

We had only 5 miles to walk on Highway 17 before turning into Nipigon. We headed to the public library and ate our sandwiches on a bench in front. Due to recent redevelopment funds Nipigon has nice new sidewalks, benches, trees and street lamps. They've also built a new municipal building, with the library attached, plus the delightful Paddle-to-the-Sea Park.

It was easy to picture Nipigon in its heyday. Historical photos and signs on many of the buildings show what they looked like in the 1920s and '30s. The train used to be the lifeline bringing people and goods to town. The highway has replaced that.

We headed to the Nipigon River Trail, happy to walk away from the busy Highway 17. The Paddle-to-the-Sea Park extends down a road closer to the river and to the marina. The new park, of course, delighted Mike and his own little "Paddle Lake Superior." Nipigon is the town mentioned in the Holling C. Holling book *Paddle-to-the-Sea*, so it's a natural place for the themed playground. There was the larger than life "Paddle" statue above waterfalls that we sat in, model lighthouses, a giant frog and heron, and patterns of blue that mimicked the water as the children climbed, slid, and moved through the variety of playground equipment. Mike took photos of his little Paddle Lake Superior and I tried out the swings and monkey bars.

Down at the Nipigon River Trail, it started out easy – wide and grassy, with nice observation decks of the river and wetlands beside them. Signs noted these as "Provincially Significant Coastal Wetlands." A man running down the trail with his dog stopped to talk. He lived near the trail and used it a lot. In winter, he ran on another trail headed toward Lake Nipigon because the snowmobiles pack this trail, but "there's so many wolves, you have to watch out," he cautioned. We'd like to see wolves, we said, and told him about the deer. The white-tails been showing up more in the last 10 years, he said.

The Nipigon Loop of the trail became more like the Voyageur Trail we knew. Sawmill Point is a place where loggers once cut trees for railroad ties, and the ground was thick with sawdust and bark. We could see Red Rock ahead on the shore, but then the trail turned and became narrow, root-lined and rocky. And it began to go up. Way up. Ropes tied to trees were meant to help, but it was still difficult. The stairs in place seemed to reach to the sky. Climbing steep inclines, natural or artificial, is my least favorite activity. I had to stop at every landing to let my heartbeat return to normal. I was getting light-headed and it didn't help that Mike was already at the top as I struggled – hot, sticky and out of breath.

"Why, oh why, do we always seem to have climbs at the end of a long day?" I whined to myself as yet another set of stairs loomed after I thought we'd mounted the last ones. Then after the stairs, we still had to climb more rocks. We met Amanda and Tobias on a flat rocky ridge. Amanda was taking photos of the gorgeous view from Eagle Overlook. Tobias was searching for a geocache, but discovered it was too well hidden in the brush. We worried about him being too close to the edge. (We'd had enough of cliff-falling accidents on this trip.)

Continuing on, still climbing upward, we finally found the downward path - hard on the toes and knees, but not the heart and lungs. Mike highly recommends this trail for anyone who does not mind some climbing for its "great views and a sense of wildness."

The town of Red Rock has an unusual history involving the fur trade, as prisoner of war camp, in forestry and mining, and now with a popular folk music festival. It was a company town for sure, with many identical houses. We saw two schools – one public, one Catholic, side by side – and a tiny business section.

We returned to the Nipigon campground, and Amanda set about making dinner. She was disappointed to discover that the Boboli pizza bread was moldy, but we used the basil tomato tortillas instead. She also heated up the frozen chili – making some of our best homemade pizzas and chili on the trip.

> Everything was going somewhere, everything except Paddle.
> He seemed to be sitting in one place, rocking up and down.
> Yet all the time he had been traveling.
> Paddle-to-the-Sea, Holling Clancy Holling

After Thoughts
Meals

Here's a six-day sample of our daily food diary:

August 26	Breakfast	Pie and coffee
	Lunch	1.5 oz. cheddar chips, 2 jerky, 1 sesame seed bar, organic root beer
	Dinner	1 burrito, 1 cup spaghetti, 1 cup salad, 1/2 cup beans and rice, wine
August 27	Breakfast	Pie and coffee
	Lunch	BLT and coffee and donut
	Dinner	2 brats, 3 perogis, beer and wine
August 28	Breakfast	coconut tart, Italian perogi
	Lunch	Pepperette (like beef sticks) & tomato
	Dinner	1/3 rack BBQ ribs, fries, gin & tonic
August 29	Breakfast	Donut and egg sandwich
	Lunch	1/4 chicken, rice veggie soup. Veggie mash potato, rhubarb pie
	Dinner	taco, cheese, salsa, tequila
August 30	Breakfast	Finnish pancake, 2 eggs, bacon, OJ
	Lunch	Ice Cream cone, pepperette
	Dinner	salad and two ears of corn
August 31	Breakfast	granola, coffee
	Lunch	PBJ, granola bar, meat stick
	Dinner	Taco, cheese, salsa, tequila

For snacks, we munched trail mix, candy bars and jerky.

Mike and Sheena share a trail snack.

235

FOURTEEN
All South from Here

In places without water, gods are not present.
Unknown

Kate:

August 18, about 3½ months into our journey, the sun was shining as we headed across the road to our first stretch of decommissioned railroad track to Dorian. Mike drove down the road to show Amanda where the Hurkett crossing was, so she'd know where to meet us. Then we found the Hurkett Dock, a public boat launch looking out onto Black Bay. Black Bay is one of the most remote and difficult areas to get to (we like the fact that it seems so wild) – no roads, no trails, just lots of boggy terrain extending in to a large natural bay like a big "T" and only accessible by boat. The bay has shallow water with good fishing and wild rice, but it remains a mystery to us.

On Everard Road, we found the old Canadian National track that runs parallel to the active Canadian Pacific tracks. We crossed over the Black Sturgeon River on an old wooden trestle. The abandoned track bed still had its ties sticking up askew. The rock base on the sides varied in width, often forcing us back on to the ties where a mix of goldenrod, raspberries and other flowering plants now bloomed.

A couple of CP trains passed, and we could hear Highway 17 in the distance. Mike caught up with Tobias, who had stopped to watch spruce grouse, or as the man who owns Birchwood campground told us later, "We call

236

them partridge." So we had three partridge in an aspen tree. We heard a broad winged hawk flying above the treetops as we had every day for the past week. They were migrating south with us.

Not far from Hurkett, we met Amanda and Sheena and had lunch at the Hurkett Dock, where a small group of older teens was fishing. Mike and Amanda talked to the adult leaders and learned that the kids were studying fishing and where food comes from. They'd been to a fish hatchery earlier in the day.

After lunch, we returned the abandoned track. Tobias ran ahead, and Mike found a beaten-down path beside the railroad grade. Something or someone had walked it regularly. I was guessing bear. Canine scat that included a lot of hair led us to believe wolves or coyotes frequently visited as well.

When a lovely medium-size black bear appeared out of the bush, it walked across the tracks in front of Tobias.

"STOP!" Mike yelled. He wanted to get a picture of the bear. Tobias and the bear both looked up at the same time, scaring each other. Poor bear, it was out ambling on its afternoon walk, as it probably does every day, and suddenly these frightening humans show up. It shot off into the brush, and Tobias, after his initial fright was elated to have seen a bear.

The end of the track crossed a road. The GPS unit indicated this was the road to Dorian. We had done six miles in a little more than two hours. We expected to see Amanda, but there was no sign of her, so we walked back down the road to Highway 17 and came out at the Dorian gas station store. Sitting at a picnic table near a little French fry stand, we tried to figure out how we'd missed her. A few minutes later, across the road, we saw Amanda with her camera aimed toward us, so we waved. We were sure she saw us, even though she didn't wave back. A few minutes later she arrived fairly agitated. She couldn't' figure out how

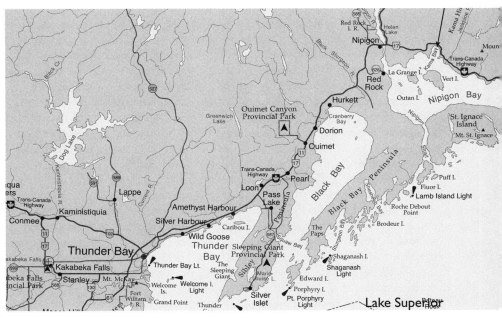

237

she had missed us. Then we said, "But we saw you across the road and waved at you." She said she hadn't seen us and had been taking photos of the building behind us. Later when she looked at her photos; Mike was in the bottom corner.

This was Tobias' last night with us .After dinner he and I talked about his life. In some ways he feels like he was born in the wrong place and time. Singapore is about as urban as a place can be, but he dreamed of being a mountain man and living in the wilderness. Hiking with us and seeing land (and shoreline) that few other people see fed the part of his soul that is passionate about nature. He has so many talents it's hard to say where life will take him.

The next day, Mike went to the café and came back with a raspberry pie. Then he announced he would start walking the road to our next campground. I drove to the post office in Nipigon a little after 10 a.m. We were still expecting some checks in a package sent by our neighbor, but, unfortunately it hadn't arrived. Our cash flow was turning into a trickle and we needed to replenish our account. When I told the woman behind the counter it had been mailed in Minnesota a week ago, she said, "Oh, that doesn't mean anything. It could even take two weeks, depending. It could be at the border where things get hung up."

I asked if the package could be forwarded to Thunder Bay. She said yes, but we learned later when we went back on Saturday that it would cost money to do this. So we knew we'd be backtracking again on Monday.

Todd Starling, one of our Ontario partners, met us at the Wolf River Campground tucked into a hairpin turn in the Wolf River not far from Hurkett. Amanda had moved the RV there during the morning hours. When we returned, Tobias was busy repacking his bag. We wished him a good journey, thanked Todd for being the shuttle and then parted ways. We had become used to people coming in and out of our trip and it became as natural as getting up in the morning and starting out to discover what the new day would hold. A long stay like Tobias's was more difficult because we had a routine for living and with the addition of a fourth person we had to find a new equilibrium for the team.

The morning was bright, sunny and chilly, and the abandoned railroad track had loose ties and lots of vegetation. Just another day on a 1,555-mile walk.

Despite the pleasant weather, the only wildlife we saw was a woodchuck. We heard a pileated woodpecker, a vireo, a raven, some flickers and another broad-winged hawk. For birders, hearing counts as much as seeing. Mike found a single ripe thimbleberry, which he ate. I'd been hoping we'd find lots of them by this point of the trip, but we saw few bushes on the Ontario side of the lake and those didn't have berries. Thimbleberries, which resemble large raspberries and are sometimes called salmonberries, flourish in the Upper Peninsula.

Near the end of the abandoned track, we watched two loons swimming in a small lake. We ate snacks and decided to follow the road into the much more agricultural landscape. When we reached the end of the day's walk (12 miles) we found Amanda waiting in the car on the edge of the road. She was still beaming from the excitement of seeing a bear. Sheena's bark alerted her, just as it ran across the road and down into a ditch. It wasn't until the bear heard her camera clicking that it realized it wasn't alone.

Driving back to the campground, we stopped at a self-serve garden and fresh eggs stand we'd spotted on our morning walk. The small shed was a treasure trove of baskets filled with multi-colored beans and colorful buckets of cucumbers and squash. Besides the fresh eggs, a refrigerator held bags of heirloom carrots, German butter potatoes, pattypan squash and zucchini. On a shelf above it were berry preserves, jams and bread and butter pickles, which I couldn't resist. We put $12 into the honor-system can, and I walked away wearing a big smile and an armload of produce.

At the Dorian store, we picked up more produce – locally grown sweet corn. Mike and I had been talking about corn earlier and how we hoped to get some when we went home on Labor Day. We cooked the ears on our Coleman stove outside on the picnic table, while Amanda fried everything else on the stove in the RV. Not quite the same as what we find growing farther south, but this sweet corn still satisfied our craving.

The next morning I suggested that if we were going to go back to Nipigon to get our mail we should stop back at Birchwood campground for breakfast. Remember this was the pie place, but it also had excellent and very reasonably priced breakfasts. We were up early and told Amanda she could sleep in if she wanted, and take her time driving to our next campground - Sleeping Giant Provincial Park, about 22 miles southeast of Dorian.

At Birchwood, we went into the café and said, "We're back. You can't get rid of us." We had spent four evenings sitting in their porch like dining room, catching up on internet messages, since this was the only spot at the campground that had service. I had seen the breakfasts they served on our last morning and was sorry we hadn't taken advantage of it while we were camped there. We ordered the Traditional – 2 eggs over easy, 3 pieces of bacon, home fries and brown toast.

The room was mostly empty, except for another couple at one table and a long-distance biker sitting by himself. We struck up a conversation, an easy thing with the shared camaraderie among travelers, we'd found. He was a Brit - a geography teacher going from New York City to San Francisco. We talked about the difficulty of riding on 17 with semi trucks and cars so close to the edge. "You know," he said, "the truckers have been brilliant, giving me a lot of clearance." We talked about our walking adventure. Intrigued, he asked for our website address. Before leaving we offered to take a photo of him with his camera. Then we bid each other safe travels.

We drove back to Nipigon and, still finding no mail, decided to take advantage of the Internet access from our parked car outside of the public library. We had been sharing one laptop – mine, ever since the end of our Voyageur canoe trip. Mike's computer had a serious 'breakdown' and went home with fellow paddler and IT specialist, John Oehler. We quickly learned how difficult it was for two people to share one laptop. Giving Mike his turn, I took time to wander through a few nearby shops looking for keepsakes and unique Christmas presents. I found some Canadian dish soap that sounded ecological, as best I could tell from the French words on the bottle; the fun of exploring stores in another country. Then it was time to drive south to Sleeping Giant Provincial Park on the Sibley Peninsula, which is across the bay from the city of Thunder Bay. The peninsula resembles the "sleeping giant" after which the park is now named. The giant is said to be the stone form of Naniboujou, who lay there and turned to stone either after the secret of silver on Silver Islet, at the end of the peninsula, was revealed to white miners or for darker reasons, depending on which narrative you hear.

We would be spending four days hiking through this park, the last large one of our Lake Superior journey. It was raining when we arrived and after finding Amanda and the RV in the campground, Mike looked at some maps to determine where we could walk in this weather. The cold rain and a blustery wind prompted us to put on our long underwear under our rain pants. Amanda decided to brave the weather and go with us. Though it wasn't raining hard, I put up my umbrella. We were fully suited out in rain pants, rain jackets and hats. On a narrow trail through the forest and wet trees, I worried we'd get totally soaked. Thankfully, the trail was much wider, although rocky and full of roots. Much of it was in the woods, but eventually we heard the waves on the lake. Emerging onto Middlebrun beach and into the steady rain, we tried videoing the lake from under the dripping umbrella – a new experience. A cluster of shorebirds were the only other living creatures sharing the beach with us three (and Sheena).

The map showed the trail going to the next bay. At the end of the beach, we entered the woods again. It looked and felt like a scene from "Lord of the Rings." Abundant black spruce trees stood draped in grayish green "old man's beard" lichens. Some trees had fallen across the trail. After ducking under the second fallen tree, Mike stopped to check his GPS (we also brought an older GPS unit). When Amanda caught up we decided to continue despite the rain and the trail barriers, but we found Finlay bay uninspiring in the grey sky with the water murky from suspended sediment. Still, we had walked 7 miles more on this difficult to access portion of the peninsula.

Amanda was soaked and concerned about her camera. With one hand holding Sheena's leash, she couldn't protect herself from the rain and her umbrella had broken in the wind. Mike took Sheena's leash. The dog seemed unsure of what to do at first, with Amanda behind her. She lagged behind Mike, but was soon trotting beside him, trying to avoid big puddles all the way back to camp.

Mike and I went right to the showers. The hot water felt wonderful, as did our dry clothes. Amanda didn't get that same luxury, since she wanted to get dinner started. The plan called for pork tenderloin, the little German butter potatoes and heirloom carrots – all cooked in foil, so no pans would get dirty. Good plan, but when we came back from our shower, smoke was seeping from the oven. Amanda opened the oven door, and thick choking smoke poured out. We opened all the RV windows and turned on the fans. Apparently grease from the meat had leaked through the foil and created the mess. After an attempt at cleaning it up and finding new foil, we gave up on the original meal plan and just foraged in the refrigerator.

After dinner, Mike decided to drive around to find reporter Sam Cook, an outdoor writer and columnist for the *Duluth News Tribune* who was to meet us here to spend some time hiking with us and taking photos for an article he would write. We'd seen a red car with *Duluth News Tribune* on it go by earlier.

Apparently Sam had been driving around, trying to find us. After Mike had been in the car for awhile, he looked in his rearview mirror and saw a red car following him. Sam had seen our Minnesota license plates. That's how we met up.

We put the barking Sheena in the car so Sam could come inside the RV to visit. As we talked, a light tapping sounded on the door. We opened it, and there stood Todd Starling holding Mike's computer. Oh, what joy! Todd, Carolyn and Sierra had made a special trip to deliver it to us. They couldn't stay, though, because they needed to get back to Thunder Bay.

At 7 a.m., we were up and ready, but no Sam. At 8:45, I found him sitting at his picnic table putting on socks. I asked if he'd remembered to change to Eastern Time. Nope. Poor Sam was embarrassed and apologized sincerely. "No problem," we assured him. Lucy, his yellow Labrador retriever would walk with us too. An attractive, well-behaved animal, her eyes and face matched those of our late yellow lab, Sigurd, so it was love at first sight.

Sheena became defensive, barking and growling when she got into the car and saw Lucy in the back seat. Amanda held Sheena tightly in her arms and tried to calm her down. Lucy looked at Sam and seemed reassured by his command to 'lay down'. The sky was cloudy, but I had seen some blue patches by the time we reached Sawyer Bay Trail. This was west of where we had walked the day before and at the foot of the Sleeping Giant. The trail, an old logging road, looked like it had been mowed. It met another wide, rocky and hilly trail. I chose this direction because, on paper, the trail looked like it had fewer steep hills, including the last, long one at the end. "How high could it be?" I thought.

Mike walked ahead with Sam, and I hung back with Amanda. We reached Sawyer Bay and went out to the rocky beach for a look. Amanda turned back at this point, because she was going to drive to the other end and start walking back to meet us. The trail to the Thunder Bay Lookout paralleled the shore going through fairly thick second growth. We walked single file, and Lucy ran ahead. Whenever we'd come to an opening to the beach, Sam would send her out for a drink or a swim. The sun had returned and we were getting hot.

Lucy patiently waits for Sam Cook to get his pack together.

The trail was flat and fairly easy. At one beach, we looked across the water and saw the city of Thunder Bay. It sparked some longing. Like seeing Duluth for the last time behind us, or seeing the wind farms near Sault Ste. Marie, the Thunder Bay cityscape was another indicator of how far we'd come and, now, that we were headed home.

Earlier on the trail, I'd heard the distinctive song of a peewee (whose name reflects its call) and a loon's tremolo. Mike spotted a pileated woodpecker close by the trail. The sun hit its magnificent red cap as it flew one tree stump away. Frustrating Mike's photographic efforts, the bird just kept moving one tree ahead of us, flitting next to a mountain ash, where it fed on the bright orange red berries.

I often look down as I walk to secure my footing and on this trail, I suddenly spotted a good size garter snake. I was surprised that it was still there because Mike had already walked past. I called him back to look at it, but by then the snake had had enough with us tourists and slithered effortlessly into the undergrowth. It stood out, like the garter snake in Pukaskwa because these and a few turtles were the only reptiles we saw in Ontario.

At an opening where we could see out into the lake, something strange in the water caught our attention. It appeared to be a tree branch with a wake behind it. Birds on a branch maybe? I borrowed Mike's binoculars, and "What….. the…. heck?"

"Is it a deer swimming?" Mike and Sam caught on at the same time I recognized antlers.

I got out my video camera and went to the beach for a better shot. The deer spotted the two guys and remained short of shore, submerged to its chest, staring at Mike and Sam. All of a sudden, it turned. "Oh no," I thought, "it's going to go back out." I climbed back up on the trail. It started swimming parallel to the beach, headed toward me.

Well hidden by some shrubbery, I stood directly across from it, seemingly invisible. It stood half out of the water, but didn't seem in a hurry to get out. It just kept staring toward the guys. I crouched down to get a better view, but before long my knees complained. I stood up and peeked through the branches. It remained still. I worried that if I went ahead on the trail, it would see me and I didn't want to spook it back into the water. Carefully, I ducked through an opening in the vegetation, watching over my shoulder. The deer looked at me, but didn't move. What a regal animal with the sun shining on his tawny coat.

I found Mike and Sam on the beach. Sam was still taking photos with his long lens and Mike was sitting on a log. All this time, Lucy obediently sat quiet on the trail where Sam had told her to wait.

We went out to the rocky beach a few more times. The deer was still standing there.

Eventually we found a spot with a pile of driftwood trees and logs – a good place for lunch. Sam had Lucy "stay" as we ate. It was hard not to look at her, with her tongue hanging out and her big brown eyes focused on what we were eating. Sam threw her some apples. Then he dragged over a big thick board to use as a table to cut his block of cheese and sausage.

We could still see the deer, standing in the same place for well over an hour. It probably was chased into the water by wolves, we decided, and was extra cautious. How could it stand in that cold water for so long without its legs going numb?

Sam certainly got some photos of a lifetime. He is an easy-going companion, down to earth and self-deprecating. It's what makes him a good reporter. After eating, though, I turned the tables and interviewed him. He talked about moving from Kansas to work for a canoe outfitter in Ely 30 years ago. It was that experience of the wild north woods that contributed to his taking the job in Duluth. And the rest, as they say is history.

We had gone more than 8 miles by this time. The trail turned away from the beach and began gradually going up, past rock walls. The ups and downs became rockier and slippery, reminiscent of the trail in Lake Superior Provincial Park or of the Voyageur Trail in general. We had to use caution and help one another down some. One had a big thick, moss and algae covered rope to use. Sam's photo of Mike using the rope made it later into his newspaper article.

Amanda and Sheena appeared on the trail. People camping on a rock had told her about encountering wolves on the trail and suggested she shouldn't have her dog, it would draw the wolves. Amanda would definitely defend her "baby" against wolves, I knew, but how would the wolves respond?

The trail came out on a large rock outcrop. Two people were down by the water and one man was standing near the top. He told Mike that two wolves had come out at different spots and seemed to be stalking them. His said that a friend, who is a ranger in the park won't bring his dogs on the trail in the fall because of the wolves. After that, Sam put Lucy on her leash. We were skeptical about wolves stalking them, but knew both dogs could be vulnerable.

The man chatting with Mike had read about our walk somewhere. Then he looked at Sam. "Are one of you from the Duluth News?"

"I am," said Sam.

"Are you Sam Cook?"

"Yes."

"I recognize your mug."

The man had been the editor of the Thunder Bay newspaper for 33 years. They shook hands, and while they talked, the man and woman who had been down by the water came up.

"Where did you start out?" she asked. We conversed about our trip for a while then finally headed off on a big, slightly sloping slab of rock covered with reindeer lichen and moss. It didn't connect with the trail, and we had to backtrack to the same spot with the same people. We asked for help, and one of the men asked where we were headed next. Mike told them of our anticipated route through Thunder Bay.

"That goes right past my house," the fellow said.

"Have a cold one ready," Mike joked.

Back on the trail, it got boggy. We lost it for a bit, then came to a steep ascent. I had Sam and Lucy go by me. I'd be very slow, I told Sam. And I was. Even with poles, the going was tough. Far behind the others, I had to keep stopping to let my heartbeat return to normal and let the light-headedness pass. Climbing high boulders tested my strength and stretch, but I did it. Soon, the voices of the others ahead of me faded away. When I reached the point that looked like the top, Amanda came up with her camera. I really didn't feel like smiling. It still wasn't even the end of the trail.

Sam and Lucy were sitting on the ground in the shade.

"Where you from?" Sam teased.

"Hell," I shot back, and he laughed. He'd chided me earlier when I grumbled at the beginning of the ascent. I had been telling him earlier about trying to learn patience. "Remember Kate," he'd said, "live in the moment."

"This is one moment I won't miss," I'd said, thinking about how glad I'd be when it was gone.

Finally we reached the parking area and shed our packs. We'd walked 16 miles. Mike dug out a BeneVia (our nutritional drink sponsor) for Sam and a beer for himself, which we shared with Lucy. Sam didn't know if she'd drink it. The poor dog was so beat and thirsty, she would drink anything, but we only gave her a small drip. Sam gave her water out of a squirt bottle. She stared longingly at the car. Before leaving, we wanted to go to the lookout to take a picture of Paddle there, but we couldn't find him.

"Didn't you have Paddle on the blue tarp by the door of the RV yesterday?"

"Yes."

"Are you sure you didn't leave it in the RV?"

"Maybe."

We went to the overlook without Paddle. (We found him later on the table in the RV.) The overlook is amazing, but daunting. A platform cantilevers beyond the cliff. It's scary for anyone with acrophobia and might make everyone else at least a little uneasy.

Returning to our campsites, we stopped first at Sam's tent. Looking up through the car window, I saw hundreds of nighthawks overhead. Soaring and swooping, their bent wings and white markings etched the pale blue-gray sky – a thrilling sight.

Restored after a hot shower followed by a hearty meal of leftover spaghetti, potatoes, carrots, pork tenderloin and a package of freshly cooked bacon, we got our things together for our 8 p.m. program at the visitor center. This would be our sixth public program of the trip.

Families with lots of children crowded in the audience. The Park was having its Miss Sleeping Giant 2010 Contest program and had done a good job of promoting it. Mike went behind the screen to give the projector operator our thumb drive and their shadows went up on the screen where other slides were being shown. The kids in the front rows booed, but Mike and the other person were unaware of their images on the screen until someone went back and told them. They moved aside.

Sam sat down behind us. Mike sat on the ground between the two rows, his legs resting on the bench in front of him. We watched the five contestants – Miss Leach, Miss Water Strider, Miss Pitcher Plant, Miss Porcupine and Miss Vulture – compete. The show was entertaining and educational; a great job by the park staff who came up with fun costumes. I learned things about leeches and tiger swallowtails even I didn't know. The winner, Miss Porcupine was chosen by the 'applause meter' method.

It was a hard act to follow, but Mike talked about our freshwater emphasis and I did a quick synopsis of our journey to date. When we said we'd passed 2,000 kilometers, there was applause. We felt like winners, too.

We said goodnight and good bye to Sam at that point. He and Lucy would do some solo hiking the next day and then they'd head back to Duluth.

The next morning, August 21, loons were calling as we got dressed and ready for the day. It was already warm, and we decided to do the road sections that we missed when coming to the park.

The first took us past some cottages. The shore at this spot was all marshy and not good for walking. Then the road dead-ended at what looked like a fisherman's shack. Some people were standing in front of the shed talking. Mike asked if they had any fish to sell.

"No, stopped fishing a few weeks ago," one man said. "But we'll go back out in September."

We ended up walking on Grann Road and could see the lake occasionally down power corridors or driveways. There was no access to walk the actual shore.

An immature broad-winged hawk floated overhead, circled and landed in a dead birch on the side of the road, not 40 feet away. Mike and Amanda had their cameras up and clicking before the bird had settled its feathers. I had binoculars trained on it and could see the details of its brown and beige plumage and its dark beak. Even birds pant in the hot sun. It seemed content to sit there, until someone came up the driveway in their ATV with the family dog eagerly trotting alongside.

I started walking off, but turned to find Amanda and Mike with cameras pointed down into the ditch. A rabble of butterflies had caught their attention, and that pretty much describes the rest of our walk down this dirt road lined with wildflowers and butterflies galore. Many were in the sulfur family, with wings the same bright yellow as the nearby mullein flowers, goldenrod and birdsfoot trefoil. The pink -tipped sulfur butterflies have a smudge of rosy orange along the edges of their wings, but it's difficult to see when the wings are folded. Mike had never seen so many butterflies getting nectar from the white pearly everlasting flowers.

There were cabbage butterflies, a monarch, white admirals, painted lady, and a buckeye with amazing large owl-like "eye spots" – one on each wing.

A man out mowing his driveway waved hello as I passed; when Mike went by him, the man asked if we were "new around these parts." Mike explained what we were doing and to confirm that we were not some crooks casing out the area, he gave him a business card. Reassured, the man wished us well. We also discovered a picket fence of massive mullein with dense floral spikes looking like a Midwestern version of saguaro cactus. Some were at least 7 feet tall with multiple branches (or arms) and sage green fuzzy leaves like rabbit ears. Even with all these wonderful floral entertainments, neither of us had any enthusiasm for walking dirt roads far from the lake on a hot August afternoon. Though we tried, we could not find a good alternative route.

We drove out to Silver Islet to get groceries at the general store. This charming little hamlet at the end of Sibley Peninsula runs completely off the grid. Everyone has to power their homes on generators, windmills or solar panels.

After dinner, Mike sat in the passenger seat of the car with it reclined and his legs up, trying to relax. I was working on the computer at the picnic table and looked up as a small black bear passed by our site. I got Mike's attention and he hurried to get his camera and alert Amanda. All three of us started down the road after it. The cub, maybe 4 feet long and less than 100 pounds, seemed to know where it was going.

Two women at another campsite said the bear had eaten two of their citronella candles, the kind on poles, like it was corn on the cob. Then it licked out one that was in a pot. Sure enough, the bear headed right to their site, but they were ready this time. They banged on pots and yelled at it. About the same time, a park truck drove by and blasted an airhorn to chase the bear away.

In this park, white-tailed deer were as tame as dogs. They browsed near the campsites and the comfort station. When I went for a shower, a doe with her nearly grown fawn were standing by the recycling cans. "Don't mind me," I said, just a few feet from them. "I'm just throwing some stuff away." The doe casually looked up and moved around a picnic table. Then she stood on her hind legs to reach the leaves on an alder shrub growing below a birch tree. She got a branch in her mouth and pulled it down, stripping the leaves. When deer overpopulate, such eating habits can make them a true problem.

The sunshine helped improve my mood when I was feeling less than inspired when 7:30 a.m. arrived on August 22 – 116 days into our trip, Mike had whimpered, moaned and muttered most of the night.

The sound of pressurized air came from the other room. When I stepped in there, Amanda was aiming a can at her computer. She'd spilled coffee on it and now it wasn't working. She kept spraying it and tapping the keyboard without success. I suggested it might heal itself like her camera had done when it got wet, but she said Apple products are sensitive to moisture. I ate my breakfast in the tense silence. She had turned off the computer and ate her breakfast on the couch. She seemed on the verge of tears, but I didn't know what else to say.

Amanda drove us to the trailhead for the Kabeyun Trail and seemed in a better mood as we left. She dropped us off and returned to camp to give a 10 a.m. program. This, of course, was one reason her computer was so critical. Amanda had been doing children's programs in some of the parks and locations on our trip, as well as updating the "Where is Paddle" section of our website.

We walked down a wide grassy trail and came to a sign announcing the "Sea Lion" side trail. It led to a fenced area and a great view of a diabase dike that sticks out into the lake. The arch was covered with orange lichen, but it didn't look like a sea lion to me. Signs with detailed graphics explained the geologic forces that created the famous arch. The "head" of the lion had fallen into the lake years ago, and there are black-and-white photos of it, with a head, at the small Silver Islet General Store.

Six loons swam on the water, hooting to one another. The air was cool at that time, but we knew it was going to be a warm, humid day. Back on the main trail we heard something behind us. A young woman and some kind of spaniel were coming up fast. It surprised both of us. They passed us, then later we passed them when she'd veered down to the water to let the dog drink. Before long, they were behind us again. A big dog on a leash can pull you along at a pretty good pace. When they caught up, Mike said, "How far are you going?" She didn't know, and he said, "Just wondering how many times we're going to leapfrog."

"That's his water bottle out there," she said, pointing at the lake. "I didn't bring one for him."

Reaching Tee Harbour, we walked the beach and shore until we came to another trail out to a large flat area made up of black diabase rock and covered with orange lichens. Without any breeze, it was a too warm to hang out, so we took two pictures of ourselves, then took the trail to Lentinen Bay. Here we found an amazing array of black and gray stones – smooth, flat and mostly oval or round in shape – absolutely perfect skipping stones, the best we'd seen on all of Lake Superior. I can never resist these sorts of 'toys'. We also found an amazing monument to Guinness beer. Someone had built an intricately stacked hollow pillar of stones more than 5 feet tall and placed a few empty Guinness cans on top. We could have used a few cold ones by then.

Farther up the beach, we sat almost in the shadow of the Sleeping Giant and ate jerky and dried fruit. This massive red stone wall rose behind us and stretched out in front of us. From this angle the Sleeping Giant was just a massive wall of volcanic columns that dominated the west and felt powerful, the way a spirit giant should.

Peregrine falcons were calling near the rock face and a cawing pair of ravens flew above it. We walked on the boulders near shore rather than going back to the interior trail. When we finally cut in, we found the trail to be a narrow path, with roots to climb over and an interesting, challenging terrain.

Cloudy and stormy looking, the next morning found us on the trail near the spectacular cantilevered lookout that is at the end of the road and the trail. This is where we had ended our hike with Sam Cook. The trail here is actually an old road, easy to walk and mostly downhill. Our rain pants protected our legs from all the tall vegetation on the trail.

Again, a loon was calling, and a pair of ravens heard us and started squawking. I made my raven call, and they really got worked up, flying overhead slowly, their big wings whooshing through the air. I kept up my calls, and one even turned and flew back to check us out again. That usually doesn't happen, but I like it when it does. Quite a few yellow-shafted flickers appeared on the trail, flying ahead of us, and we heard a pileated woodpecker and saw a broad-winged hawk fly over.

We passed an old overlook that had a chain link fence in front of it and on the other side a cross that said, 'In memory of Shawn Petersen'. Beyond that and through the trees we could see the Lake and the end of the bay where we would be walking the next day. This trail took us north by Pass Lake and to where the peninsula became part of the mainland. Our next trek would begin here – moving west towards Amethyst Harbour and Thunder Bay. Amanda had gone ahead in the morning and found the Thunder Bay KOA and rented a space. They had Wi-Fi, happily, and we all got online that evening.

During the day, Mike had called the Nipigon post office and when I heard him exclaim, YES!, I knew our mail had finally arrived, so before going to the KOA, we made one more drive back to Nipigon and collected the long sought treasure, including the now desperately needed checks. Since we passed the Birchwood once more, Mike had to stop and buy one last pie, telling the owners that he was Sure, this would be the last time they'd see us for a long time.

The following day, we stayed on the road as long as we could, then got back on the old railroad bed. It was in poor condition with some ties pulled up. At one point, Mike stopped and pointed at an animal ahead of us. A pretty red fox trotted toward us until it caught our scent or saw us and hopped off the track. Later, a couple of guys on dirt bikes rode past. We crossed the McKenzie River on a short old wooden trestle. The river had exposed rock and not much water.

Every inch of shore here was privately owned, though Mike crossed one property because he really wanted to see Amethyst Harbor. Private development is common from this point on the shore, all the way down to Duluth.

The day seemed to pass quickly, but I was really dragging the last part of the hike down the railroad grade. When we finally reached the road where Amanda picked us up, we had done 15 miles.

The next day at the Silver Harbour Conservation Area, we met reporters from a local TV station. Mike had suggested this harbor because it was scenic and better than the roads and train track on which we'd be walking. A pretty spot, with Sibley Peninsula in the background.

Todd Starling and his family arrived, including his mom, Penny. We walked the road, stopping to talk to a woman with two little kids working in her yard.

"Where are you walking to?" she asked, and we told her to Duluth. She was on maternity leave from Parks Canada. She and her husband owned a little cabin here and then bought the wooded lot next to them as a screen when a new neighbor began building a huge two-story house, quite out of character for this neighborhood. The big-house owners also removed the trees on their lot.

We told her about our observations of the cabins, or cottages as they call them, on the Ontario side of the lake, how they seemed more modest. We didn't know that in Canada your mortgage interest payments are not tax deductible, so people only get the home they can afford. She felt that the lack of tax incentives made Canadians think twice about the size of their lake cottages.

When we told her the route we planned, she suggested an alternative. "You can go down here until you come to the end, and then there's a trail through the "bush" (I love the Canadian way of saying "woods"). That should take you through to the other bay and you can follow that a long ways."

We switched from the road to the train track then back to the roads, but that allowed us to see the lake through people's yards, at least. Todd, Mike and I met with the others in our group close to Amy's Organics, the roadside vegetable stand we'd seen earlier. We bought more fresh produce.

The cottages here face the big bay with a nice view of the Sibley Peninsula and a variety of mesa-shaped islands filling the horizon. Here is where I found my favorite place name of the trip: Ishkibibble Road. I love the way the word spills out of my mouth. Train track and roads continued to be our trails for the afternoon. We passed a Smurfit-Stone plant, and Mike asked about using the road there. It was private, we were told, so we returned to the train track until we tried another road that led to another dead end gate and industrial site. The whole group of us continued on the tracks, aware that this close to Thunder Bay, the track was active. Luckily, only one of the two was in use.

It was the end of the day, my feet hurt and Mike was confused about our destination, too. He thought we were walking to the Marina Park, which I believed was several miles away. We crossed the other set of train tracks and found a dirt track out to the street and to our car. While the rest of the group walked down to look at the river, Penny and I crossed the main street and walked to the car.

Nice temperatures, a breeze and sunshine would make any day a good one for the walk, but it was the company that made the day. We did 13.4 miles, and little Sierra deserved the most praise for riding in the backpack for six hours and keeping a good attitude most of the way.

The next morning before 8 a.m., the phone rang. Brian Turner at KTCZ, the Twin Cities radio station was calling an hour and half earlier than we expected to do an interview. It was always fun to talk to BT on his morning show. He is always full of energy and curiosity and wanted to know where we were, how far we had walked, and what the scene was like where we were connecting. He was a good cheerleader who would join us on our last day walk.

We were also expecting a call from a CBC reporter named Amy (we don't recall her last name). When she called, we made plans to meet her at noon at the Marina Park in downtown Thunder Bay. Walking on the sidewalk of the busy street, we took pictures of local signs and other sights we found interesting.

Amy arrived by cab and walked with us to find a quiet spot in the park to conduct the interview. She was animated and asked good questions, but really wanted to know how we liked Canada. Of course, we loved it and said how nice the people in Ontario had been. So the story was about how far we had come, when we would end and what we had seen. She wanted to know what the water quality was like, but we were not testing the water, we could only say that the Lake Superior Binational Forum Areas of Concern needed to be addressed and that we were concerned by the invasive species. Then she had us walk away from the camera so she could record the sound of our boots crunching on gravel – a nice touch. We asked Amanda to give Amy a ride back to her office, which meant we needed to take Sheena with us. We left with Sheena tugging on the leash, looking over her shoulder for her mistress.

On busy Fort William Drive with cars, trucks and buses just half a foot away from us, we stuck to the sidewalk. At every parked blue car we passed, Sheena veered over to sniff the doors to see if Amanda was inside. (Who says dogs are color blind?). Or whenever she saw a young woman with glasses and a phone to her ear, she pulled on the leash to check. When Amanda found us, we were by a store that sold specialty doggie biscuits. The two of them went to shop and we continued down the street.

Thunder Bay was formed in 1970 from two older cities, Port Arthur and Fort William. The location has a long history of human habitation, with some artifacts dating back more than 11,000 years to the Paleo-Indians, who had settlements near the newly formed lake. Copper tools, such a fish hooks, found here date to 4,000 to 5,000 years ago. European settlements came with the fur trade in the 1700s. Today, Thunder Bay, with a population of about 109,000, is the largest city on Lake Superior.

As a child Mike came up here almost annually when it was still two separate cities so that his grandmother could go to the Hudson's Bay store. Today the vibrant downtown includes a casino complex and even better, the restored waterfront. We always visit the old districts around Hoito Restaurants and the Finnish Canadian complex in Port Arthur. In addition, there is the original Fort Williams with its churches and structures bringing back the Eastern European heritage of the post fur trade development. We love lingering in Thunder Bay, though on this trip we would cross it relatively quickly.

At Main Street, we turned left and headed up a bridge and crossed over towards an industrial area. Amanda arrived before we got on the next bridge. We drove to an area called the East End, the site of the original Fort William. A historical marker at the end of one street listed all the dates from the late 1700s through the 1800s for the English trading companies – the Hudson's Bay Company and the North West Company. The houses here were all modest, built close together and with three churches within a block of one another. One was Ukrainian, another was Slovakian and the third had also been Slovakian, but now stood empty. Two had onion-dome roofs.

We met and talked with a young bespectacled Diocesan priest at the Slovakian church. He invited us to come in, and let Mike take photos of the beautiful stained glass windows.

Mike stopped a man walking down the street to ask questions about the area. When I joined them, I asked if I could record what he had to say. His name was John and modestly added, "I'm not a historian or anything."

He had lived in the neighborhood all his life and gave insights into the different ethnic groups (Slovakians, Italians and Ukrainians) who lived there in recent decades, although "a lot of them moved away to southern Ontario or Alberta," adding that "a lot of them have assimilated."

"Originally it was the English, Irish and Scottish people who settled here," he said, "but first there were the aboriginal people."

After taping him, I videotaped other portions of neighborhood, the train and tracks and a tunnel under the tracks to the business district. When we left, we noticed all the streets had Scottish or Irish names, which we attributed to the fur trade where these nationalities were common among the leaders.

We'd been in contact with Josephine Mandamin, an Ojibwe woman who launched the "Mother Earth Water Walks" that would eventually take her and a few others on the roads around the Great Lakes to call attention to freshwater issues. We planned to meet her at Mount McKay on the Fort Williams First Nation reserve later in the evening. It was difficult finding our way in the dark with the directions we'd been given, which did, however, peg the "rickety" (though I'd say more clickity) bridge just before the base of the mountain. We crossed that bridge and came to a T intersection, then couldn't see any signs to go right or left.

Pulling into a gas station to ask for directions, Mike asked a woman in a nearby car how to get to Mount McKay. A man washing the windows of a van closer to us said, "Just go out this road here and then …" and he swung his arm sharply to the right, which we took to mean take the road to the right. We drove out and down the dark road, past homes of this small community and saw a police station. Mike stopped, knocked on the window and then rang a bell. A policeman came to the door. "Can you tell us how to get up to Mount McKay?" Mike asked.

The officer came outside. "Go down this road and you'll come to a Y at the bottom of the mountain and you go right and keep following that road and you'll go to the top." But then he continued, "Take this road and it will start to curve to the east and you will come to a Y and take a right …" and he finished by saying, "If you can't find it come back here, and I'll lead ya up."

We found the Y and started up the asphalt road filled with lots of potholes.

We reached the overlook with a view of the city and the lake under a nearly full moon. Behind us rose the massive rock with sheer sides that reminded me of a short, wide Devil's Tower (the one in Wyoming). Some handmade signs near the top said: This is a Sacred Mountain. Respect it and don't leave Trash. Three other cars were parked at the overlook facing the edge. I saw a woman get out of a truck and knew it was Josephine.

We introduced ourselves and Mike presented her with a package of tobacco, a sign of respect and thanks for meeting us. "Miigwetch," she said, which is Ojibwe for "thank you." She wore a fleece jacket and a long skirt. Her long gray hair was clipped up behind her head. We stood at the back of her truck, talking about the walk that she'd done. She, along with others, had carried a bucket of water traveling on the roads around Lake Superior. She described how the calluses grew on her hands. Then we shared stories about both of our walks, what we'd seen and experienced. Josephine comes here to the mountain often and has a favorite spot by some trees and a picnic table where she makes offerings. While we talked a couple of ATVs roared by. We all looked at them before commenting on the noise and how hard it is these days to find quiet in our world.

It was nice to talk with Josephine, who also represented what our walk was about and the connection with First Nations. She was a fascinating person whose gentle aura masked her determination and dedication. Born on Manitoulin Island in Lake Huron, she has lived in the Thunder Bay area since the 1970s. She has always lived by the water, is a member of the Fish Clan and was born under the sign of Pisces. She has had dreams of swimming with fish and snakes and in the dreams she can breathe underwater. Josephine seems well suited to call attention to water concerns "People seem to be sleeping," she said, "not paying attention to what is around them. … The water is always flowing, it never goes backwards."

We'd been standing the whole time at the back of the truck. Mike's legs were hurting, so finally I said we needed to get going to walk tomorrow. "You have to get up at 3:30," she said. We all laughed as I explained that we're much later risers than she and her companions. She hugged us before we left, and we retraced our way down the curvy road back to the hotel and to bed.

The Farmers Market in Thunder Bay was packed with people this late August morning selling local products, bakery items, meat, pastries and coffee. We wandered around and bought a couple delicious lemon/coconut/raspberry tartlets. I spent way too much for three tomatoes ($3 U.S.), but they looked homegrown and I hadn't had any yet this summer. We also bought three cucumbers for Mike and six ears of corn and some jerky and pepperettes (like beef sticks) for our lunches.

Resuming our walk, we crossed a bridge with three delightful metal fish sculptures arrayed along the bridge railing. It was road walking until we crossed an old lift bridge for cars and trains. The bridge mechanism had massive steel half wheels and a concrete weight at the top. At the end of the bridge, I looked down at my feet and saw a dead dragonfly – a big blue darner. I picked it up by a wing and thought I'd drop it into the water, so it could feed another creature, but when my hand went over the side, the "dead" dragonfly grabbed my little finger and wouldn't let go. I carried it with me, examining it carefully. It appeared to have a crack in its thorax. I decided I'd take it to the marsh where we were headed, but then it changed its position on my hand and suddenly fell off. I looked all around me, in the grasses and on the road edge, but it had completely disappeared. It was a special, mystical ride for both of us.

The mix of industrial and pastoral was striking. We passed ditches filled with waving cattail leaves. Under some transmission towers, an old tugboat leaned on its side. Factories loomed to our right. Balsam poplar trees lined the road. We reached a parking area where people were kiteboarding (or kitesurfing) out on the water.

I got jealous watching them, with the "kites" catching the wind and hauling them high into the air. Sometimes they did fancy 360-degree spins. Liam, one of the kitesurfers, told us his GPS clocked him at 50 kmh. That's 30 mph. Watching with my binoculars, I could see the guys holding onto the trapeze bar with just one hand – a beautiful ballet on water. A windsurfer rode the waves, too, but by comparison that seemed old-fashioned and slow. We ate our Farmers Market lunch of beef pepperettes and expensive tomatoes on the grass while we watched the water show, Amanda, Corlyn and Sierra joined us.

I met the windsurfer, a man in his 50s, whose first name was Danny. He shared his memories of a time when the bay in front of us had 30 or more ships moored in it. Talking more about the history of Thunder Bay, he mentioned the melting pot of eastern Europeans, French, British and his own ancestry saying, "I'm Italian on the outside, and all Irish on the inside – plus the blue eyes."

Before resuming our walk, Mike wanted to visit the side of the river where a red-and-white tugboat was moored. After parking at a Robins Donuts shop, and ordering a suitable energy treat, we walked down the sidewalk and under the railroad track to the waterfront park.

A large stainless-steel sculpture filled the center of the plaza. It was called "Anikii," or "Eagle," and there were quotes around the circular base in English, Anishinabe and Cree.

The tugboat had seen better days, but Mike, who has had a love affair with tugboats since he was a little boy, shot lots of photos. We took the pathway by an old passenger train parked on the tracks. It was a hot afternoon, and we were all sweating by the time we got back to the cars.

We drove to Squaw Bay, which is east of Mount McKay, to begin our walk on to Brule Bay. Both are on the First Nations' reserve. Along the way, we found an old, but pretty, white-and-blue church with boarded up windows perched on a hill. There were no signs indicating what denomination it had been, but it was definitely abandoned. The doors were open, so we went in and found an empty room, with partially dismantled walls, but a graceful blue-painted tin ceiling. The altar area was painted white and blue. It was a shame to think that this might all be lost. The intricate designs in the ceiling included a Eucharist inside a circle at the top of the ceiling above the sacristy.

Out in the bay, a series of big wooded headlands poked into the lake. The wind was blowing hard, so it was comfortably cool. We came to Brule Bay, which had been divided by the road. A minivan with two older folks in it slowed down behind us. The man rolled down his window. "Are you that couple that were in the paper?"

Yes, we said, though we hadn't seen the paper.

"You're doing a good job," he said. We thanked them and said we'd have to try to get a copy of the paper. "Just go down to the *Sentinel*," he said, "and they'll give you some copies."

We reached Chippewa Park after a couple hours of walking and exploring and cut through a picnic area near the beach. As we walked the path, a lady focused on me, smiling. I figured she'd seen us somewhere on the media recently. I smiled back, and when we got closer, she said, "Are you the ones I saw on TV?" We told her yes.

"That's amazing," she said. "How's it going?"

"It's been going great."

That evening, we went back to Silver Harbour for our scheduled program, but the only ones waiting to hear us were Carolyn, Todd, Sierra and Amanda.

It was a clear, warm and calm evening. Carolyn took out her guitar and began to play and sing. An animated performer, who wrote her own folk songs, she caused people to stop and come closer. After Carolyn stopped playing,

Period-clothed interpreters bring history alive at Fort William Historical Park in Thunder Bay.

one couple came up with a spaniel on a leash. "Are you disappointed about the turn out?" said the woman, who lived nearby on the shore and worked for Northwest Ontario Tourism. Poorly attended events were good for our egos, Mike pointed out later, or at least for keeping our egos humble. With so many people recognizing us, we did sometimes feel a little "famous."

The next day we spent time at Fort William Historical Park, a re-creation of a North West Fur Company Post, where the staff dress in period costumes from the early 1800s. The buildings and the re-enactors do an excellent job transporting visitors back in time. Todd had arranged for us to have a table in the Provision Store, a big, barn-like building with doors on both sides and a nice breeze blowing through on this hot day. We moved some tables closer to the door, so we could see people coming by and talk to them.

As visitors strolled by the table, we explained who we were and what we were doing. That brought most of them in for a closer look at our maps, to listen to our commentary and to ask questions. One woman who had been following us on Facebook brought her two young sons to meet us. She was impressed with what we were doing and tried to explain the significance to the boys, who were probably 5 and 8 years old. A re-enactor came around to announce an event taking place at the waterfront. Todd said he'd stay at the table and suggested we go to watch. When we got there, a young man dressed in knee-length pants and a loose shirt asked if I would be his partner for a dance. How could I refuse? To the accompaniment of fiddle music, we formed two lines and danced forward and back, kicked, stomped and skipped around the lines.

After the dance, the main show began. The company's clerk was going to be leaving on a smaller voyageur canoe that the Metis women carried down to the water. Guests and performers gathered together as the company partners talked about the upcoming journey. They all made toasts, the young man climbed into the middle of the canoe then they shoved off. There was one male voyageur in the stern and four "Indian" women at the other paddles. They used the commands "*Prépare*" and "*Avant*," as Chris taught us on our voyageur canoe trip. A cannon was fired, which made me jump and Sierra cry.

When we returned, we were delighted to learn that Todd had arranged for us to have a traditional meal in the commissary. Mike, Amanda and I walked to a building used for staff and found a table bearing a feast. A big black cast iron pot had wild rice/vegetable soup in it and there were platters and bowls of roast chicken, mashed potatoes with vegetables (a Scottish dish called "clapshot"), freshly baked white bread and a rhubarb pie. We ate until we could eat no more.

The next morning, we met Amanda at the Hoito Restaurant for breakfast – apparently just in time. Half an hour after we arrived, people were lined up outside the front door of the Finnish restaurant. We ordered their famously thin Finnish pancakes, which look like crepes, but are huge and delicious.

Heading out of town, we stopped at a Can-Op, and Mike bought ice cream treats, which served as our lunch for the day. Neither Mike nor I were inspired for this road-walking day. It didn't help that it was hot outside and we would be walking next to a freshly tarred surface.

As we walked on Ontario Highway 61 out of town, we discovered drivers were not nearly as considerate as they had been on Highway 17. Few moved over toward the center line, except for the big trucks. I didn't have to give out many waves on this section, but quite a few scowls were deserved.

We passed farmland and farmsteads with fields of hay and corn surrounded by forest and backed by the massive rock cliff faces of the Nor'wester Mountains – a dramatic setting for agriculture. A lone immature red-tail hawk sat on a power line above the road. As we approached one crossroad, a healthy looking black bear ran across the highway ahead of us. Mike crossed over, hoping to catch a glimpse of it, but all he got was a distinctive whiff of "eau de bear."

We met Amanda 6 miles up the road and were relieved to stop walking, even for a short time. It was hot, but a strong south/southwest wind helped to cool the sweat on our bodies. We sat in the car, rested our legs for a half hour, then set off again.

Walking by some road construction, a green pick-up truck slowed down on the other side of the road, and a woman rolled down her window. "Getting closer to home every day, eh?"

We agreed, and she wished us good walking and drove away. Such encounters always perked us up and reminded us that people were paying attention, to us and, we hoped, to our messages.

When we reached our set mileage of 10 miles for the day, we got into the car and drove to the Pigeon River Visitor Centre parking area, where we'd left the RV. When we finished our dinner, we cleaned up and got ready to drive over the border, not knowing what to expect since we'd had quite an unusual trip. Mike and I went first in the car, handed the border protections officer our passports and explained what we'd been doing (He had asked where we were coming from and Mike said, "Sault St. Marie.") Mike told him our support vehicle was behind us, so the officer suggested we park and that one of us go into the building. He'd probably have an officer come out to check the RV, he said. I sent Mike in because my all-day headache was getting worse. Amanda parked, too, and carried a muzzled Sheena inside.

Before long, I heard their voices, and then Mike said, "Kate, come on out. Officer Hong wants to meet you." A man with white hair shook my hand and asked if I'd autograph the back of our business card for him. It was the first time anyone asked for our autograph, I told him, and he seemed genuinely surprised. Mike told me later that inside the office, the officers said, "These are the people who are walking around the lake" and "We've been waiting for you." One officer brought our website up on the computer while another brought up Sam Cook's article. We were definitely celebrities of the moment. So much for fretting; it was unlike any other border crossing we'll ever have and made Mike laughed most of the way to Grand Portage.

It was getting dark by the time we pulled into the RV campground at the Grand Portage Marina. Mike stopped at the gas station to see where to register and bumped into Travis Novitsky, a member of the Grand Portage Band of Chippewa who works at the Grand Portage State Park and is a well-known nature photographer.

The last day of August, we were retracing our way back up Highway 61 (Minnesota and Ontario) and through customs again. We had a final Ontario section to cover. We drove down Mink Mountain Road and finally came to a resort office and parking area for the trails on the mountain.

The woman in the office gave the three of us (Amanda and Sheena joined us) some cold bottles of water. She'd been in Rossport and seen us, the "lake walking couple" and was excited to have us here. The sun was out by the time we started walking down Island Road. We followed this until we came to a trail sign and began our climb to the top of Mink Mountain (600 feet). We hiked single file up a narrow, steep path marked with good signage. The view from the top was magnificent with islands scattered on the water and fog clinging to their bases, giving everything a mystical appearance.

The change in season was becoming more evident by the amount of crunchy leaves on the ground and lots of color showing up in the branches. The sarsaparilla leaves were a pretty mix of maroon with green veins. The trail stayed on top of this mountain for quite a ways and fencing kept people from the sheer precipice. Then we started down to find the portion of the trail called "Lake Walk". This proved more difficult as we followed a wide old logging track that dead-ended. Turning back, we came to a gravel road, then turning right, we found the lake and a wooded path close to the shore. Walking behind Mike, I could see the ground depress under his step and spring back when his foot moved forward. No wonder hiking these trails was so much easier on our joints; it was like walking on a springboard.

A kingfisher, annoyed by our presence, flew chattering along the shore. After passing a dock with a fishing boat, we came to Picnic Point. The trail was reminiscent of the Kabeyun in Sibley Provincial Park – going up and sliding past rock faces. It even had a rope "trick" to get down one steep section. We got back to Island Road and walked uphill to the parking lot and car. Only the wind saved us from severely overheating.

We didn't have much time left in the day, but we still had to get to the Finger Point Lookout in Pigeon River Provincial Park, right at the border. It was not a long trail, but it did have a steep climb to the lookout. As usual, I had to stop a couple times to let my heart beat slow and to gulp down liquids. Mike was already at the top when Amanda, Sheena and I got there. Sometimes there's no stopping him. The view was 360 degrees at the top, and there was a long, dark metal sculpture and a thick, 6-foot-long wooden bench cut in the shape of Lake Superior. We took turns sitting, lying and walking on it. The metal work depicted scenes of the human history on the lake with an emphasis on boats. We soaked in the view, and I video interviewed Mike and then Amanda about their thoughts, feelings and memories of being in Ontario; and to add to our YouTube collection. Back at the car, Mike and I prepared to walk – not drive, across the border.

Crossing the bridge over the Pigeon River, we got in line with cars in front of and behind us. When it was our turn, we presented our passports, and the officer asked if we'd had a good time. Then he sent us on with best wishes. As we got out into the sun, I took my baseball cap off and tossed it into the air. Mike and I hugged and kissed and we walked towards the car. We were back in Minnesota and we knew for certain we – both of us – would finish our Full Circle.

We had arranged to interview Travis Novitsky at the Spirit Little Cedar (or Witch) Tree. It would be shady this late in the afternoon, but it is a sacred quiet spot. Taking the main trail through the woods, we passed trees draped with old man's beard lichen. Then down the wooden stairs and walkway to the platform that looks down at the tree. Travis climbed over the railing and told us to follow the path through rocks, around trees and down to the water and the cedar. We each left tobacco for the tree, a 400-year-old gnarled survivor on the edge of Lake Superior. I put my hands on its trunk to express admiration for its perseverance and longevity. It is a work of nature's art and understandably important to the Ojibwe people.

> They, hand in hand, with wandering steps and slow,
> Through Eden took their solitary way.
> Paradise Lost, John Milton

After Thoughts

Sprawl

Mike:

Our survey gave voice to a concern we discovered as we walked some sections of the shore – 63 percent of those who took the survey did not think the current laws and regulation do enough to control development. The majority answering the question live or have cabins on the shore.

We took photos of signs along the way because, like pictographs, they tell about our world and the messages we send. But one photo we did not take, but should have, was of the "For Sale" signs – the most common sign we saw. These signs may tell several stories. One is economic – increasingly desirable lakeshore property becomes a tax burden for those who bought it when it was not worth much. The other story is that when those properties sell, the new, wealthier owners often want larger homes or commercial developments. We found bulldozers making way for new cabins, while older cabins remained for sale. It would make more sense to use the old before building the new.

The lake needs protection from overdevelopment. We loved the stretch from Pancake Bay Provincial Park through Neys Provincial Park along the eastern Ontario shore – one of the most protected parts of the entire lake. We wish we could travel back in time to see what the shore looked like before development (especially to see those ancient stands of towering pines), but we are not against lake homes. Hey, we are admittedly jealous of those who own them, but we do advocate managed growth and land-use planning.

Often more wooded inland habitat gets separated from Lake Superior by too many homes and roads that create a physical obstacle. So when a bear wanders from the forest to the lake, it's considered a nuisance because it encounters temptations we put in its way. A moose that wants to cool off in the lake and to ease the itch of ticks and insect bites encounters highways and fences.

If we were making the rules, we'd leave more lots left intentionally vacant. Planning committees could call them animal (or people) access points and require them in each development under zoning laws. There could also be tax incentives for people who retain their forest and natural landscape. Call it a "lawn mower tax" – those who remove the forest and field to install lawns certainly add to erosion, runoff pollution and other negative impacts. A tax break for the untouched lot would protect the lake and keep the natural ties from land to water.

258

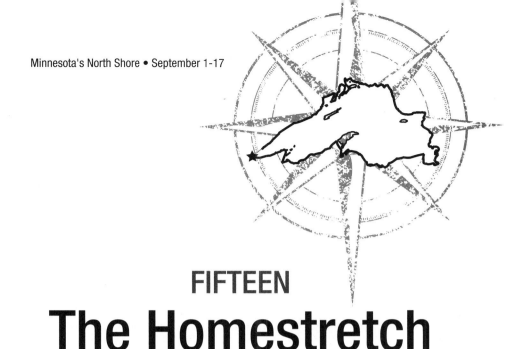

FIFTEEN
The Homestretch

*Capo, my first golden retriever, so loved to swim
she once jumped off a cliff to get into Lake Superior.*
Sara Paretsky

Kate:

Travis Novitsky, a naturalist at Grand Portage State Park, gave us a sneak preview of the new visitor center. A huge, colorful tile turtle is set into the floor right inside the entry, underneath a big circular skylight. The turtle's head points east and the design is encircled by the four sacred colors, aligned with their directions – yellow for east, red for south, black for west and white for north. It was good to learn that the Ojibwe of Grand Portage were so involved in this state park and sharing their history there. It was also a good way to start September and our home stretch.

We stood with Travis on the new wooden deck overlooking the Pigeon River and wetlands while eight eagles circled and soared. Then we took our poles and smaller packs and started walking towards Mount Josephine. It was a long hill with a gradual rise, and Mike was walking very slowly because of sore legs. Mount Josephine is one of the peaks in the Sawtooth Mountain range in Minnesota. It offers views of Lake Superior, Pigeon Point, Wauswaugoning Bay and, on clear days, Isle Royale and the Susie Islands. At the first overlook we could see the wind patterns on the lake. Staring into the distance, I wondered how it could be possible that we had walked on a shore beyond the horizon, just three months ago.

Amanda met us and drove us to the gas station near the band's casino for lunch. Band Chairman Norman Deschampes came into the building, and Mike visited with him – the Band was one of our sponsors. Then the cook in the deli came out and asked Amanda, "They look familiar. Are they the ones walking around the lake?" The cook said she'd been following us in the news and was proud of us.

Our walk resumed at the parking lot, from where we had visited the Spirit Little Cedar. We walked down the road with the bay on our left until we could get to the beach. Ahead of us, Travis, Allan Aubid and his boys, Jaden and Biidaash (which means 'blown by the wind'), waited for us. The two boys were digging in the sand on this narrow strip of beach. The wind, still blowing big and hard, launched rows of whitecaps in the bay. Allan, a young father, is fluent in the Ojibwe language and his boys are learning it now.

Jaden, a talkative 10-year-old and the older of the two, told me that he has about four or five forts built into the brush next to his house. His main fort, he explained, was a lab where he invents stuff like "a birch-bark vest." He tested it by using an air gun and proudly announced that the vest repelled the assault. Four-year-old Biidaash was quieter and had a hard time keeping up.

We came to a sandwich board sign written in English and Ojibwe that warned kids not to swim in the lake. It didn't explain why, but Allan said it was because e-coli had been found in the water. Later in the day, we walked on rocks coated with a smelly, slimy, grayish brown sludge on the other side of the bay.

At the end of our walk, Allan gave us a small bag containing tobacco he had grown from seed and dried himself. He pointed across the road to his house, and we saw some of the big green leaves hanging from the rafters of his front porch. We thanked him and told him we would use it to make an offering to the lake at the end of the trip.

Travis told Mike we could walk the shoreline around the point that we could see from the front of the Grand Portage Lodge and had shown him an access road. We started at the beach in front of the hotel and looked up the shore to the point, but it didn't look that accessible. Waves were washing in and the substrate was not sand, but looked like slippery clay. So we started out on a

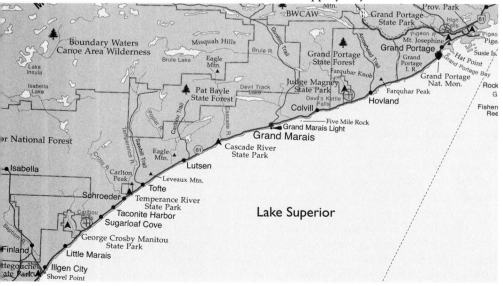

wooded path, which quickly evolved into bushwhacking. We could see that it had once been an old footpath, but had not been maintained for a long time. Climbing over downed trees and pushing through the branches of balsam firs that had grown over the path, we stumbled along and tried to go out on the rocks, but were forced back into the woods. At one point, in an especially bad tangle, Mike asked if we should go back or forward. I figured we had gone far enough that I didn't want to back track and hoped that we would soon get out on the shore. "Let's go ahead," I said.

We finally broke through the forest onto a space wide enough to avoid the mucky, yucky tan coating on the rocks. When the shore turned right, we were met with the full force of the wind. Even with the sun shining, it was chilly, but the rocks were bigger and easier to walk on. Nearby, wild rose bushes were thick with bright scarlet hips. The rocks were a different kind of volcanic formation with lots of holes (gas bubbles), indicating it had been a surface flow.

As we walked, we saw one spotted sandpiper – my personally designated shorebird of this lake. Except for the rocky Canadian shore, they had been constant companions. At first they had been new arrivals, but now they were preparing to leave, as we, too, were ending our journey. We also saw huge numbers of dragonflies, the beautiful, big darners. They were moving south, a rare example of a migratory insect. Our day ended after 12 miles at the campground next to the Grand Portage lodge.

Weigh-in morning, and Mike, naturally, lost a couple more pounds, his skin was noticeably looser in places, but his blood pressure remained high. I lost six more ounces, still two pounds away from my goal of 10 pounds. My blood pressure had consistently dropped, though, and now was about 120/80, which is close to ideal for my age.

The wind was really cranking – a September nor'easter – as we put on all our raingear and packs and told Amanda to meet us 5 miles up the road. Around 10 a.m., Jim Radford pulled in front of us. He left his wife, Donna, in the car and began to walk with us. After walking on the cobbled beach for some minutes, Mike asked how Jim would like to walk on this for four hours as we had on the beach above McClain State Park in the Keweenaw and many other locations.

"No thanks," he said. "I'll leave that to the pros."

"More like the foolish," said Mike.

Neither Mike nor I had brought our poles. I was wearing my bigger pack and suddenly my left foot slipped on some small rocks and I fell forward, the weight of the pack pushing me down. I landed on my hands and knees. I wasn't hurt, but realized how much difference a full pack made and that my poles might have prevented the fall. Mike asked if I was OK. I was. We climbed back up onto the road, which was right next to the beach just before we got to a small cabin 15 feet from the water. This turned out to be a commercial fisherman's camp.

A short distance from this cabin, a black SUV pulled into a driveway in front of us. The vehicle turned around and three people got out of the car to ask if we were "the walkers."

"We were really hoping to see you!" they said with big grins and hands out. Cassie and Bill Gamble have a cabin on the shore, and Kris Garey is the pastor of the Trinity Lutheran Church in Hovland. "Bless you," they all said, and "This is so wonderful" and "Everybody is so excited about what you're doing."

We agreed to stop at the Gambles' cabin the next day for coffee. We were tickled by their enthusiasm and wondered how many more encounters we would have like that on the Minnesota shore – our home territory.

At another driveway Ben Petz was waiting to greet us next to a beautiful diamond willow mailbox post he had carved. The Gambles were also waiting by our parked car and told us we should get our lunch at the Chicago Bay Marketplace. We took their advice and ordered fresh-baked pizzas. While we waited for our food, Mike and I took turns going outside to record the audio commentary for Jim's video project.

After lunch, Amanda drove us back to continue our walk. Cars honked and people waved as they passed us. Two cars slowed down and pulled in behind us. One belonged to Mary Petz, Ben's wife, who walked down to tell us how pleased she was to see us. A short time later, another car stopped ahead of us. A woman got out and walked towards us, saying she had hoped to see us on her drive to Grand Portage. Mary Rademacher is a psychologist who grew up in Grand Marais and moved away at 19. She's always been drawn back to the lake, and at 62 decided she wanted to do something important for the lake and the people on it. She got involved with the charter school on the reservation and comes up every other week to work with the kids who need extra help.

We realized our schedule on this shore might be altered by all our encounters. Just before we got to the Marketplace at Chicago Bay Road, a woman walking up the hill saw us and said, "Are you the ones walking around the lake?"

"Yes."

"Wait 'til I tell my husband I saw you!" She said, adding "Bless your hearts" and, as she patted our arms, "Oh, you kids." (One of my favorites from the trip.)

From the road, we could see the rocks out in Chicago Bay, something neither of us had ever noticed before despite passing this way driving many times. We also noticed the elegant rock-and-wood sided Trinity Lutheran Church. We were pleased by our newfound image of Hovland, gotten by choosing a different way to travel.

Amanda met us at the Java Moose in Grand Marais and drank coffee while we waited to be interviewed for the Grand Marais paper. Rhonda Silence hadn't heard anything about our walk until recently, but was highly complimentary of our website. Everyone in her office had said, "I want to do that." Mike asked if she wanted to walk with us to Duluth. Her response was a hearty laugh.

I caught up with Mike at the Lake Superior Trading Post, where was chatting with two of his former Hamline students he'd bumped into. Meeting all of these people reinforced that crossing the border had brought us home.

We decided to go to Hughie's Tacos, where Amanda treated us to dinner. Their tortillas are like Indian fry bread and overflowing with ingredients. I had the beef and sauerkraut, which doesn't sound remotely Mexican, but was great. Amanda would be leaving us for the rest of the journey until Duluth and this was our farewell dinner.

It rained all night and continued in the morning. At Naniboujou Lodge about 14 miles northeast outside of Grand Marais, we parked and did a quick shuttle with Amanda. We gave her a hug, and she and Sheena drove off up the hill. From now on, we'd be using Mike's bike to do our shuttles.

Almost as soon as we started walking, we heard someone calling. A young man in his 20s wearing shorts was running to catch up. "Are you the ones walking around the lake?" Ben Hatter had a firm handshake and said he'd walk with us for a ways. He and his dad were doing the Lake Superior Circle Tour by car and were on their homestretch, too. He was from McGregor, Minnesota, and was a college friend of our dentist's son. Mostly he wanted to tell us how impressed he was with our walk. We told him we were glad he and his dad had gone around the lake together. After walking with us for awhile, he shook our hands again and turned back. We shook our heads at the enthusiasm people were showing for this crazy walk.

The Gambles' dark gray wood-sided home set well inside the trees. The rocks facing the water are almost flat ledge rock, perfect for sitting and watching the lake. They built this place more than 30 years ago when shoreline property was selling for $6 a front foot, they said. Today in some places around the shore, prices can range as high as $500 to $800 a square foot.

Cassie came to the door and was just as enthusiastic as yesterday. "Oh, you came! Come in!" Bill is a retired surgeon and a professor emeritus from the University of Minnesota College of Surgery. We sat at their long wooden dining room table, looking out the picture windows at their bird feeders and the lake. We talked about our trip and their lives. Bill, 76, asked lots of questions. Cassie retains the pretty features of her youth, but with creases deepened by her constant smile. Bill is a philanthropist, involved with a non-profit that helps provide water for people in water-strapped Tanzania, as well as medical assistance.

Outside, waves crashed onto the rocks, and Cassie asked Mike to identify a mystery in her garden, which turned out to be cotton aphids. She thought that they were a fungus or plant and was surprised to learn that they were insects. Mystery solved, we took photos and said goodbye - picking our way carefully over the angled, dark rocks covered with lichens and moss. We had our poles along, but they weren't much help on damp rocks. It was slow going, and I didn't trust my boot soles, especially after slipping on one rock. I looked ahead at the distance we'd have to go and said, "I think we should go back up to the road." This is where we began to notice that our shoes were worn out. They looked good above, but had no tread left. These were our original pairs.

Early Labor Day weekend traffic was heavy and the pressure to get somewhere was obvious in the drivers. Few moved over to give us room and one roared within a foot of us as it passed another car going our direction. We realized traffic was just going to get worse all weekend and we were glad that we were going home to take a break for the holiday, when we'd also be celebrating our grandson's birthday.

A car slowed down on the other side, and we knew we had another well-wisher to meet. A woman wearing a bright yellow rain poncho got out and yelled across the road. "Are you the ones walking around the lake?" Jeannie Hanson has a cabin on the shore and lives in the Twin Cities. She'd read about us in the North House Folk School newsletter.

We reached Naniboujou Lodge around 12:30 p.m., and Mike went in to see owner Tim Ramey. Tim was in his office in a motorized wheelchair. He has not been able to walk since a tragic accident 12 years ago when a portion of a building fell on him when he responded to a call as a volunteer firefighter. We met Tim more than two decades ago, and after chatting about our trip, he asked, "Could I buy you lunch?" An offer we would not refuse. Naniboujou has amazing food and a mind-blowing dining room, painted in all the primary colors based on a Cree design.

Back down in Grand Marais, the Lake Superior Trading Post agreed to get us new shoes. Bill and Beth Blank, our advisors who had taken over as support drivers when Amanda took a break in Michigan, invited us to their home. Then we were driving toward our home, watching growing cloud formations and sunset colors spreading over them. On the other side of the lake in Ontario, 10-foot waves were reported by Montreal River. In Muskallonge State Park near Newberry, Michigan, campers had to be evacuated because of tornado-strength winds. It is indeed a big lake with its 350-mile east-west stretch.

During our Labor Day weekend hiatus, both of us slept soundly in our own comfortable bed. We awoke to a clear, but chilly morning. I wondered what the yard and flower beds would look like in the daylight after about four months of neglect. Overgrown best defined them. The bird feeders were empty, except for the hummingbird feeder, which drew no customers. We attended a wedding of young friends on Saturday afternoon, enjoyed our grandson Matthew's birthday and caught up with mail and laundry.

Heading back up to Lake Superior on Tuesday, September 7, the day after Labor Day, our car was nearly full again as we drove north through rain.

Going past Grand Marais, we began to see patches of blue between the clouds. After finding a place to hide Mike's bike on the side of the road, we drove to Naniboujou Lodge. We had wanted to interview Tim Ramey but just missed him as he headed out for his daily bike exercise.

After walking across the bridge over the Brule River, we came to Manitoo Road. Taking any opportunity to get off of Highway 61, we turned on to it. By the time we got to the end of this road and back to 61, I had taken off my fleece layer. We saw a spot where we could get to the shore, made up here of gravel and cobbles. Low swells rolled into shore and a gray light spread softly on the water. On the beach, the waves made a great rhythmic rattling as they pushed up onto the rocks and swept back down.

There were trees to go under and over along the way, and hunks of bedrock to climb, but mostly it was just loose rock. A spotted sandpiper flew out over the lake, calling as it went.

Ahead I could see people standing on the shore. Mike stopped to take off his jacket and answer his phone. It was Mike Simonson of Wisconsin Public Radio. Letting Mike handle the interview, I started to walk and saw Tim Ramey pedaling by on the road edge. I waved and called his name, but he kept going, so I ran up the bank, calling louder. Finally Tim slowed down.

Every day Tim rides about 8 miles on his three-wheeled, hand-pedaled bike. I wanted to do a video interview, even though the side of the busy road wasn't the best location. Ahead, a man got out of a pick-up truck and walked to us carrying two water bottles. He offered us the bottles with without saying a word. We thanked him and he went back to his truck. Tim didn't know him either; he was just a kind stranger.

Tim talked about how he and his wife, Nancy, bought Naniboujou Lodge in 1985. The previous owners' two sons, 23 and 28, died tragically in a canoe accident on the Brule River. The lodge seemed to have a cursed, yet fascinating history. The idea of the place was launched in 1927 as the "Naniboujou Holding Company" to be a private club on 3,330 acres about 125 miles northeast of Duluth. The company had members from around the country, among the most famed being homerun hitter Babe Ruth, former world heavyweight boxing champion Jack Dempsey and New York newspaperman Ring Lardner. A French artist was commissioned to paint the distinctive dining room designs. The lodge was christened in July 1929 but was in deep trouble by October 1929 with the stock market crash igniting the Great Depression. Eventually, Naniboujou would be bought by owners who made it an open-to-the-public resort.

A few miles southwest of Naniboujou, the Lake Superior Hiking Trail comes down from a ridge to the beach on a stretch called the Lake Walk. Out on the round cobbled shore, the only person I saw was a young man wearing a big backpack and adjusting his walking poles. The lake shimmered in silver. More bedrock, covered in lichens, created the shore beyond a nearby point of rock. It was a good spot to stop for lunch. Around us blue harebells were in bloom, as were the small yellow flowers of the cinquefoil. Raptors flew overhead – merlins, kestrels, broad-wing hawks and an eagle. We were walking southward in concert with the raptors on their migration.

The boardwalk at Tofte links Bluefin Bay Resort and the Tofte Commercial Fishing Museum.

As we ate our sandwiches and gazed out at the calm water, I realized once again how lucky we were to have this chance to be on Lake Superior and in an intimate way that we would never repeat. We had the joy of discovering the less-traveled places, like the small clearing with four or five cedar trees where I found big black feathers on the ground and what looked like a wood duck box attached to a tree. It was a perfect little spot for a tent and a great hiding place.

We passed people looking for rocks. The woman, casually smoking a cigarette, stood in the water in hip waders. Her companion sat in a folding chair on the rocks just a few feet up the beach. There were buckets around them. She said she was looking for "pretty rocks." It struck us how people enjoy the lake in different ways.

The Lake Walk is 1.5 miles long and makes a nice diversion from Highway 61, but we kept going past the designated trail exit because we could still see shore to walk. Cabins came into view, and suddenly there was a gypsy wagon, the roof covered with a tarp. It was set back in the woods. Authentic looking, it seemed homemade and definitely was a surprise to find here.

Near the Kadunce River, we saw a man with his tent spread on the ground. He was drinking a can of soda. "Are you walking all the way around the lake?" He was from Blaine, Minnesota, and had been coming to the cabins by Colvill since he was a little kid. He was up for the weekend, and a co-worker had shown him our website. "Maybe you'll run into them!" his friend told him.

The gravel and cobbles were taking a toll on Mike's knees. A falcon flew across the road, then over the lake, chasing a smaller bird. It made a quick turn back to shore and dove hard. A small songbird flew just a foot or so ahead of the winged predator; it barely made it into the safety of the shrubbery. The falcon had to swoop up and fan out its tail to slow down. We know a falcon's got to eat, but we couldn't help but root for the underdog (or in this case, the underbird).

Kestrels swooped from one side of the road to the other, sometimes perching in trees near the road. One seemed to play leapfrog with me, perching in one place as I walked by it, then flying ahead and perching again.

Having done his bike shuttle back to the car, Mike drove up as I got to the Devil's Track River bridge and the stone house that I so love. It is like a fairy tale cottage. Hard to imagine how long it took to build with all those round cobble stones. We drove back to town and went to the East Bay Suites, where we had been given an anonymous gift of a luxurious suite of rooms. I soaked in a lovely hot bath, with a row of candles flickering on a shelf as I let the heat seep into my sore feet and hips.

Our second day back on the shore, we woke up with sunshine streaming in the windows and Beth Blank drove us to the Devils Track River to start the day's walk. She also gave us cherry tomatoes to eat and a container of fresh watermelon. An immature bald eagle and several vultures soaring over the streambed greeted us when we got out of the car. The eagle flew off and landed in a tree, while the vultures continued to circle under a beautiful blue sky.

Bill and Cassie Gamble's black SUV stopped. "We needed one more hug," Cassie said. We told them we'd be giving a talk that night at East Bay, and they thought they'd come. Shortly after they left us, the phone rang. It was Dennis Lien of the *St. Paul Pioneer Press* wanting an interview. It was good to have such interest continue along the way – and not always easy because cell phone service can be spotty along the shore.

The water whispered as it slipped up and down on the gravel beach in front of the Best Western and the East Bay Suites. We crossed the parking lot by the Coast Guard station, walked over to Main Street and on to North House, where our friend Kelly Dupre came in carrying some papers.

She looked questioningly at Mike as he was walking away from her. Then she saw me. "You didn't realize that was Mike, did you?" I said.

"No," she said. "I was just thinking 'Who's the guy wearing the weird shorts.'" Mike wore his knee braces under his shorts, like leggings.

Then she said, "It's cold out there today."

And for most people it was, but Mike has a history of wearing shorts in temperatures others would consider outside that range.

After we left North House, we continued towards Cutface Creek. A horned lark rested beside the road and another immature bald eagle soared overhead. Out on the lake, I spotted my first big freighter since somewhere close to Gros Cap, Ontario, and the Sault Ste. Marie area. We didn't see any freighters on our journey across the northern shore of the lake, even while we were in the voyageur canoe.

Cutface Creek has recently renovated the rest area, with picnic tables and clean outhouses. We did a point count out on the beach, where other people were sitting or looking for rocks. We ate the little cherry tomatoes and caramel apple suckers.

Walking uphill to Terrace Point, we passed Mike's favorite rock face. It has layers of different volcanic flows over layers of sandstone. According to the Minnesota Geology website there are two very different layers of rock. The lower red layer is sandstone, 130 feet thick. The upper gray layer is basalt, 160 feet thick at this point. This layer contains the mineral thomsonite, a highly sought pink, green and white gemstone.

Just nearby is the Thomsonite Beach Resort, where we asked permission to go to the beach. The owner gave us his permission, though he didn't think we could walk the shore because of the rocks and other private lands. He was right. Where his property ended, a sign said "Private property," so we turned back and crossed a lawn being probed by a flock of yellow-shafted flickers.

That night, we had Sven and Ole's pizza with Karen Halbersleben and her husband, Jack, who had worked with Mike at Northland College. They joined about a dozen others for our presentation in the East Bay lounge, where a fireplace filled the room with warmth.

Mike's former student and friend Andrew Slade joined us for a day of hiking along the Cascade State Park Lakeshore Trail. Andrew is a strong advocate for environmental issues and is the author of hiking, skiing and camping guides to the North Shore. This particular rocky shore is one we have walked in all seasons and is yet another favorite.

We continued down the trail to the rocky shore. It felt so good to be next to the water and exploring again. Bright orange lichens and all the intrusive lines of orange and white in the black basalt entertained our eyes. After crossing the Cascade River, we walked to the Cascade Lodge to see owner Michael O'Phelan.

Michael was enthusiastic about our adventure and came with us to the beach, where I interviewed him.

Looking out at the lake that drew him north, he said "I was tired of the corporate life, 45 years old and we were looking for something. We decided we were going to make a jump and once we saw Cascade Lodge our eyes never turned to anything else."

"All my life I remember driving up here on the old road, getting out of the car in the middle of the night, breathing that fresh north shore air, and laying on the hood that was so warm and looking at those millions of stars and it just gets in your blood."

"That was pretty painless," he said when we'd finished. We tried to walk along the shore from that spot to the Cascade Beach Road, but could see cabins close to the rocks and didn't want to antagonize anyone. We went back up to Highway 61 for a stretch until we turned onto the Beach Road. The day was warming up.

Solbakken Resort was our next stop, where Scott Benson a longtime employee and friend, was working. The O'Phelan's bought Solbakken from Bill and Beth Blank a few years ago, and we are so happy they are keeping it in the same small-scale operation. Scott offered us candy bars and pop, and I interviewed him on the porch.

With busy Highway 61 behind him, he reminisced, "I've worked at the Lodge 19 years. I moved up here in 1978."

"I like to say that my first trip up here was when my mom was seven months pregnant and we came up here every year…I grew up coming to the North Shore. The Lake was a huge draw."

When we finished he repeated Michael O'Phelan's opinion, stating, "That was pretty painless."

We crossed the highway and got onto a well-used trail that parallels Highway 61 all the way down to Clearview Store. We had been invited by Andrew's parents for dinner, but we cleaned ourselves up first at the Blanks.

Dick, Andrew's dad, was standing outside with Hammo, an enthusiastic yellow lab who came charging over to welcome us and then charged back into the shrubbery. Ella brought out corn chips, guacamole and hummus. (Should you invite us to your house, do not put guacamole in front of Mike or me; we have no control.) Ella must have had an angel whisper in her ear because she had made pot roast, Mike's all-time favorite dish. She also served fresh steamed green beans and pasta noodles. For dessert, there was a mouthwatering apple pie with a cream cheese layer on the bottom. Before leaving, we made plans to meet Dick the next morning, as he would take us along their shore and through their property.

The Blanks had generously invited us to stay with them for a few days as we walked this stretch of the shore. It's always a treat to sit beside their big living room windows and stare out at the lake in its many moods. Bill has become friends with a crow that he calls Big Bird. It comes to their deck every morning. Dutifully he carries out a tray with a mixture of cat food and bird seed to the deck table while the crow stands on the deck railing waiting. Then Bill sits down and the crow hops along the edge of the railing until it decides to land on the table and delicately pick up the tiny pieces of food.

We met Dick Slade at the Caribou River parking lot under a mix of blue skies and clouds. Hammo came along and was straining on his leash. Down the path along the Caribou, we came to a sign and gate that said, "Magney." This is the family of Judge C.R. Magney and they own property on the north side of the river.

On the south side was the home of Frank Wright, another famous North Shore resident. Magney and Wright were responsible for getting most of the rivers and parks along the shore protected as public land – a state park near Colvill is named for the judge – but they kept this stretch along the Caribou River private. We walked down a grassy path until we came to a bridge over the river. A good amount of water was flowing and we could see waterfalls we had never before seen along this stretch. On the other side, we negotiated a thickly overgrown path up a hill until we came out on a driveway that took us by a house then down some steps to the rocky beach and mouth of the Caribou River.

Hammo was desperate for someone to throw something for him. He kept looking at the rocks and then at me, so I threw a few. Then I found a stick and threw that. The waves splashed onto the gravel. It looked to be the beginning of another beautiful day on the shore.

Dick, who is 80, started up the rocks before us. I watched nervously as he balanced precariously. His walking stick lacked a rubber tip, and we knew from experience those could be useless on rocks like these. Hammo raced up and down, back and forth, like a yellow streak on extra caffeine. Bright orange lichens covered the rocks, and the wind and sun beat down on us.

At the end of the day, Dick told me that his balance isn't what it used to be. Is there any 80-year-old who has the balance they once had? I wondered what causes us to become less steady on our feet – fading eyesight, slower reflexes? Mike certainly was getting a better idea of aging joints with every mile, and his balance, too, was threatened by his worsening eye.

One gravelly beach had scattered pieces of driftwood. Dick told us that the well-known Ojibwe abstract artist George Morrison used to come here to collect pieces for his earlier works.

Then Dick tumbled backward. His sunglasses fell off and slid down the rocks, one lens coming out as it hit. We retrieved the glasses, but not the lens. Luckily, Dick hadn't hurt himself, but it shook me up. "They weren't prescription glasses," he said, assuring us that he was fine.

We came to what Dick called the "Least Manitou River," a small flow that cut a large crevice in the shore. Next we climbed into the shrubbery and took a path to his driveway.

Dick's father bought 5,000 acres in 1938 when Dick was 8 years old. In the height of the Depression, the price that seems outrageously low today was a fortune then. His father built a massive stone house on the shore and came up every August to stay. The road was built in 1924, but they didn't have an electrical hook-up for a couple years after that.

Ella, who still likes to look for agates and other pretty rocks despite the

number of years she's been on the shore, joined us on their beach. She brought a walking stick and a box of rocks she was returning to the beach. Mike walked ahead with Dick and I stayed back with Ella, a down-to-earth lady who, like all grandparents, enjoys talking about her grandkids and I, also a grandmother, enjoy listening.

Hammo had found a water-logged tennis ball and was in yellow-lab heaven. We took turns throwing it into the lake. He would charge out, catching waves in the face and surfing them back into shore. Dogs love Lake Superior. We followed along the beach before starting up the slope through the vegetation. Hammo by this time had lost his energy and was walking sedately near Dick, still carrying his precious tennis ball. The high rocky cliffs offered good views over

The aptly named Cascade River flows through its state park namesake. Minnesota's North Shore parks offer memorable hiking experiences.

the lake as we progressed. The trail had unexpected dips and rocks and roots hidden by thick vegetation.

We crossed the Manitou River on a bridge. The gorge below was one of the deepest we've seen on the Minnesota shore. Walking on this elevated edge, we saw only the third waterfall of our walk that ended right at the lake. The other two were Spray Falls in Michigan and the one at the campsite across from Otter Island in Canada

Following the trail, we came out on a road and took it to the Slade family house set on a cliff overlooking the lake. It resembled a French chateau and is built of flat stones from the area. Workers out in front were repairing the original stone pillars. Hammo, refreshed, ran to them, and they threw the ball for him.

We sat on a bench and ate lunch while gazing out at the vast blue body of fresh water. Then we walked to the front of the house and up the road to another path through the woods. This used to be a pasture where a lone milk cow was kept, Dick said. His dad felt that by having a cow, the caretaker would stay onsite. The cow, after all, had to be milked every day. When his dad bought the land and built the house in 1938, he hired locals to do the work. The craftsmanship was superb. "This was the first cash money these people had seen in a long time," Dick recalled.

This path led us to another road, to another property on a high bluff, through the woods, and back out on the rocks. Hammo, tired of waiting for us, dropped his tennis ball on these rocks then ran down after it into the surging waves. The dog seemed to have a frightening time getting out of the lake, and for a moment Mike thought he would have to go down to rescue him. Hammo made it out, but without the tennis ball. It was gone for good.

Dick said we should bushwhack up the hill until we came to an old driveway. Mike led the way. We crossed a track cleared for a powerline, but found no driveway and the vegetation got thicker. Dick said try going left, but still no luck. We continued uphill, spooking two good-sized white-tailed bucks. Overhead, low clouds were rushing by and, above them, cirrus clouds indicated a change of weather coming. At a ridge, we found a track but couldn't tell whether it was old or new. Following it to the south, we gradually went downhill and came out close to Highway 61.

Mike continued walking down the road, since we still needed to get in 4 more miles to reach our 12 mile goal. When Ella came to pick up Dick, she saw Paddle and wanted to know what it was. When I told her, she got very excited. She had bought a carved Paddle at a toy store in St. Paul and had it sitting on the mantel in the cabin. She even had the drawings for the carving, done by a fifth-grade Hmong boy. We stopped to take photos of the two Paddles.

The next day, flying gulls made dark silhouettes against the flat gray sky. We began the day by meeting the owners of Lutsen Resort on Lake Superior, Scott Harrison and Nancy Burns, who invited us to join them for brunch in their historic lodge dining room. Lutsen Resort may be Minnesota's longest operating resort, established in 1885 by a young Swedish immigrant, Charles Axel Nelson.

After breakfast, we met our friend John Wolforth from Willow River. Walking across part of the Superior National Golf Course to a nature trail, we passed rain-swollen streams rushing toward the lake. Thick clouds and fog surrounded us. The trail popped out on an old road that led to the Gitchi-Gami State Trail, a new, paved pathway for non-motorized use such as bicycles or walkers. Along the way culverts spouted white and brown water into Lake Superior, vivid examples of potential non-point pollution sources.

We continued on the paved trail and crossed the Onion River. The Gitchi-Gami trail goes downhill and away from the road by the Cobblestone Cabins. At the cabins' driveway, Mike called out "Jan!" to the man there. They exchanged handshakes and a hug; Jan was an old friend of Mike's from 1975. Yet another friend along this shore.

The sun broke through the fog, and it was warming up. The vegetation sparkled with silver pearls of water shining in the sun. I tapped longer grasses with my pole, creating showers onto the path.

We finished by traversing Tofte Park, with its little marina and picnic grounds. We also came upon a surprising little section with handmade cobblestone bridges, built in the early 1900s and repaired and rebuilt almost 100 years later. Next to the Coho Café and Bakery, there is the small Tofte Commercial Fishing Museum. Inside we found this understated quote by an old Scandinavian fisherman: "I always loved the lake, you know, but it's a bad one at times." Helmer Aakvik of Hovland (1896-1987) should know. The Norwegian immigrant nearly died going out in his small fishing boat to save his young neighbor from a sudden Lake Superior storm in November 1958. He couldn't save him and was found, mostly ice-encased, on the water. He earned the Carnegie Award for Heroism and his description of that day recorded in his own accented English is one of the treasures of this museum.

As we continued, I knew Mike's knees hurt, but he said we'd drive back to Lutsen and finish the walk to the Lockport store. We needed to do it, but I felt cranky by this time, probably from lack of sleep and fluids.

We'd never been to the Last Chance Studio & Gallery, where Beth Blank works, so we stopped and met Tom Christiansen, the owner and a metal-working artist. His whimsical sculptures are scattered around the building. One wonderful bronze bench has two people sitting next to each other. Another sculpture, designed to look like a mosquito, was made with a fire extinguisher body and sunglasses for eyes.

Rhea Kontos, a tall, lean and friendly angel who we met at a fundraiser before our walk, decided to join us the next day. She is a Nordic Walking instructor, who procured the poles and rubber tips that became so important during our walk. (Nordic Walking, or pole walking, involves the use of such poles to increase the intensity of a fitness walk.) We met at Temperance River State Park and Mike left his bike at the Caribou River rest area.

We walked through the park campground until we found a path down to the rock shore. Big darner dragonflies swept back and forth, their diaphanous wings glinting in the sun, and a water pipit (a small grayish brown bird) hopped on the rocks. The waves splashed and crashed on the shore. In a few spots, the waves shot upward like geysers. Rhea had never walked this difficult a shore, but easily kept up – not surprising considering her level of fitness and training.

The Taconite Harbor power plant loomed ahead, and Mike felt we could get all the way to Schroeder, but we were moving slowly, having to climb down steep sections. At the Temperance River mouth, we took the foot bridge across the stream, before returning to the shore, where we walked the gravel beach and took photos of kids in the water, squealing as waves splashed them.

We were near Father Frederic Baraga's cross – a stone cross marking the spot where Baraga and his canoe paddler supposedly landed after safely crossing Lake Superior from Wisconsin during a storm in the mid-1800s. We had to go down a steep rock and dirt slope to get to the water and encountered a narrowed path. Mike went first, then Rhea. I tried to time our sprint between the waves. We didn't quite make it and we got wet shoes. Rhea was getting the full experience.

At the next gravel beach, people were looking for rocks. One man remarked about our ski poles and lack of snow – not an uncommon quip. When we headed to the other side, he said, "You can take the road up, it's much easier."

"Yeah," Mike replied, "but this way is much more inspiring."

Crossing more boulders and a slope, we finally reached Baraga's cross on a promontory above the mouth of the Cross River. Below, a large fish tried to swim up the river.

The Cross River wasn't deep this time of year, but it flowed fast. In spring or after lots of rain, it can be torrential. We decided that since our feet were already wet, we'd cross it. I filmed from the top as Mike scared one fish into jumping out of the way. People sitting on the shore watched with amusement. I handed the woman one of our business cards, and told her we were walking around the lake.

"The whole lake?" she said, looking a little shocked.

After more waves and more splashes, we finally reached the campground for Lamb's Resort, which is near Schroeder and about 80 miles northeast of Duluth. (Still quite a ways to go!) Rhea was to meet her husband in Schroeder so we walked up to the road and came out at the town post office. Rhea walked a short distance on Highway 61 with us, but she turned back because she was not comfortable with all the close traffic. We understood perfectly.

Our road walk took us 4 miles southwest from Schroeder to Sugarloaf Cove Nature Center, operated by the Sugarloaf: The North Shore Stewardship Association and where my brother's RV was parked. Tom and Susan were having their lunch, so we joined them. After eating, Tom, Mike and I walked down the trail to the water, where Mike and I did our point count. Sugarloaf Cove has a wonderful recovery story for the once heavily logged area. The cove features 1.1 billion-year-old lava flows and a beautiful bay. There is an interpretive building with staff and volunteers.

The afternoon took us along a section of the Superior Hiking Trail, which soon will link from south of Duluth all the way to the international border. What a treat it was to walk among the trees on a soft, well-groomed dirt path with many views of the lake. This is birch forest, and many of the trees were bent or had broken trunks from previous ice storms, but their golden leaves, in full autumn splendor, lit up the day.

The Caribou River was really flowing fast as it approached a long drop into a wide pool. We took a long set of stairs down to the pool where the canyon walls are high. At 4:30 p.m. at the bottom, the sun was already hidden from view. Susan took off her shoes and waded tentatively into the pool. A native Californian, this was her first exposure to cold North Shore waters. She said it felt good even as she gasped. Tom and Mike went back up the steps to the parking lot, where Tom persuaded Mike to let him ride the bike back to fetch the RV.

It was 3:30 a.m. on Monday, September 13, and I was awake. I had slept fairly well the first few hours of the night, but woke up and realized Mike was not in bed. I figured he was on the couch in the Blank's living room, trying to get some sleep.

Through the living room window, I could see a line of lights off in the blackness on the lake. I pressed my face against the glass and wondered if it was a freighter. I'd never seen one lit up and down its whole length. The clear sky was filled with constellations and the waves continued to crash on the shore.

At 5:40 a.m., a light orange-pink line formed over the lake's horizon. Dark, scattered puffs of clouds floated above the color, but it was still dark out the window. The mountain ash tree framed the view, and, at 6:38 a.m., the sun broke above the horizon.

We went to the Lockport store for breakfast with Tom. Nan, at the counter, was asking, "Is Kate coming?"

"Here she is," Mike said as I came in. Nan asked if I had changed my hairstyle. Maybe I lost weight in my face at least. I had gotten my haircut last in Thunder Bay, but it was the same short style I always wear.

The year before our walk, we'd visited with Nan Bradley and Deb Niemisto, owners of the Lockport. At that time, Nan had said, "You be sure to stop in, and we'll give you breakfast." She was true to her word. There was a copy of the St. Paul newspaper on the counter, and photos of us covered a full half of the front page and most of the back, too.

After a breakfast, we headed to Tettegouche State Park. Bryan and Kat Wood were waiting there. Bryan, a co-director at the Audubon Center of the North, took over when Mike retired. He's also a former student of Mike's and a good friend. He and Kat, who is a talented artist from Germany and a biologist, had brought their dog, Nellie. We were happy to have another canine companion, though Nellie is a most unusual looking mutt with almost rabbit-size ears and a small pointed face. With her slender body and long legs, she looks like a wild dog from Africa. She was alert and friendly and would become the cause of my falling on the trail.

On one of the park boardwalks, Mike and Bryan walked ahead of me while Kat, with Nellie on the leash, walked behind me. I stopped to take video of an ancient-looking cedar that had embraced a huge boulder. As I stepped off the boardwalk, Nellie decided to step off beside me. I saw her just as I stepped down and began to step on her. I'm not sure what happened next, if I tripped on her leash or tried to avoid her, but I went down, landing on my left hand with my right hand holding the camera in the air. Bryan and Kat rushed to me. "Are you all right?" Yet another lucky fall with no injuries.

274

We walked the paths to get to Shovel Point. The park has a lot of boardwalk in place to keep people on the paths as the park is trying to restore vegetation. This area and Palisade Head, about a mile southwest of the park, are popular rock climbing sites. We saw some of the permanent metal anchors set in the top of the point's cliff.

When we got to the point, Mike continued on down a narrow path, skirting the edge of the cliff. This was the way to Shovel Point, he said, even though I was sure we had just been on the point. The path came frighteningly close to the edge in places – a sheer drop off a 100-foot cliff. I was glad Nellie was on a leash.

We continued going over rocks and through woods until we came to a bay and had to turn back. This gorgeous coastline with lots of headlands and their sheer drops were made more spectacular by the dragonflies that filled the air above us, zipping back and forth to catch insects.

After finding our way down to the cobble beach, we came to the mouth of the Baptism River. A lone fisherman stood near the river. We walked over to see the pink salmon he'd caught. He pulled one out of a bucket, and its belly had a subtle pinkish/silver tinge with greenish silver lines. It was sad to know this beautiful creature was headed for the grill – though we would happily have cooked and eaten it.

At the top of Palisade Head, I interviewed Bryan and Kat as we looked out over the lake where the wind had begun to kick up lines of waves.

Bryan started, "I got introduced to the outdoors by my dad. In college I went to UMD and that's where I really got familiar with Lake Superior. I got used to seeing it every day and when I moved away it felt really strange."

Kat who is from Germany remembered, "I first got to see the Lake in January when the edges were frozen and cold. And it was hard to believe that people would voluntarily live here, but then I saw it later when it was not frozen."

Bryan continued, "I hope that as much of the natural primitive character of the shoreline can stay that way permanently. This (lake) demands our respect and treating it with the best practices that we can."

Kat is a biologist and an artist, so it's not surprising that she had this observation. "One of the things I really liked about it was the color. I had never seen anything that was that color. I remember standing by the Split Rock Lighthouse and the snow was hitting the rocks. It looked like the snow was coming up at us. And when I talk to the people at home I call it Lake Superior blue – this mix of turquoise and light blue and dark…"

At the end of the day, we returned to Lutsen Resort and its Watersmeet Spa. Laura Bernhardson, a woman we've never met, gave us a gift certificate to the spa. It was a wonderful way to end a day's walk and Laura, if you're reading this, thank you.

When Jennifer Morawitz, a massage therapist and registered nurse, finished with Mike, she came out and asked me to return to the room so she could explain what she had done. Mike was "really messed up, muscularly speaking," she said. One side of his back had been swollen an inch higher than the other side. Most of the massage, therefore, had been painful, until she got his back to relax. Mike noticed a definite improvement in the amount of pain in his legs.

At 6:24 a.m. the next morning, an amazing glowing pink sunrise spread over the eastern side of the lake, with lots of gray clouds to the south. There were no waves, just a riffled surface, and swells, moving south to north. A large raptor went winging over the water heading southwest. The pink kept spreading across the bottoms of the clouds, reaching to the south. It was a new baby sky with its magical mix of pink and blue.

Walking along the bike trail toward Split Rock Lighthouse State Park, I noticed big flocks of blue jays flying across the road, headed in a southwesterly direction. They seem to migrate at the same time as the kestrels and darner dragonflies. Large flocks of sparrows flew back and forth across the path, too, but their somber brown plumage made them impossible to identify specifically.

Mel Aanerud and his son Eric pulled their car behind ours at the Split Rock Lighthouse. Eric is one of Mike's former students. From the lighthouse's visitor center, we went down the old tramway steps to the rocky beach. Mel and Eric followed, although Mel had a hard time walking on the boulders and uneven rocks. By this time, most people were at a big disadvantage when they walked with us on rocky beaches. It was second nature for us now.

At the picnic grounds, Mel turned back to fetch their car and later picked up Eric in the campground parking area. We've walked this shore countless times, mostly in winter, but were shocked to see how low the water was between the mainland and the bird refuge island. It was the first time we had ever seen the rocks sticking out of the water and creating a dry land route from the end of the beach to the island.

The crisp fall breeze rustled golden aspen leaves above us. We walked past

Day Hill up the shore from the lighthouse. The water in the bays sparkled. This trail eventually took us to the Gitchi-Gami State Trail and to where Mike parked the bike. I continued walking while Mike rode the 4 miles back to the car. At Gooseberry Falls State Park, I waited for him out on the rocks of the middle falls. Very little water was going over the falls, and I lay on the warm rocks with the sun on my left side and tiny bits of water spraying me. A good day overall.

Seeing the iconic Split Rock Lighthouse reminded us how close we were to our full circle goal.

Up at 5:45 a.m., I was treated to another pink Lake Superior sunrise. It started out deep rouge, but gradually washed into pastels. A pretty sunrise, but it made me remember, "Red sky in morning; sailors take warning." True to the rhyme, we had a rainy day.

After coffee and freshly baked scones at the Spirit of Gitche Gumee, where we had spent the night we drove to Gooseberry Falls State Park, left the car near a gravel beach, then walked south on the ledge rock. The blustery gray day was invigorating; it is weather we both enjoy. We crossed a streambed, which was mostly dry, and continued to follow the shore. The water in the lake was a mix of blue, green and gray.

Neither Mike nor I have ever walked this part of the park, which is surprising since Mike has explored so much of the North Shore during the past 40 years. We came to a point with houses ahead and signs that said: "All shoreline is private" and "Private beyond this point." We moved into the vegetation and bushwhacked our way back to the streambed. From there we took a narrow pathway to a big group camp clearing. Raindrops began to fall as we followed the Gitchi-Gami trail back to the parking lot. On the way, we passed a massive old birch tree with branches that circled the trunk and grew outward like big long arms. Another outstanding tree to add to our growing list.

The Rustic Inn has an unimpressive brown exterior that hides a welcoming and comfortable establishment. We were in the mood for pies – actually Mike is always in the mood for pies – and he characteristically ordered a berry. I ordered the lemon angel, ignoring the calorie count.

Owner Beth Sullivan came to our table, and we raved about her creations. Mike told her about our trip. She asked if we had gotten permission to cross the Encampment Forest Association property. We told her, "No."

"I know the caretaker. Would you like me to call and ask him?"

"Yes, please."

So Beth went off and came back a short time later, telling us he had said it was OK. Just like that, thanks to helpful people, one more stretch of shore was opened to us.

This day especially, walking Highway 61 was just plain awful. Cars would not move and the shoulder was narrow. At Encampment Forest Preserve, we put on our rain gear and walked to the river past signs that warned of private property and advised that the sheriff would be called on trespassers.

The Encampment River is a rocky stream. There wasn't much water in it, but the path on the side had lots of slippery rocks. Mike was thrilled at the chance to walk on this property that he had so long wondered about. The path took us through a forest with thick, bright green moss all around our feet. In a lot of ways it reminded us of the Huron Mountain Club and, indeed, it is similarly a private collective of properties established in the 1950s that spans a generation or two of same-family owners. All the cabins were built of logs. Most were quite modest and looked old.

The path took us out to the shore where Encampment River enters Lake Superior. Out the driveway and onto the main road for Gates 1-4, we eventually ended back on the miserable highway. Walking in the rain made it worse.

We headed toward the Silver Creek Cliff tunnel and up the path around it. Great graphics on a panel installed along the path document the history of the cliff and construction of the tunnel, which opened in 1994. Mike remembers climbing the cliff with a friend. He came close to falling. "It didn't look as difficult back then," Mike said.

Several raptors swooped by us on this cliff side. They landed, then took off again, dipping low and swinging up. A bad day for thermal air columns, but the birds were definitely moving. Mike retrieved his bike from the bushes and rode back to the car. I worried about him riding on the edge of that damnable busy highway. Of 19 cars that passed him, Mike said only five gave him extra room.

I had almost walked to Betty's Pies restaurant before Mike caught up. The wind was blowing hard at my back, and I had to keep my umbrella angled so it wouldn't turn inside out. We made it into Two Harbors this day – only 26 miles to our goal.

That night we stayed at Cove Point Lodge, where we had been offered a room in exchange for giving a talk to their guests. Even though I don't know of any Scandinavian genes in my body, there must be some lurking somewhere because I absolutely love Cove Point's Scandinavian breakfast of pickled beets, herring, cucumbers, sliced tomatoes and thin meats and cheese. Steve Hillestad, one of the co-owners, joined us and talked about the activities the lodge offers to engage people with the area. Unfortunately, few people walk out to the point and no one, it seems, goes up the Superior Hiking Trail, which has an access point right at the property. Steve often has a campfire set up in front of the lodge for guests to view the wide starry sky. Too often, he says, he looks up at the lodge and sees a blue glow of televisions from most rooms.

After an interview with Cathy Wurzer of Minnesota Public Radio, we drove to Two Harbors. Mike hid his bike in the bushes, and we drove back to Burlington Bay, one of the two harbors of Two Harbors, the other being Agate Bay. In the parking lot, a lady in another car saw the Full Circle Superior sign on our car door and commented about how we were "almost done."

We walked up the hill and on the bike trail until we found a foot path closer to the lake. The sun nearly blinded us with its intense reflection off the crashing waves. The breeze carried a chill, and we both wore our jackets and Granite Gear packs, appropriately since this is the community where Granite Gear is headquartered.

Mike Creger, a friend and reporter with the *Lake County News Chronicle*, the Two Harbors newspaper, rode up on his bike and took photos, first of us coming through the vegetation and again on the flat rocks out in front of the lighthouse. This has always been one of our favorite spots for walking by Lake Superior.

The water was hitting, spraying and splashing on the rocks. With the end coming up quickly now, both Mike and I realized how much we would miss seeing Lake Superior every day. Later in the day, as we were dining at Larsmont Cottages, I would look through the window at the water. "I'm missing you already," I thought out to the lake. There's no way to describe the euphoria or peace that this majestic body of water can create in a person.

After parting from Mike Creger, we walked through Two Harbors, up side streets down to a dead end. A path led us to the railroad yards, and we followed the tracks. I was not excited to be walking the tracks again, but Mike was happy to be in the woods, avoiding the highway. The tracks curved, and I knew we'd be coming to a crossing soon, having seen it often from the road. At that point, Mike turned right to get the bike and I turned left to walked farther down the road. When Mike returned with the car, we drove to Knife River and hid the bike there. We stayed on Old North Shore Road, the scenic drive between Two Harbors and Duluth that paralleled the major highway and closely hugged Lake Superior. It was a quiet walk, and we could see the lake through some of the driveways. We came to a candy store, interestingly called "Great! Lakes Candy Kitchen," on the side of the road. A sign advertising nutty ice cream bars stopped me. Mike said, "Do you want to go in?" Too late, I was already climbing the steps. (The sisters who own and operate the store, it turns out, buy the ice cream and then tip it into coconut and salted peanuts, using their father's recipe.)

A new bridge crosses the Knife River, and flower boxes along the length of it make it the prettiest bridge I can remember seeing. We reached the bike's hiding place, and I continued walking while Mike went back for the car.

We spent the night at Larsmont Cottages. At dinner that night, a woman sitting at the table behind us wanted to say how much she admired us and what we'd done. Victoria was working the front desk, and when Mike introduced me to her, she said effusively, "I bow down to you." Earlier in the day, another woman, who had been at our talk at Cove Point, said how much we had inspired her and her husband. "We really appreciate hearing that," I told her. We truly hoped we inspired others to get out in nature, to protect Lake Superior and all waters, and, of course, to follow their dreams.

Reporter Sam Cook planned to meet us on the shore with newspaper photographer Bob King. While Mike drove ahead to park the car and bicycled back, Sam and Bob met me across from Nokomis Restaurant about 10 miles outside of Duluth on the Scenic North Shore Drive. When Mike returned, we headed to the shore, where Bob could shoot photos. The poor guy had to run ahead over uneven rock slabs and through loose gravel to get in front of us for the angles he wanted. Eventually, Bob went on the road to get far enough in front. Mike and I just kept walking, we needed to make our miles to finish early. It was fun walking on this shore and great to be off the road again. Mike didn't have his poles since he couldn't carry them on his bike, but we managed to get over and around the rocks pretty easily, though some were wet from the rain in the night. Sam tried to take notes while negotiating this uneven, difficult surface.

We crossed over the French River bridge and decided to walk on the road the rest of the way to the car because of the steep red clay bank to the water. When we reached our cars, Bob came stumbling up the bank. He had expected to see us coming down the shore and was all ready for some long-distance shots. We, by then, were on the road. We placated him by going back down on the rocks and posing.

We said goodbye to Sam and Bob, and Mike drove ahead some miles, rode his bike back to me, then turned it around and walked with me, pushing the bike. This day we used multiple bike shuttles, leap frogging with the car. It was our most complex arrangement, and one that had us walking or biking solo most of the time. Mike had gotten down on the shore and called on the cell phone to tell me. Later I could see the entrance to Brighton Beach Park on the outskirts of Duluth ahead, so I found a way back down to the shore to finish the walk. I called Mike to tell him where I was and my proximity to Brighton Beach.

It was great to walk on the rocks with Duluth and the park so close. When I reached Brighton Beach, I climbed up to the grassy area and found a spot to sit down and wait. And wait. And wait. Still, it gave me time to savor the moment. We were just 9 miles from the finish line, and there was no doubt in our minds that we would finish our full circle the following day. I looked at the Duluth harbor and could hardly believe it had been a little more than 4½ months ago that we had set out from that beach.

Mike called me to say that it must have been more than a mile from the water plant. I decided to start walking back to the car, but when I got to the top of the park driveway, a white station wagon curved to a stop in front of me. It was Dan Mettner, our angel who'd helped us land on Wisconsin Point. He had seen Mike up the road and had talked to him. Dan said he'd be with us tomorrow, just as he had been with us the first day.

Back at Larsmont Cottages, we found our friends from Colorado. Mick Sommer was Mike's first employee at the Audubon Center some 40 years ago. He and his wife, Nancy, had flown in to be with us on our momentous day. We changed clothes, and all four of us went to the firepit patio where Adirondack chairs were set up and an employee was getting the fire ready to go. We visited with a half dozen of the guests and sipped red wine in the waning afternoon sun. Then we made arrangements to meet my mom, two brothers and sister at Emily's restaurant in Knife River for a celebratory dinner. Our spirits were bubbling over with pleasure – at what we had accomplished and at the joy of celebrating the closure with so many of our closest friends and family.

A waterfall is but an episode in the life of a whole sing stream.
Ansel Adams

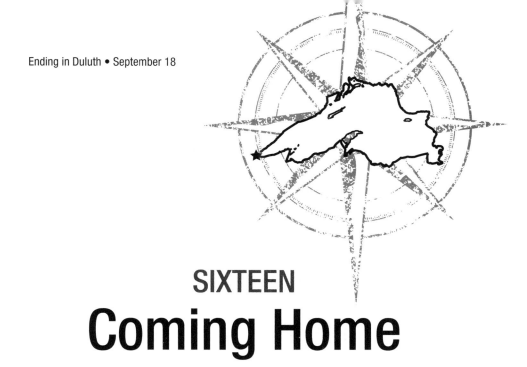

SIXTEEN
Coming Home

Won't you come now and walk along with me
Sing Hallelujah
When we get there, we'll be strong and free
Sing Hallelujah
Long Journey, Unitarian Song Book

Mike:

It was the last day.

The weather was gorgeous – when we gathered with friends and family in Brighton Beach Park on the outskirts of Duluth. Just 8 more miles, and we would close an amazing chapter in our lives. This time, of course, we would not be walking alone.

A great sense of accomplishment filled us and we were overwhelmed with thoughts of all the friends we had made around the lake. Thousands of people had followed us on Facebook and our website. We felt their presence that last morning as we gathered at the park and prepared for the last steps of the long walk.

For nearly all of the second half of our Lake Superior circle, we'd wondered and hoped that my knees would keep bending, that I would make it. Now there was no doubt, no hesitation; walk, crawl or hop, we would reach our goal.

Brighton Beach Park was a good place to begin the end. From here, we could look back to the shores of Minnesota and Wisconsin, see where the lake widened and the horizon dipped toward Sault Ste. Marie, our midway point. The lake was beautiful (of course) and we had many of Kate's family with us, as well as some hardy friends who had followed us by our web postings. It was a grand reunion.

281

We walked beside the water's edge, as we had tried to do the entire trip, but this time felt the elation of our companions. Every day that we posted website and Facebook notes, we had been eager to see the comments of friends and followers. Now, finally, we could meet some of them face-to-face instead of Facebook-to-Facebook. What could be better?

We had just taken our first few steps when two people emerged from a parked car and stopped us in our tracks. There could not have been a bigger – or more pleasing – shock. It was our son, Jon, and his wife, Kristin, all the way from Bozeman, Montana. Our newest grandchild, Teagan, was there, too – inside her mom and only three weeks from entering the world.

We were nearly speechless, first amazed and then a little concerned.

"Don't worry, Dad," Jon said. "We Googled every hospital along the way." The broad smiles never left our faces from Brighton Beach all the way as we trekked the rocks and streets toward Canal Park.

At the Lester River, which enters Lake Superior at 61st Avenue East, our friend Dan Mettner said, "Are you going to cross?" There was, after all, a bridge.

But wet feet were part of our entire journey; shouldn't they be wet at the end? Of course we would cross, through the water.

As we slogged forward, some of the people leaned over the bridge. Their expressions of "Are they going to go through the water when there is a bridge here?" turned into "They are going to cross the river and there is a bridge here!"

As we continued, passing cars honked, some people stopped and jumped out to walk a few feet with us, some stopped and shook hands. A video camera caught our thoughts. We alternately walked with one another or with friends. We tried to share every step, every emotion, but of course we couldn't. How to express in a few words the totality of 144 days of experience that suddenly welled up inside me?

More and more friends, family and well wishers on our last miles entering finally into Canal Park.

I laughed, smiled, waved and felt like I would burst. I wanted to squeeze Kate's hand, to transfer the rise of my many emotions to her, but even that was not possible. Yes, we'd shared an incredible journey together and had common memories, but the hike also had affected each of us in our own way.

Just past the huge Congdon Estate, we drifted back on to the lakeshore trail again. Listening to the lapping waters, feeling each footfall as I negotiated the cobblestones, I realized that I did not want this to end. I had grown to depend on the daily simplicity of our walk. The outside world rarely imposed on our daily regime: Get up, eat, figure out where we could walk, and then, walk!

Each day ended with dinner, a shower, some computer time and sleep – if the pain was not too bad.

Now here I was, a few miles shy of the point where I would not have to push my old and aching body, and yet, I did not want to stop. I already missed having a goal, as though this one already had been completed and shelved. There would be more to explore and to do, but I felt a sense of loss along with my elation during those last miles.

Kate was not thinking this. Proud of our accomplishment so far and knowing we would achieve our goal, she was ready to end the hike. She was satisfied.

We walked along shore with the Aerial Lift Bridge, essentially our goal, in view. We had put the word out for people to meet us in Leif Erikson Park, about a mile from our end point, and there they were, hanging over a bridge, leaning on the fence. So many people wanted to touch our adventure that lifted us. It had been this way, I realized, along our entire route and I flashed back to the multiple chance encounters, the encouraging words, the smiles, the help. So many people cared about us and about the lake, so many walked beside us in spirit and embraced the thought of two old-timers hiking along the shore.

We hugged, greeted and invited them to join us as we finished our dream – as if they weren't already there to do just that. Among the crowd was our grandson Matthew and my daughter Julie, becoming part of the ending as they had been part of the beginning and of the middle on our trek.

We walked, but I did not feel the ground and, most miraculously, I did not feel my pains. The love and attention of all these great people inflated me like a balloon. I floated. Kate seemed to feel the same. We came past Fitger's Brewery Complex, where we had had our pre-trip party, then continued past the train tracks and Veterans Memorial, making the last corner of the Lakewalk with enough people to make it seem like a parade.

Then, much too soon for me, we were back where we began, where the dream commenced. Once again there were the cameras, the people, the emotions. Our little carved friend Paddle Lake Superior was with us. Once again, too, we offered tobacco, gifted to us by Allan Aubid of Grand Portage. The tobacco recalled to me a pipe ceremony near here 21 years before, when we honored the memory of my son Matthew.

Soon we'd be going into Canal Park Lodge where a celebration was waiting for us, organized by *Lake Superior Magazine* as a chance to celebrate and to reconnect with friends.

But before that, we needed to deliver a good message, to celebrate the lake, the earth and the years to come. So many thoughts welled inside me. Walking beside it, I felt as intimate now as one could be with Lake Superior – a shining entity so big and beautiful, yet fragile. It inspired us with its moods and mass, but I knew better now than ever that it also requires our care. It belongs to all of us and we all must put our care for it into action. Our grandchildren and everyone's grandchildren now and in the future require us to care for and protect it. I wanted to say all of this to those who came to share our "homecoming."

I wanted to tell them all that we loved the hike, we continue to love the lake and thank everyone, those there that day and those who could not be there, for sharing this adventure with us.

We spoke to the gathered crowd and shared a few readings.

Then Kate took the smooth, round quartz stone she had carried for 1,555 miles and nearly five months around the world's largest freshwater lake. On it was painted "Walk Around Lake Superior." Holding the stone in her palm one last time, Kate took aim. She threw it high over the sparkling blue waters. It arched and splashed and we watched as its ripples drifted outward. We hoped that our ripples – word of our journey and of our concerns for the lake – also were spreading outward.

They, hand in hand, with wandering steps and slow,
through Eden took their solitary way.
Paradise Lost, John Milton

After Thoughts

Miles Logged

Day	Date	Location	Day Mi.
1	4/29	MN Point, WI point to Camp Amnicon	18
2	4/30	Bracketts Corner to Port Wing	13.1
3	5/1	Port Wing to Cornucopia	16.1
4	5/2	Camp Amnicon to Brule River	13.3
5	5/3	Cornucopia to Sand Point	15.4
6	5/4	Sand Point to Red Cliff	14.4
7	5/5	Red Cliff to Port Superior	12.9
8	5/6	Port Superior to S of Washburn	13.3
9	5/7	S of Washburn to Bad River Res.	13
10	5/8		OFF
11	5/9		OFF
12	5/10	Bad River Reservation	22.3
		Missed shoreline	
13	5/11	Saxon Harbor to Porkies	16.4
14	5/12	Porcupine Mountains (reverse)	17.1
15	5/13	Porcupine Mountains trail head to Union River	7
16	5/14	Union River towards Ontonagon	10.5
17	5/15	Half way creek through Ontonagon and Firesteel River to Ontonagon River	15.6
18	5/16	Firesteel River to 14 mile lighthouse to Misery Bay river	15
19	5/17	Agate Beach and Freda to Houghton Canal	16
20	5/18	Agate Beach to Freda	11.5
21	5/19	McClain SP to north of the waterworks for Calumet River	7.5
22	5/20	Off	5
23	5/21	North of waterworks to Eagle River	16.5
24	5/22	Eagle River towards Copper Harbor	16

Day	Date	Location	Day Mi.
25	5/23	West of Copper Harbor to Fort Wilkins. Fort Wilkins to Horseshoe Harbo	8 4.5
26	5/24	Boat to East end of peninsula Bete Grise to Oliver Beach	9 6
27	5/25	Oliver Beach to Gay	13.5
28	5/26	Gay Rd. to Muddy River beach BootJack Rd. – Muddy River to Canal across from SF	8.6 8.5
29	5/27	Sturgeon River Refuge to Keweenaw point	15
30	5/28	Keweenaw Point to Baraga State Park. Baraga SP to L'Anse	13.9
31	5/29	Abbaye Point to Second Sand Beach	16.3
32	5/30	Second Sand Beach to L'Anse	8.4
33	5/31	Huron River to Skanee (reverse)	15.9
34	6/1	Huron Mountain club	19.3
35	6/2	Big Bay area	7.5
36	6/3	Past Granot Loma and between little and big Presque Isle, Marquette	13.7
37	6/4	To Northern Marquette	5.5
38	6/5	Presque Isle through downtown parks	4.5
39	6/6	Marquette	6
40	6/7	Marquette towards Munising	16
41	6/8	Making progress to Munising	13
42	6/9	Still going to Munising	6.7
43	6/10	Finally Munising and then Miners Castle to Munising falls	15
44	6/11	Sand Point to Munising (reverse)	4.2
45	6/12	Little Beaver Lake to Miners Castle (reverse)	15.4
46	6/13	Little Beaver Lake to Log slide	19.3
47	6/14	Log slide to Grand Marais	6.5
48	6/15	Grand Marais to Lake Superior SF campground beach	17.9
49	6/16	Lake Superior beach to Muskellonge	6.2
50	6/17	Little Lake to Muskellonge (reverse)	14,4
51	6/18	Tahquamenon River to Naomikong Overlook	12
52	6/19	Little Lake to Vermilion and Paradise to Tahquamenon River	17.4
53	6/20	Vermilion Point to Whitefish and Paradise	18.9
54	6/21	Last of Palisade, Naomiking to the shallows	10.4
55	6/22	Shallows to Iroquois Lighthouse	11.9
56	6/23	Off In Sault Ste Marie, MI	2.5
57	6/24	Sault Ste. Marie to Sherman Park (reverse)	2.9
58	6/25		OFF
59	6/26	International Bridge	3.5
60	6/27	Brimley	4

Day	Date	Location	Day Mi.
61	6/28	Iroquois light to Brimley SP	10.8
62	6/29	Birch Point to Brimley (reverse)	4.5
		Birch point to Brush Point	6.5
63	6/30	Pancake Bay	4
		Missed Miles	
64	7/1	Pancake Bay to Batchawana (reverse)	13.2
65	7/2	Visitor center Sault Ste Marie to airport road	8.6
66	7/3	Red Rock to Gros Point	14.1
67	7/4	Kelly Creek to Goulais River	4
		Coulais Mission around Goulais Bay (reverse)	7.4
68	7/5	Goulais point to Knight Bay	13.7
69	7/6	Batchawana River south of Chippewa River	7
70	7/7	Chippewa River to Harmony	5
71	7/8	Haviland Bay North side of Goulais to Harmony	13.5
72	7/9	Pancake Bay to Hibbard Bay	4.5
73	7/10	Deadman Cove to Mica Bay	10.7
74	7/11	Mica Bay to Montreal River	12.7
75	7/12	Montreal River to Agawa Beach campgrounds	12.4
76	7/13	Pictographs to Agawa picnic grounds (reverse)	7.8
77	7/14	Sinclair Cove to Catherine Cove	8.1
78	7/15	Gargantua to Chantrell Cove and back	14
79	7/16	Henry Lake to Rabbit Blanket (reverse)	7
80	7/17	Orphan Lake to Catherine Cover (reverse)	7.9
81	7/18	Orphan Lake to Rhyolite and back	7
82	7/19	HWY 17, Henry Lake to Wawa	7.9
83	7/20	Off	7
84	7/21	Sandy Bay to Naturally Superior	3
85	7/22	Paddle to Hattie Cove	
86	7/23	Paddle to Hattie Cove	
87	7/24	Paddle to Hattie Cove	
88	7/25	Paddle to Hattie Cove	
89	7/26	Paddle to Hattie Cove	
90	7/27	Paddle to Hattie Cove	
91	7/28	Paddle to Hattie Cove	
92	7/29	Paddle to Hattie Cove	
93	7/30	Paddle to Hattie Cove	
94	7/31	Paddle to Hattie Cove	
95	8/1	Paddle to Hattie Cove	

Day	Date	Location	Day Mi.
96	8/2	Paddle to Hattie Cove	115
97	8/3	Wawa	3
98	8/4	Drive to Pukaskwa	6
99	8/5	Marathon to Hattie Cover (reverse)	15
100	8/6	Marathon to Coldwell	10
101	8/7	Coldwell to Neys	9
102	8/8	NEYS West on HWY 17	12.6
103	8/9	Black Fox Lake past Jackfish	14.4
104	8/10	HWY 17 Past Terrace Bay	14
105	8/11	Terrace Bay to West Hydro (Voy trail)	12.8
106	8/12	Lakeshore Drive past Rossport	8.3
107	8/13	Rossport to Gravel River	15.1
108	8/14	Scheiber to Rainbow Falls (VT)	10.9
109	8/15	Gravel River to Kama Overlook (17)	15.3
110	8/16	Overlook towards Nipigon (17)	13.2
111	8/17	Ruby Creek to Red Rock 17 and Nipigon River Trail	13.5
112	8/18	Abandoned RR to Dorion	13.6
113	8/19	Dorion to Rd 5	12.8
114	8/20	Silver Islet to Findlay Bay	7.9
115	8/21	Sawmill trail Thunder Bay lookout	16.2
116	8/22	NE Sibley Peninsula and Portage Road	8.4
117	8/23	S Sibley Tee Harbor Kabeyuna trail	12.6
118	8/24	Thunder Bay lookout to highway	11.1
119	8/25	E Nelson Point to Silver Harbour Rd on RR	15
120	8/26	Silver Harbour to Centennial Park McIntyre River	13.5
121	8/27	Centennial Park towards Mission Marsh	7.9
122	8/28	Farmers Market to Mission Marsh and Squaw Bay	9
123	8/29	Fort William Historical Park	3
124	8/30	Moose Hill and south on HWY 61	15
125	8/31	Pigeon Point and Mink Mountain	13
126	9/1	September 1 Border south on 61, hat point around bay	14
127	9/2	Reservation to Hovland	12
128	9/3	Hovland to Naniboujou	8
129	9/4	OFF	
130	9/5	OFF	
131	9/6	OFF	
132	9/7	Naniboujou to Devils Track	13
133	9/8	Devils Track to S Grand Marais	13

Day	Date	Location	Day Mi.
134	9/9	Grand Marais to Cascade	12
135	9/10	Cascade to Lutsen stores	13
136	9/11	Lutsen stores to Tofte and Temperance River	13
137	9/12	Tofte to Temperance River and HWY 1	13
138	9/13	Tettegouche and Palisade Head to Beaver Bay	13
138	9/14	Beaver Bay to Gooseberry	12
140	9/15	Gooseberry – Split Rock to Two Harbor	12
141	9/16	Two Harbors to Knife River	12
142	9/17	Knife River to Brighton Beach	10
143	9/18	Brighton Beach to Canal Park	8
		Total	1555.5

SEVENTEEN
Two Years Later

This is my place.
Hardly a ripple,
so silent.
This is the place I wish I could always be.
By the Lake, Ciana Parker

It's been two years since we started our walk around Lake Superior and after two years we can honestly say that we have not gone a day without thinking about the hike.

It truly was the highlight of our lives – with the exception of our children and grandchildren.

This adventure exceeded all others and our love of the Lake and our concern for freshwater only continues to grow.

A quick update on two people who became such vital parts of our Full Circle story.

Our main support person, Amanda Hakala, returned to her family life in Cromwell, Minnesota, and is now pursuing a doctorate degree. We look forward to the day we'll be calling her Dr. Hakala (though she'll continue to be our Mandy).

Nic, the young man injured on our canoe adventure, recovered from his injuries through surgery and physical therapy. Sadly we know that he cannot continue to pursue his dream of playing in the NFL and, despite efforts to keep in touch, we have not had much continued contact.

As to our own adventures, we are delighted that people continue to visit our website and our Facebook site and we will continue to add to both as long as anyone is interested.

Our concerns about the quality of the environment and water have not lessened. We also worry that not enough people realize that air and water cannot be compromised. As an extension of this walk – and of our plans for the future – we are keeping contacts with the people we met and are sharing our thoughts, inspiration and observations at presentations to a variety of audiences. In turn, we are proud and inspired by the reaction of the people who hear our story and who love the fact that two seniors would take on such a challenge.

We have been fortunate in that we could bring in our family at the beginning, middle and end of our adventure. This is something that many adventurers cannot do and we felt so lucky to have been renewed by and connected to our family in Duluth and Sault Ste Marie.

Our life has changed since the walk because it gave us status (and responsibility) among people interested in water quality and other environmental or health issues. Since the walk, we've been honored with an environmental education award from the Izaak Walton League, a lifetime achievement award from the Minnesota Association of Environmental Education, a stewardship award from the Lake Superior Binational Forum and, along with Josephine Mandamin, with an achievement award from *Lake Superior Magazine*.

The walk has allowed us the opportunity to speak to many crowds and to have more than 2,000 people following us on the internet. We have given 70 talks and a dozen school presentations in Minnesota and Wisconsin since the end of the trip and hope to continue to share our stories and hope other people will also want to leave a legacy for the future. The walk also resulted in Mike being appointed to the Minnesota Coastal Management Council and the state River Advisory Board. It has not changed our dedication, but it has enhanced our ability to share.

What's next for us? Can you take a voyageur canoe down the Mississippi River? Hmmmm.

We continue to exercise on foot, bikes and skis, but it is not the same as a dedicated walk. Mike misses that day-to-day commitment and consistency. He knew he would on the last day as we moved towards the culmination of the hike. Like astronauts, athletes, and probably presidents, there can be a peak experience in life that is so satisfying you never want it to end so you continue to find new outlets for your drive and energy. We expect to do many things in the future, but we do not expect to match the intensity of this walk.

Since leaving the trail for home life again, Mike had five eye operations, one knee operation, two hip replacements and multiple steroid injections in his back. We consider 2010 the year of the trip and Mike calls 2011 the year of the operations and hopes that it does not carry over to 2013, when we've got a new adventure planned.

We've decided to continue to bring attention to freshwater issues with a 4,500-mile trip by bicycle and boat along the Mississippi River to the Gulf in 2013. Part of the trip will stray from the river to include key designated bike routes. We look forward to understanding better the river and the people who depend upon it for life and livelihood.

We're excited by this future journey, along which we will conduct sampling and photographing in the Mississippi River Flyway – one of the most important birding regions in the world.

So our 1,555-mile walk around Lake Superior, intended initially to celebrate and commemorate the end of one chapter in our lives, may well only be a new beginning.

The adventure for us will continue and we will flow along with new waters.

**I sit by the lake on this wondrous day,
watching the reflection of flowering trees,
rippling past watching appreciative eyes.**
Afternoon At The Lake, Sandi Vander Sluis

Final Thoughts
The Thank Yous

Mike & Kate:

There are so many people who helped us in one way or another as we prepared for and did the Walk Around Lake Superior. It would be impossible to list everyone. So for those whose names are not included, we apologize, but thank everyone immensely for your contributions to making it a success.

Major funders:

BeneVia, Medica Insurance Company, Anytime Fitness, Anderson Insurance Agency, Lois and Tom Woodman, Betsy and Alex Johnston.

Equipment/food/supplies/services:

Dan Cruikshank, Granite Gear; Steve Piragis, Piragis Northwoods Outfitters; Eric Humphries, Lake Superior Trading Post; Kent Hering, Littlbug stove; Dick and Connie Glattly; Rhea Kontos, Gabel Trekking poles; Cherry Republic; Jennifer Ashley, BeneVia health drinks; Craig Thorvig, Chris's Fairway; Joyce Hakala; Beth and Bill Blank; Niko Economides; Mike Landmark; Bad River Band of Lake Superior Chippewa; Jennifer Edlund; Gateway Clinic; Mercy Hospital; Drs. Paul and Dan Dewey; Jim Radford; Tobias Tan; Todd and Carolyn Starling; Voyageur Lodge and Cookhouse; Douglas and Bryan Wood; Jerry and Mary Phillips.

Lodging (in the order of our travels):

Canal Park Lodge (beginning and ending), Camp Amnicon in Wisconsin, Wilderness Inquiry in Wisconsin, The Rittenhouse Inn in Bayfield, Wisconsin, Best Western Houghton, Michigan, Huron Mountain Club, The Landmark Hotel in Marquette, Michigan, Falling Rock Lodge and Café in Munising, Michigan; Holiday Inn in Sault St. Marie, Michigan; Naturally Superior Adventures in Wawa, Ontario; The Rossport Inn in Ontario, Grand Portage Lodge in Minnesota, East Bay Suites in Grand Marais, Minnesota, Spirit of Gitche Gami in Little Marais, Minnesota, Cove Point Lodge in Beaver Bay, Minnesota; Larsmont Cottages in Minnesota.

Fundraising help:

Nicci Sylvester, Melissa Eggler, Karen Shragg; Marilee and Dave Anderson; Carolyn and Pete Hendrixson; Bill and Mary Crowley; The Great Lakes Aquarium, Liz Sivertson and John Gruber. There were many, many people who made financial contributions through our website and our fundraising events. Without their help we couldn't have made it.

We must also thank all of our family who were our cheerleaders and part of the inspiration for undertaking this adventure – Julie Link and Matthew Lyon; Alyssa, Troy, Aren, Ryan and Annalise Carlson; Jon, Kristin and Teagan Horn; and all of the Crowleys.

Special thanks to our major sponsor and supporters:

Cindy, Paul, Konnie, Siiri and all the other staff of *Lake Superior Magazine*.

And finally, a heartfelt thanks to Amanda Hakala for supporting and sharing our adventure.

From Lake Superior Port Cities Inc.
www.LakeSuperior.com

Lake Superior Magazine
A bimonthly, regional publication covering the shores along Michigan, Minnesota, Wisconsin and Ontario

Lake Superior Travel Guide
An annually updated mile-by-mile guide

Lake Superior, The Ultimate Guide to the Region – Second Edition
Softcover: ISBN 978-0-942235-97-5

Hugh E. Bishop:
The Night the Fitz Went Down
Softcover: ISBN 978-0-942235-37-1

By Water and Rail: A History of Lake County, Minnesota
Hardcover: ISBN 978-0-942235-48-7
Softcover: ISBN 978-0-942235-42-5

Haunted Lake Superior
Softcover: ISBN 978-0-942235-55-5

Haunted Minnesota
Softcover: ISBN 978-0-942235-71-5

Beryl Singleton Bissell:
A View of the Lake
Softcover: ISBN 978-0-942235-74-6

Bonnie Dahl:
Bonnie Dahl's Superior Way, Fourth Edition
Softcover: ISBN 978-0-942235-92-0

Joy Morgan Dey, Nikki Johnson:
Agate: What Good Is a Moose?
Hardcover: ISBN 978-0-942235-73-9

Daniel R. Fountain:
Michigan Gold, Mining in the Upper Peninsula
Softcover: ISBN 978-0-942235-15-9

Chuck Frederick:
Spirit of the Lights
Softcover: ISBN 978-0-942235-11-1

Marvin G. Lamppa:
Minnesota's Iron Country
Softcover: ISBN 978-0-942235-56-2

Daniel Lenihan:
Shipwrecks of Isle Royale National Park
Softcover: ISBN 978-0-942235-18-0

Betty Lessard:
Betty's Pies Favorite Recipes
Softcover: ISBN 978-0-942235-50-0

Mike Link & Kate Crowley:
Going Full Circle: A 1,555-mile Walk Around the World's Largest Lake.
Softcover: ISBN 978-0-942235-23-4

James R. Marshall:
Shipwrecks of Lake Superior, Second Edition
Softcover: ISBN 978-0-942235-67-8

Lake Superior Journal: Views from the Bridge
Softcover: ISBN 978-0-942235-40-1

Howard Sivertson
Driftwood: Stories Picked Up Along the Shore
Hardcover: ISBN 978-0-942235-91-3

Schooners, Skiffs & Steamships: Stories along Lake Superior's Water Trails
Hardcover: ISBN 978-0-942235-51-7

Tales of the Old North Shore
Hardcover: ISBN 978-0-942235-29-6

The Illustrated Voyageur
Hardcover: ISBN 978-0-942235-43-2

Once Upon an Isle: The Story of Fishing Families on Isle Royale
Hardcover: ISBN 978-0-962436-93-2

Frederick Stonehouse:
Wreck Ashore: United States Life-Saving Service, Legendary Heroes of the Great Lakes
Softcover: ISBN 978-0-942235-58-6

Shipwreck of the Mesquite
Softcover: ISBN 978-0-942235-10-4

Haunted Lakes (the original)
Softcover: ISBN 978-0-942235-30-2

Haunted Lakes II
Softcover: ISBN 978-0-942235-39-5

Haunted Lake Michigan
Softcover: ISBN 978-0-942235-72-2

Haunted Lake Huron
Softcover: ISBN 978-0-942235-79-1

Julius F. Wolff Jr.:
Julius F. Wolff Jr.'s Lake Superior Shipwrecks
Hardcover: ISBN 978-0-942235-02-9
Softcover: ISBN 978-0-942235-01-2

www.LakeSuperior.com
1-888-BIG LAKE (888-244-5253)
Outlet Store: 310 E. Superior St., Duluth, MN 55802